Metropolitan College of NY
Library - 7th Floor
60 West Street
New York, NY 10006

FOCUS ON CIVILIZATIONS AND CULTURES

WESTERN CIVILIZATION IN THE 21ST CENTURY

FOCUS ON CIVILIZATIONS AND CULTURES

Additional books in this series can be found on Nova's website
under the Series tab.

Additional e-books in this series can be found on Nova's website
under the e-book tab.

FOCUS ON CIVILIZATIONS AND CULTURES

WESTERN CIVILIZATION IN THE 21ST CENTURY

ANDREW TARGOWSKI

Copyright © 2015 by Nova Science Publishers, Inc.

All rights reserved. No part of this book may be reproduced, stored in a retrieval system or transmitted in any form or by any means: electronic, electrostatic, magnetic, tape, mechanical photocopying, recording or otherwise without the written permission of the Publisher.

We have partnered with Copyright Clearance Center to make it easy for you to obtain permissions to reuse content from this publication. Simply navigate to this publication's page on Nova's website and locate the "Get Permission" button below the title description. This button is linked directly to the title's permission page on copyright.com. Alternatively, you can visit copyright.com and search by title, ISBN, or ISSN.

For further questions about using the service on copyright.com, please contact:
Copyright Clearance Center
Phone: +1-(978) 750-8400   Fax: +1-(978) 750-4470   E-mail: info@copyright.com.

NOTICE TO THE READER

The Publisher has taken reasonable care in the preparation of this book, but makes no expressed or implied warranty of any kind and assumes no responsibility for any errors or omissions. No liability is assumed for incidental or consequential damages in connection with or arising out of information contained in this book. The Publisher shall not be liable for any special, consequential, or exemplary damages resulting, in whole or in part, from the readers' use of, or reliance upon, this material. Any parts of this book based on government reports are so indicated and copyright is claimed for those parts to the extent applicable to compilations of such works.

Independent verification should be sought for any data, advice or recommendations contained in this book. In addition, no responsibility is assumed by the publisher for any injury and/or damage to persons or property arising from any methods, products, instructions, ideas or otherwise contained in this publication.

This publication is designed to provide accurate and authoritative information with regard to the subject matter covered herein. It is sold with the clear understanding that the Publisher is not engaged in rendering legal or any other professional services. If legal or any other expert assistance is required, the services of a competent person should be sought. FROM A DECLARATION OF PARTICIPANTS JOINTLY ADOPTED BY A COMMITTEE OF THE AMERICAN BAR ASSOCIATION AND A COMMITTEE OF PUBLISHERS.

Additional color graphics may be available in the e-book version of this book.

Library of Congress Cataloging-in-Publication Data

ISBN: 978-1-63482-302-9

Published by Nova Science Publishers, Inc. † New York

Contents

Preface		vii
Foreword		ix
Part I: Civilizing and Globalizing Society		1
Chapter 1	Civilization Index and Western Civilization	3
Chapter 2	Spatio-Temporal Boundaries of Western Civilization	49
Chapter 3	The Life Cycle of Western Civilization	85
Chapter 4	Legacy of Western Civilization	95
Chapter 5	Western Civilization in Transformation to Global and Virtual Civilizations in the 21st Century	129
Part II. Globalizing and Virtualizing Culture and Infrastructure		149
Chapter 6	Culture Fragmentation of Western-Global-Virtual Civilization	151
Chapter 7	From Multiculturalism to Hybrid Culture in Western-Global-Virtual Civilization	169
Chapter 8	The Expanding Infrastructure of Western-Global-Virtual Civilization	191
Chapter 9	Western-Global-Virtual Civilization and the Clash of Civilizations in the 21st Century	231
Afterword		253
Index		259

PREFACE

This book took the task of conceptualizing Western civilization in the 21st century. It examines Western Civilization and its encounters from a viewpoint of the impact of rising Global civilizations in the 21st century. This political and technological success of Western civilization in the last 500 years triggered a dream of spreading around the globe Democracy and liberal Capitalism. Western society was held together by Christian morality (regardless whether someone was a believer or a non-believer or agnostic).

The medicine for all shortcomings faced by Western civilization in the 21st century is offered by Al Gore in his book "The Future: Six Drivers of Global Change" (2013). He thinks that inventions and technology will save Western civilization. The author of this book argues that vice versa, the rise of certain technologies are the main reason for the decline of Western civilization. These kind of issues will be investigated in this book and the message is not optimistic, since Westerners, when are poor are wise, and when are better off are stupid. Hence, without practicing wisdom, Western civilization cannot be revived.

FOREWORD

Since the Italian Renaissance, in other words in the last 500 years, Western civilization has won the contest with other civilizations in terms of economic, technological and societal perspectives. Through several Revolutions such as the English (1688), American (1776), French (1789), Mexican (1910), and Polish (1989) and wars such as the American Civil War (1861-1865), World War I (1914-1918), World War II (1939-1945), and the Cold War (1945-1991), human progress in Western civilization has been marching toward freedom and prosperity. People have been liberating themselves from religion dogmas, societal hierarchies, and political tyranny. Eventually in the second part of the 20th century, Westerners, mostly in North America and Western Europe as well as in Australia and New Zealand, were successful in developing a more balanced society in terms of wealth and opportunities supported by effective management of business and national governance which regulated cruel competition based on Darwinistic instincts.

This success of Western civilization triggered a dream of spreading universal *Democracy* and liberal *Capitalism* around the globe. Western society was held together by Christian morality (regardless whether someone was a believer or non-believer or agnostic). Also it seemed that the sky was the limit, but only if competition is not constrained by unnecessary regulations. The prerequisite was a national governance driven by the check-and-balance-driven political system. A country which propagated such a dream society was the United States of America. It is a matter of fact that in the 1960s-1970s the U.S. was at its peak of development and most of the people in the world wanted to immigrate to this country. This desire was strengthen by the miserable standard of living offered by the Soviet Block which was practicing *Communism* through totalitarian dictatorship of a close group of political leaders being in the Political Bureau and in the secret police (NKWD and later KGB). Most educated people in the world knew that "America" is a "heaven" and "Soviets" are from "hell."

Eventually the Westerners won the Cold War in 1991, *Communism* was discredited and *Democracy* won, perhaps forever. A leading American politolog, Francis Fukuyama, even proclaimed (although too soon) the *End of History and the Last Man* in 1992 (just one year after the fall of *Communism*) since the ideals of the American and French Revolutions remained valid and uncontested. Very quickly President George H.W. Bush Sr. announced the New World Order (NOW). Supposedly, this meant that the world would be peaceful and prosperous. Both were wrong. Since instead, as of NOW, we are facing the New Word Disorder (NWD).

The United States which de facto won the Cold War became the sole superpower in the world, and as the hegemon it feels responsible for sustaining a global order based *Democracy* and *Capitalism*. The reality, however, is different. In the 21st century Western society has become drained, suspicious, and pessimistic, and it is losing ground. The democratic dream has been replaced by fatalism and powerlessness that whatever Western governance is doing, it is resulting in a wrong solution.

For example, the Vietnam War was lost in 1975; the 9/11 attack on New York's World Trade Towers could not be prevented despite some early signals; the Iraqi War in reality was lost and the Afghanistan War was lost as well. Even worse, the threat from Islamist Freedom fighters has grown larger and larger in the 21st century. It has become very apparent that Arab nations, despite the Arab Spring (2012-2014), are not going to be democratic any time soon. Certainly the rising China as the world economic power does not like liberal *Democracy* and *Capitalism* since it inclines towards authoritarian *Capitalism* (called in China as market *Socialism* with Chinese character) (Targowski and Hun 2014).

The world is a complex of several civilization such as: Western, Eastern, Chinese, Japanese, Islam, Buddhist, Hindu, and African. Each one has a different religion, society, culture and infrastructure and is not yet ready to apply the same political system of *Democracy* and *Capitalism* due to different heritage and circumstances. It is apparent that not only nature and people like diversity, but polities like diversity too. Perhaps it is healthy for the world to be differentiated and not closed and stagnant in one political solution, run by the World Government. Particularly, *Democracy* and *Capitalism* in its actual form in the 21st century does not remind one of these ideologies when they were at their peak about 50 years ago and had a human face. Why?

The Americans and Western Europeans (particularly Italians, French, Spanish, Greeks, and Portuguese) lost faith in their message. However, they do not know why. This happened since Western civilization has been transforming into Global civilization in the 21st century (Targowski 2014). As late Arnold Toynbee, the British Father of the study of civilization teaches us, a religion defines a civilization; hence the question is: what is the religion of Global civilization? Its religion is business with its values such as superconsumerism and relentless unregulated competition. Needless to say this religion is supported by corporate lobbying and corruption. It used to be that what was good for society was good for business. Nowadays it is vise-versa; what is good for business is good for society. Even the market economy was extended to the market society, where everything is for sale and the common good is diminishing since it is unprofitable.

This transformation of civilizations and their religions put Western society in a spiritual collapse. The Westerners lost faith in their ideology and polarized society around social justice issue like rising inequality[1]. It even looks as though Western civilization is perhaps facing some sort of social revolution such as some countries of Eastern Europe, Asia, and Latin America have already passed through. Without the vivacious faith Westerners cannot lead the world as used to. Even more, they cannot lead their own civilization. The symptoms

---

[1] Deregulated taxation of corporations resulted in a declining share of paid taxes by corporations; in 1952 it was 33% and in 2014 it was 10.5% and the corporate profit after tax was $1.8 trillion, an all-time high in 2014 (Time September 22, 2014, p. 26). The new trend is in moving corporate headquarters abroad to avoid taxation, causing the state to live upon the individuals' taxes while outsourcing even their jobs since they are too expensive a labor force, and the later complaining that the demand for business is declining in the U.S. as well as in the EU too.

of declining Western civilization are seen everywhere, not only by the elite but by others as well, particularly by the former members of the Western middle class which is disappearing due to the economic globalization.

The best diagnosis of what is going on today in Western civilization is provided by two American intellectuals: Samuel Huntington in his book *The Clash of Civilizations and the Remaking of World Order* (1996) and Thomas Friedman in his book *The World is Flat* (2005).

Samuel Huntington states that NOW is controlled by the clash, and in fact the war, between Western and Islam civilizations and that such a war is driven by supposedly the superiority of a given civilization's values. This is not a war against terrorism because terrorism is just a weapon of the weaker side. Likewise during the Cold War, it was not a war against the Atomic Bomb; it was only a war between *Capitalism* and *Communism*. Hence, the war/clashes of civilizations go far beyond the boundaries of one country as it used to be in traditional wars between nations in the past.

Thomas Friedman argues that the world is flat since wealth is passing from developed to developing nations due to outsourcing manufacturing (or jobs in general) from Western nations to Asian nations with cheap labor forces. He even motivates the Westerners to outsource their jobs and be free; unfortunately he does not explain how to pay the bills and what else to do if a job has been outsourced since not everybody is married to a billionaire spouse as he is. Though in his next book (co-authored with M. Mandelbaum) *That used to be us: how America fell behind in the world it invented and how we can come back* (2012), he argued that for educated people there are plenty of jobs in the United States. Really? Perhaps for 30 million there are jobs, but what about jobs for remaining 130 million members of the American labor force who do not have a college education?

The remedy for all shortcomings faced by Western civilization in the 21st century is offered by Al Gore in his book *The future: six drivers of global change* (2013). He thinks that inventions and technology will save Western civilization. This author thinks that vice versa, technology, like the Internetization, is the main reason why Western civilization declining.

These kind of issues will be investigated in this book. The message is not optimistic, since Westerners, when poor are wiser, and when stupid are better off. Hence, without practicing wisdom (Targowski 2014) Western civilization cannot revive!

REFERENCES

Friedman, Th. (2005). *The world is flat*. New York: Farrar, Straus and Giroux.
Friedman, Th. and M. Mandelbaum (2012). *That used to be us: how America fell behind in the world it invented and how we can come back*. New York: Picador/Farrar, Straus and Giroux.
Fukuyama, F. (1992). *The end of history and the last man*. New York: Penguin Group.
Gore, Al. (2013). *The future: six drivers of global change*. New York: Random House Trade Paperbacks
Huntington, S. P. (1996). *The clash of civilizations and the remaking of world order*. New York: Simon & Schuster.

Targowski, A. (2013). *Harnessing the power of wisdom*. New York: NOVA Science Publishers.
Targowski, A. (2014). *Global civilization in the 21st century*. New York: NOVA Science Publishers.
Targowski, A. and B. Han (2014). *Chinese civilization in the 21st century*. New York: NOVA Science Publishers.

Part I: Civilizing and Globalizing Society

Chapter 1

CIVILIZATION INDEX AND WESTERN CIVILIZATION

ABSTRACT

The *purpose* of this investigation is to define the political decisions which shaped Western Civilization and its role with respect to the rising Global Civilization in the 21st century. The *methodology* is based on an interdisciplinary big-picture view of Western civilizations' development and interdependency with other civilizations. Among the *findings* are: Western civilization is about 1200 years old and is one of the youngest civilizations with a consistent Christian religion, society, culture and infrastructure among contemporary civilizations. *Practical implication:* Western civilization's Index of development is 91% which means that it is saturated and is therefore pushing towards the development of globalization to allocate its material and financial output. *Social implication:* economic globalization and the clashes with Islamic and Eastern civilizations weakens Western civilization and forces it to transform into Global civilization. *Originality:* This investigation defined the Civilization Index of Western civilization which allows predictions of its behavior today and in the future.

INTRODUCTION

Human civilization emerged 6000 years ago after the climate warmed on Earth. Civilization first appeared in the Middle East and then spread to the Mediterranean and the Chinese Sea in the form of several religion-based civilizations which began as city-states eventually became empires. The biggest and best-known was the Western Roman Empire (44 B.C – 476 BCE), which survived over 520 years. The Roman Empire in turn paved the way for Western Civilization (born in 800 CE), which to this day stands in the forefront of Global Civilization. Chronologically speaking Western Civilization formed during the first three centuries after the fall of Rome (476), in other words in the era of "Old Europe". Later it expanded to Young Europe, America, Australia, and New Zealand. Western civilization has lasted about 1200 years and together with Classical civilization (Greek and Roman civilizations), it has lasted about 2700 years, if not formally then at least informally through the development of its society, culture, and infrastructure.

This development of Western civilization will be investigated with a focus on its political processes which shaped it and has led to its transformation into Global civilization in the 21st

century. The consequences of this transformation will be evaluated and will lead to predictions of the civilization's future.

A COMPOSITE DEFINITION OF CIVILIZATION

Perhaps it is the time to combine *early* and *contemporary definitions of civilizations* (Targowski 2009b) by emphasizing these following important attributes:

1) Large society
   a. Specializing in labor
   b. Self-differentiating
   c. Sharing the same knowledge system
2) Space and Time
   d. Autonomous fuzzy reification
   e. Distinguished and extended area or period of time
   f. Reification not a part of a larger entity
3) Cultural system, values and symbols driven
   g. Communication driven (e.g., literate and electronic media)
   h. Religion, wealth and power driven
4) Infrastructural system, technology-driven by, first, at least one of the following:
   a. Urban infrastructure
   b. Agricultural Infrastructure
   c. Other infrastructures (Industrial, Information and so forth)
5) Cycle-driven
   d. Rising, growing, declining, and falling over time

Based on these attributes, the composite definition of civilization is as follows:

Civilization is a large society living in an autonomous, fuzzy reification (invisible-visible) which is not a part of larger one and exists over an extended period of time. It specializes in labor and differentiates from other civilizations by developing its own advanced cultural system driven by communication, religion, wealth, power, and sharing the same knowledge/wisdom system within complex urban, agricultural infrastructures, and others such as industrial, information ones. It also progresses in a cycle or cycles of rising, growing, declining and falling.

A graphic model of civilization is illustrated in Figure 1.1.

THE WESTERN CIVILIZATION AMONG OTHER CIVILIZATIONS

In this study of civilization we begin with the construction of the empirical model of civilization development. Figure 1.2 illustrates this model and indicates that the world civilization has a continuous character, and it can be also perceived as a mosaic of autonomous civilizations.

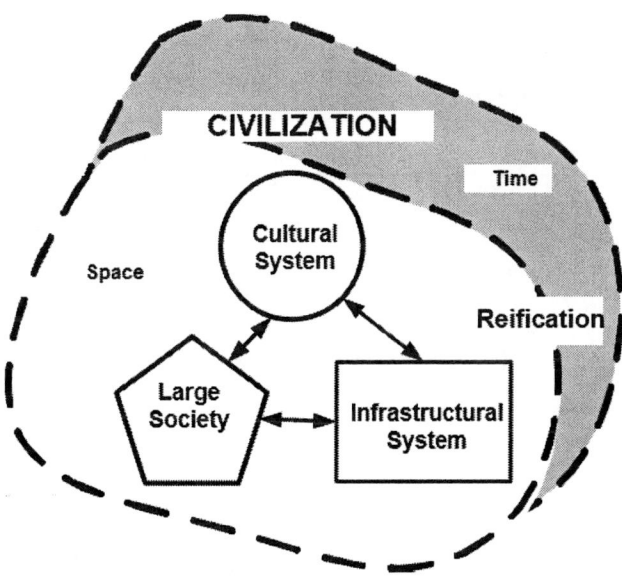

Figure 1.1. A model of civilization.

The world civilization as a continuum never dies—it only evolves from one stage to another. This evolution takes place through the life cycle of autonomous civilizations. At the very beginning of human civilization, there were several successful formations of living processes that could be considered initial autonomous civilizations. The first autonomous civilization was the Mesopotamian Civilization (including Sumerian), which emerged in the valley of the Euphrates-Tigris rivers in the Middle East about 4,000 B.C. In the Far-East, the first autonomous civilizations rose inland: Sinic (Chinese) about 3,000 B.C. and Indus (Harrappan) about 2,500 B.C. In Africa the initial civilization formed about 2500 B.C. and later the Berberic-Carthagean Civilization emerged around 600 B.C. and, in South America early autonomous civilizations included the Andean Civilization that emerged about 1500 B.C. In Central America the first autonomous civilization was the Meso-American Civilization which rose about 1000 BC. Both Central American civilizations fell about 1600 AD.

Autonomous civilizations rose in a response to physical challenges of nature (ecosystem). Humans began to organize themselves into a society, which provided exchangeable and specialized services, such as food from hunting, food production, house building, road construction, transportation, health care, entertainment, and so forth. These services and growing human communication led towards the formation of cities. These types of autonomous civilizations we will call societal civilizations.

In addition to the environmental challenges, societal civilization as a whole has been threatened by its own internal structure involving power, wealth creation, beliefs enforcement, family formation, leadership, and so forth. As societal civilizations evolved into more complex entities, they were managed by cultural manipulation. This type of autonomous civilization we will name cultural civilization. By culture, we understand a value-driven patterned behavior of a human entity.

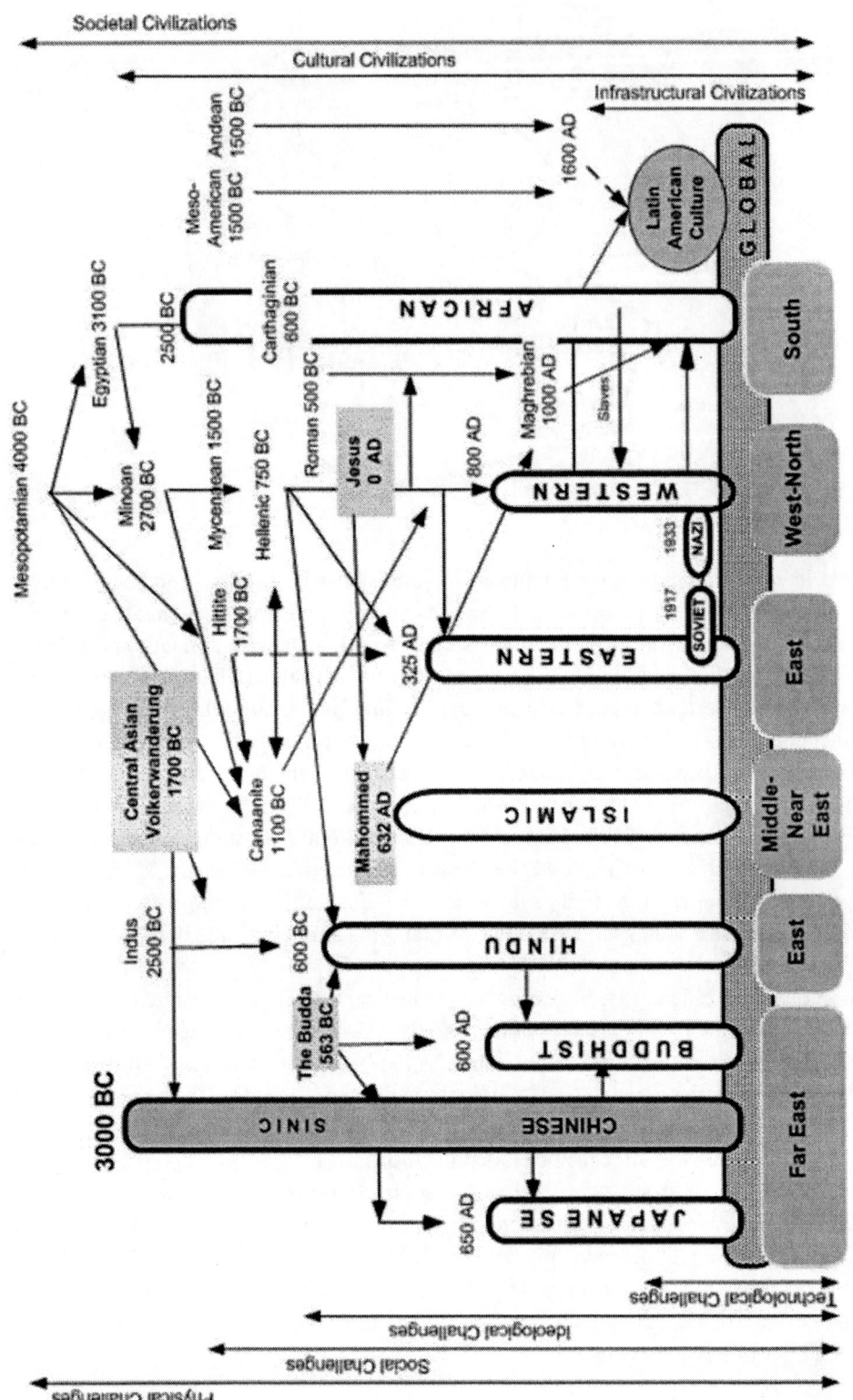

Figure 1.2. The Development of Chinese Civilization among other civilizations.

Ever since religion was transformed from beliefs in magic to beliefs in poly-gods and then to a mono-god, cultural civilization has applied religion as the main tool of cultural control. Religious and military forces were the foundations of the power apparatus that maintained society as a governed entity. These forces civilized society and moved it into higher levels of organization. Among cultural civilizations one can recognize about 16 cases, such as the Egyptian Civilization 3100 B.C., the Minoan 2700 B.C., the Mycean Civilization 1500 B.C., the Sinic (Chinese) Civilization 3000 B.C., the Canaanite Civilization 1100 B.C., the Hellenic Civilization 750 B.C., the Hindu Civilization 600 B.C., the Hellenistic Civilization 323 B.C., the Roman Civilization 31 B.C., the Eastern Civilization 325 A.D., the Ethiopian Civilization 400 A.D., the Buddhist Civilization 600 A.D., the Islamic Civilization 632 A.D., the Sub-Saharan Civilization 800 A.D., the Western Civilization 800 A.D., and the Maghrebian Civilization 1000 A.D. Cultural civilization evolves into a civilization with challenges generated by intra and inter-civilizational issues of war and peace. These types of issues have been managed by technological means of domination. Such a civilization we will call infrastructural civilization.

Infrastructural civilization's purpose is to expand spheres of influence with the means of technology. Technology drives the development of infrastructural civilizations. The prime target of technology applications has been a war machine which supports the main values of a given civilization. By-products of military applications of technology affect the civilian part of its infrastructure. Among eight infrastructural civilizations one can recognize the oldest and still acting Sinic-Chinese Civilization 3000 B.C., the Hindu Civilization 600 B.C., the Japanese Civilization 650 A.D., the Western Civilization 800 A.D., the Eastern Civilization 350 A.D., the Buddhist Civilization 600 A.D., the Islamic Civilization 632 A.D., and the African Civilization 1847 A.D. after the international treaty which established borders of states during the conference in Berlin in 1884-1985[2].

THE EVOLUTION OF WESTERN CIVILIZATION IN THE FIRST 1000 YEARS

The Rise of Europe

Europe is one of the Earth's seven continents; it is a Eurasian peninsula bordering the Atlantic in the North and West (counting Iceland) and separated from Africa by the Mediterranean in the South. In the East the divider between Europe and Asia are the Ural

---

[2] On November 15, 1884 at the request of Portugal, German chancellor Otto von Bismark called together the major western powers of the world to negotiate questions and end confusion over the control of Africa. At the time of the conference, 80% of Africa remained under traditional and local control. What ultimately resulted was a hodgepodge of geometric boundaries that divided Africa into fifty irregular countries. This new map of the continent was superimposed over the one thousand indigenous cultures and regions of Africa. The new countries lacked rhyme or reason and divided coherent groups of people and merged together disparate groups who really did not get along. At the time of the conference, only the coastal areas of Africa were colonized by the European powers. At the Berlin Conference the European colonial powers scrambled to gain control over the interior of the continent. The conference lasted until February 26, 1885 - a three month period where colonial powers haggled over geometric boundaries in the interior of the continent, disregarding the cultural and linguistic boundaries already established by the indigenous African population. By the time independence returned to Africa in 1950, the realm had acquired a legacy of political fragmentation that could neither be eliminated nor made to operate satisfactorily.

Mountains and Caspian Sea. The Black Sea belongs to Europe. Covering 10,400,000 km^2 (2 percent of the Earth's surface), Europe is the second-smallest continent after Australia. Population-wise (710,000,000, 11 percent of the global population) it comes third after Asia and Africa.

Figure 1.3. The border between Europe and Asia.

Most debatable part of Europe's geographical borders are the eastern frontiers. According to the *National Geographic Society (NGS)*, the border between Europe and Asia runs along the Ural range and through the middle of the Caspian Sea, leaving the Black Sea in Europe but the Caucasus Mountains and Turkey outside – despite the fact that the frontier cuts right through Constantinople, making three percent of Turkey European. According to Russian geographers, the European-Asian border runs along the Caucasus range, which would place parts of Caucasian states to the west of the Black Sea like Georgia, Azerbaijan or Armenia, as well as Kazakhstan in Europe, as together they lie to the west and north of the Caspian Sea. However, these countries are traditionally not considered European (especially Kazakhstan, which has no ties at all to European culture). Politically things may look different as Georgia strives for membership in NATO and Turkey negotiates its EU accession, but will we consider them European once they join? Figure 2 illustrates the European-Asian frontier.

From Europe to Western Civilization

Europe's sub-division into countries has probably been more debated than on any other continent. Depending on the author, we can even distinguish several different "Europe concepts". Davies[3] believes "Europe" to be a relatively late concept which replaced the "Christian" vision dominating intellectual perception from the 14th to the 18th century. It was not until after the Great French Revolution that the term "Europeans" came into use in place of "Frenchmen", "Spaniards" or "Germans."

Historically we can distinguish three main development phases in Western European civilization (Figure 1.4):

- *Early Europe.* The Greek and Roman era began around 1300 BC with the Mycenaean culture, which spread from the Greek mainland to the nearby islands Sardinia, Sicily, Crete and Cyprus. This was followed by the 753 BC foundation of the city Rome, the nucleus of Italy and its Roman Empire embracing Spain, Gaul, Britain and the Balkans (to name only its European dominions), which in fact was Early Europe although it still functioned in classical civilization.
- *Old Europe.* Its beginnings date back to the 800 AD foundation of the Frankish Empire by Charlemagne as a crowning of unity processes taking place on the continent from the 5th to the 7th centuries. This was a rather "dark" period in European history, marked by chaos, high crime and civilizational regression brought on by the downfall of the well-organized Roman Empire (even the famous Roman roads fell into decay). The response to this disorder and disintegration was the Migration Period during which Europe's peoples sought new territories and a new fate. The first to settle were the Franks, who under Charlemagne's excellent leadership formed so-called Western Europe, which ranged from the Atlantic to what was then known as Bohemia (today's Czech Republic). Old Europe laid the ground for Atlantic Civilization.
- *Young Europe.* Young Europe emerged to the east of Old Europe about two centuries later and stretched from the western borders of Germany to the Ural Mountains and from the Baltic to Black Sea. Moczulski[4] termed this territory "Isthmus."

---

[3] Norman Davies. Europe. Oxford. 1996. s. 7.
[4] Leszek Moczulski. *Geopolityka* (Geopolitics). Warsaw 1999.

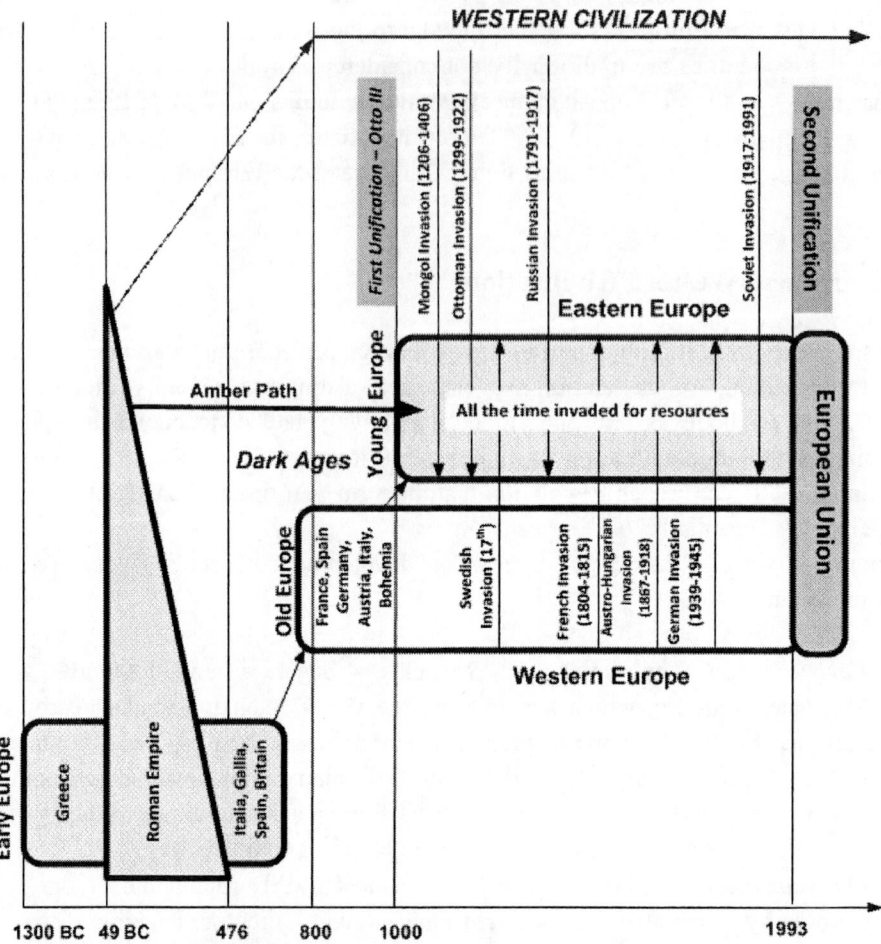

Figure 1.4. The birth of Europe and its development (time not in scale).

The relationships between Old and Young Europe reminds one of the relationship between older and younger sisters who furiously fight for inheritance but sometimes share some unexpected sentiment of being close members of the same family. In addition to these difficult relations between these two Europes, Young Europe, through her 1000 year history, experienced several invasions from the East and Far East (the Mongols) which added strong disadvantages to its well-being in the comparison with Old Europe's development. This bad "luck" of Young Europe has ended after being incorporated into European Union (2004-2007) about 1000 years after the German Emperor of the Roman-Holly Empire, Otto III, for the first time in the European history attempted to unite it.

WESTERN CIVILIZATION IN OLD EUROPE

Much of Western civilization in Old Europe was determined by the power of the Christian church, the Franks, and the Germans after the breakup of the Roman Empire in 476. The increased supply of silver from the Slaves gave the Franks the means to enlarge and fuse their power and helped pave the way for the supreme ruler of early medieval Europe: Charles the Great or Charlemagne (768-814). There were three aspects of Charlemagne's control that were particularly imperative: his conquests, his attempts to recover Roman civilization in what is known as the Carolingian Renaissance, and the resumption of the Roman imperial title. By the end of his reign, Charlemagne's empire contained most of Western Europe: France, Germany, Austria, Bohemia (The Czech Republic), half of Italy, the Low Countries, and Denmark. The size of his empire was the primary basis for the rise of Western Civilization since he was crowned Roman emperor by the pope on Christmas day, 800 AD as Roman emperor. The real status of this revived title diminished fairly early after Charlemagne's death and did not regain its luster until 961 when the ruler of Germany, Otto I, was crowned emperor by the pope. For next 850 years, Germany would be known as the Empire, or the Holy Roman Empire.

The most important mark Charlemagne's reign is that it was a shifting point in history when for the first time scholars began to treat Europe as a united culture and polity. After Charlemagne, Western European civilization would no longer be a simple imitation of Roman civilization. Ever since, it has defined its own institutions, culture, and infrastructures in its own standings. Western Civilization, at this time, was born and it has lasted 1200 years up unto the present.

The following centuries of Western Civilization in Europe (9th to 21st) were characterized by power, creeds, scientific, artistic, social, economic, technological, and military ferments full of wars and revolutions. They are characterized in the book's following chapter due to their complexity and importance which requires drawn out considerations. Here in a short synthesis one can distinguish the following key strategic events which gradually defined Western civilization in Old Europe from the 8th to 21st century:

1. **Christian religion** (8th century[5]) - the rising popularity, inspirational and organizational power, regardless of its schism, divisions, inquisition, and institutional problems.
2. **Feudalism** (8th century) – decentralized economy and clusters of hierarchical economic-power-community relationships.
3. **Colonialism** – (15th – 20th century) – expanded world and Old Europe's wealth.
4. The Scientific Revolution (16th – 17th centuries) – open minds and truth about the universe and planet's nature.
5. The Italian Renaissance (14th – 17th centuries) – humanity and beauty in art and architecture.
6. **High Culture** (since 14th century) – good taste and aspiration level.
7. The Enlightenment (17th – 18th centuries) – social progressive ideas inspiring coming revolutions.
8. The English (1688), American (1765-85), French (1789-1799) Revolutions - parliament, democracy, citizenship and equality.
9. The Industrial Revolution (since the 19th century) – engine, electricity, capital, factory, products, labor, Bourgeois society, class conflicts.
10. **Industrialization** (20th century) – spread of manufacturing, bureaucracy, technocracy and meritocracy.

---

[5] It includes the time from 8oo.

11 **Capitalism** (19th century) – free market, entrepreneurship, competition, efficiency, effectiveness, and inequality.
12 **Socialism** (20th century) – social-oriented distribution of wealth.
13 The Scientific and Technological Revolution (29th century) – car, airplane, medications, landing on the Moon, computer, the Internet.
14 **Mobility** (20th century) – easiness of engine-driven movement of people and material.
15 **Education** (20th century) – enhancement of judgment & choices, and attitudes of society
16 **Nationalism** (since 19th century) – ethnic pride, belonging, and sacrifice.
17 Two World Wars (1914-18) and (1939-1945) – Humanity won with modern barbarism.
18 **Independence** (second part of 20th century) – end of colonialism.
19 **Science** (20th century) – the foundation for advancement in civilizational development.
20 **Technology** (20th century) – the Technology society and conquered culture
21 The rise of the United States as the world-super power in the 20th century as the world hegemon controlling the world order.
22 The Cold War (1945-1991) - Capitalism has disqualified Communism.
23 **Democracy** (second part of 20th century) – dissemination around the world as the best political system.
24 **Pop Culture** (20th century) – vulgarization and counter-activation of society.
25 European Union (1993) – common market, currency (17 countries), laws, and peace.
26 The application of Internet (2000th) – free flow of ideas world-wide.
27 The **Information Wave** (end of the 20th century).
28 **Civilization clashes** (20th century) – values-driven conflicts and war between Islam and Western civilizations.
29 **Globalization** – free flow of ideas, capital, products, services.
30 The Global civilization (21st century) - super-consumerism, turbo-Capitalism, and huge inequality.
31 **Super-consumerism** (21st century) – more is better and strategic resources depleting.
32 The Virtual civilization (21st century) – active life beyond reality.
33 **Virtualit**y (21st century) - unlimited freedom and social chaos.
34 **Liquid times** (21st century) – uncertainty about today and tomorrow.

This set of the key strategic events through 1200+ years of civilizational development in Old Europe has defined the attributes for the rest of territories within the reach of Western civilization. Figure 1.5 illustrates how, from the Dark Ages, Western civilization transformed Old Europe to the Liquid Times, in other words moving from old regressive to new progressive uncertainty. Was it worth it? A great ancient Greek sage, Plato (424/423 – 348 BCE), was right that ideas control the development of the society; however, despite many good Western ideas, wisdom must be present in this development, of which there is a deficiency in the more advanced stages of Western civilization.

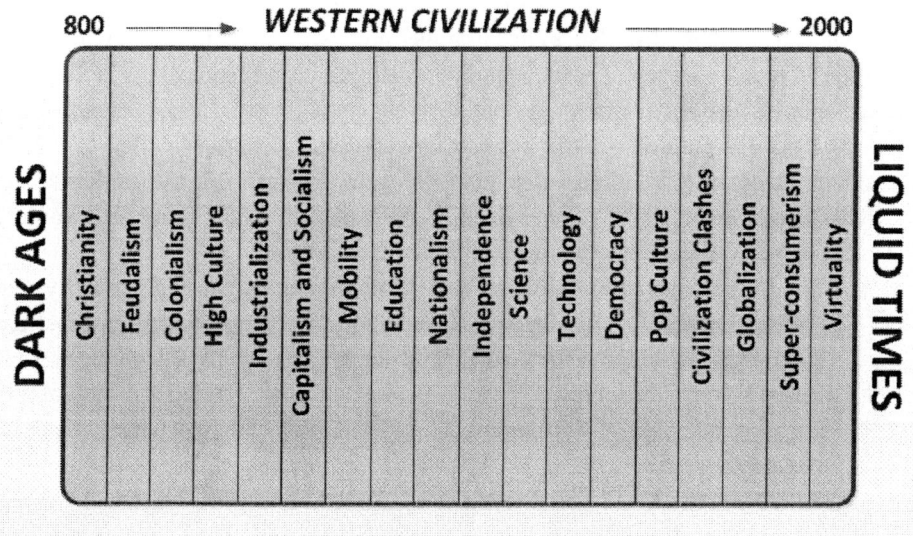

Figure 1.5. The development of Western civilization in Old Europe.

WESTERN CIVILIZATION IN YOUNG EUROPE

The First Nine Centuries of Young Europe

Young Europe is one of the world's "youngest" historical theatres and, although it was never a major part of either Global Civilization or its subcomponent Western Civilization, itis the most conflict-ridden region in the world.

Why did Young Europe attract more attention than other parts of the world? Doubtless the wars waged against it were driven by the need for material and human resources, which well-established Old Europe decided to satisfy by exploiting its weaker neighbor Young Europe. Young Europe owed its weakness to religion and geography. The Reformation's 1517 division of Christianity into Protestantism and Catholicism (and the earlier, 1054 Orthodox schism) resulted in the formation of industrious societies in the West and moralistic ones in the East. The first ate better, the second slept better, which in the West's case led to the earlier emergence of human rights, education, science, technology, trade, commerce and industry. Also, Old Europe was better located, and its access to the Atlantic allowed for the colonization of the non-European world, which ensured an almost unlimited supply of natural resources and slave labor (especially in the 16th-19th centuries).

Young Europe's first nine centuries were marked by wars and oppression, hence its present leanings towards defensiveness, nationalism and patriotism. It is no wonder that most of the huge migration wave from Europe to the U.S. between the years 1880 and 1914 came from Young Europe – its peoples were fleeing poverty and desolation in search of a better life in a New World.

Young Europe's first 900 years prompts to the following conclusions:

1. Due to its long isolation from the mainstream of Global (Greek-Roman) Civilization, Young Europe's main weakness lies in governing skills and education, which is still visible in today's Poland, Czech Republic, Slovakia, and Hungary.
2. Permanent internal conflict considerably weakened Young Europe, making it easy prey for foreign empires seeking resources, slaves and women.
3. Poland, territorially the largest state in 16th-century Europe, lost its position due to:
   a. Commitment to the over-demanding mission of civilizing Lithuania and Ruthenia, then a part of the Republic of Two Nations.
   b. The *Liberum veto* rule and elections of foreign monarchs. This gradually steeped Polish statehood in chaos and allowed the rise of absolutistic monarchies in Russia, Prussia and Austria, which eventually divided the disintegrating Polish state between themselves. Poland's weakness soon infected the rest of Young Europe, with only the Hungarians and Czechs thriving under the Austro-Hungarian rule.

Young Europe – The 20th Century

Young Europe's inferior geographical position and its dependence on stronger states helped create a geopolitical concept. Leszek Moczulski[6] defined geopolitics (power over time and space) as overlapping layers – physical, civilizational and political – which give birth to a political doctrine. In the 20th century, geopolitics was the driving force of political strategy in Germany, the Soviet Union and the U.S. The fundamentals of geopolitics were laid down in the 1880s by the German geographer Friedrich Ratzel, who first defined the *Lebensraüm* concept entailing the "enlargement of vital living space" by societies with "growing cultures". This idea was subsequently adopted by Nazis Germany in World War II. In the 19th century Ratzel's concept of geopolitics was further developed by the Swedish scholar Rudolf Kjellen; however, the idea won broader attention only after Kjellen's 1916 book *The State as a Form of Life*.

In the 21th century geopolitics controls the entire world, but it owes its emergence to the early-20th-century situation in Young Europe. One of the most influential contemporary geopolitics theoreticians was the English geographer Halford Mackinder, who outlined his views in a paper entitled *The Geographical Pivot of History*, delivered in 1904 before the Royal Geographical Society. At the time Mackinder said that history was and will remain an effect of the pressure suffered by the peoples locked away in Young Europe and Western and Central Asia (Mackinder 1904).

These territories possessed the resources and natural conditions that attracted imperial economies and their military machinery, and, as Russia was a natural heir to the Mongolian Empire, its expansionism was, perforce, its *reson d'etre*.

Mackinder reminded everyone that nine-twelfths of the globe's surface was taken up by oceans and seas and the remaining three-twelfths by the World-Island of Europe, Asia, Africa, America and Australia-Oceania. Of these three-twelfths, two-twelfths fall to Europe, Asia and Africa and one-twelfth to America and Australia-Oceania (whose frontiers are not easy to attack). Mackinder split the world into four parts (Figure 1.6); the **Heartland**

---

[6] Leszek Moczulski. *Geopolityka* (Geopolitics), Warsaw, 1999.

embracing Young Europe and West-Central Asia, the **Marginal Lands** including Western Europe and Southeast Asia, **Deserts** (the Mideast and North Africa) and **Islands and Other Continents** (America and Australia-Oceania). This division led him to formulate the following rules:

1. Who rules Young Europe commands the heartland,
2. Who rules the Heartland commands the World-Island,
3. Who rules the World-Island controls the world.

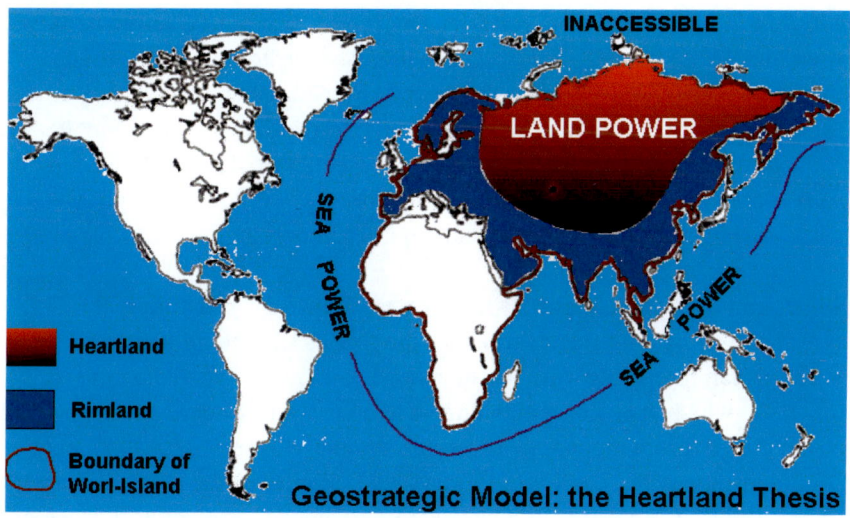

Figure 1.6. The world according to Halford Mackinder (1904).
(Photo: www.birminghamwarstudies.wordpress.com).

Mackinder suggested a sanitary cordon between Russia and Germany to prevent the Heartland's (Germany's) expansion. This idea was put to practical use by U.S. President Woodrow Wilson in the 1919 Versailles Treaty. The new states, from Finland down through Poland, Czechoslovakia, Hungary, Romania, Bulgaria (last two founded earlier, respectively in 1878 and 1908) and Yugoslavia were to keep Communism away from Old Europe. The Teheran and Yalta Treaties of 1943 and 1945 again placed the countries of Central-East Europe in the role of a safety cordon around communism and its threats to Old Europe.

Germany applied Mackinder's theory before Yalta to first attack Poland in 1939, and then, in 1941, the Soviet Union (the heartland) with the aim of gaining control of the World-Island, and subsequently the entire world. German geopolitics has many fathers. Its official founder is Karl Haushofer, a geography professor at Munich University whom Hitler later promoted to head the German Academy of Science. Haushofer helped Hitler write *Mein Kampf* in his Landsberg prison and dedicated his own book, *Contemporary World Politics*, to Rudolf Hess. Karl Haushofer adapted the heartland doctrine to promote a German-Russian alliance aimed at integrating Central and Young Europe. It is this concept that produced the notorious 1939 Ribbentrop-Molotov Pact. On September 26, 1939, three days after the pact was signed, Haushofer even published an article entitled *Hitler's World Revolution* in the British weekly *New Statesman and Nation*. After Germany's 1941 invasion of Russia, Haushofer fell out of grace and was replaced by Alfred Rosenberg, a pathological enemy of

Russia. Professor Haushofer was a typical German theoretician (like Marx or Luxemburg) who failed to foresee the tragic consequences of his teachings. To do him some justice, he did commit suicide after the war.

While World War I was fought mainly in Old Europe and on Polish-Russian ground, World War II took place chiefly in Young Europe and, towards its close, on Old Europe's northern and southern outskirts. This was a terrible war which cost 55 million lives mostly in Young-Europe and especially in Poland. In all about 240 million people perished in Europe's 20th-century wars, revolutions and the Spanish flu epidemic (Ferguson 2006)[7].

A first attempt at analyzing Germany's invasion of the Heartland (Russia) was *The 1812 Campaign in Russia* by General Carl von Clausewitz. According to Clausewitz Napoleon lost because he was unable to gain control over Russia's vast territory. Also L. Tolstoy's *War and Peace* contains a motif about drawing the enemy into forestland. In their war against the Soviets the Germans were not afraid of Russia's territorial vastness and compared the hardships of accessing the Ural Mountains with Napoleon's troubles with reaching the Rhine. The Germans were convinced their advanced technology would take them as far as India. They miscalculated because they forgot about another important heartland factor – its severe climate.

The Soviet empire's strengthened position after World War II forced the U.S. to adopt new strategies for dealing with the Heartland – the Soviet Union and its satellites. Already in 1944 America began preparing for World War III. Among the plans was a long-range bomber, the B32, which had no application in the war still underway at the time. Some Americans envisaged dropping an atom bomb on the Soviets. The U.S. elite's attitude towards Communism was marked by fear, very much similar to the onetime fear of Genghis Khan's hordes. The Polish general Władysław Anders hoped to lead Old Europe against the Soviets in 1945-47, which he admitted in his memoirs entitled "No Last Chapter". This last chapter was to be the crusade against the Soviet Union.

In 1945 the U. S. had sixty times as many combat-ready divisions as the war-decimated Red Army. In 1944, fearing a protracted war with Japan, U. S. President Roosevelt drew the Soviets into the conflict. For this he paid with Young Europe, which he handed over to the Soviet Union in Yalta. This move in a sense strengthened the Heartland (in Mackinder's variant), hence it had to be replaced by a new doctrine.

A new American doctrine keeping the Heartland at bay and simultaneously putting the world under The U. S.'s control was developed in 1944 by the Dutch-American geostrategist Nicholas Spykman, head of the International Relations Institute at Yale University. According to this doctrine the one who controls the **Rimland** rules the world (Figure 1.7). Necessary in this case was an alliance between the sea powers, Great Britain and the U. S., and the land power, the Soviet Union, in order to conquer Germany and Japan. After WWII was won, the possession of the Rimland by the West would enable it to encircle the Soviets and prevent communism from spreading around the world. Taught by the defeats of France and Germany in 1812 and 1945, America did not wish to interfere in the Heartland's (Russia's) inner affairs but only neutralize it by encirclement and control over the Rimland.

---

[7] Ferguson, Neil. (2006). *The War of the Word, Twentieth-Century Conflict and the Descent of the West*. New York.

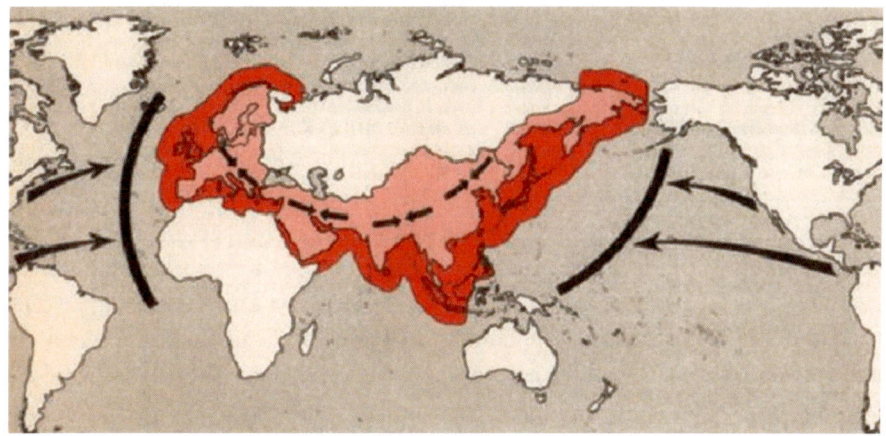

Figure 1.7. The world according to Nicholas Spykman (1944). Who controls Rimland controls the world.
(Photo:www.alainet.org).

So it seemed that for the first time in centuries Young Europe would cease to be a source of global conflict. Always on the peripheries of World Civilization, it had now evolved into a mega-periphery, a kind of "disease area" everyone wanted to avoid. Then came the Cold War (1945-1991), which, however, was to bring quite unexpected effects – moreover, they were to come from Europe's "diseased" part.

Attempts to surround the Soviet Union by democratic countries and their allies resulted in an arms race in space begun by the Soviets, who decided to avert circumvention threats by developing inter-continental missiles. The first of these was the renowned Sputnik. Launched in 1957, it signaled that the Heartland planned to protect itself from the West by attacking its distant outskirts (the Rimland and the New World).

The communist onslaught in South America proved successful only in the case of Cuba (1956), which in 1962 almost became the hotbed of a Soviet-U. S. conflict over plans to install Soviet nuclear silos on the island. But America's young president, John F. Kennedy, refused to be led astray by the wily Soviet leader Nikita Khrushchev and the Soviets agreed to withdraw from Cuba, in return for which the U. S. resigned plans to build nuclear silos in Turkey.

Meanwhile Young Europe was proving increasingly reluctant to adjust to the Cold War and its demands. In 1956 public revolts broke out in Poznań (June), Budapest and Warsaw (October), after which Soviet domination in this part of the continent began to erode.[8] This surely pleased the man in the street but was very worrying for the communist elite. In the early 1970s, in an attempt to reinforce its authority, the Soviets began to prepare for an inner-European conflict. This way the geopolitical focus had again moved from Asia and Cuba to Young Europe – a periphery and at the same time a geopolitical hotbed, as only here did democracy neighbor so closely on totalitarianism.

In 1971 the Warsaw Pact was preparing an invasion of Western Europe. According to the plan, Soviet tanks equipped with extra fuel tanks were to attack western cities from East

---

[8] Targowski Andrzej, *Informatyka klucz do dobrobytu* (*IT – the Key to Prosperity*), Warsaw 1971. Targowski Andrew, *Chwilowy koniec historii* (*The Momentary End of History*), Warsaw 1991. Targowski Andrzej, Andrzej Ajnenkiel (Ed), *Losy Polski i Świata* (*The Fate of Poland and the World*), Warsaw 2000.

Germany at a time when most U.S. officers were away from NATO bases. Success was to be guaranteed by the Soviets' clear supremacy in tanks and infantry, as NATO would never attack its own cities with tactical nuclear bombs. NATO would, however, atom-bomb Poland, Czechoslovakia, Hungary and Romania to cut off supplies for the Warsaw Pact forces already in Western Europe. The Soviets foresaw this and were prepared to ship supplies via the Baltic Sea.[9]

These plans got into the hands of a Polish staffer in the Warsaw pact HQ, Col. Ryszard Kuklinski, who quickly realized that he and his loved ones, not to mention the Polish people and the country's armed forces (which under the plan were to gain control of Denmark), could well meet a fate similar to the inhabitants of Hiroshima and Nagasaki. Losing no time, Col. Kukliński told the U. S. about these plans. At the time the West was flourishing and, fearing the specter of war, replied with a *détente* policy under which it granted the Soviet bloc over $100 billion in credit, of which 30 billion went to Poland. The then Soviet leader Leonid Brezhnev allegedly responded to this with the words, "why wage war when we have what we wanted?" In 1972 U.S. President Nixon and his aide Henry Kissinger visited Poland underway to Moscow and promised economic aid, including computer hardware, which at the time was embargoed.

The Polish communist party secretary Edward Gierek and his deputy prime minister for economic affairs Tadeusz Wrzaszczyk promptly purchased license rights for 300 new products and industrial processes and quite effectively knocked out the country's centrally-steered economy, which collapsed under its own weight and the "medication" it had been applied. The situation soon got out of control, although for a short time living standards actually did improve, and Poles began to harbor hopes for a better future and even prosperity (from Targowski's book *IT – the Key to Prosperity*). This revelry, however, soon came to an end. Already, 1974 witnessed the beginning of severe economic shortages ultimately crowned by the 1981 Solidarity revolt and communist Poland's fall in 1989. In the years between, about 1.2 million Poles emigrated from the country.

This huge historical process was set in motion by Col. Ryszard Kukliński, a man of frail build and Great Spirit, who not only saved his army, companions and their families from a terrible death, but also initialized the slow and painful agony of communist Poland, like a classical catalyst which speeds up processes without participating in them.

Poland in the year 1980 saw the emergence of Solidarity, a trade union which began the large-scale print of underground press and literature. This and the homeland pilgrimages of Polish-born pope John Paul II woke the Poles and with them the rest of Central-East Europe, which in 1989 freed itself from the Soviet yoke. Two years later, in 1991, came the demise of the Soviet Empire itself.[10] Figure 1.8 shows Young Europe as a 20th-century geopolitical center. A periphery of Western Civilization, it also neighbored on the East, which throughout the 20th century stood in conflict with the West.

---

[9] These fears were not unfounded. An acquaintance at a U. S. college, who in 1971 was in command of U.S. nuclear installations in West Germany, told me that they were on constant alert and ready to fire A missiles at us within 10 minutes. In 2005 I had a chance conversation with a former U. S. pilot who told me that at the time he had been given targets to destroy Young Europe.

[10] This is described in greater detail in related literature; therefore, I only mention it here.

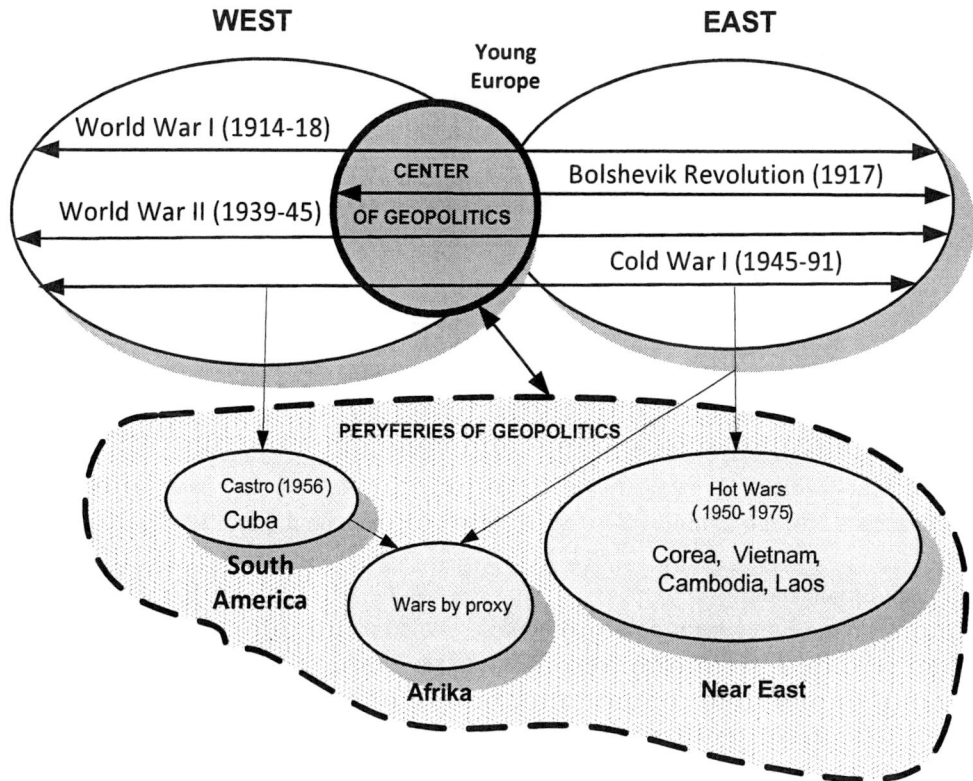

Figure 1.8. Young Europe as the center of Geopolitics in the 20th century.

A side-product of the Cold War was the Internet, devised as a communication tool for the "day after" the nuclear holocaust (Targowski 2006).[11] The Internet has become what books were in the 15th century. It revolutionized information flow and communication and helped build today's "electronic global village" with very "revolutionary" consequences for humanity and geopolitics.

Young Europe's last hundred years has led to the following conclusions:

1. In the words of the eminent British historian Norman Davies,[12] New Europe, especially Poland, evolved into a "God's Playground" on whose territory (playing field) all and sundry pursued bloody and fiendish games.
2. Despite its peripheral position Young Europe was a 20th-century geopolitical center where:
   a. Capitalism, Communist and Nazism were experimented with and two world wars took place.
   b. The Genocide and Holocaust were committed.
   c. Subjugated societies showed that moral values can be more important than material welfare and even worth dying for.

---

[11] Targowski Andrzej, "Polsko-Amerykańskie aspekty Internetu." (The Internet - Polish-American Aspects), *Rocznik Polonii*, No. 1/2006, pp. 122-138.
[12] Norman Davies, *Heart of Europe, A History of Poland*, New York 1986. Norman Davies, *God's Playground, History of Poland*, New York 2004, rev.ed.

d. The abovementioned extremes were discredited to the benefit of all humankind.
3. Old and Young Europe have united after a millennium of armed conflict. This time they united peacefully and willingly, with Old Europe ready to atone for the wrongs done to its "younger sister".
4. Europe united within the EU has a chance to live better, and a lot of Europeans have become an example of peaceful cooperation between countries for the rest of the world.

Young Europe in the 21ST Century

Europe's 2004-2007 reunion was a process of huge macro-historical importance as it marked Young Europe's breakaway from the victim's role it had played over its first thousand years. Thus, the future of Young Europe will depend on the following strategies:

1. In the short term:
   a. Young European politicians should avoid conflict within the EU in order not to estrange Old Europe and inspire it to seek its future in a "real Europe" limited to Germany, France, Britain, Italy, Belgium, Holland and Luxembourg.
   b. The societies of Young Europe must make use of their chance to learn from Old Europe. Also, they should elect pro-European representatives to national and EU legislation bodies.
2. In the long term:
   a. Young Europe must unite with Old Europe permanently and irrevocably.
   b. Young Europe's future should also be the future of Old Europe. This will probably take effect in the wake of the already beginning global battle for energy sources.

WESTERN CIVILIZATION IN EUROPE AFTER WORLD WAR II

After World War II the 20th century witnessed Old and Young Europe's evolution into political Western and Eastern Europe. Figure 1.9 illustrates Europe's political and geographical division into "West" and "East".

The civilizations of Europe can be divided into (Figure 1.10):

- Western Europe (Western Civilization-Christianity-oriented)
- Northern Europe (Western Civilization- Christianity-oriented)
- Central Europe (Western Civilization- Christianity-oriented)
- Eastern Europe (Eastern Civilization-Christianity-Orthodox-oriented)

Europe's fundamental division into Old and Young was sufficiently deep to survive the whole 2nd millennium. Periodically reinforced, it is still visible today. Still in 2004-2005, U.S. Secretary of State Donald Rumsfeld resorted to this division when commenting on Europe's stance towards the Iraq invasion (although instead of 'Young Europe" he used the term "New Europe"). In one of his lectures Norman Davies split Europe into "better" and "worse". I think a much more adequate division would be into "richer" and "poorer".

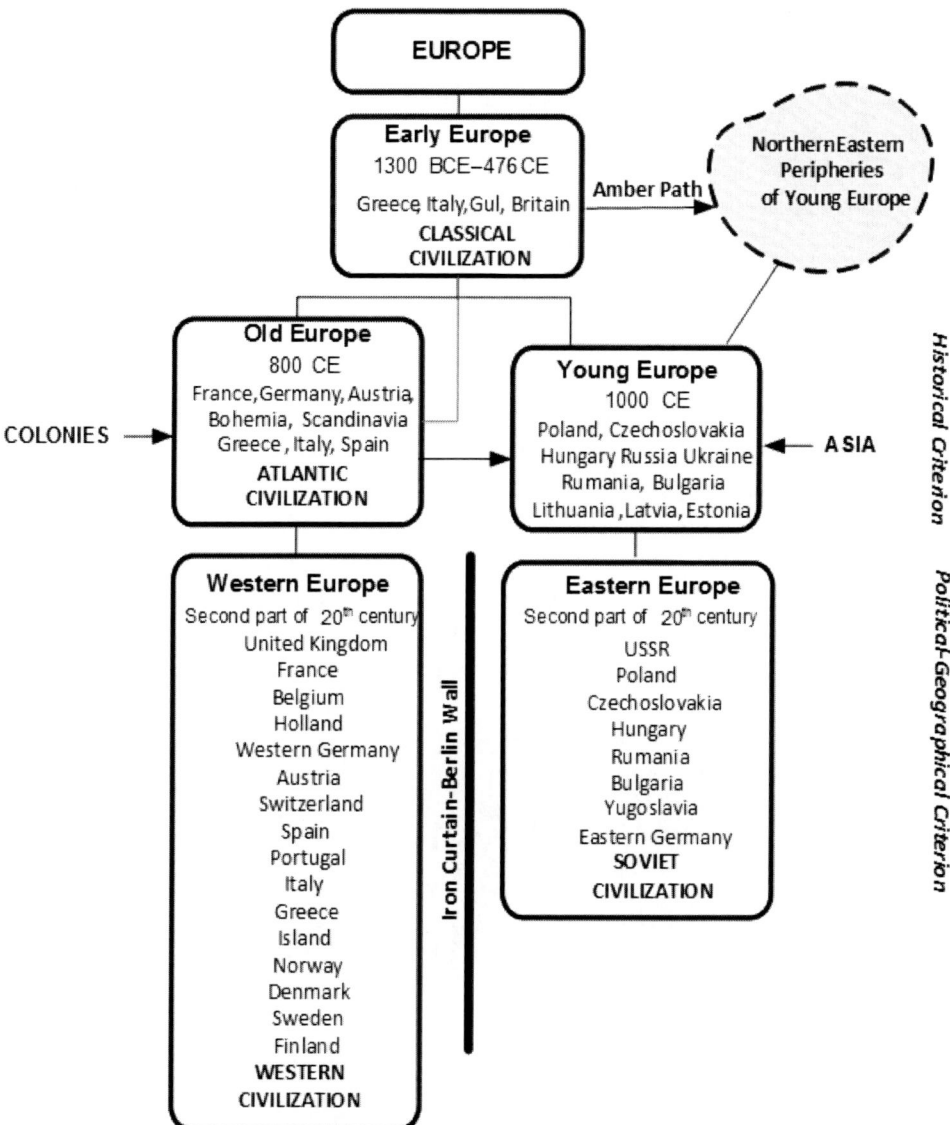

Figure 1.9. The states evolution of Europe after World War II (1939-1945).

Many – perhaps too many – efforts have been undertaken in the past to unite Old and Young Europe. One rather vague attempt was made in the year 1000 by Otto III, the son of a Greek princess hence an Easterner on his mother's side and a student of Sylvester II, the pope who founded Poland's first bishopric and, more interestingly, gave European civilization the ZERO, which laid the foundations for modern information technology development. Otto's efforts, however, quickly proved quite futile. Decidedly premature, they were founded more on an intellectual concept than any real civilizational or geopolitical necessity. Old and Young Europe were to really unite in early 2007, a whole 1007 years later.[13]

European Union

France after losing in devastating wars three times to Germany in 1871, 1914-18, 1940-45, wanted to curtail any other hostilities of Germany which was once united with France in the empire of the Franks. A French diplomat, Jean Monnet, and Józef Retinger[14], a Polish émigré-diplomat and founder of the Bilderberg Group in 1954 behind the scenes at a club of very influential active and former politicians[15], and who eventually became the Honorary Secretary General of the European Movement (Figure 10.10), inspired the formation of the European Coal and Steel Communality (ESCS) in 1951. It drew together the chief continental Western consumers and producers of coal and steel, the two materials most essential for the rebuilding of Western European civilization. It members were France, West Germany, Luxemburg, Belgium, Holland, and Italy. These six countries thus became the core countries of the coming Western European unity. Their project was to place the German industrial complex, the center of German industrial power, under international control and at the same time promote cooperation, reconciliation, and economic strength.

Very soon in 1956 the North Atlantic Treaty Organization (NATO) was formed as an alliance of national military forces in response to the formation of the Warsaw Pact, the Soviet-led alliance of Young Europe's military forces in 1953 aimed at Western Europe during the times of the Cold War between the West and East.

Figure 1.10. Those who inspired the process of unifying Europe after World War II.
A French diplomat Jean Monnet (1888-1979) and a Polish Diplomat Józef Retinger (1888-1960).
(Photo: Public domain).

---

[13] Romania and Bulgaria joined the EU in 2007.
[14] J. Retinger was never mentioned in official and popular publication on the birth of United Europe. He completed a PhD degree at Sorbonne at 20 years old, the youngest ever for an alumni of Sorbonne.
[15] Among other pioneers of united Europe were: Robert Schuman, Konrad Adenauer, Alcide De Gasperi, Paul-Henri Spaak, and Aliero Spinelli.

Eventually, following the successful beginning of Western Europe's integration, the next similar organizations were formed: The European Atomic Energy Community (Euratom) and European Economic Community (EEC also known as the Common Market) were formed in 1957. These organizations became the launch pad for the further integration of Western Europe, aiming to compete with the United States and generate again the prosperity and power that Europe had in the 19th century. In 1973 the original Six were joined by Great Britain, Ireland and Denmark. The Nine now began calling themselves the European Community (EC). By 1986 Spain, Portugal, and Greece were admitted to the EC after three years of preparations to fit the rules of the EC. In 1993 the European Union was created with a common currency (among 17 nations only), law and restructured European Parliament, European Commission, European Council, and Courte of Justice to follow the classic three branches of government, needless to say originally formulated in Europe by a French philosopher Baron de la Bréde de Montesquieu in the 18th century. Through the next process of acquiring new members from political Eastern Europe (Young Europe), the common market embraced 28 countries and 600 million consumers in 2004-2007. It constitutes the largest single trading entity, conducting one fourth of the world's commerce and has becomethe strongest common market in the world, measured by its purchasing power.

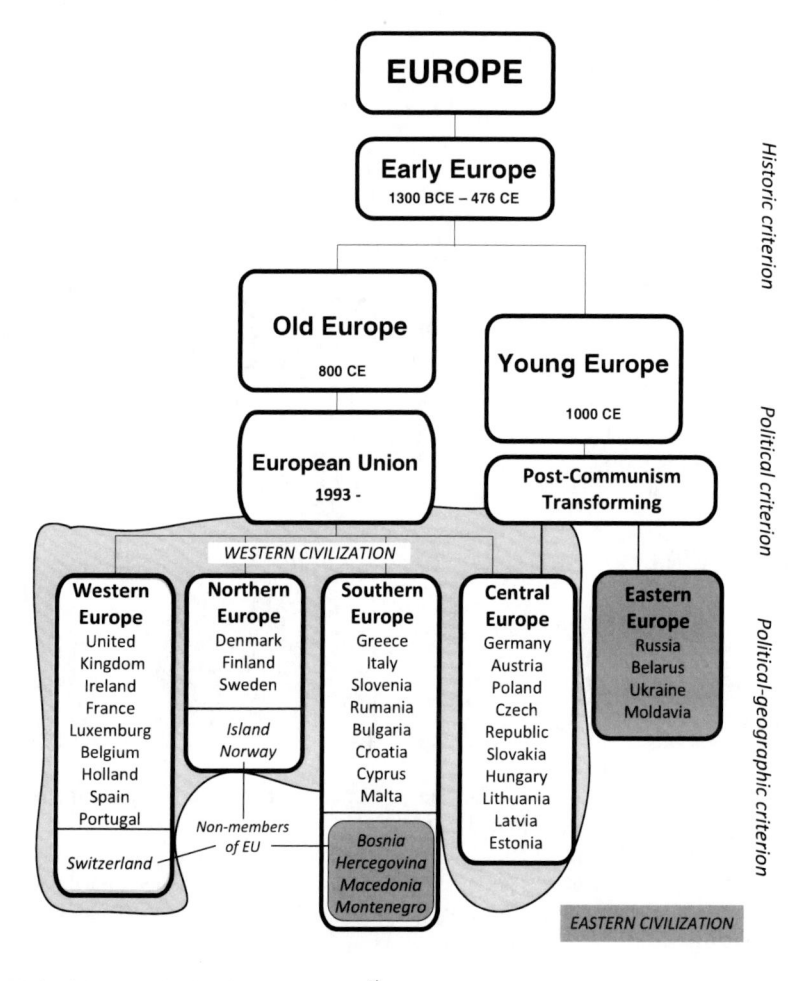

Figure 1.11. United Europe in the dawn of the 21st century.

Figure 1.11 illustrates the birth of United Europe in the 21st century.

Belarus, Ukraine and Moldova belong to East Europe, though in 2014 the Western Union and Russia staged a silent tug-of-war trying to pull all three over to "their side". The intellectual elites in these countries would like to see them closer to Central Europe; however, Russia cannot allow for losing those countries which share Eastern Civilization (Orthodox) and belong to the former Soviet Empire.

The fact that Old and Young Europe have been united in the 21st century after 1000 years of such attempts is proven by the fact that four Polish politicians took leadership of the whole of Europe (both Old and Young) by a free election organized according to European Union rules (Figure 1.11). It was done with the exception of John Paul II who has been elected by the Church's Cardinals from the whole Christian world.

Figure 1.12. Polish politicians from Young Europe who changed geopolitics (by eliminating *Communism* from Young Europe) and shaped Europe after 1000 years of attempts. Pope John Paul II (1920-2005), Lech Walesa (1943-) Leader of Solidarity and first democratic President of Poland after WW II, Poland's Prime Minister Jerzy Buzek (1940-) and President of European Parliament (2009-2012), Poland's Prime Minister and President of the European Union (2014-) Donald Tusk (1957-). (Photo: Public domain).

Table 1.1. A Framework of American civilization history 1000-1788

Epoch *(long-term segment)*	Period *(determined by political aims)*	Phase *(ruled by the same political paradigm)*	Interphase *(transitional interaction)*	Stage *(ruled by same political shade)*
Agriculture Wave 8000 B.C.-	Asian Migration to America 30,000-13,000 B.C.	Early Medieval European Expansion 900-1100 A.D.	European Crusades in the East 1095-1291	
	Viking Voyages 1000-1015 A.D.			
	Growth of Local Tribes 1000 - 1500 A.D	Growth of Feudal Europe 1000s-1400s	Age of European Exploration & Renaissance 1400-1600	
Pre-colonial 1000-1607	Discovering a New World 1492-1607	Clash of Cultures Indian vs. European in a New World 1500s-1800s	New Monarchies Merchant Capitalism 1460s-1700s	Wars with Indians in a New World 1490s-1800s
Globalization Wave I Colonial 1607-1783	Exploring North America 1607-1772	Settling & Colonizing 1607-1667 Jamestown-1607 Mayflower-1620 Boston-1630 Maryland-1632 Connecticut-1639 Massachusetts-1692 Virginia-1707 New Netherlands-1614 New Amsterdam-1625 New Sweden-1638		Harvard College-1636 New York 1665-
			Anglo-Dutch Naval War 1664-1667	
		Colonial Affairs 1668-1776	Revolutionary Approach 1762-1774	
	Birth of a Nation 1773-1788	War of American Independence 1775-1783 Final Struggle For Political Independence 1776-1783	Revolutionary War "Boston Tea Party" 1773	First Continental Congress-1774
				Battles of Lexington and Concord-1775
				Second Continental Congress 1775-1776
				Declaration of Independence-1776
				Constitution 1787-1788 Bill of Rights-1789

THE EXPANSION OF WESTERN CIVILIZATION TO AMERICA

The huge continent of America was populated by people coming from Asia through the land-bridge connecting Asia with America about 30,000 years ago, where today there is the Bering Strait. These people created the original and vigorously developed civilizations of the Indians, Incas, Aztecs, and Mayans. About 1002 the first European Vikings led by Leif Ericsson from Scandinavia (Norway today) came to Northern America and settled colonies of ruthless raiders which did not survive to see the next wave of discoveries of America in the 15th century.

Table 1.2. A Framework of Americanized Western civilization history 1778 – 1900

Epoch (long-term segment)	Period (determined by political aims)	Phase (ruled by the same political paradigm)	Interphase (transitional interaction)	Stage (ruled by same political shade)
Globalization Wave II Founding a Nation 1788-1900	Testing a Union 1788-1865	The Young Republic 1789-1861	*Agricultural Wave* 1607-	First President G. Washington 1789-97
				Federalists 1789-1801
				Jeffersonians 1801-1829 (Louisiana Purchase 1803) (Lewis & Clark 1804-1806) (War with Britain 1812-1815)
			Innovation Wave 1830s- "Yankee Ingenuity" --------------------- *Continental Expansion* 1835-1910s --------------------- *Industrial Wave* 1840s- --------------------- Civil War 1861-1865 Spanish-American War Approach 1895-	Jacksonian Democracy 1829-1848
				(War with Mexico 1846-1848 *Westward*)
				Slavery and Southern States Issues 1848-1861
				"Robber Barons" 1840s-1900s
				Monopolistic Capitalism 1860s-
				First Gilded Age 1865-1900s

Table 1.3. A Framework of Americanized Western civilization history 1901 – 1990

Epoch *(long-term segment)*	Period *(determined by political aims)*	Phase *(ruled by the same political paradigm)*	Interphase *(transitional interaction)*	Stage *(ruled by same political shade)*
Globalization Wave III Building a Superpower 1898-	Expanding Resources 1898-1945	Imperial Dreams 1898-1914 War against Spain in Cuba and Philippines-1898 Annexation of Hawaii 1898 and Panama Canal-1903 Intervention in Nicaragua-1912-1925 Mexico-1914,	World War I 1914-1919 Parity with England, Germany & France	Regulated Capitalism 1910s- (income taxes & Federal Reserve Board)
				Fordism 1907- *assembly lines* Labor Movement Full Speed Ahead
			----------------------	All Jazzed Up 1919-1929
		Economic Instability 1914-1941	World War II 1941-1945 (Entering the War in 1941) Dominance over Europe & Japan	Depression 1929-1933
				New Deal 1933-1941
			----------------------	War Effort 1941-1945
	Emerging as a World Power 1946-1991	Age of Affluence 1945-1960	Cold War 1945-1991	Korean War 1950-1953
				Vietnam War 1959-1975
		Long Strange Trip 1960-1969		Civil Rights 1960s
		Out of Gas 1970-1980	*Information Wave 1980s-*	Oil Crisis 1974- Liberal Capitalism
		Masters of the Universe 1980-1988 *(Reagan Era)*	--------------------- Fall of Communism 1991	Second Gilded Age 1981-2000s

The next wave of Westernizing America took 6 centuries (1000-1607) and can be called the Pre-colonial Era full of civilizational clashes with Indian civilization. The First Globalization Wave aimed at the exploitation of American resources including the colonization by the British Empire and a war which ended by the formation of the United States in 1776 (Declaration of Independence). These times and events are provided in Table 1.1.

In the following their independence, the United States passed through many stages of brutal development at the political, social, and economic levels which is characterized in Table 1.2.

The birth of the USA eventually Americanized Western civilization since the New World became the winner of Wars I and II and the world's extraordinary leader in industrial and military manufacturing supported by the strong development of science and technology as it is illustrated in Table 1.3.

Figure 1.13. George Washington (1732-1799) made the United States possible—not only by defeating a king, but by declining to become one himself (Wikimedia Commons and Photo too). The decolonization of North America was 180 years prior to a similar world-wide process which took place after the World War II in the 1960s.

Figure 1.14. Abraham Lincoln (1809-1865) freed the slaves and presided over America's second unification. Thomas Jefferson (1743-1826) the author of the five most important words in American history: "All men are created equal."

Figure 1.15. The American Giants of Technology who changed Western civilization and beyond: Thomas Edison (1847-1931) put electricity to homes, Orville Wright (1871-1948) and Wilbur Wright (1867-1912) invented airplane, Andrew Carnegie (1835-1919) developed the large steel industry, Henry Ford (1863-1947) invented inexpensive cars and assembly lines as the way of Americanizing of the mass production and market, Alexander Graham Bell ((1847-1922) invented the telephone and opened the age of telecommunications, thereby "shrinking" the world.
(Photo: Public domain).

The American civilization in the 21st century is losing its steam due to economic globalization and the clash of Islam and Western civilization as it is characterized in Table 1.4.

The presented model of American Civilization history allows for the following observations:

A. Why was America discovered in the 15th century?
   1. Human curiosity, geographical explorations, and scientific theories defined in the Renaissance led to a new world view and modernity, which motivated sailors to open new routes to the Indies and (by accident) across the Atlantic to the Americas.

Table 1.4. A Framework of American civilization history 1990 – 2008

Epoch (long-term segment)	Period (determined by political aims)	Phase (ruled by the same political paradigm)	Interphase (transitional interaction)	Stage (ruled by same political shade)
Globalization Wave IV Building a Superpower 1991- "Flattening World"	Emerging as a Sole Remaining Superpower 1991	New World Order 1991-2001	Information Wave 1980s- ------------------ War of Civilizations New York 2001--	"Persian Gulf War" 1990-1991
				War in Afghanistan 2001-
				War with Iraq 2003-
		Globalization of the U.S Economy 1990s-		Managerial Capitalism 1980s-
				Off-shore Outsourcing 1980s-

Figure 1.16. President Theodor Roosevelt (1858-1915) shortened the power of Big Business in the U.S. and President Franklin Delano Roosevelt (1882-1945) eliminated the threat of Nazism with temporary help from Soviet Communism and spread democracy beyond the U.S.
(Photo: Public domain).

2. The growth of New Monarchies (Portuguese, Spanish, British, and French, the first modern bureaucratic states) in the 15th and 16th centuries helped to grow merchant capitalism and supported geographical explorations, eventually leading to the discovery of America and acquisition of new resources and wealth.

B. Why did the U.S become the world's superpower within 220 years (1788-2008)?
   1. The international impact is the critical factor in the attainment of hegemonic power by the U.S. in the 21st century:
      Proof:
      - The Globalization Wave I (geographical discoveries) brought Europeans to a New World, which they colonized, leading to the birth of a nation (1774-1788).
      - The Globalization Wave II (Immigration Wave – 1870-1914) populated the vast country and strengthened its continental destiny (Into the West 1840s-1910s) and Yankee ingenuity (Innovation Wave 1830s-).
      - The war with Spain, the annexation of Hawaii and the Panama Canal, the occupation of Nicaragua, the intervention in Mexico (19th/20th centuries), and winning World Wars I (1914-1918) and II (1939-1945) as well as the Cold War (1945-1991), gave the U.S. self-confidence and a powerful ability to guide the world.
      - The Globalization Wave IV (after winning the Cold War 1945-1991), the spectacular victory in the Persian Gulf War (1990-1991) and an active engagement in the War of Civilizations (2001-) guides the internal and external politics of the U.S from the sole superpower position.
   2. The ability to generate progressive political advances (republicanism and democracy (Constitution 1788), social equality (Bill of Rights, Civil and Human Rights, achieved after some struggle and even Civil War) and American scientific-technological leadership (innovation: Industrial Wave 1840s-, Innovation Wave 1830s-, Information Wave 1980s-), and business leadership (evolutionary, large-scale market economy, best business schools in the world) are the second most critical factors in attaining hegemonic power in the 21st century.

      The 220 years of dramatic events stretching from 1776 to the War for Independence, creation of the Republic, continental expansion, industrialization, two victorious World Wars, victory over communism, computerization and finally to the War of Civilizations gave the American citizens a sense of shared pioneering, successful experience, and pride of unity and achievements.

In summary, one can say that the critical ability to gain from international relations, progressive ideas, and a sense of unity led the U.S. to become the hegemonic power in the 21st century after a short 220 years. However, that this has worked in the past does not guarantee it will work in the future.

The historic American capacity of the state to engage successfully in international issues contradicts the lack of interest in this kind of issue shown by the majority of citizens, who would prefer international isolation to an active role in the world. Perhaps this contradiction has something to do with the current level of American politics, which is seen by many Americans and foreigners as disastrous (antagonization of Islamic states and talking at others from a military position, avoiding dialogue in conflicts).

Figure 1.17. The American Giants who built the technological foundation for America to become a superpower and the President who used it skillfully. Enrico Fermi (1901-1954) provided the scientific foundation for the development of the atomic bomb, Paul Baran (1926-2011) invented the Internet which can connect all people and goods in the world, and President Ronald Reagan (2011-2004) beat Communism without a battle due to the persuasiveness of American power.
(Photo: Wikipedia).

Western Civilization in Central and Southern America

With the arrival of the Europeans following Christopher Columbus' voyages in the 15th century, the native ethnic tribes, such as the Incas and Aztecs, lost power to the heavy European invasion. The effective Hernándo Cortés grabbed the power of the Aztec elite with the help of local groups who had favored the Aztec elite, and Francisco Pizarro eliminated Incan rule in Western South America. The European powers of Spain and Portugal colonized the region, which was divided into areas of Spanish and Portuguese control by the line of demarcation in 1494, which gave Spain all areas to the west, and Portugal all areas to the east (the Portuguese lands in South America afterward became what is today Portuguese speaking Brazil)

By the end of the sixteenth century Spain and Portugal had been joined by others, including France, in occupying large areas of North, Central and South America, ultimately extending from Alaska to the southern tips of the Patagonia. Western European civilization, including culture, customs and government, was introduced with the Roman Catholic Church becoming the major economic and political power to exercise authority over the traditions of the region, eventually becoming the only official religion of the Latin Americas during this period.

Epidemics of diseases brought by the West Europeans, such as smallpox and measles, killed a large portion of the native population in Latin America. Historians cannot define the number of natives who died due to European diseases, but some put the figures between 25% and 85%. Due to the lack of written records, specific numbers are difficult to prove. Many of the survivors were forced to work in European plantations and mines. Intermixing between the native peoples and the European colonists was very common, and, by the end of the colonial period, people of mixed ancestry (mestizos) shaped nations in several colonies.

By the end of 18th century, Spanish and Portuguese power declined on the global scene as other European powers took their place, particularly Britain and France. Antipathy grew among the population in Latin America over the limits forced by the Spanish government, as well as the dominance of native Spaniards (Iberian-born) in the major social and political establishments. Fighting soon broke out between juntas and the Spanish colonial authorities, with initial victories for the advocates of independence. Eventually these early movements were crushed by the royalist troops in 1810, including those in Mexico, and later in Venezuela in 1812. Under the leadership of a new generation of leaders, such as Simón Bolívar "The Liberator," in South America, the independence movement gained strength, and by 1825, all Spanish America, except for Puerto Rico and Cuba, had gained independence from Spain. Brazil achieved independence with a constitutional monarchy established in 1822.

Losing the North American colonies at the end of the 18th century left Great Britain in need of new markets to supply resources in the early 19th century (Donghi 1970). In order to answer this difficulty, Great Britain turned to the Spanish colonies in South America for resources and markets. In 1806 a small British force surprise attacked the capital of the viceroyalty in Río de la Plata (Donghi 1970). The British were able to capture numerous amounts of precious metals before a French naval force intervened on behalf of the Spanish King and took down the invading force. The next year the British attacked once again with a much larger force attempting to reach and conquer Montevideo (Donghi 1970). This newly gained British dominance slowed down the development of Latin American industries and strengthened the dependence on the European trade network. Britain now replaced Spain as the region's largest trading partner (Colegio Woodville 2013). Great Britain invested significant capital in Latin America in order to develop the area as a market for processed goods coming from her Industrial Revolution. From the early 1820's-1850 the post-independence economies of Latin American countries were lagging and stagnant (Donghi 1970). Eventually, improved trade among Great Britain and Latin America led to state developments such as infrastructure improvements including the construction of railroads by engineers coming from Europe (mostly from Poland). These improvements of roads and railroads helped the trades inside and between the countries of Latin America (Racine 2010).

The struggle for independence after 1810 by the Latin American nations evoked a sense of unity, especially in South America where, under Simón Bolívar in the north and José de San Martín in the south, there were cooperative efforts. Francisco Morazán briefly headed a Federal Republic of Central America. Early South American Pan-Americanists were also inspired by the American Revolutionary War, where a suppressed and colonized society struggled, united, and gained its independence. In the United States, Henry Clay and Thomas Jefferson set forth the principles of Pan-Americanism in the early 19th century, and soon afterward the United States declared through the Monroe Doctrine (1826) a new policy with regard to interference by European nations in the affairs of America.

Brazilian President, Getúlio Vargas, wanted to industrialize Brazil, allowing it to be more competitive with other countries. He reached out to Germany, Italy, France, and the United States to act as trade allies. In effect, many Italian and German people immigrated to Brazil many years before World War II began thus creating a Nazi influence. The immigrants held high positions in government and the armed forces. It was recently found that 9,000 war criminals escaped to South America, including Croats, Ukrainians, Russians and other Western Europeans who aided the Nazi war machine. Most, perhaps as many as 5,000, went to Argentina; between 1,500 and 2,000 are thought to have made it to Brazil; around 500 to 1,000 to Chile; and the rest to Paraguay and Uruguay (Hall 2012).

As the result of this European immigration and involvement in supplying food to Germany during the World War II, Argentina flourished after the war as well as Uruguay and Chile. Therefore today these three countries would like to be considered as not belonging to Latin but to South America due to their better development.

Colonialism and post-colonialism instituted huge inequalities in Latin America that are difficult to eliminate since the differences between initial endowments and opportunities among social groups have constrained the poorest peoples' social mobility, thus causing poverty to become transmitted from generation to generation, resulting a vicious cycle. Children in Latin America are often forced to seek work on the streets when their families can no longer afford to support them, leading to a substantial population of street children in Latin America. According to some estimates, there are 40 million street children in Latin America (Tacon 1982).

In 2008, According to UNICEF, Latin America and the Caribbean region had the highest combined income inequality in the world with a measured net Gini coefficient of 48.3, an unweighted average which is considerably higher than the world's Gini coefficient average of 39.7. Gini is the statistical measurement used to measure income distribution across entire nations and their populations and their income inequality. The other regional averages were: sub-Saharan Africa (44.2), Asia (40.4), Middle East and North Africa (39.2), Eastern Europe and Central Asia (35.4), and high-income nations (30.9) (Ortiz and Cummins 2011)

According to a study by the World Bank, the richest 1% of the population of Latin America earn (HDR 2104) 48% of the total income, while the poorest 10% of the population earn only 1.6% of the income. In contrast, in developed countries, the richest 1% receive 29% of the total income, while the poorest earn 2.5%.

Figure 1.20. (Continued).

Civilization Index and Western Civilization 35

Figure 1.20. Slums on the outskirts of a wealthy and impressive skyline of urban area in São Paulo, Brazil are an example of poverty and inequality common in Latin America. Buenos Aires looks like Paris; however, Argentina is a bankrupt state in 2014.
(Photo: Wikipedia and www.argentinastravel.com).

Figure 1.21. Latin America due to its climate an ethnic diversity created a very recognizable and beautiful culture: A Roman Catholic Easter procession in Comayagua, Honduras, Casapueblo, Carlos Páez Vilaró's *citadel–sculpture* near Punta del Este, Uruguay; Mexicans dancing Jarabe Tapatío in Guadalajara, Mexico; Salsa dancing in Cali, Colombia; A couple dances the Argentine Tango.
(Photo: Wikipedia).

THE EXPANTION OF WESTERN CIVILIZATION OUTSIDE OF EUROPE IN THE LAST 200+ YEARS

Western Civilization in Canada

Canada is a country in North America consisting of ten provinces and three territories. Located in the northern part of the continent, it extends from the Atlantic to the Pacific and northward into the Arctic Ocean. Canada is the world's second-largest country by total area and the fourth-largest country by land area. Its common border with the United States is the world's longest land border shared by the same two countries. The land that is now Canada has been inhabited for millennia by numerous Aboriginal peoples. Beginning in the late 15th century, British and French colonies were established on the region's Atlantic coast. As a result of various encounters, the United Kingdom enlarged and lost North American territories until it was left in the late 18th century with only what is today Canada. The English crown, like Elizabeth II, is the Head of State of Canada today.

Canada is a developed country and one of the wealthiest in the world, with the eighth highest per capita income globally and the eighth highest ranking in the Human Development Index. It ranks among the highest in international measurements of education, government transparency, civil liberties, quality of life, and economic freedom. Canada also ranks among the world's most educated countries, and was ranked first worldwide in the number of adults having tertiary education with 51% of adults having attained at least an undergraduate college or university degree according to OECD's 2012 survey.

Since the early 20th century, the growth of Canada's manufacturing, mining, and service sectors has transformed the nation from a largely rural economy to an urbanized, industrial one. Like many other developed nations, the Canadian economy is dominated by the service industry, which employs about three-quarters of the country's workforce.[16] However, Canada is uncommon among developed countries in the significance of its primary sector, in which the logging and petroleum industries are two of the most prominent components (Easterbrook 1995). This means that manufacturing is not a large part of Canada's economy. Canada, being so great an exporter of energy (oil), lumber, and wheat, can afford to import manufactured goods.

Canada is a participant in the International Space Station (ISS) and is a pioneer in space robotics, having constructed the Canadarm, Canadarm2 and Dextre robotic manipulators for the ISS and NASA's Space Shuttle. Since the 1960s, Canada's aerospace industry has designed and built numerous marques of satellite, including Radarsat-1 and 2, ISIS and MOST.[17] Canada has also produced a successful and widely used sounding rocket, the Black Brant; over 1,000 Black Brants have been launched since the rocket's introduction in 1961.[18]

---

[16] "Employment by Industry". Statistics Canada. January 8, 2009. Retrieved May 22, 2014.
[17] The Canadian Aerospace Industry praises the federal government for recognizing Space as a strategic capability for Canada". Newswire. Retrieved 9-02-2014.
[18] Black Brant Sounding Rockets". Magellan Aerospace. Retrieved 9-02-2014.

Figure 1.22. Trans-Canada trains define this country's developed infrastructure and hockey defines Canadian culture.
(Photo: www.telegraph.co.uk and www.nicolascanada.blogspot.com).

Figure 1.23. Opera House in Sydney and the new Parliament House in Canberra are symbols of Australian modern civilization.
(Photo: www.hartransom.org).

Western Civilization in Australia

The Australian Aborigines reached Australia from the Asian Continent from 60,000 to 40,000 years ago. They may have arrived by boat through shallow waters or across land bridges no longer present. Aborigines were the first people to live on the Australian continent. Their traditional territory extends over mainland Australia and Tasmania. At the time of European settlement on the east coast of Australia in 1788, there were about 1 million Aboriginal inhabitants. The British landed in Australia in order to establish a penal colony. In the century that followed, the British established other colonies on the continent, and European explorers ventured into its interior. Indigenous Australians were greatly declining, and their numbers diminished by introduced diseases and conflict with the colonists during this period.

Gold rushes and agricultural industries (exporting wool and wheat) were the source of prosperity for the relatively few on such a vast territory. Autonomous parliamentary democracy began to be established in six colonies in Australia from the mid-19th century. The colonies in Australia voted by referendum to unite in a federation in 1901, and modern Australia came into existence. Australia battled on the side of Britain in the two World Wars and became a long-standing ally of the United States when endangered by Imperial Japan during World War II. Trade with Asia increased and a post-war multicultural immigration program received more than 6.5 million migrants from every continent. The population tripled in six decades to around 21 million in 2010, with people originating from 200 countries sustaining the world's 14th largest national economy today.

Figure 1.24. Melbourne's Central Business District - it has become the employment giant sucking jobs from the suburbs. The city has gone away from manufacturing towards financial and business services which means an increase in jobs in the center of the city, like in New York and London.
(Photo: news.domain.com.au).

Western Civilization in New Zealand

New Zealand is an island country in the southwestern Pacific Ocean. The country geographically comprises two main landmasses – that of the North Island and the South Island, and numerous smaller islands. There are 4.5 million people and about 50 million sheep which interact for the greater benefit of the former.

About the 8th century CE, squads of canoes or rafts from the Society Islands and other parts of eastern Polynesia had sailed thousands of miles to the southwest and by chance discovered the two large islands that today make up New Zealand. Their success is evidenced by the large numbers of Maoris – the people descended from the Polynesian seafarers - who lived in the islands when the Europeans first came to stay in the late-18th century.

In 1840, the British Crown and Māori signed the Treaty of Waitangi, making New Zealand a British colony. Today, the majority of New Zealand's population of 4.5 million is of European descent; the indigenous Māori are the largest minority, followed by Asians and Pacific Islanders. Reflecting this, New Zealand's culture is mainly derived from Māori and early British settlers, with other elements arising from increased immigration. The official languages are English, Māori and New Zealand Sign Language, with English being the predominant language.

Figure 1.25. Elizabeth II, Queen of New Zealand, and her vice-regal representative, the Governor-General Sir Jerry Mateparae, the second Māori person to hold this office ever.
(Photo: Public domain).

The country's economy was historically dominated by the export of wool, but exports of dairy products, meat, and wine, along with tourism, are more significant today.

Figure 1.26. The Parliament and Government's building are in place to rule 4.5 million people and 50 million sheep in New Zealand.
(Photo: Wikipedia).

Western-Jewish Civilization

Why are the Jews considered as belonging to Western civilization, especially given that Judaism is not a religion of Western civilization based on Christianity (e.g., Catholicism and Protestantism)? The answer is that the Jews, living Near East about 2000 years ago, spread in many places in the world but mostly in Northern Africa and Europe where through two Millennia they contributed significantly to Western culture development. This is a similar case to the Greeks who by the Orthodox religion should belong to Eastern civilization (Russia, Bulgaria, Ukraine, Moldavia, and Belarus), but due to their early role in the development of the civilizational foundation of Europe 2700 ago, they belong to Classical civilization (including the Romans too) and therefore belong to Western civilization today.

Among the Jewish contributions to Western civilization one can mention just a few out of many:

- *Nobel Prizes* - At least 193 Jews and people of half or three-quarters Jewish ancestry have been awarded the Nobel Prize, accounting for 23% of all individual recipients worldwide between 1901 and 2013, and constituting 37% of all US recipients during the same period. In the scientific research fields of Chemistry, Economics, Physics, and Physiology/Medicine, the corresponding world and US percentages are 27% and 39%, respectively. Among women laureates in the four research fields, the Jewish percentages (world and US) are 38% and 50%, respectively. Of organizations awarded the Nobel Peace Prize, 23% were founded principally by Jews or by people of half-Jewish descent. Since the turn of the century (i.e., since the year 2000), Jews have been awarded 28% of all Nobel Prizes and 32% of those in the scientific research fields. (Jews currently make up approximately 0.2% of the world's population and 2% of the US population.)[19]
    - Chemistry (36 prize winners, 22% of world total, 33% of US total)
    - Economics (29 prize winners, 39% of world total, 50% of US total)
    - Literature (13 prize winners, 12% of world total, 27% of US total)
    - Peace (9 prize winners, 9% of world total, 10% of US total)
    - Physics (51 prize winners, 26% of world total, 37% of US total)
    - Physiology or Medicine (55 prize winners, 27% of world total, 40% of US total)
- *Physics* - Jews played a major role in the development of twentieth century physics. Any reasonably objective listing of the twenty-five most influential physicists of that century would probably include, at a minimum, the following fifteen individuals of Jewish descent: Albert Einstein, Niels Bohr, Wolfgang Pauli, Max Born, Hans Bethe, Felix Bloch, Lev Landau, I. I. Rabi, Eugene Wigner, John von Neumann, Richard Feynman, Julian Schwinger, Murray Gell-Mann, Steven Weinberg, and Edward Witten. According to a recent monograph by the distinguished theoretical physicist Roger Newton, Albert Einstein and Niels Bohr were "the true revolutionaries ... two men whose ideas would dominate most of physics for the 20th century."[20]
- *Atomic Bomb* - In addition to work on the conceptual foundations of physics, Jews have also been significantly involved in the development of its practical applications like the development of the atomic and hydrogen bombs; such Jews such as Leo Szilard, Eugene Wigner, Sir Rudolf Peierls, Sir Francis Simon, Hans Bethe, Victor Weisskopf, John von Neumann, Robert Oppenheimer, Edward Teller, Stanislaw Ulam, Alvin Weinberg, Hyman Rickover, Yuli Khariton, Vitaly Ginzburg, and Yakov Zeldovich (the latter three in the Soviet Union) played a dominant role in the development of nuclear power. The nuclear reactor was first conceived of and then co-invented by Leo Szilard. The pressurized water reactor (PWR), the nuclear reactor design that dominates both naval and commercial nuclear power generation, was proposed by Alvin Weinberg, based on earlier work by Eugene Wigner.[21]
- *Music* - Western classical music is an outgrowth of the Gregorian chant, which had its origins in the liturgical chants of the synagogue service. In modern times, Jews

---

[19] http://www.jinfo.org/Nobel_Prizes.html, Retrieved 9-6-2014
[20] http://www.jinfo.org/Nobel_Prizes.html, Retrieved 9-6-2014
[21] http://www.jinfo.org/Nobel_Prizes.html, Retrieved 9-6-2014

have played a major role in music as performers, conductors, and composers.[22] Of the one hundred leading virtuoso performers of the twentieth century listed,[23] approximately two-thirds of the violinists, half the cellists, and forty percent of the pianists were, or are, Jews. Of the one hundred leading conductors of the twentieth century listed,[24] approximately one-fourth were, or are, Jews. Among the leading classical composers, the Jewish representation is only about ten percent, the most notable having been Felix Mendelssohn, Jacques Offenbach, Gustav Mahler, Arnold Schoenberg, George Gershwin, and Aaron Copland. Jewish composers have, however, played a predominant role both in the development of the American musical theater and in the development of film music; approximately forty percent of the membership of the Songwriters Hall of Fame is Jewish.

Figure 1.27. Albert Einstein (1879-1955) the Man of the 20th century (by TIME), John von Neumann (1903-1957) contributed to the development of American atomic bomb and first computer with a stored program; George Gershwin's (1898-1937) compositions spanned both popular and classical genres, and his most popular melodies are widely known world-wide as American music genre.
(Photo: Wikipedia).

The Jews, due to their world experiences, are easily able to find a new way of thinking and experiencing and a new way of understanding and feeling the world, so much so that it may be said with some justice that some of their ideas, such as those in science and medicine, are opening minds and new horizons for the development of Western civilization.

THE COMPLEX OF WESTERN CIVILIZATION

The complex of Western civilization is charted in Figure 1.28. It contains four sub-civilizations and 13 cultures. These cultures are predominantly old ones with one exception - American culture - which grew from the Anglo-Saxon culture into own as the result of a

---

[22] http://www.jinfo.org/Music.html, Retrieved 9-6-2014
[23] http://www.muzieklijstjes.nl/100players.htm
[24] http://www.muzieklijstjes.nl/100conductors.htm

strong mix of almost all cultures of the world due to the intensive and broad scope of the ethnicity of immigrants. However, the dominant religion of American culture is Christianity.

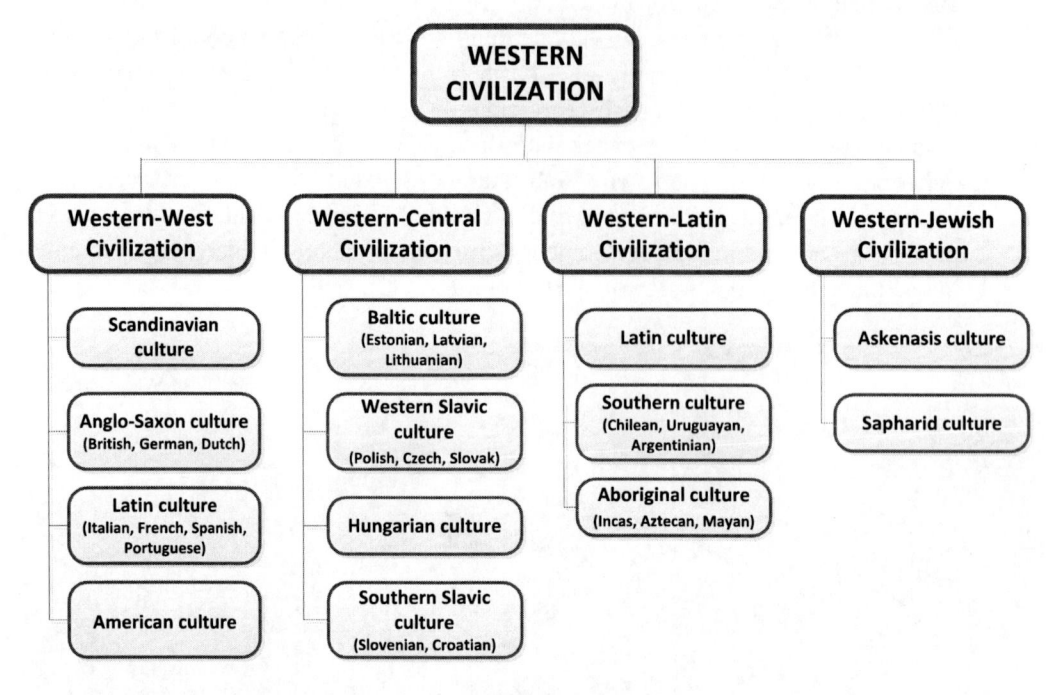

```
                          WESTERN
                        CIVILIZATION
    ┌──────────────────┬─────┴──────┬──────────────────┐
Western-West      Western-Central   Western-Latin    Western-Jewish
 Civilization       Civilization     Civilization      Civilization
    │                   │                │                 │
Scandinavian      Baltic culture     Latin culture    Askenasis culture
  culture         (Estonian, Latvian,
                   Lithuanian)
    │                   │                │                 │
Anglo-Saxon culture  Western Slavic   Southern culture  Sapharid culture
(British, German,     culture         (Chilean, Uruguayan,
  Dutch)           (Polish, Czech,     Argentinian)
                    Slovak)
    │                   │                │
Latin culture      Hungarian culture  Aboriginal culture
(Italian, French,                    (Incas, Aztecan, Mayan)
 Spanish, Portuguese)
    │                   │
American culture   Southern Slavic
                    culture
                  (Slovenian, Croatian)
```

Figure 1.28. The complex of Western civilization in the 21st century.

THE CIVILIZATION INDEX AND WESTERN CIVILIZATION

Examples of Contemporary Civilizations

According to Samuel Huntington (1996) the following civilizations exist in the post-1990 world: Western, Latin American, African, Islamic, Sinic, Hindu, Orthodox, Buddhist, and Japanese. A slightly updated set provided by Targowski (2008) contains the following civilizations in the post-2000 world: Western (Western-West, Western-Latin, Western-Central, and Jewish sub-Civilizations), Eastern (Russia, Ukraine, Belarus, Bulgaria, Moldavia), Chinese, Japanese, Islamic, Buddhist (Cambodia, Laos, Thailand, Sri Lanka, Tibet, Mongolia, Bhutan, Nepal, and Afghanistan), and African.

In the 21st century infrastructural civilizations have become civilizations responsible for influence and domination in entire world hemispheres. Hence, Western Civilization dominates the Western Hemisphere, Eastern and Hindu rule the Eastern Hemisphere, the Islamic Civilization rules the Near and Middle East Hemisphere and some parts of the Far East Hemisphere, the Japanese Civilization governs some parts of the Far East Hemisphere, the Chinese Civilization influences the majority of the Far East Hemisphere, and the Buddhist civilization influences a small part of the Far East Hemisphere.

Furthermore, nowadays, Western and Chinese civilizations are the main organizers of Global Civilization, which has a horizontal character and invades other civilizations as its new layer of civilizational *modus operandi*.

Index of Civilizations

Each civilization has its own dynamics, which determines its behavior. The civilizational dynamics are formulated by the scope of interactions among civilizational systems. Let's analyze them looking at the General Model of Chinese Civilization shown in Figure 1.6.

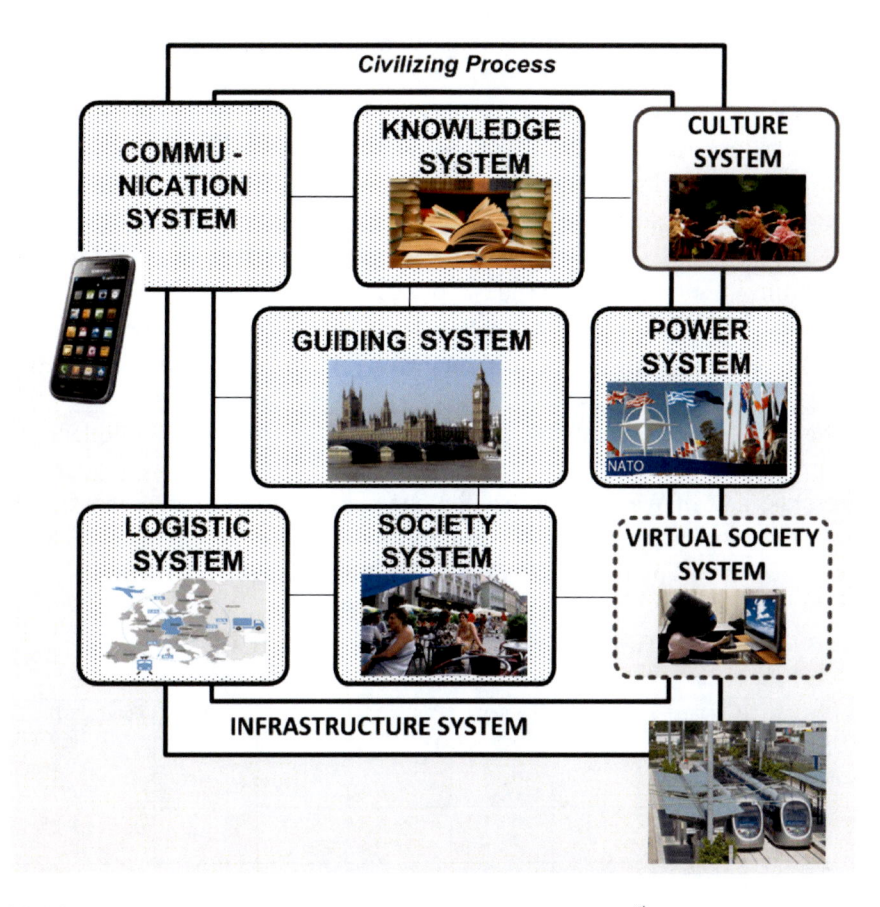

Figure 1.29. The generic system model of Western Civilization in the 21st century.

A civilization is autonomous because it has a guiding system, which through a structure of feedbacks keeps a civilization in a functional balance. Thus, an autonomous civilization protects itself by counteractions against factors that could destroy it. The clashes with terrorism in the 21st century is in fact the confrontation of values between Western, Eastern and Islamic Civilizations. An autonomous civilization tends to protect its existence through prophylactic measures against challenges coming from other civilizations and through control if challenges are coming from within it. The guiding system touches all system components of a civilization (Figure 1.29).

The first level of civilizational operations generates awareness of events and challenges by the knowledge system. The more mature and experienced a knowledge system is, the more advanced the generated awareness of the challenges faced by the civilization is. Once awareness is passed to the guiding system, it triggers a reflection which is communicated as a response to stimuli. Civilizations with a weak guiding system do not generate strong enough reflections and interactions between the communication, knowledge, and power systems reflect a reactional way of being.

The second level of the guiding system involvement deals with threats coming from the society system and all signals from other civilization systems sent to this guiding system. These signals are guided by the reflectional responses of the guiding system. The quality of the society system depends upon the level of available resources. Every autonomous civilization begins with some level of resources; however, along with its existence this level may decline or rise. If a civilization does not have enough resources, then it begins to search for them in the boundaries of other civilizations. This was the case of the Japanese Civilization in the first part of the 20th century, and it is the case of Chinese Civilization in the 21st century (with the rapid growth of the Chinese economy, China is contracting almost the whole Africa to secure the supply of needed resources such as oil).

As the history of civilization indicates, the application of the power system (in the war mode) was the main solution in this quest for resources. The stronger power system was usually victorious in determining the outcome of the war and the well-being of the civilizations involved. This was the case of Germany in WWII (1939-1945) which was motivated by the assumed right for a bigger space (*Lebensraüm*) for "higher culture." Germany therefore pushed towards the East (*Drang nach Osten*), taking the land of weaker states.

To assess the state of Western Civilization one must compare it with other contemporary civilizations which are active in the 21st century, by applying the Civilization Index which evaluates each major system of a civilization (Table 1.5).

Table 1.5. The Civilization Index (CI)

CIVILIZA-TION	Society System	Communication System	Knowledge System	Guiding System	Power System	Logistic System	Infrastructure System	Total	CI as% of Potential (77)	Ranking
Western - West	29	7	7	7	7	6	7	70	0.91	1
Western-Jewish	27	7	7	7	6	6	7	67	0.87	2
Japanese	21	6	6	7	5	6	7	58	0.75	3
Western-Central	20	5	4	6	5	3	4	47	0.61	4
Eastern	23	5	5	1	7	3	3	47	0.61	5
Western-Latin	15	4	4	6	3	2	4	40	0.52	6
Chinese	17	4	2	2	6	1	3	35	0.45	7
Islamic	13	3	2	4	4	3	4	33	0.43	8
Hindu	13	2	3	7	3	1	3	32	0.41	9
Buddhist	9	3	3	5	2	1	2	25	0.32	10
African	8	1	1	1	1	1	1	14	0.18	11

Source: Targowski (2004b).

The Civilization Index (CI), applies the following criteria (Targowski 2004b) weighted on the scale 1 to 7:

- Society system
- Communication system
- Knowledge system
- Guiding system
- Power system
- Logistic system
- Infrastructure system

The results are provided in Table 1.5.

A comparison of civilizations at the end of the twentieth century permits us to draw the following conclusions:

1. The Western-West civilization is at the stage of "saturation," indicating that it is either ready to expand into other civilizations or to enter into social unrest. This civilization has an almost perfect Index: CI = 91%. Therefore this civilization pushes for the development of Global Civilization.
2. The Western-Jewish (CI=87%) and Japanese civilizations (CI = 75%) are very well developed and will approach the "saturation" point in the near future. Needless to say that these civilizations are strong participants of Global Civilization.
3. The African civilization is either at the beginning of the developmental process or at the stage of disastrous development. Taking into account its very short and tumultuous history, both statements may be correct (CI = 18%).
4. The remaining civilizations have a good prospect for further development or redevelopment. This is presently taking place in the case of the Western-Central civilization after the collapse of the Soviet civilization. Civilization Indexes of these civilizations vary from CI = 32% to 61%.

The Chinese civilization has CI = 45%. This means that there is plenty of "room" for intensive civilizational development, and therefore this civilization is the biggest beneficiary of Global Civilization. The latter uses this civilization's cheap labor to make huge profits, but at the same time Chinese civilization is getting stronger and stronger.

CONCLUSION

One can draw the following conclusions about the role of Western civilization's development among other civilizations since its birth till the present and particularly in the 21st century:

1. Western civilization takes place on the central territories of the world such as Europe and America as well as peripheral lands too, like Australia and New Zealand. All the people on those places are integrated by shared values, culture, and infrastructure despite local specific differences. This means that Western civilization is widely accepted by those people and developed in close inter-relations in the last 1200 years, leading other civilizations in terms of modernization and Westernization. Although,

while the latter is accepted only by Hindu and Japanese civilizations, others such as Eastern, Chinese, Islam, Buddhist, and African civilizations are impacted by Western modernization but with respect to values and culture, they reject its dominance and "superiority."

2. The here-presented interdisciplinary approach to the political aspect of Western civilization shows that despite its location on the outskirts of that civilization, Young Europe was for a about two thousand years a major invasion target for foreign empires and states and, during the dramatic 20th century, the center of geopolitics. This had a negative influence on its civilizational development in comparison to Old Europe. The belief that Poland was the "conscience of the world," often was considered as a sign of Polish megalomania, and this belief finds some justification in light of the present study. It must be remembered that over its more than thousand-year history, Poland enjoyed relative peace only for a mere 200 years (1410-1606), which means that for over 80 percent of its history it was steeped in conflict, war or chaos. Only countries like Korea, Vietnam or Cambodia, who suffered aggression by China, Japan, France and the U. S., can compare their fates to Poland's. Unfortunately even such comparisons would be to Poland's "advantage." However, this "advantage" led the Polish Solidarity revolutionaries to win the 1980-1989 battle against Soviet *Communism* and led to the unification of Old and Young Europe in 2007.

3. The fall of Berlin Wall and Soviet Empire as well as *Communism* in 1991 led to the New World Order and the so called "End of History" (Fukuyama 1992) and everlasting liberal *Capitalism* with *Democracy* everywhere. Eventually, in the 21st century, Russia led by Vladimir Putin waged a second Cold War invading the territories of former satellites such as Georgia (2009), Ukraine (2014), destabilizing Moldavia and Latvia, and confronting NATO and Western civilization, including the U.S.

4. The globalizing world's future is increasingly dependent on shrinking natural resources, especially energy sources, which would imply that the geopolitical center in the 21st century is shifting from Young Europe to the oil-rich Middle East. This translocation is driven by the mounting civilization clashes between Western Civilization and Islamic Civilization, in which Western traditional weaponry is attacked by terrorism, which is bringing incalculable harm to the entire world.

5. The globalizing world in the 21st century transformed China into the World Factory and the second largest (or soon to be first) world economy. This has led Western and Chinese civilizations towards the probable clash of *Liberal Capitalism* with *Authoritarian Capitalism* and *Democracy* with *Authoritarianism*. The *Authoritarian Capitalism* in China secures power by the political mono-party elite with some wealth at the lower level of the society; it looks as though it may have an advantage over *Liberal* or rather *Turbo-Capitalism* and lobbyists-led *Democracy* in the eventually coming clash between those two civilizations since a dictator has a broader scope to make decisions than an elected leader who is limited by the voters preferences and opposition's opinion.

6. The world of the 21st-century is going from partitioned to global but is non-united; hence tolerance for cultural difference is a necessity. In effect, peaceful coexistence should be founded on tolerance-oriented cross-culture communication skills which

are lacking. The increasingly globalized world has thus become a kaleidoscope of various "frontier zones" constituting a new challenge for the dynamically-growing world and its peoples. In this world, centers evolve into a network of frontiers, which calls for mutual understanding and coexistence. Perhaps the center, which supposedly was Western civilization, is turning into a frontier driven by a "bottom-up" strategy instead of the "top-down" strategy to which the center is accustomed. An example is the dwindling political position of the United States, heretofore a global center resembling Rome, which despite their military might, evidently cannot handle many of the world's frontiers. A case in point is the difficult relations between the U. S. and EU, or the U. S. and Russia, Iran, Syria, Iraq or North Korea.
7. Taking into account all these conflicts, clashes, and wars one can state that the long expected defeat of *Communism* at the end of the 20th century did not bring in the New World Order but rather New World Disorder and such international and intra-national complexities that are far beyond societies' ability to control them. Furthermore, despite better education and ruling experiences in the 6000 years of civilization, are humans too limited as creatures of nature to continue the game of survival within their space in the universe?

REFERENCES

Bosworth, A. (2003). "The genetics of civilization: an empirical classification of civilizations based on writing systems," *Comparative Civilizations Review*, 49(9).

Colegio Woodville (2013). *Latin American history from 1800 to 1914*. Colegio Woodville, http://www.woodville.org/documentos/130506latinamericanhistory-summary.pdf, Retrieved 9-5-2014.

Coulborn, R. (1966). "Structure and process in the rise and fall of civilized societies," *Comparative Studies in Society and History*, VIII-4(404).

Dexter, R. (2014). China wants its people in the cities. *BloombergBusinessWeak*, March 20.

Donghi, T. (1970). *Historia contemporánea de América Latina* (2. ed.). Madrid: Alianza Editorial:148-149.

Easterbrook, W.T.(1995). Recent contributions to economic history: Canada. *Journal of Economic History* (19):98.

Fernandez-Armesto, F. (2001). *Civilizations, culture, ambition, and the transformation of nature*. New York: A Touchstone Book.

Foster, J.B. and H. Holleman (2010). The financial power elite. *MONTLY REVIEW*. 62(1).

Fukuyama, F. (1992). *The end of history and the last man*. New York: Penguin Group.

Hall, A. (2012). *Secret files reveal 9,000 Nazi war criminals fled to South America after WWII*. London: Mail Online. Retrieved 6-12-2014.

Hord, J. (1992). Civilization: a definition part ii. the nature of formal knowledge systems. *The Comparative Civilization Review*, (26):111-135.

UNDP (2014). *Sustaining human progress: reducing vulnerabilities and building resilience*. New York: Human Development Report.

Huntington, S. P. (1996). *The clash of civilizations and the remaking of world order*. New York: Simon & Schuster.

Ortiz, I. and M. Cummins (2011). *Global inequality: beyond the bottom billion*. UNICEF. p. 26.

Racine, K. (2010). This England and this now: British cultural and intellectual influence in the Spanish American Independence Era. *Hispanic American Historical Review*, Vol. 90(3):423–454.

Tacon, P. (1982). *Carlinhos: the hard gloss of city polish*. UNICEF news.

Targowski, A. (2004a). From global to universal civilization. *Dialogue and Universalism*, XIV(3-4), pp. 121-142.

Targowski, A. (2004b). The civilization index. *Dialogue and Universalism*, XIV(10-12): 71-86.

Targowski, A. (2004c). A grand model of civilization. *Comparative Civilizations Review*. (51):81-106.

Targowski, A. (2009a). *Information technology and social development*. Hershey, PA & New York: IGI Publishers.

Targowski, A. (2009b). Towards a composite definition and classification of civilization. *Comparative Civilization Review*. (60):79-98.

Toynbee, A. (1935). *A study of history*, 2d ed. Oxford: Oxford University Press.

Chapter 2

SPATIO-TEMPORAL BOUNDARIES OF WESTERN CIVILIZATION

ABSTRACT

The *purpose* of this investigation is to define the roots of the Western civilization and its role with respect to the rise of Global civilization in the 21st century. The *methodology* is based on an interdisciplinary big-picture view of the Western and Global civilizations' developments and interdependency. Among the *findings* are: Western civilization is about 1200 years old and is one of the oldest civilization with a consistent religion, society, culture and infrastructure among contemporary civilizations. *Practical implication:* Western civilization has a very complex, dynamic history generated by endless conflicts, wars, and invasions and the impact of nine Western empires which have developed this civilization. *Social implication:* It is surprising that Western civilization, which invented the Globalization Wave in the liquid times of the 21st century, is transforming to Global and Virtual Civilization, replacing its Christian values with the values of business and technology. *Originality:* This investigation defined key patterns and dynamics of Western civilization which allow predictions of its behavior today and in the future.

INTRODUCTION

The purpose of this investigation is to define the roots of the Western civilization and its role with respect to the rise of Global and Virtual civilization in the 21st century. Western civilization is one of the oldest civilizations among contemporary civilizations. It has been the leading civilization of the world's many civilizations during the times of modernity in the last 500 years. Why was Western civilization able to develop the modernity of the world and maintain its leadership for such an extended period of time? This question has motivated this author to seek answers and suggest what went wrong and what went right in the course of its development.

The emphasis in this investigation will be placed upon the key events, processes, and leaders in the history of Western civilization in order to keep the big-picture consistent.

THE EUROPEAN PENISULA AFTER THE ICE AGE OR DURING AN INTERGLACIAL PERIOD KNOWN AS THE HOLOCENE[25] WHERE ITS FIRST CIVILIZATIONS WERE BORN

The European peninsula, recently called Europe, is the hub of Western civilization. However, this peninsula became inhabited by humans "recently" in comparison to other lands. Neanderthals (a subspecies of *homo sapiens*, differing from us by only 0.12% of the DNA set) were the first humans who lived here during the Glacier Age; they were "replaced" by Cro-Magnons coming from Asia about 40,000 B.C.E. An alternative to the theory that Neanderthals went extinct is that Neanderthals were absorbed into the Cro-Magnon population by interbreeding. This would be in opposition to strict versions of the Recent African Origin theory, since it would imply that at least part of the genome of Europeans descended from Neanderthals. In this author's opinion Cro-Magnons won against Neanderthals since the former communicated better by developed languages and therefore were better organized socially.

The process of intensive and continuous inhabitation of this peninsula took place during the great warming period between 15,000 to 11,000 B.C.E. when people came from Asia and moved toward the West, rounding the Mediterranean Sea. At the East of this peninsula people were settling too, and from the Stone and later Bronze Age their influence is felt up to the present. This is the region of contemporary Greece, whose Hellenic period gave birth to Classic Civilization which is the civilization that transformed (about 800 C.E.) into Western civilization. The civilizational impact upon the Eastern European peninsula (where there is Turkey today) under the form of agriculture was coming from the Mesopotamian (Sumerian) Civilization at the Indus River about 3500-3000 B.C.E. in what is today Pakistan.

As far as the flow of people is concerned, those Hellenes were coming from the continental interior and took control of the Aegean seashores in what is today Greece (including the Peloponnese peninsula in Southwestern part) and Turkey (Asia Minor). The Aegean Sea is full of islands such as Crete and Rhodes. Many of the islands in the Aegean have safe harbors and bays. In ancient times, navigation through the sea was easier than travelling across the rough terrain of the Greek mainland (and to some extent the coastal areas of Anatolia, Turkey today).

The island rich Aegean Sea forced people to travel by boats and frequently among islands to trade and pass believes, ideas, art (culture), and technology (infrastructure) among dispersed societies of diversified people. The Cyclades and Crete islands played the central role of disseminating culture (Cycladic, Minoan) and giving rise to civilization among all parts of this area.

---

[25] The Earth has been in an interglacial period known as the Holocene for more than 11,000 years. It was conventional wisdom that the typical interglacial period lasts about 12,000 years, but this has been called into question recently. For example, an article in Nature (Barbante 2004) argues that the current interglacial might be most analogous to a previous interglacial that lasted 28,000 years. Predicted changes in orbital forcing suggest that the next glacial period will begin at least 50,000 years from now, even in absence of human-made global warming.

Figure 2.1. The rising of Minoan (2000 B.C.E.) and Mycenaean (1600 B.C.E.) Civilizations in South-Eastern European Peninsula as the first ones in future Europe.
(Photo: www.forumbiodiveristy.com).

    The Minoan Civilization, named after the legendary Cretan ruler Minos, was founded by people who emigrated from Asia Minor to Crete around 3000 B.C.E. Within 1000 years they made the transition from the Neolithic stage to the age of metals; by 2000 B.C.E. they developed cities and an early form of writing. While the Minoan Civilization of Crete was flourishing, a related one was emerging on the mainland of Greece. Around 1900 B.C.E. Indo-European people who spoke the earliest form of Greek invaded the Greek peninsula, and by 1600 B.C.E., they established a trade-driven relation with Crete and its Minoan Civilization. As a result of this relation, the mainland and island triggered the rise of Mycenaean Civilization (McNall et al. 1982).

    The Mycenaean kingdoms of main land Greece and Peloponnese consolidated their position and prospered thanks to the systematic exploitation of agriculture resources (for example by draining Lake Copais) and a highly centralized, bureaucratic system. In effect, the marine powers of Crete and the Cyclades were beaten, and the Mycenaean kingdom took over the Aegean Sea region. Between 1400 and 1200 B.C.E. Mycenaean trade was developing in the Central and Eastern parts of the Mediterranean Sea, triggering the move towards permanent settlements. This resulted in the spread of Mycenaean Civilization into Italy, Sicily, Sardinia, Asia Minor, Cyprus, Syria, Palestine, and Egypt. In 1200-1100 B.C.E. the invasion of the Dorian tribe destroyed the central administration of Mycenaean kingdom (civilization), resulting in the disintegration of Mycenaean Civilization.

The Dorian "barbarians" came from the north-western mountainous regions of Greece, ancient Macedonia and Epirus. They spoke 'new' Greek and had iron weapons which the bronze-weaponed Mycenaeans could not withstand. It took a while for the new invaders to learn civilized ways, and so there followed a "dark age" for Greece. Greece had broken up into separate city-states (like Sparta, Athens and others) ruled by the most important families through the next several centuries, developing philosophy and art.

THE RISE OF ETRUSCAN CIVILIZATION OF ANCIENT ITALY IN THE CENTRAL MEDITERRENIAN REGION (768 B.C.E.–264 B.C.E.)

Etruscan Civilization is the modern name given to a civilization of ancient Italy in the area corresponding roughly to Tuscany, western Umbria, and northern Latium. The ancient Romans called its creators the Tusci or Etrusci.[26] Their Roman name is the origin of the terms Tuscany, which refers to their heartland, and Etruria, which can refer to their wider region.

The historical Etruscans had achieved a state system of society, with remnants of chiefdom and tribal forms. In this they were different from the surrounding Italics, who had chiefs and tribes. Rome was in a sense the first Italic state, but it began as an Etruscan one. It is believed that the Etruscan government style changed from total monarchy to oligarchic republic (as the Roman Republic) in the 6th century B.C.E., although it is important to note this did not happen to all the city states. The Etruscans, like the contemporary civilizations of Ancient Greece and Ancient Rome, had a significant military tradition. Warfare was a considerable economic boom to Etruscan civilization.

Etruscan architecture made lasting contributions to the architecture of Italy, which were adopted by the Romans and, through them, became standard to Western civilization. Rome itself is a repository of Etruscan architectural features. Etruscan art was strongly connected to religion; the afterlife was of major importance in Etruscan art (Spivey 1997).

CELTIC CIVILIZATION OF THE CENTRAL-NORTHEN EUROPEAN PENISULA AND ITS IMPACT ON OTHER PARTS OF THE EUROPEAN PENNISULA (1200 – 60 B.C.E.)

An Indo-European people called Keltosi (Celts) by the Greeks and Gauls by the Romans had lived north of the Alps (today Switzerland and Austria) since before 1200 B.C.E. They had expanded westward into what is now France and Spain and northward into the British

---

[26] According to Félix Gaffiot's *Dictionnaire Illustré Latin Français*, the term Tusci was used by the major authors of the Roman Republic: Livy, Cicero, Horace, and others. Cognate words developed, including Tuscia and Tusculanensis. Tusci was clearly the principal term used to designate things Etruscan; Etrusci and Etrūria were used less often, mainly by Cicero and Horace, and they lack cognates. According to the Online Etymological Dictionary, the English use of Etruscan dates from 1706.

Isles. By 500 B.C.E. they were beginning to soak across the barrier of the Alps into Italy. Their rise is linked to the end of the Bronze Age, when increased metal production led to hoarding and inequality of wealth, and also to the appearance of heavily armed professional soldiers in the style of the ancient Greek infantryman. The iron tools improved the agricultural production, clearing new land and arming the surplus population that was making inroads into Italy and would soon be expanding over the entire Mediterranean.

Celtic mercenaries, in their contacts with local populations, introduced new techniques both in art and in production: compasses, the porters' wheel and the rotary millstone were the most popular inventions.

The Roman conquest chased the Celts out of Italy by the end of the last Millennium B.C.E., then out of southern Gaul which led to the birth to a civilization based on hills forts stretching from Brittany to Hungary.

ROMAN CIVILIZATION AND ITS CONTRIBUTION TO FUTURE WESTERN CIVILIZATION (753 B.C.E. – 476 C.E.)

The activities of Roman Civilization can be divided into three useful periods or episodes. The years 753-509 B.C.E. concern the years of Rome's origins. By 509 B.C.E., Rome had established itself by pushing the Etruscans out of northern Italy. The era of the Roman Republic falls between 509 B.C.E. and the Battle of Actium in 31 B.C.E. Rome under the Republic consolidated both its power at home and abroad, especially during the Punic and Macedonian Wars. The Republic is also the period when Rome developed its distinctive forms of law and government. Finally, the period from 31 B.C.E. to 476 C.E. constitutes the era of the Roman Empire. It is this period that most people think of when they are reminded of the grandeur that was Rome. Thanks to the greatest of all the Roman emperors, Augustus Caesar, Rome was able to capture and control all of modern day France, Spain, Greece, Asia Minor, Palestine, North Africa (including Egypt) and Great Britain. Of course, the Empire is also the period in which Christianity made its appearance as another mystery cult among the lower orders of people. However, it quickly became apparent that Christianity was something more than just another mystery cult and was indeed a new religious phenomenon that had to be reckoned with (Kreis 2006).

Since 27 B.C.E. under Emperor Augustus the era of *Pax Romana* ("Roman Peace") characterized by long peace and prosperity began. Imperial Rome was a centralized police state with an elaborate government and potent army. The Roman leaders undertook large-scale public works (aqueducts, roads, bridges, schools, and so forth). They used slaves to do difficult jobs and were bringing valuable resources from conquered territories such as gold, silver, amber, gemstones, grain, timber, wool and so forth. Many Roman-styles cities were built and were connected by a network of sophisticated roads. In its peak (100-180 C.E.) trade reached as far as China and its oriental vicinity.

When Rome reached a good quality of life, social disorder propagated, values and morality declined, and *dolce vita* became a popular modus operandi. The economy switched from being monetary-driven towards local barter. Unpaid soldiers, particularly from the northern Germanic tribes, eventually took over this Imperium.

Figure 2.2. Gaius Julius Caesar (100-43 B.C.E.) was a Roman general, statesman, Consul, and notable author of Latin prose. He played a critical role in the events that led to the demise of the Roman Republic and the rise of the Roman Empire. Nowadays, fresh flowers are put every day on his memorial tomb in central Rome.
(Photo: www.bbc.co.uk).

THE FALL OF ROMAN EMPIRE AND CLASSIC CIVILIZATION INTO THE DARK AGES (476 C.E. – 15TH CENTURY)

The Fall of the Roman Empire under the Siege of Barbarians

For centuries, Germanic people from the North had been pushing against the borders of the Roman Empire but without a sustainable success. But in the meantime Rome, due to a culture of *dolce vita*, had been weakened by military self-proclaimed and unqualified commanders for some time. Emperor Diocletian decided to split the Roman Empire into the Eastern and Western halves in 286 C.E.. Emperor Constantine I had enough intrigues in the West and in 330 C.E. moved his capital eastward to Constantinople, nowadays Istanbul, calling it "a New Rome," which soon became the center of the Byzantine world.

Meanwhile, "Old Rome" and the Western Empire went into hands of corrupted leaders and unpaid soldiers. Around 370 C.E., nomadic Huns from the East, very mobile on horses and lightly equipped, attacked Rome while the Vandals from the North (from the banks of Vistula River, nowadays Poland) went into Gaul (nowadays France) and northern Africa, and despite getting their autonomy, attacked the Roman Empire. Another tribe, the Goths first acquired the Balkans (belonging to the Roman Empire) and took the city of Rome in 410. The Romans abandoned Britain since they could not face the attacking Scots, while the Huns, led by the legendary Attila, invaded Gaul and Italy. Lastly, in 476, the German's chieftain Flavius Odoacer (433-493) deposed the last Western Roman Emperor Romulus Augustus (460-500) and proclaimed himself king. It was the end of the once powerful Roman Empire.

This also marked the end of the ideas and ways of behaving of Classic Civilization which integrated contributions of Greek and Roman Civilizations. However, those contributions have not been lost since fortunately they were absorbed within the next 300+ years by the emerging Western civilization, founded by Emperor Charlemagne of the Holy Roman Empire around 800. This new empire was in fact the German empire, since the Germans were decisive in conquering and beating the Roman Empire.

The Dark Ages of the Middle Ages (476-1453)

The Dark Ages is a historical periodization used originally for the Middle Ages which emphasizes the cultural and economic deterioration that supposedly occurred in Western Europe following the decline of the Roman Empire (Oxford English Dictionary). The period of history which lies between ancient times and modern times, from the fall of the Western Roman Empire to the fall of Constantinople and the end of the Eastern Roman Empire, is generally known as the Middle Ages. It was a period when the removal of the strong, central government of Rome left Europe in chaos. The mighty empire was fragmented into small kingdoms, and in many places rule was by local lords, each of whom exercised power only in the immediate vicinity of his own castle.

This was a time of migrating people who looked for better conditions of living. Ever since people first began migrating, they have always attempted to accomplish this same goal. In the years between 500 and 700 C.E. Slavic tribes were settling in central and eastern Europe (particularly in eastern Magna Germania), gradually making it predominantly Slavic (Kobyliński 2008). Additionally, Turkic tribes such as the Avars were migrating too. In 567, the Avars and the Lombards destroyed much of the Gepid Kingdom.[27] The Lombards, a Germanic people, settled in northern Italy in the region now known as Lombardy. The Central Asian Bulgars had occupied the Pontic steppe north of Caucasus since the second century, but after, having been pushed by the Khazars, the majority of them migrated west and dominated Byzantine territories along the lower Danube in the seventh century.

During the early Byzantine–Arab Wars the Arab armies attempted to invade southeast Europe via Asia Minor during the late seventh and early eighth centuries but were defeated at the siege of Constantinople by the joint forces of Byzantium and the Bulgars. During the Khazar–Arab Wars, the Khazars stopped the Arab expansion into Europe across the Caucasus. At the same time, the Moors (consisting of Arabs and Berbers) invaded Europe via Gibraltar (conquering Hispania—the Iberian Peninsula—from the Visigothic Kingdom in 711), before being halted by the Franks at the Battle of Tours in 732. These battles largely fixed the frontier between Christendom and Islam for the next millennium. The following centuries saw the Muslims successful in conquering Sicily from the Christians.

---

[27] Gepids were sometimes known as the Gepidae to Roman writers; this East Germanic tribe never came into particularly close contact with the Roman Empire. For about two hundred years from the first century AD, they were located on the eastern bank of the Vistula (today Poland), with the River Bug forming a loose southern border, and it seems likely that they migrated there alongside the Goths, to whom they were closely related. They followed the Goths on their slow migration south-eastwards, ending up in the Pannonian basin where they formed a short-lived tribal kingdom known as Gepidia. The capital of this kingdom was Sirmium (modern Sremska Mitrovica in Serbia), but Gepidia was destroyed by the Langobards in 567, effectively ending the existence of the Gepids as a recognizable people.

This was a time too, of poverty and hardship; with the lack of wealth and consequently of people able to act as patrons, there was a decline in learning. In the Near East, however, learning flourished and the religion of Islam was to prove a unifying force, while in Asia (Chinese) and in the Americas complex independent civilizations flourished (Aztecan and Mayan).

However, the European picture was steadily improving from the dark one. Gradually there was a growth of nationalistic feelings, and strong kings began to make countries of their lands. Finally, the steady growing message (*love your neighbor*), power, and wealth of the Christian Church provided another unifying force and gave some men leisure to pursue lives of scholarship and study.

THE CONTRIBUTION OF CLASSIC CIVILIZATION TO THE FUTURE WESTERN CIVILIZATION

The Greek and Romans both gave many important contributions to Western civilization. While the Romans copied many aspects of Greek culture, they also made distinct contributions. Greece had the first democracy, and all citizens could participate in the government. Rome built on the Greek democratic government and established a sharing of the administration with checks and balances. Both the Greeks and Romans believed in justice and the equality of people to a certain extent.

Greece and Rome have worked together to provide Western civilization with substantial contributions. Some great Roman structures are the Pantheon and the Colloseum. The Greeks had a polytheistic religion. Greece and Rome have also made tremendous contributions to Western civilization with art and architecture. All of these philosophies have contributed to modern thought.

Rome produced many works of art and architecture, created Christianity, and added on to Greek philosophy and government administration. The Assembly of Tribes and the Tribunes were Plebeians.

Figure 2.3. Three great ancient Greek philosophers; Plato, Socrates, and Aristotle. (Photo: peminggirkota.blogspot.com).

Figure 2.4. The Greek theater Epidaurus built in 4th century B.C.E. and Roman Colloseum, amphitheater in Rome, built by the Roman emperors between 75 and 80 C.E. as a place of entertainment; it was a scene of gladiatorial combat. The most common form of Greek secular architecture was the theater, but the most common Roman form was the amphitheater.
(Photo: ancient.eu.com, and www.telegraph.co.uk).

The Greeks invented the column, the arch, and the dome. The Greeks started philosophy, seeking true knowledge. The Romans took these Greek features with some of their own, such as the new composite material, concrete, and created marvelous structures. Both civilizations' architecture have been influential and have served as examples for those following them. They believed that many anthropomorphic deities ruled over them in daily life. The Cynics, Skeptics, and Epicureans searched for happiness in simplicity, spiritual, and intellectual activities. The Stoics, believing in the equality of all people, were influential in both Rome and Greece.

Figure 2.5. Roman aqueduct as a great example of advanced engineering of Romans which after 2000 years still is staying.
(Photo: Wikipedia).

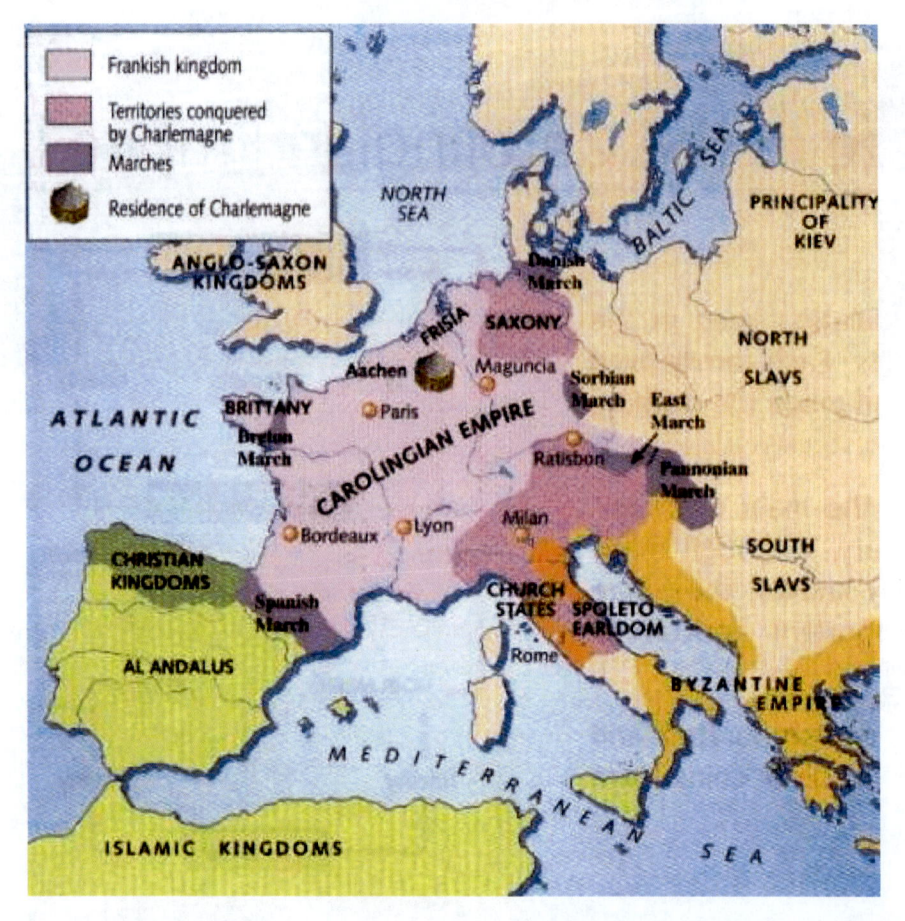

Figure 2.6. Charlemagne's Carolignian Empire in 800 as the first step towards the rise of Western civilization.
(Photo: www.historiasiglo20.org).

CHARLEMAIN EMPEROR, ROMAN HOLY EMPIRE, CHRISTIENDOM AND THE RISE OF WESTERN CIVILIZATION (8TH CENTURY)

Charlemagne Emperor As the Founder of Western Civilization (800)

If Western civilization were assigned a starting date, Christmas Day in the year 800 would be a very good choice. The ambitious Frankish monarch, Charlemagne (742–814) had recently restored Pope Leo III to his seat at the Vatican as a separate state. On that day, to the astonishment of the assembled multitude, the Pope interrupted the service to place a crown on Charlemagne's head, and declared him emperor over a restored Western Roman Empire, more known as the Carolingian Empire. What came to be called soon the Holy Roman Empire was the first great power to emerge in the new rising Western Christian civilization; it was an attempt to recreate the glory of the realm of the Caesars, but in a Christian, rather than a pagan, setting.

The Rise of High Culture in Western Civilization

Although Charlemagne was illiterate himself, he ardently supported scholarship, literature, the arts, and architecture. In fostering a renewal of learning, he called an English scholar Alcuin of York (735-804) to the court to establish a school that became the heart of the Carolingian Renaissance.

The effects of this cultural revival, however, were largely limited to a small group of court literati: "it had a spectacular effect on education and culture in Francia, a debatable effect on artistic endeavors, and an unmeasurable effect on what mattered most to the Carolingians, the moral regeneration of society," (Contreni 1984:59).

Figure 2.7. Lorsch Abbey gatehouse, c. 800 an example of the Carolingian architecture style. (Photo: Wikipedia).

Carolingian art extents to about a one-hundred-year period from about 800–900. While it was brief, but it was an influential period. Northern Europe embraced classical Mediterranean Roman art forms for the first time, setting the platform for the rise of Romanesque art and finally Gothic art in the West. Charlemagne, who was particularly interested in music, began a period of intense activity in the monasteries of the writing and copying of treatises in music theory and related topics. Carolingian architecture promoted by Charlemagne has the roots in Roman, Early Christian and Byzantine architecture with its own innovation, resulting in a unique Northern European character, more "heavy" than Southern Europe where one is more impacted by the warm weather.

The Holy Roman Empire – As the Second Step in Emergence of Western Civilization

The Holy Roman Empire (RHE) was a loose federation of states in central Europe. It was basically the area covered by modern Germany, Austria, Switzerland, and northern Italy, though its boundaries varied greatly over the centuries.

The second attempt to unite the empire was made by the German King Otto I, the Great, who came to the throne in 936. It was his ambition to revive the glories of the old Roman Empire, which had been briefly renewed by Charlemagne in 800 in the first attempt to activate this empire. In 962 Otto I had himself crowned as "Emperor Augustus," founding a line of emperors which endured until Napoleon I[28] abolished the Empire in 1806. The title "Holy Roman Empire" was assumed by Frederick Barbarossa in 1157.

Only under the very strongest rulers did the Empire have any cohesion or real power, and by the 1700s it fully justified the French writer Voltaire's quip that it was "neither holy, nor Roman, nor an empire." The Holy Roman Empire through 9 centuries was led by German emperors who tried to unite Europe.

Figure 2.8. The Holy Roman Empire (936-1806).
(Picture: history.howstuffworks.com).

The third attempt was made by Otto III who wanted to expand his empire towards the East. He was the son of a Greek (the Byzantine) princess and naturally he was planning to extend its Empire eastward. He settled in Rome, and tried, unsuccessfully, to revive its past glories. In 1000 he paid a visit to Poland and established the first Christian metropolis in Gniezno (western Poland) as the first step to establishing the Polish Kingdom which could take care of the eastern part of the Empire where the pagans were living. In fact by 1025 his

---

[28] Napoleon Bonaparte tried to transform his "Carolingian" feudal and federal empire into one modeled on the Holy Roman Empire but it lasted only 10 years (1804-1814) since his many wars eventually were not successful.

plan had been implemented and a Polish prince, Boleslaw Chrobry (967-1025) became the first Polish king in 1025. Unfortunately Otto III (980-1002) died so young that he could not accomplished his great plan. The RHE lasted through 8 centuries of changing configurations of states until 1808 with the military defeat of the Austrian-Russo Army by Napoleon at Austerlitz (2 December 1805).

The fourth attempt to unite Europe was done by the Austro-Hungarian Empire (1867-1918) which ruled Austria, Hungary, Czechoslovakia, republics of future Yugoslavia and southern Poland. This empire was a successful empire but of small scale in comparison the old Holy Roman Empire.

The fifth attempt was done by German Emperor (Kaiser) Wilhelm II who waged World War I (1914-1918) together with Austria-Hungary in an attempt to rule Europe and the world as was once done by the Holy Roman Empire.

The sixth attempt to rule the reborn Holy Roman Empire was done by Adolf Hitler in 1939-1945 when he ruled almost the whole Europe with exception of a few countries such as Great Britain, Portugal, Spain, Switzerland, Sweden, Italy, and Lichtenstein. However, the real unification of Europe took place about 1000 years after the first attempt, under a form of European Union with 28 countries-members in 2007. Needless to say, the EU is dominated today by the Germans, particularly by its Chancellor Angela Merkel.

Christendom

After the dissolution of the Roman Empire, the idea arose of Europe as one large church-state, called Christendom. Christendom was thought to consist of two distinct groups of functionaries: the sacerdotium, or ecclesiastical hierarchy, and the imperium, or secular leaders. In theory, these two groups complemented each other, attending to people's spiritual and temporal needs, respectively (Encyclopedia Britannica).

The rise of Christianity, from the hills of Galilee to the crowned heads of Europe, must be regarded as one of history's most extraordinary events, especially given the persecution of early Christians and the overwhelming secular power directed against them. For while the Roman Empire did not at first regard fledgling Christianity as a serious threat, it had taken the life of its founder, Jesus of Nazareth, and its officials in Palestine were susceptible to complaints against them leveled by other Jews. From our early 21st-century perspective, it is difficult to imagine how absolutely Rome ruled her far-flung dominions (Scalgier 2012).

In the centuries to follow the birth of Western civilization, which can also be called Christian civilization, there were many challenges — barbarian invasions, socioeconomic collapse, schisms, the rise of Islam, and periodic waves of heresy; however, never again was it to suffer an existential threat like during the early centuries of the Roman Empire. By the time of Charlemagne's Christmas coronation, although portions of Europe remained pagan, especially in the far north and east, it was apparent that Christian civilization, against all odds, had triumphed over the greatest worldly powers and was on the Earth to stay (Scalgier 2012), flourish and contributing strongly to the great successes of Western civilization up to the present.

THE ITALIAN RENAISANSE THE REBIRTH OF WESTERN HIGH CULTURE AND INFRASTRUCTURE (14TH -16TH CENTURIES)

The Renaissance was hailed as a new style, yet its name – meaning "rebirth" – shows a historical bend. In the classical part, 15th and 16th century designers such as Michelangelo, Palladio, and Brunelleschi found models of ideal form. But the Renaissance was also a modern age of exploration and invention. People began to build again, released from the Dark Ages, and used science and nature to achieve a cultural rebirth. No Renaissance man exemplified the spirit of this era more than Leonardo da Vinci – scientists, innovator, and artist of world-renowned works such as the Mona Lisa.

Figure 2.9. Leonardo da Vinci (1452-1519) and his great artwork, the Mona Lisa, the most famous artist and inventor of the Renaissance.
(Photo: Wikipedia).

Figure 2.10. The printing press invented by Johann Gutenberg in 1453 fueled Western civilization with new ideas contained in books in an accelerated manner and was key factor behind the changes in world civilization for the next 500 years, until the birth of the Internet (1983-2000) since it is now supposed that e-books are "better".
(Photo: Wikipedia and Huntington.org).

From the miraculous domed cathedral of Florence to urban places and rural villas, the Renaissance captures the new world view that spread from Italy throughout Europe – to English country houses, French chateaux, and German town-halls. It chronicles the achievements of the period along with the architectural styles, furnishings, fashion, art, designers, and notable buildings.

The distinctive aspect of the Renaissance was a changed view of history. Attentiveness of modernity was established and an appreciation of the present as diverse from the classic-ancient past. Rather than being viewed as random unfolding events, history was understood as having a structure and purpose. The Renaissance which developed modernity gave some opportunity to comparative thinking about humanity. Melancholy created the dream of Arcadia,[29] recreated in the pastoral life with the harmony with nature. Optimism for the future life created a vision of Utopia,[30] expressed as an ideal society built somewhere on an island in the Atlantic Ocean.

Standards of living were rising in sunny Italy which afforded wider access to comfort and wealth as well to art and beautiful architecture. Urban economies of many Italian cities benefited from mercantilism based on merchant-driven trade with northern Europe and Asia Minor. It only was triggering dreams for "better business" with distant but still unknown lands. The merchants and diplomats traveling around the Mediterranean were disseminating cultural and political ideas. European monarchies were in transition from the feudal to sovereign model and state-serving bureaucracies were emerging in this sea-oriented region.

The exploratory mind of the Renaissance led to steady decline of Christendom, since its misbehaving (in economic terms) led to the Reformation in the Northern-west and the Counter Reformation in Catholic regions.

The invention of gunpowder in Europe and discovery of propulsion principles[31] affected the design of fortresses and cities. But the invention of printing with movable type was the most radical invention of the Renaissance. Johann Gutenberg first[32] produced printed books in Mainz around 1453. Books had previously been for the elite only, because manuscripts were rare and costly to produce. Now a new map of ideas was opened to a broader spectrum of readers. One of them had developed theoretical science and technology which became the driving force of developing Western civilization in centuries to come.

The challenge of fresh ideas conveyed by the books and maps gave impetus to explorers, who began to open new lands and trade routes.

---

[29] Arcadia (Greek: Ἀρκαδία) refers to a vision of pastoralism and harmony with nature. The term is derived from the Greek province of the same name which dates to antiquity; the province's mountainous topography and sparse population of pastoralists later caused the word Arcadia to develop into a poetic byword for an idyllic vision of unspoiled wilderness. Arcadia is associated with bountiful natural splendor, harmony, and is often inhabited by shepherds.

[30] The term utopia was coined in Greek by Sir Thomas More for his 1516 book Utopia, describing a fictional island society in the Atlantic Ocean.

[31] The thrust of all moving propulsion systems comes from the same principle reaction, as expressed by Newton's second law of motion: force = mass x acceleration.

[32] The first printing, using wood-blocks carved by hand, was done by the Chinese in the 700s C.E.

THE AGE OF EXPLORATIONS AND EXPANTIONS IN SPACE OF WESTERN CIVILIZATION OVER THE OCEANS AND SEAS *PAX PORTUGANNICA* AND *ESPANNIA* 1500-1837

With good reason the Renaissance has been called the Age of Exploration. The voyages of Christopher Columbus, Amerigo Vespucci, Vasco de Gama, Francisco Pizarro, Hernando Cortes, and Bartolomeu Dias opened new routes to the Indies and across the Atlantic to the Americas and around Africa to India and China. Together with Nicolaus Copernicus and Galileo Galilei's speculations about the heavens, they forever changed humanity's view of the world.

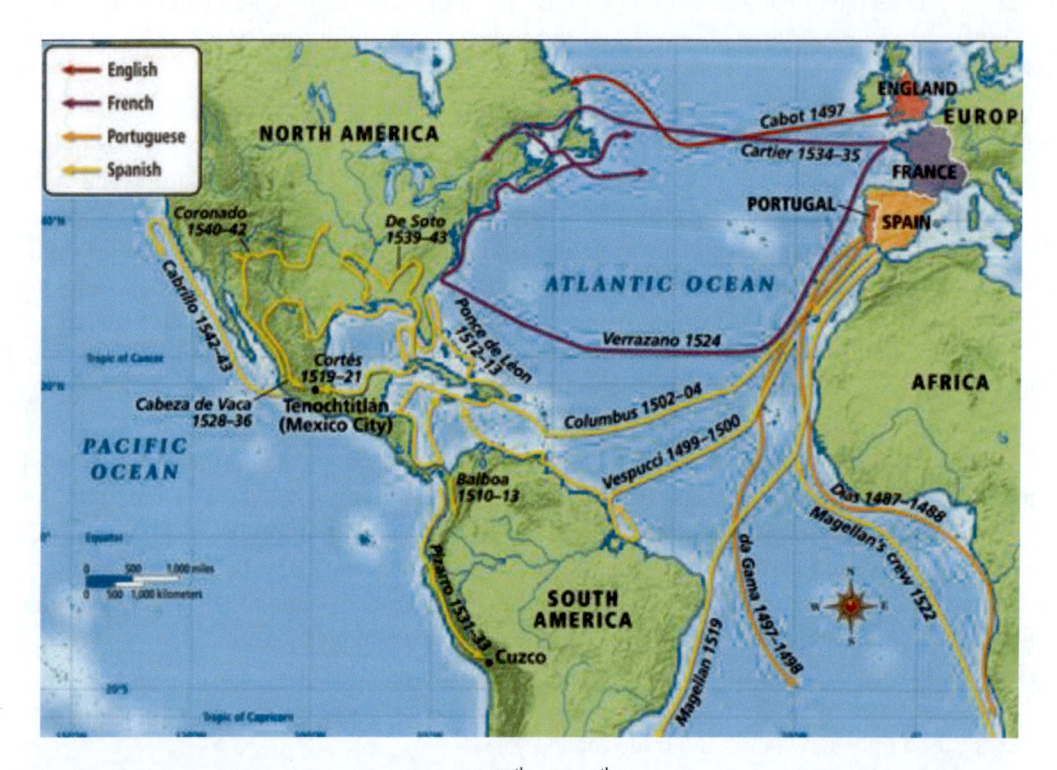

Figure 2.11. The first European explorers in the 15th and 16th centuries extended Western civilization through wars with other civilizations like the Aztecan, Mayan, Incan, African, Hindu, and Chinese. (Picture:www.historicalhoney.com).

In the 1400s there was a great impetus to explore in order to open trade routes which has carried through to today, as in the 21st century global business expands the globalization process into undeveloped countries. From the time of Prince Henry the Navigator, Portuguese seamen were exploring the west coast of Africa, seeking a sea route to India. The Portuguese were successful in that coastal trade and often used military force to secure their interests. The Africans welcomed Portuguese merchant and missionaries and embraced Christianity, only to lose faith in the foreigners when Portuguese slave traders made deals with their enemies. Portugal enjoyed a virtual monopoly of the Atlantic slave trade for over a century, exporting around 800 slaves annually. Most were brought to the Portuguese capital Lisbon, where it is estimated black Africans came to constitute 10 per cent of the population (Anderson 2000).

By 1700 the Portuguese had been surpassed in the slave trade by the French and English. Eventually the Portuguese discovered Brazil (1497-1500), occupied Angola and Mozambique and established some colonies in Goa (1510, India) and Macau (1513, China).

Since in those times the Portuguese sailors were the best in the world, due to the School of Navigation at Segers, Spain relied on them and other nationals in conquering the Americas. Spanish colonization of the New World began in the Caribbean, where Columbus and others founded settlements on Hispaniola (the island shared today by Haiti and the Dominican Republic), Puerto Rico, Jamaica, and Cuba. Spanish settlers demanded labor and tribute from the native people they called Indians, who suffered severely from exploitation by colonists and the diseases they introduced. As Indians died out in the Caribbean, Spaniards brought enslaved African to labor on plantations, and the population became largely African-American. The same process occurred in Portuguese Brazil. By 1750 Spain had colonized Mexico, including Florida, Texas, and New Mexico. The French colonized Louisiana and Canada, while the English colonized the central-east of North America. Even the Dutch colonized the ports of New York and Philadelphia, which later in 1664 were seized by the English who had developed them into thriving commercial centers.

Figure 2.12. The slave trade enriched and wounded America.
(Photo: Wikipedia and www.americanrtl.com).

The colonization process of the Americas was in fact based on a war between the several centuries old Western civilization with the older Indian, Aztec, Mayan, and Incan Civilizations. The colonization of the Americas by the Europeans supposedly led to a more advanced civilization. It is a matter of fact that emerging North American Civilization (or West-Western as a subset of Western civilization) eventually in the second part of the 20th century became the most advanced civilization in the world, due to democracy and capitalism with a human face and highly developed technology. Also the Latin-American Civilization became the subset of Western civilization, although at a lower level of advancement than the

North-American Civilization. The latter's slowed civilizational progress perhaps is due to the long and dangerous route of fighting for independence from Portugal, Spain, and France.

The slave trade and colonization of Africa did not implement Western civilization in Africa, expect in the case of the South African Republic. What is more, Sub Saharan Africa (SSA), due to these devastating processes including Westernization, is today in a situation where every second habitant of SSA has no access to clean water and electricity. Africa is due to actively implement the Africanization process again, as was formerly the case since modern humans originated in Africa.

The Pax Portugannica and Espania lasted until 1837 when Pax Britannica[33] took leadership over the world.

PHILOSOPY AND SCIENCE-ORIENTED ENLIGHTEMENT AND BETTER COGNIZING SOCIETY OF WESTERN CIVILIZATION (17TH -18TH CENTURY)

Progress of Philosophy or Thinking through Reasoning

The Enlightenment originated in the 17th century; it was ignited by philosophers Francis Bacon (1562-1626), René Descartes (1596-1650), Baruch Spinoza (1632–1677), John Locke (1632–1704), Pierre Bayle (1647–1706), Voltaire (1694–1778), Francis Hutcheson (1694–1746), and David Hume (1711–1776).

In France, the Enlightenment was based in the salons and culminated in the great *Encyclopédie* (1751–72) edited by Denis Diderot (1713–1784) and (until 1759) Jean le Rond d'Alembert (1717–1783) with contributions by hundreds of leading intellectuals who were called philosophes, notably Voltaire (1694–1778), Rousseau (1712–1778) and Montesquieu (1689–1755). Some 25,000 copies of the 35 volume encyclopedia were sold, half of them outside France (Sootin 1955).

These new intellectual strains would spread to urban centers across Europe, notably England, Scotland, the German states, the Netherlands, Poland, Russia, Italy, Austria, and Spain. It was also very successful in America, where its influence was manifested in the works of Francophiles like Benjamin Franklin and Thomas Jefferson, among others. It played a major role in the American Revolution. The political ideals of the Enlightenment influenced the American Declaration of Independence, the United States Bill of Rights, the French Declaration of the Rights of Man and of the Citizen, and the Polish–Lithuanian Constitution of May 3, 1791 (Palmer 1964).

The major contribution of this movement was that *reason* is the main tool of humans. It is best exemplified by the Frenchman René Descartes (1596-1650) who said "I think, therefore I am" (*cogito ergo sum*). His book on *La Méthode* (1637) provided the foundation for rational (scientific thinking), where the first rule is to doubt, the second rule is to divide a big problem into small problems, and the third rule is to solve the problem step by step from the small to the large. This method of pro-foundational skepticism is considered by some to be the start of modern philosophy and science.

---

[33] This date is associated with the beginning of the reign of Queen Victoria.

Progress of Science and Truth about the Universe and Nature

Scientific progress occurred in three major areas: astronomy, biology, and chemistry. The former was concerned with the issue of the solar system; the latter was concerned with the basics of physiology and anatomy. The third area challenged ancient alchemy. Galileo Galilei (1564-1642), the Italian scientist, caused a furor when he asserted the truth of the theory put forward a hundred years earlier by the Polish astronomer Nicolaus Copernicus (1473-1543) that the Earth is not the center of the universe, but revolves around the Sun. The Inquisition forced Galileo to recant such "heresies." Johannes Kepler (1571-1630) formulated the mathematical model of orbiting planets on the ellipse trajectories. The ellipse was the key to making Copernicus' system work. Sir Isaac Newton (1642-1727) was an Englishman; he formulated the law of gravity watching apples fall from a tree. Newton's theory of gravity was, in a certain sense, as if make-believe. He was proposing invisible forces that could not be detected. But the model worked and has been expanded by Albert Einstein in the 20th century, who formulated the concept of relativity.

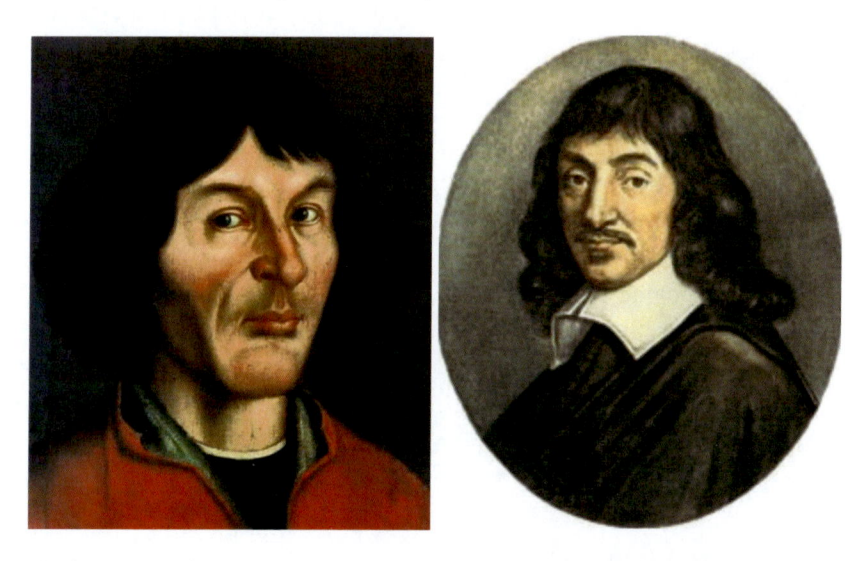

Figure 2.13. Nicolaus Copernicus questioned the Church's theory about the Universe and René Descartes followed the Polish Priest and defined *La Méthode* whose first rule is to have doubt. Both great scientists encouragement of thinking gave the foundation for the knowledge-driven development of Western civilization within the next 500 years.
(Photo: my.vanderbilt.edu, and www.edublox.com).

In the field of biology, the writings of Roman physician Galen had dominated European thinking in the subject for over a millennium. However, the Italian scholar Vesalius first demonstrated the mistakes in the Galenic model. His anatomical teachings were based upon the dissection of human corpses, rather than the animal dissections that Galen had used as a guide. Human anatomy, *De humani corporis fabrica*[34] was published in 1543, and was a groundbreaking work of human anatomy in the emerging modern medicine. Further groundbreaking work was carried out by William Harvey, who published *De Motu Cordis* in

---

[34] Page through a virtual copy of Vesalius's *"De Humanis Corporis Fabrica"*. Archive.nlm.nih.gov. Retrieved on 5-21-2014.

1628. Harvey made a detailed analysis of the overall structure of the heart, going on to an analysis of the arteries, showing how their pulsation depends upon the contraction of the left ventricle, while the contraction of the right ventricle propels its charge of blood into the pulmonary artery (Harvey 1978).

Chemistry, and its antecedent alchemy, became an increasingly important aspect of scientific thought in the course of the 16th and 17th centuries. English chemist Robert Boyle (1627–1691) is considered to have refined the modern scientific method for alchemy and to have separated chemistry further from alchemy. Boyle is also credited for his landmark publication *The Sceptical Chymist* in 1661, which is seen as a cornerstone book in the field of chemistry. In the work, Boyle presents his hypothesis that every phenomenon is the result of collisions of particles in motion. Boyle appealed to chemists to experiment and asserted that experiments denied the limiting of chemical elements to only the classic four: earth, fire, air, and water.[35]

Even calculating machines were a subject of advanced inventions in those times. Blaise Pascal (1623–1662) invented the mechanical sequentially computing calculator in 1642 which challenged bankers who were afraid that it would trigger unemployment. Gottfried Leibniz (1646–1716), building on Pascal's work, became one of the most prolific inventors in the field of mechanical calculators; he was the first to describe a pinwheel and the computing calculator in 1685. He invented the Leibniz wheel, used in the arithmometer, the first mass-produced mechanical calculator. He also refined the binary number system (to recognize God-1 from others-0). In the 20th century this system was called the binary system (invented by Claude Shannon (2016-2001) and it provided the foundation for all modern computers (Targowski 2013).

The progress in thinking and science paved the way to the Industrial Revolution which is the most important accomplishment of Western civilization and humans (so far).

THE AGE OF IDEAS AND REVOLUTIONS AND THE RISE OF EQUAL WESTERN SOCIETY (1688-1789)

The Glorious Revolution (1688-1689)

The revolution settlement established the supremacy of parliament over the crown, setting Britain on the path towards constitutional monarchy and parliamentary democracy. Over the course of the reign of William III (1689-1702) society underwent significant and long-lasting changes. The Bill of Rights was defined and made into law. It affirmed a number of constitutional principles, such as the illegality of prerogatives suspending and dispensing powers, the prohibition of taxation without parliamentary consent and the need for regular parliaments. Pressure from William also ensured the passage in May 1689 of the Toleration Act, granting many Protestant groups, but not Catholics, freedom of worship. Parliament gained powers over taxation, over the royal succession, over appointments and over the right of the crown to wage war independently, concessions that William thought were a price worth paying in return for parliament's financial support for his war against France (Vallance 2006).

---

[35] Robert Boyle, http://understandingscience.ucc.ie/pages/sci_robertboyle.htm.

The revolution, however, failed to limit the powers of the parliament and failed to create a body which could protect constitutional law. The revolution also fostered the growth of slavery by ending the Royal African Company's monopoly on the trade in 1698. For the non-white inhabitants of the British Atlantic Empire, the Glorious Revolution represented not the broadening of freedom but the expansion of servitude (Miller 1999).

But, regardless of this revolution's shortcomings, it paved the road to the parliamentary democratic system which eventually would become the political mark of Western civilization and its recommendation for the rest of the world.

The American Revolution (1776-1789)

The American War for Independence ended up as a revolution since it implemented a new society in the New World. In this war, 13 of Britain's North American Colonies broke away from rule by the mother country. Americans rejected the oligarchies common in aristocratic Europe at the time, championing instead the development of republicanism based on the Enlightenment's understanding of liberalism. Among the significant results of the Revolution was the creation of a representative government responsible to the will of the people defined in the Constitution (1788) and Bill of Rights (1791). The American shift to liberal republicanism, and the gradually increasing democracy, caused an upheaval of traditional social hierarchy and gave birth to the ethic that has formed a core of political values in the United States (Wood 1992).

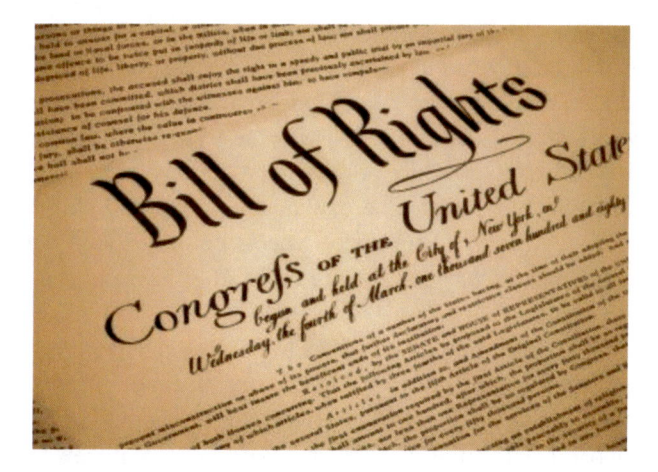

Figure 2.14. The American Bill of Rights (1791) the most important document of Western civilization (Photo: www.shestokas.com).

The French Revolution (1781-1789)

The French Revolution follows the case of the American Revolution and overturned the dictatorship of the French king and put forward the ideals of "Liberty, Equality, and Fraternity." Also, the Frenchman was transformed from a king's subject to a free citizen. This Revolution did not sustain itself, but the ideals remained influential through the next century on both sides of the Atlantic and were in some ways implemented in France within the next 100+ years. After the French Revolution, France became an aggressive state. The French tried to export Republicanism to other parts of Europe through the Napoleonic Wars which resulted in the collapse of the French Empire (1814/15).

x x x

The movement of revolutionary ideas in the 17th and 18th century persisted through the 19th century, replacing the Enlightment's reason and natural law by Romanticism which favored emotions in art, music and in the societal ideas of the French Revolution.

THE INDUSTRIAL REVOLUTION, NEW WESTERN CIVILIZATIONAL INFRASTRUCTURE AND THE RISE OF WESTERN BOURGEOIS SOCIETY
PAX BRITANNICA 1837-1914

The Industrial Revolution first began in the 1700s in Great Britain since that country was united (Scotland with England), free from wars and becoming the dominant colonial power. The British Empire was territorially enlarged: from France, gaining Newfoundland and Acadia, and from Spain, Gibraltar and Minorca. Gibraltar, which is still a British overseas territory to this day, became a critical naval base and allowed Britain to control the Atlantic entry and exit point to the Mediterranean. This means that British people were generally prosperous, and thus had money to buy manufactured goods, and at the same time enlarged colonies were a good market for any products from Great Britain.

The invention which started the revolution was the flying shuttle, made by John Kay in 1733. This enabled weavers to produce cloth more quickly and in greater widths. Fast spinning machines came 30 years later. The new machines were too big to drive by hand, so factories were built besides rivers where water-wheels could provide power. By the 1800s, nearly all spinning and weaving was done in factories, after having been a home process for thousands of years.

The first steam engines built in the late 1600s to pump water were very inefficient. James Watt, a Scottish engineer, devised the first satisfactory steam-engine in 1765, and in 1775 with Mathew Boulton he formed a company to manufacture them. This new source of power mechanized production replacing muscle power with mechanical power. The factories had been located near coal mines to shorten the transportation lines. In the early 1800s engineers also experimenting with mobile steam engines which could replace horses. The first practical modern engine was "Puffing Billy," built in Tyneside town in North-East England in 1813; it hauled coal from a mine to a riverside loading docks. The first passenger railway was built in Britain 1825, and within 10 years railways were operating in North America and Europe.

Among important industrial innovations done in Europe one can list the following:

- Automobile – in 1885/86 in Germany Karl Friedrich Benz invented the first true automobile. Gasoline automobiles were powered by an internal combustion engine: three wheels, a four cycle engine and a chassis form a single unit. At the same time

Gottlieb Wilhelm Daimler invented the first four wheeled, four-stroke engine- known as the "Cannstatt-Daimler."
- Photography – In 1816 in France Nicéphore Niépce, using paper coated with silver chloride, succeeded in photographing the images formed in a small camera, but the photographs were negatives, darkest where the camera image was lightest and vice versa, and they were not permanent in the sense of being reasonably light-fast like earlier experimenters. Several inventors through the next decades improved photography.
- Difference Engine – In 1834, Charles Babbage (the "father of computers") (1791-1871) created a machine that users could program. Like modern computers, Babbage's machine could store data for use later in other calculations and perform logic operations like *if-then* statements, among other capabilities. Babbage never compiled a complete set of designs for his next project – the Analytical Engine as he did for his beloved Difference Engines, but it's just as well; the Analytical Engine would have been so massive that it would have required a steam engine just to power it.
- Canned food – a French chef and innovator named Nicolas Appert in the early years of 1800s devised ways to preserve foods without stripping them of their flavor or freshness. Appert tested several methods to store food in containers. Before, storing food required drying or salt – treatments that didn't bode well for flavor and lasting.
- Others

Figure 2.15. The early factory system and railroad – products which defined a new industrial civilization infrastructure for the next centuries.
(Photo: findfacts.appaspot.com and Pegasus.cc.ucf.edu).

Very soon the Industrial Revolution entered the United States and continued its revolutionary innovations, through such inventions as:

- Thomas Edison (1847-1931) and his workshop patented 1,093 inventions. Included in this collection were the phonograph, the incandescent light bulb, and the motion picture. He was the most famous inventor of his time and his inventions had a huge impact on America's growth and history.
- Samuel Morse (1791-1872) invented the telegraph which greatly increased the ability of information to move from one location to another. Along with the creation of the

telegraph, he invented Morse code which is still learned and used today in navigation.
- Alexander Graham Bell (1847-1922) invented the telephone in 1876. This invention allowed communication to extend to individuals. Before, the telephone businesses had to rely on the telegraph.
- Elias Hower (1819-1867) and Isaac Singer (1811-1875) both were involved in the invention of the sewing machine. This revolutionized the garment industry and made the Singer Corporation one of the first modern industries.
- Cyrus McCormick (1809-1884) invented the mechanical reaper which made the harvesting of grain more efficient and faster. This helped farmers have more time to devote to other chores.
- George Eastman (1854-1932) invented the Kodak camera. This inexpensive box camera allowed individual to take black and white pictures to preserve their memories and historical events.
- Nicola Tesla (1856-1943) (a Serbian-American was a collaborator of Thomas Edison) invented fluorescent lighting and the alternating current (AC) electrical power system. He also is credited with inventing modern radio. The Tesla Coil is used in many items today including the modern radio and television.
- Charles Goodyear (1800-1860) invented vulcanized rubber. This technique allowed rubber to have many more uses due to its ability to stand up to bad weather. Interestingly, many believe the technique was found by mistake. Rubber became important in industry as it could withstand large amounts of pressure.
- The Wright brothers, Orville (1871-1948) and Wilbur (1867-1912), were two American brothers, inventors, and aviation pioneers who are credited with inventing and building the world's first successful airplane.
- Henry Ford (1863-1947) invented a business of manufacturing inexpensive cars in assembly lines in mass volumes.
- John Mauchly (1907-1980) and J. Presper Eckert (1919-1995) built the first working electronic computer ENIAC in 1946.
- The international team of American, Hungarian and Polish physicists built atomic and hydrogen bombs in 1945.
- Modern medications were invented by several inventors and pharma businesses.
- Others

The Industrial Revolution changed the face of the countryside. The new machines were housed in large factories, and towns sprang up around these to provide homes for the workers. Before the revolution, most workers could grow their own food. In new towns, they lived in cramped conditions with no gardens and depended on their wages for everything. This new demand and money pool created a growing service industry and urbanization development. Very soon a new workers' class (lowest class) was created which entered the endless paths of conflicts with the owners of factories and businesses as members of the rising bourgeois society and its large stockholders with capitalists as members of the upper class. It was the beginning of the rising class consciousness among social activists. The whole economy functioned as a capitalistic system, supposedly the best economic system ever invented. The results of the Industrial Revolution controlled by capitalism are as follows:

Figure 2.16. Model T Ford and the Bleriot XI airplane – products which made people mobile and look for more supporting products and services in the industrial economy.
(Photo: www.boldride.com and www.wright-brothers.org).

- The quality of life in Western civilization has risen 16 times from the 1700s up to the present, and we live almost 3 times longer (Fogel 2004, Maddison 2000).
- The mechanization and automation of mass-scale production in the 20th and 21st centuries created the policy of constant economic growth and a habit of super-consumerism which causes the growth of population and hence the decline of the reserves of strategic resources like: water, oil, gas, coal, uranium and others which if depleted, world civilization may stop functioning. In 1820 the population of the world was around 1 billion and by 2014 it had grown to 7 billion; thus, in the short span of about 200 years, it had grown by a factor of 7, while from the year 1000 to 1820 the population within this 800 year span had grown only about 4 times (Maddison 2000:28), in other words, 16 times slower.
- Might the early triumph of modernity in the 19th – 20th centuries trigger the collapse of Western civilization in the 21st century?

WORLD WAR I AND II AS THE INTERNAL CONFLICTS FOR RESOURCES AND DOMINANCE IN WESTERN CIVILIZATION 1914-1918 & 1939-1945

The World War I (1914-1918) As the Fifth Attempt to Expand the Holy Roman Empire

One of the chief causes of WWI was rivalry between groups of European powers over trade, colonies, naval and military power. Countries formed defensive alliances, meaning that an attack on one country automatically involved its allies. The two main alliances were the Triple Entente – Britain, France, and Russia; and the Triple Alliance – Germany, Austria-Hungary, and Italy (which very soon declared neutrality in August 1914). It was a war with mechanized weaponry such as the magazine rifle, the machine gun, and quick firing artillery, which had enhanced every soldier's killing power, especially at a distance. To protect themselves, the armies dug trenches and ended up waiting in them for death. The total number of military and civilian casualties in World War I was over 37 million. There were over 17 million deaths and 20 million wounded ranking it among the deadliest conflicts so far in human history.

This war should not have happened in Europe but the growing capital, nationalism, greed for more land and strategic natural resources, and the erratic personality of Kaiser Wilhelm II, who to certain degree reflected the rising industrial and national power of Germany, were placing Germany as the leader pushing towards the war. Wilhelm II believed "in force, and the 'survival of the fittest' in domestic as well as foreign politics..." and certainly thought that the Holy Roman Empire should be re-activated as the continuation of the German dominance in Europe during the last 1000 years with himself at the top.

Germany was not prepared for a conflict on such a scale, having to combat several nations at once. Logistically they didn't have the resources to sustain a long war and achieve the final victory. Industrial powers like the United States could stay in such extended conflicts for the long haul and win, but not countries like Germany. The striking thing about the history of German warfare in WWI are the combat zones: Germany's fighting prowess was second to none. They were good at winning battles, since they had good tactical commanders. However, logistically, they were weak. The entry of the U.S. into the war was a decisive event. With America's manpower and industrial might, the deadlock of armies staying months in the trenches was broken.

The Bolshevik Revolution (1917) As the Correction of the French Revolution through the Rising short-lived Soviet Civilization

The new industrial economy ruled by Darwinian Capitalism (born in the 19th century) was blossoming at the dawn of the 20th century with the embedded conflict between the working class and the bourgeois society which was better off.

Karl Marx's theory of capital was convincing the international movement of workers (which still is considered by many Western scholars as the right theory) to materialize Marxism in the Bolshevik Revolution in the backward Russian Empire. The revolution's goal was to reverse the French Revolution's glory of individualism by collectivism and the equal distribution of wealth (Targowski 1982). The total death count as the result of this revolution's crimes, terror and repression is in a range of 94 million (Courtois et al., 1999) which is close to the total number of deaths in the two world wars in the 20th century. This bloody revolution took place in Eastern Civilization (Russia controlled by Orthodox-oriented Christianity, and in Asian republics belonging to Islam Civilization) and Oriental Civilization (China, Vietnam, Cambodia, Laos, North Korea) with a strong impact upon Western civilization, where in Central European states alone (under control of the Soviet Empire, such as Finland, Baltic Republics, Poland, Czechoslovakia, Hungary, Rumania, Bulgaria) about 1 million were killed (Courtois et al., 1999).

In reality the Bolshevik Revolution was financed by some New York banks looking for some lucrative business, and as a result the leader of the Russian Communist party, Vladimir Lenin, was sent by the German Government from Germany to Russia in a locked train (via ferry and Finland) to trigger chaos in the Russia (among others) which was fighting against Germany in the World War II. Broadly speaking, Western civilization tried to help the future

Nazis Civilization to fight Eastern Civilization. As the result of this help, Germany, as the part of Western (in fact Nazis) Civilization, was beaten by the Soviet Civilization 48 years later. In the 21st century, is this case repeating itself with Western civilization (mostly its part Western-West or "Atlantic") now helping the Chinese Civilization to flourish economically which may result in its hegemony in the world?

Soviet Communism through 74 years (1917-1991) of practice has been discredited as an unlawful and immoral social system ruled by the powerful elite in the name of faceless masses. There is an opinion that it is pitiful that communism took place in the backwards Russian Empire instead of, for example, in Germany; however, this was rather fortunate, given what the Germans showed in East Germany under Soviet control during the Cold War (1947-1991). Communism with German flavor perhaps would have persisted through the present in a totalitarian-barbarian (Nazis Germany showed what they were able to do) system which would surpass even George Orwell's imagination and North-Korea's current (21st century) regime.

On the other hand, the fact that Communism had its chance to be practiced on a large scale in a relatively long period of time gave the rest of the world a laboratory to test supposedly socially perfect political system. The test's result is negative. Communism looks good on paper but in practice is anti-human and ineffective in using strategic resources. This result was achieved at the cost of 94 million lives. Was it worth? Western civilization's prosperity owns much to those people who paid such a high price to invalidate Communism through real life experience.

In fact, Soviet Communism functioned as the Soviet Civilization with a secular religion (new collective morality and values), a new society (of supposedly all equal citizens), and new infrastructure, with large scale municipal projects and cosmos conquering space for keeping Capitalism away from that civilization. However, when Mikhail Gorbaczev (1931-) in the 1980s slightly changed the Soviet's values, goals and strategy and asked the citizens to re-built the state, Soviet Civilization collapsed first with the Polish Revolution (1980-89) and later by the removal of the Berlin Wall in 1991.

Figure 2.17. Soviet Civilization's liturgy controlled by W. Lenin (187-1924) and J. Stalin (1878-1953). (Photo: www.youtube, and www.notre-planet.info).

The World War II (1939-1945) As the Rise of the Super-Nation of the Short-Lived Nazist Civilization or the Sixth Attempt to Activate the Re-engineered Holy Roman Empire

The Treaty of Versailles (1919) in particular severely punished Germany which lost one-seventh of its land and all its colonies. It had also to pay huge sums of reparations, not as a percentage of GDP but in absolute amounts. In practice, Germany was so impaired by the war that it never did pay off those required huge sums. This issue was one of the main causes of an economic crisis (1923-1933) in Germany after the war which led to the unexpected rise of Adolf Hitler (1889-1945) as the legally elected Chancellor of Germany (1933) and World War II.

Hitler's approach to war was based on the anthropogeography theory [founded by Germen professors Friedrich Ratzel and Karl Haushoffer (Targowski 2014c)] that living space for the Germans should expand as their culture develops and the growth of the German state should be supported by the incorporation of smaller polities which have no rights to exists. Hitler defined the *Lebensraum* policy as an alternative for feeding the people by means of global trade. Hence, "the Push towards the East" (*Dranh nacht Osten*) strategy planned to settle people of Nordic origin (composed of Celtic[36] and Germanic people[37]), often called Anglo-Saxons, as far as the Ural Mountains. These people would form the *Übermensch* nation, a biologically superior "Aryan" or Germanic master race. It became a "scientific" foundation for the National Socialist ideas. The Nazi notion of the master race also laid the idea that "inferior humans" (*Üntermenschen*) such as Jews, Slaves, Gypsies and others, should be dominated and enslaved.

Hitler organized Nazis Germany as a new civilization with own secular religion (symbols, "liturgy," new morality and so far), a new society of masters and even new infrastructure like a system of concentration camps, highways, a eugenic program and so forth. This Nazi Civilization was spreading on a large territory but fortunately lasted only 12 years.

Figure 2.18. Nazis Civilization's new liturgy controlled by Adolf Hitler, the master of ceremonies. (Photo:ww2today.com and nickyand manvir.blogspot.com).

---

[36] Celts come from a terrene around today Vienna, Austria (Hitler was an Austrian)
[37] Including Angles, Saxons, and Jutes, collectively known as the Anglo-Saxons.

Hitler was aware that he is developing a new civilization; he asked his chief architect, Albert Speer, to plan a new Berlin and later asked him to design ruins of it to see how within a millennia they would look in comparison to how the Roman ruins (*Forum Romanum*) looked during his time.

Hitler not only wanted to enlarge Germany's living space but also wanted to use slaves from conquered countries, as it was practiced by the Roman Empire almost 2000 years ago. Therefore the Germans did not accept a warm welcome by the Ukrainians in 1941 since their plan to "clean" their land and settle Germans from overcrowded Germany together with slaves (Poles and others). Hitler had a far reaching plan for how the world would be ruled by the Nazis "Holy Roman Empire." Therefore, he let the British (including the French) Army (338,000 soldiers) return unharmed on 27 May-4 June, 1940 after it lost the battle at Dunkirk. This retreat is called the "miracle of Dunkirk." There are several explanations of Hitler's "*Halt Order*." This author thinks that Hitler wanted to save other Anglo-Saxon nation's in order to rule the world together in the near future (Figure 2.18), particularly knowing how the British were strong in other parts of the world. Contrary to this kind of soft approach to a beaten enemy, Hitler was the largest executioner of people in world history.

Hitler's racism led to the Holocaust of the Jews, Gypsies, and Poles (6 million of all mentioned civilians were killed in the organized manner), and the total dead as a result of WWII ranges from 60 to 85 million. Civilians killed totals from 38 to 55 million, including the loss of Chinese and war-related casualties from, for instance, disease and famine.

Nazis Germany lost the war since its goal and strategy were based on the morality of one nation's superiority, and the enslaving of the remaining nations united the majority of the world and put it on high alert, resulting in the total destruction of the Nazis Holy Roman Empire. The U.S. again intervened in Europe and was the decisive military and political power in the next (after WW I) annihilation of Germany.

Figure 2.19. Charles Edward (1884-1954), Duke of Saxe-Coburg and Gotha, a part of Germany, the youngest grandson of Queen Victoria, during WWI fought against Great Britain and during WWII supported Hitler as a Nazi General, with a role in the Nazi Euthanasia Program: He was the head of the German Red Cross (1933-1945) and the Prosecution of Mentally and Physically Disabled. (Photo: Public domain).

THE *PAX AMERICANA* VERSUS *PAX SOVIETICA* THE QUEST FOR THE OPTIMAL SOCIETY ON EARTH 1945-1989/1991

The winners of the World War II, the Western-West ("Atlantic") Civilization and Soviet Civilization, immediately entered in the war of civilization, officially called the Cold War. It was a war to "save" humanity since it was the race between Capitalism and Communism or Democracy and Totalitarianism for the optimal society on Earth. Capitalism blossomed, since the post-WWII Western economy created a large demand for products and services, and confronted by labor-oriented Communism, it was behaving moderately as Capitalism with a human face. Such seducing Capitalism and democracy were embracing the political West (USA, Western Europe, Australia & New Zealand, Japan, South Korea, Hong Kong, and Singapore) and successfully optimized its internal, interacting economies for the good of current generations.

Concurrently with the *Pax Americana*, the *Pax Sovietica* was spreading its integrational politics to Eastern Europe, China, Vietnam, Cuba and some African nations, promising to build equal societies where capitalistic exploitation would be eliminated forever. But, the Soviet Block (or Soviet Civilization) did not pay too much attention to the rising and better off Western Society, since it was planning and acting not for the good of the current generations but for the future generations. However, the current generations of this Block (or civilization) did not want to wait another century and were organizing revolts in Hungary and Poland (1956), Czechoslovakia (1968), and again in Poland (and in remaining Eastern European Nations belonging to the Soviet Block, 1980-1991). Eventually, due to good and wise politicians like pope John Paul II (2020-2005), Soviet leader Mikhail Gorbaczev, Lech Walesa (1943-), Vaclav Havel (1936-2011), and others, the Soviet Block (civilization) collapsed together with the Berlin War in 1991. Capitalism and democracy won out, promising a New World Order (NOW) for humanity, which had dreamed about such a solution.

After the collapse of Communism, world-wide optimism was so great that an American intellectual, Francis Fukujama, published a book *The End of History and the Last Man* in 1992. He delivered this good message too soon. He should have waited a few years in order to see that world politics since 1991 have created a more dangerous world than during the Cold War. Another American scholar Samuel Huntington (1996) waited 5 years and published a famous book that the NOW is nothing else than the clash of civilizations (mostly among Western, Eastern, and Islam). The first years of the 21st century have shown that the NOW has even become the war of civilizations, since terrorism has almost reached an equal platform with the old fashioned military power of Western and Eastern Civilizations.

Neither Communism nor Capitalism were able to build an optimal society in the world civilization during the second part of the 20th century. There is the question of whether such a society can be developed at any point on this small and overpopulated planet Earth.

GLOBALIZATION 2000
PAX CONSORTIA AND PAX VIRUALIZIANA 2000+
THE QUEST FOR THE RICH ELITE AND POP CULTURE'S SELF-SATISFYING RESPONSE BY THE REST

The Cold War in 1962 could have become a Hot (Atomic) War since 10,000 Soviet military advisors were installing missile launchers with atomic heads in communistic Cuba. The missiles in Cuba allowed the Soviets to effectively target the majority of the continental United States. The planned arsenal included forty launchers.[38] Then, Polish-American Paul Baran (1926-2011), working at the US Air Force think-tank RAND in Santa Monica (California), was asked to plan a tele-communication systems "A Day After" atomic attack on the U.S. He recommended replacing the star-oriented tele-communication network by the grid network called also as a packet switching network without a central point (easy targeted and de-capacitating the communication), similar to a human brain anatomy. Based on this topology, the ARPANET for defense purpose was built, which in 1983 (following P. Baran advice) was split into the MILINET and Internet for public info-communication applications.

By the end of the 21st in 1990 Tim Berners-Lee, a British computer scientist and former CERN (the European Organization for Nuclear Research in Geneva, Switzerland) employee invented the World Wide Web which is a system of interlinked hypertext documents that are accessed via the Internet. With a web browser, one can view web pages that may contain text, images, videos, and other multimedia and navigate between them via hyperlinks. The first web browser Mosaic was invented in 1993 by Marc Andreessen (1971-), then a student of the University of Illinois Urbana-Champaign. This paved the way for the development and applications of the future popular browsers such as Netscape Navigator, Internet Explorer, Mozilla Firefox, Safari, and Google Chrome.

Also, behind the Iron Curtain, a similar concept was invented. In 1972-1974 a prototype of INFOSTRADA was built in Poland. Later it was translated to Information Superhighway in the U.S. and stated in an interview of Al Gore in WIRED, December 1995, p. 218. The INFOSTRADA project was conceptualized by Andrew Targowski in 1972 in Poland and is described in his books (1980, 2013, 2014a).

The Internet and simple tools to use it, such as WWW and browsers, established the Internet as the Global Information Infrastructure allowing the almost instant rise of the globalization of ideas and business flows over e-ways (infostradas) around the world. The idea of the Information Superhighway defined the strong paradigm of a New Economy based on e-commerce. Also, Marshal McLuhan's idea of the Global Village (1962, driven by television) was materialized by Andrew Targowski's idea of the Electronic Global Village (2009, 2014a, driven by computers and their networks) as it is depicted in Figure 2.19.

---

[38] On October 27, 1962 after much deliberation between the Soviet Union and John Kennedy's cabinet, President Kennedy secretly agreed to remove all missiles set in southern Italy and in Turkey, the latter on the border of the Soviet Union, in exchange for Khrushchev removing all missiles in Cuba.

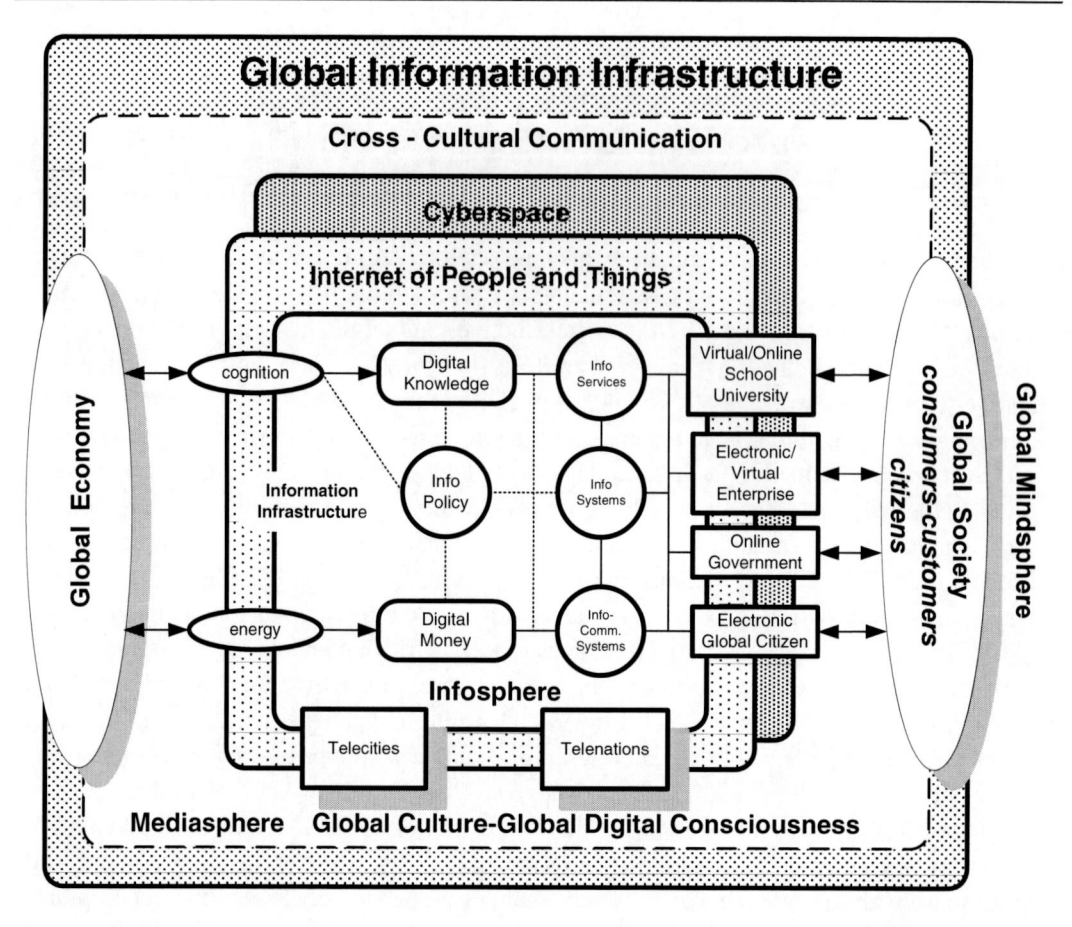

Figure 2.20. The system architecture of the Electronic Global Village as Global Information Infrastructure (Targowski 2009).

The GII (Internet) allows Western civilization (Western-West/"Atlantic") to outsource about 50,000 factories to take advantage of slavery-level labor pay in China (as well as in other countries with cheap labor) and make huge profits. This resulted in the growth of global business (*Pax Consortia*) and the decline of middle class as well as the rapid growth of the global rich elite in Western civilization. It apparently is leading to the decline of Western civilization and the re-birth of Chinese Civilization at the dawn of the 21st century. Outsourcing has contributed to a further levelling of global inequalities as it has led to general trends of industrialization in the Global South and deindustrialization in the Global North. This process was called by Thomas Friedman as *The World is Flat* in his best-selling book (2005).

In the dawn of the 21st century, the fast dissemination of the Internet and e-personal "gadgets" has led towards the rise of virtuality which is based on electronic communication and data and files storing and sharing in cyberspace (computer storing and networking distribution). This takes place mostly among the young generation which when they have some problem in reality, escape to virtuality which makes them seem "happier." Eventually, the *Pax Consortia* is confronting the *Pax Virtualiziana*, as the *vox populi* unhappy that Western civilization is declining and showing a lack of wisdom and social responsibility. Eventually the decline of Western civilization will lead towards its transformation into Global civilization (Targowski 2014a) and the rise of Virtual Civilization (Targowski 2014b), as the latter is depicted in Figure 2.19.

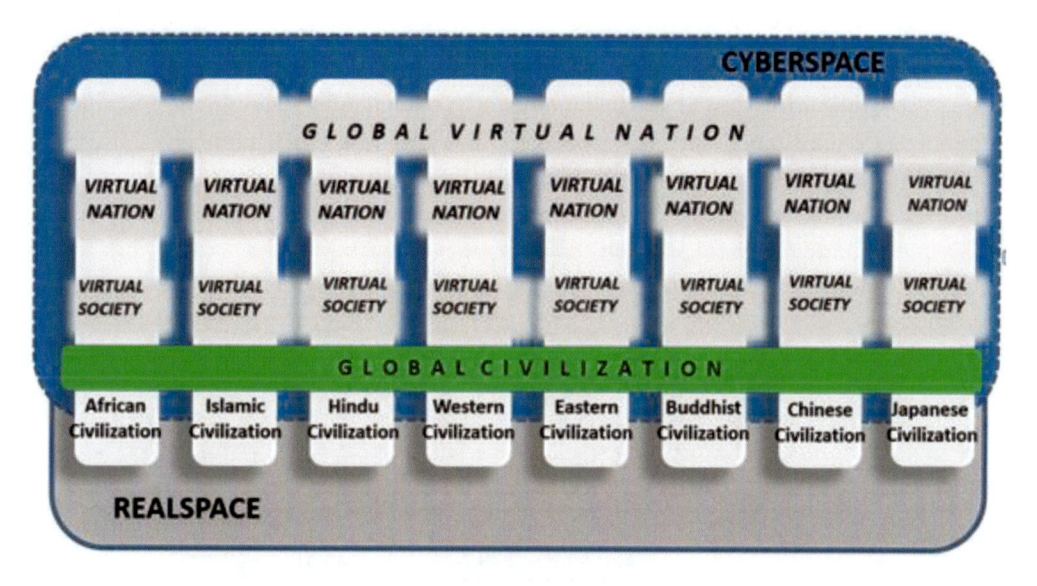

Figure 2.21. The science fiction future of Virtuality development in the context of contemporary Civilizations.

FROM WESTERN TO GLOBAL CIVILIZATION THE TRANSFORMATION OF WESTEDRN CIVILIZATION 2010+

In the dawn of 21st century, the wave of globalization led by the *Pax Consortia* is leading towards the emergence of Global civilization because this civilization meets the general criteria of civilization (Targowski 2004). For example it is characterized by:

- Global religion – Western civilization's Christianity (Protestantism and Catholicism) has been replaced by global religion, which is reflected in beliefs that business is the omnipotent power which should control society for its benefit since what is good for business is good for the society;
- The human entity in Global Society is composed of certain segments of the societies of 8 autonomous civilization (Western, Eastern, Islamic, Japanese, Chinese, Buddhist, Hindu, and African), which apply global culture and infrastructures;
- Culture has a global character, which means that certain patterns of behavior are practiced (*de facto* by certain segments of those societies only) in those autonomous civilizations, for example such practices as "English," professional and student dress codes, music, movies, food, drinks, and so forth;
- Global Infrastructure of Information (1) (the Internet and Global Area Networks) and of Material (2) (transportation, finance, and business) reaching every autonomous civilization and integrating them into an emerging Global Society and Global Economy. Furthermore, there are many international organizations (for-profit and

non-profit, official and unofficial) such as UN, UNESCO, GATT, WTO, WB, IMF, NATO, and others, which create the Global Infrastructure of Regulations.

However, Global civilization is not another autonomous civilization, which can be called *vertical* ones; it in fact *horizontally* penetrates autonomous civilizations as it is shown in Figure 2.21. Some critics might say that the reach of Global civilization in the least developed autonomous civilizations is yet very modest (for example a small number of users of the Internet or telephones). On the other hand this reach is observable and known in those civilizations, whose elites are rather active users of Global civilization.

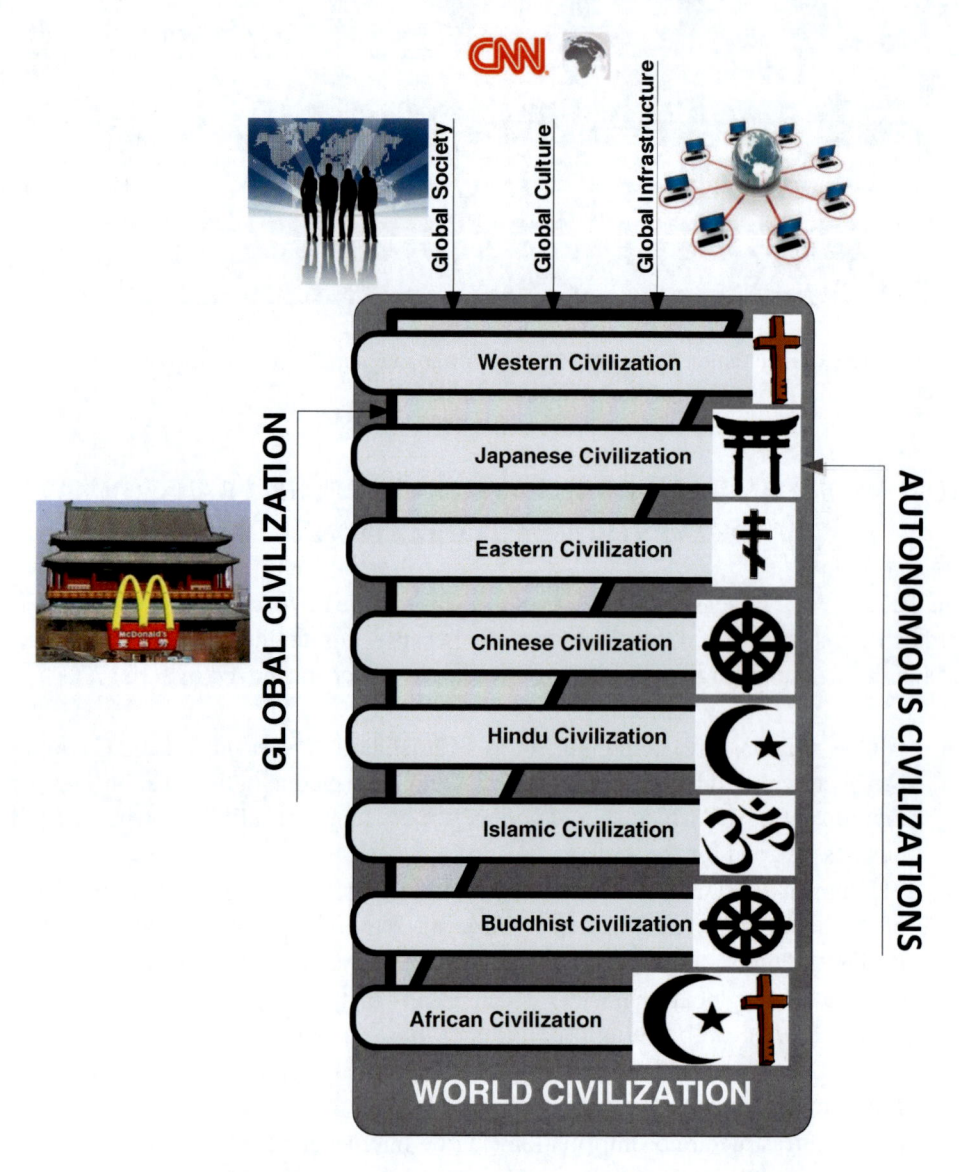

Figure 2.22. The emerging Global civilization as a new layer of the World Civilization at the dawn of the 21st century.

Conclusion

1. Western civilization is one of the oldest and largest civilizations of the world. It has lasted about 1200 years and is spreading from Poland in the Northern-east to Australia in the Southwest. In the 21st century it has a population close to 1 billion people and is the most modern and richest of all contemporary civilizations.
2. The success of Western civilization is based on: the Christian religion which asks you "to love your neighbor," a good climate, constant internal and external conflicts which create resilience and resourcefulness, the development of knowledge, skills, law, medicine, industry, technology and leisure as well as democracy and Capitalism with a human face during the Cold War (1945-1991).
3. The decline of Western civilization in the 21st century is triggered by globalization which works for global corporations but not for citizens of developed nations whose jobs are being exported to countries with low costs of labor. Also, turbo-Capitalism of the 21st century promotes super-consumerism which is leading to the depletion of strategic resources and to an unsustainable civilization. In effect Western civilization, as a declining civilization, is at the same time transforming into Global and Virtual civilizations whose *modus operendi* is just in *status nascendi*.
4. The decline of Western civilization, after reaching its peak of modernity in the second part of the 20th century, is caused by the fact that Western people are wise, when are poor and are stupid when are better off.

References

Anderson, J., M. (2000). *The history of Portugal*. Greenwood Publishing Group.
Barbante, A. L. et al. (2004). Eight glacial cycles from an Antarctic ice core. *Nature* 429 (6992):623–8.
Contreni, J.G. (1984). The Carolingian renaissance, in Warren T. Treadgold, ed. *Renaissances before the Renaissance: cultural revivals of late antiquity and the Middle Ages*.
Courtois, St. (1999). *The black book of Communism*. Cambridge, MA: Harvard University Press.
Huntington, S. (1996). *The clash of civilizations and the remaking of world order*. New York: Simon & Schuster.
Harvey, W. (1978). De motu cordis, cited in Allen G. Debus, *Man and nature in the Renaissance*, (Cambridge: Cambridge Univ. Press, p. 69.
Fogel, R.W. (2004). *The escape from hunger and premature death, 1700-2100*. Cambridge: Cambridge University Press.
Friedman, Th. (2005). *The world is flat*. New York: Farrar, Straus and Giroux.
Fukuyama, Fr. (1992). *The end of history and the last man*. New York: Free Press.
Kieffer, J. (2014). Contributions of Rome. Accessed 7-22-2014 http://www.aasd.k12.wi.us/staff/hermansenjoel/apmuseum/kiefferkerkhoff/webpage/contributions.htm.
Kobyliński, Zb. (2008). The Slavs in Paul Fouracre. *The New Cambridge Medieval History*. Cambridge: Cambridge University Press. pp. 530–537

Kreis. St. (2006). The history guide. Accessed 7-22-2014 http://*www.historyguide.org/ ancient/lecture10b.html*.
Maddison, A. (2000). The world economy, a millennial perspective. Paris: OECD.
McLuhan, M. (1962). *The Gutenberg galaxy: the making the typographic man*. Toronto: University of Toronto Press.
McNall, B. et al. (1982). *World civilizations*. New York: W.W.W. NORTHON & COMPANY.
Miller, J. (1999). *The Glorious Revolution*. Longman, 2nd edn.
Palmer, R.R. (1964). The *age of the democratic revolution*: a political history of Europe and America, 1760–1800. *Princeton*, vol. 1, 1959; vol. 2.
Anderson, S. (1995). *Civilizations and world systems*. Walnut Creek, London, New Delhi: Altamira Press.
Scalgier, Ch. (2012). Rise of Christendom. New American. Accessed 7-22-2014 http://www.thenewamerican.com/culture/history/item/13808-rise-of-christendom.
Smith, J. (2005). *Europe after Rome*. Oxfrod, UK: Oxfrod University Press.
Snider, L.D. (1999). *Macro-history, a theoreticasl approach to comparative world history*. Lwiston: New York: The Edwin Mellen Press.
Sootin, H. (1995). *Isaac Newton*. New York: Messner.
Spivey, N. (1997). *Etruscan art*. London: Thames and Hudson.
Stark, R. (2014). *How the West won, the neglected story of the triumph of modernity*. Wilmington, Delaware: ISI Books.
Targowski, A. (1980). *Informatyka, modele systemów i rozwoju* (*Informatics, models of systems and development*). Warsaw: PWE.
Targowski, A. (1982). *Red Fascism*. Lawrenceville, Virginia: Brunswick.
Targowski, A. (2004). A Dynamic Model of an Autonomous Civilization. *Dialogue and Universalism*. Vol. XIV(1-2):77-90.
Targowski, A. (2009). *Information technology and societal development*. Hershey, New York: Information Science Reference (IGI).
Targowski, A. (2013). *Historia, teraźniejszość i przyszłość informatyki* (*History, presence, future of information technology*). Łódź (Poland): Wydawnictwa Politechniki Łódzkiej.
Targowski, A. (2014a). *Global civilization in the 21st century*. New York: NOVA Science Publishers.
Targowski, A. (2014b). *Virtual civilization in the 21st century*. New York: NOVA Science Publishers.
Targowski, A. (2014c). *The deadly effect of informatics on the Holocaust*. Mustang, OK: Tate Publishing.
Toynbee, A. (1934). *A study of history*. Oxford: Oxford University Press.
Vallance, E. (2006). The Glorious Revolution: 1688 and Britain's fight for liberty. New York: Little, Brown and Co.
Van Doren, Ch. (1991). *A history of knowledge*. New York: Ballantine.
Wood, G. (1992). *The radicalism of the American Revolution*. New York: A.A. Knopf.

Chapter 3

THE LIFE CYCLE OF WESTERN CIVILIZATION

ABSTRACT

The *purpose* of this investigation is to define the life cycle (timeline) of Western civilization and its role with respect to the rising Global Civilization in the 21st century. The *methodology* is based on an interdisciplinary big-picture view of the developments and interdependency of Western and Global civilizations. Among the *findings* are: Western civilization's life cycle is not similar to other civilization since this civilization has a very complex historical pattern full of conflicts, revolutions, wars (including 3 invasions by non-Western empires), and the impact of nine Western-empires which contributed to the development of this civilization. *Practical implication:* Western civilization's life cycle pattern is original but similar to others in terms of birth and decline. *Social implication:* It is strange that Western Civilization, which invented the Globalization Wave in the 21st century, has become a victim of this wave (especially the middle class) which flattens the world in the economic dimension. *Originality:* This investigation defined the life cycle of Western Civilization through graphic modelling which allows predictions of its behavior today and in the future.

INTRODUCTION

The purpose of this investigation is to define the life cycle of Western civilization in order to learn from the history of this civilization and predict the future behavior. Since a civilization is a large social organism, it is, like history, not passive but dynamic and strongly impacts humanity and its well-being on both a small as well as a large-scale. Several great scholars of civilization worked on its patterns and cycles, but they studied past civilizations. Western civilization is a special civilization since it has a very complex path of development and functioning, defined by endless internal and external conflicts, revolutions, wars, and control by nine Western-oriented empires. In contrast, most past civilizations are one empire-oriented with a much simpler internal dynamics than Western civilization; this is characteristic particularly in modern times during the last 500 years. The graphic modeling should help in providing a clear understanding of Western civilization's elements and their relationships. If one can understand the pattern of Western civilization's life cycle than an understanding of its current and future behavior will be easier. Eventually, is it be possible that humans will show their wisdom and adapt accordingly to expected challenges?

THE EVOLUTION OF WESTERN CIVILIZATION

Western civilization has lasted about 1200 years and is spread-out from Poland in the East to Australia in the West. It began after the Dark Ages (500-800) which took place after the fall of the Western Roman Empire. Those ages were dominated by barbarian invaders, superstition, and the struggle for existence (Smith 2005). It was an age of "rapine and death." (Van Doren 1991). Most cities were uninhibited and ruined; trade had broken down, forcing societies to be self-sufficient with respect to food and goods production; education disappeared; and the quality of life went to the level of that which it was 1000 years ago.

However, this depressive situation concerned mostly the territory of the fallen Roman Empire, while remaining parts of Europe, particularly areas of contemporary England, France, Germany, and Scandinavia, were active in trade and technology development in agriculture and the making of goods (Stark 2014). This supposedly peripheral area gave birth to Western civilization, when the ambitious Frankish monarch, Charlemagne, created the Frankish Empire known as Carolingian. This process reminds one of the time when Europe had again its second "Dark Ages" after WWII and also when the United States, from the "periphery" of Western civilization, re-engineered Europe and established itself as the superpower.

In those 1200 years of history of Western civilization there were two dominant forces evolving: Germany and "peripheral" nations, even those located outside of Europe such as the United States. Germany, under different names like the Holy Roman Empire or Reich or just Germany, has been in charge of the "main field" of Western civilization. Such empires as the Portuguese, Spanish and British had the goal of colonizing the rest of the world and to certain degree neglected Europe where the Germans, in their minds, were developing a superior culture which needed more territory. Hence, the Germans waged two world wars, twice were beaten by the "peripheral" nations and twice rebuilt themselves to a higher levels of living than before those wars. This shows how able they are in transforming, time and again, "Dark Ages" into "Sunny Ages."

In that quest for the idealistic life for the higher race of *Übermensch* Germany, they transformed Western civilization into Nazis Civilization in 1933-1945 which was a natural consequence that structure follows strategy. However, Germany, beaten in 1945 and with its cities in ruins, halted the production of goods, and every other German migrating around the country was seen by the victorious Periphery as too dangerous to let it be into a situation of total freedom. The French and Italians with quite support of the Americans after 1945 formed a series of integrated European institutions, which after constant transformations, ended up as the European Union in 1993. It had two main goals: (1) to embraced Germany in a set of limiting actions by laws of the EU, (2) to enlarge the market and scale of production and services to compete with the U.S. Once again, Germany became the powerful leader of the EU, which at last understands its place in civilization but wants to control it, since it is able to do so better than others. Although, for the first time in the history, Germany is under the controlling and protecting umbrella of the bigger superpower, the United States, which commands the NATO military alliance of Western civilization. The winner of WWII does not want to risk another war within Western civilization.

What is important to notice is that Christianity was the glue which kept the coherence of this civilization, despite many internal conflicts.

In the 21st century, Western civilization invented the Internet which has transformed this civilization into Global Civilization since Christianity is being replaced by the secular business-oriented religion, where superconsumerism and greed are becoming well established values. Figure 3.1 illustrates the evolution of Western civilization and its decline-transformation.

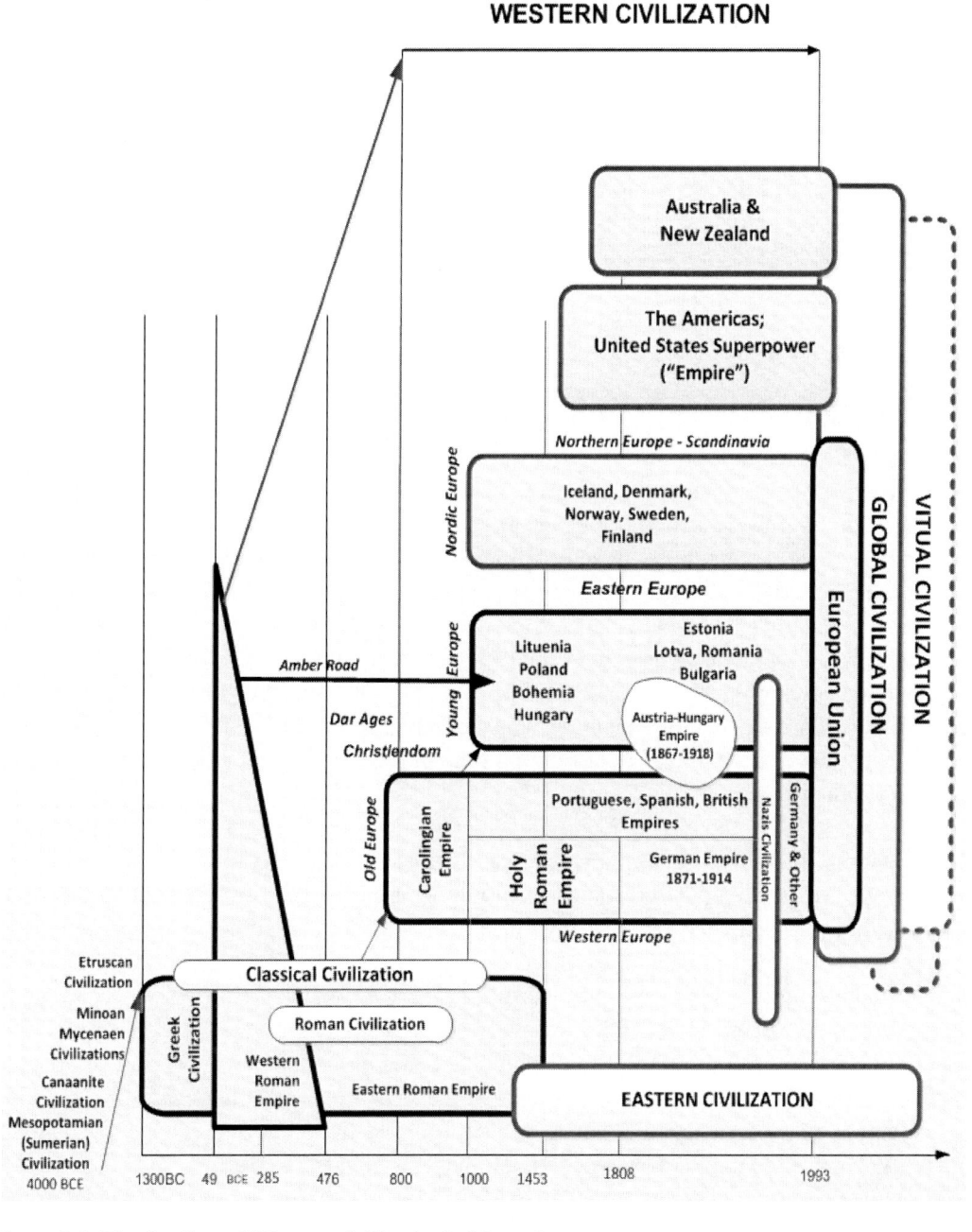

Figure 3.1. The timeline of Western civilization's life cycle.

The Western-born Internet is also transforming Western-Global Civilization into Virtual Civilization, where unreality is becoming the modus operandi of young generations.

DOES CIVILIZATION HAVE A PATTERN?[39]

We study history in order to know our past and also to learn about our mistakes how to avoid them in the so called lesson of history approach. But history is the past which cannot be reactivated even if we would like to do so. On the other hand a civilization is like a living organism, active, lasting, evolving, declining, and replaceable by the next civilization.

Therefore we would like to know the anatomy and functionality of a civilization to understand what to expect from it and how to adapt to it and eventually control it. For more than 100 years scholars have looked for patterns of civilizations. A Russian scholar Nikolai Danilevsky (1822-1885) noticed that each civilization has a life cycle, and by the end of the 19th century the Roman-German civilization was in decline, while the Slav civilization was approaching its Golden Age. A similar theory was put forward by Oswald Spengler (1880–1936) who in his *Der Untergang des Abendlandes* (*The Decline of the West*, 1918) also expected that the Western civilization was about to collapse since the lifespan of civilizations is limited and ultimately every civilization decays.

Arnold Toynbee in his *Study of History* (1934-1961) compared civilizations to organisms and perceived their existence in a life cycle of four stages: genesis, growth, breakdown, and disintegration. A mechanism of "challenge-response" facing civilizations influences them internally leading to their ability of self-determination and self-direction. However, according to Toynbee, all civilizations that grow eventually reach a peak from which they begin to decline. It seems that Toynbee's civilization life cycle is too short, since his "Breakdown of Growth" phase is in fact a point in time and the "Disintegration" phase is too pessimistic in its title, only perceiving the "Universal State" often under a form of the "Empire" as an ancient regime which only wants to maintain the status quo and is doomed to fail. History, however, shows that some civilizations may last a long time in relatively good shape, without being in panic of disintegration.

Sorokin (1937-41) argued in *Social and Cultural Dynamics* that three cultural mentalities -ideational (spiritual needs and goals), sensate ("wine, women, and song"), and idealistic (a balance of needs and ends) - are the central organizing principles of a civilization life cycle and that they succeed each other always in the same order according to super-rhythms of history. According to Sorokin, Western civilization in the last 500 years was in the sensate stage, reaching now its limit, and will pass to the next idealistic stage (which, according to this author could be Universal Civilization).

The discussion about a civilization's life cycle among contemporary researchers is still very interesting. Carroll Quigley (1910-1977) in the *Evolution of Civilizations* (1961) offered seven stages of a civilization's change: mixture, gestation, expansion, age of conflict, universal empire, decay, and invasion. Each stage is divided in further sub-stages and a characterization is provided at the levels of intellectual life, religious outlook, social group, economic control, economic organization, political organization, and military organization. Carroll Quigley perceived his famous book not as a book on history but as concerning the

---

[39] Melko (1969:168)

analytical tools assisting the understanding of history. He argued that many historic books were written about the same subject over and over without touching the main issues because the right historic tools were not applied.

Melko (1969) in his book *The Nature of Civilizations* provides a model of the stages of civilization's lifecycle: crystallization I, transition (T), complete disintegration (D), and ossification (freezing at a crystallized stage) (O). He also introduced a concept of civilization phases: primitive culture (P), feudal (F), state (S), and imperial (I). Based on these categorizations, Melko develops different "trees" of a civilization's paths, similar to formulas applied in organic chemistry. He emphasizes a strong role in the transition stage, which can lead to different stages, not necessary the same one.

Sanderson (1995) writes that "Civilizations, like symphonies, retain characteristic patterns notwithstanding fluxes of formation, disintegration, and reconstitution." This statement is corroborated by a discussion of 56 researchers, recorded in the book *The Boundaries of Civilization in Space and Time* (Melko and Scott 1987). Their main discussion was organized around the origins and termination of civilization in 32 short papers. The discussants agreed that civilizations rise and fall, but they were lost in defining the generic stages and main factors causing these stages.

Snyder (1999) made a most striking solution with respect to how to categorize the Historic Cycle of culture-systems (civilizations). He distinguished three eras: First Era 3000 B.C.-1600 B.C., Transition, Second Era 1200 B.C.- A.D. 200, Transition and Third Era A.D. 600-2000. As a parallel time division, he recognizes seven historic cycles: Proto-Formative Cycle, Formative Cycle, Classical Cycle, Renewal Cycle, Secularization Cycle, Frontier Cycle and Transitional Cycle, each lasting 300-400 years. He divided each cycle into four distinct stages of 75 to 100 years in length: reform stage, post-revolutionary stage, consolidation stage, and disintegration stage. This correlates with the traditional Chinese theory of the dynastic cycle as well as the rise and fall of dynasties postulated by Ibn Khalidun. This framework, according to Snyder, is based on his empirical study of Western European and Old World Culture-Systems. He perceives the disintegration stage not as a negative change, but one necessary for the next formative stage. He defines a culture-system or a civilization if it has at least three core cycles: Classical, Renewal, and Secularization. He analyzes the culture short-cycle (300-400 years) within the world long-cycles, such as the Classical Cycle, Renewal Cycle, Secularization Cycle, and Next Cycle, which is a very important association, but limited by the author to the Political Sub-System (dimension) only.

A Japanese scholar Naohiko Tonomura in his book *Eight major civilizations* (2013) recognizes four phases of evolution of a major civilization: confederation of tribal states, unified state, great disturbance, and world-empire.

Blaha (2002) quantifies Toynbee's cycle (growth, breakdown, and disintegration) in an elegant mathematical model with three main variables: the societal level (S), the rate of change I, the acceleration of the civilization (its growth rate socially) (A), force (F), the "mass" of civilization (m) and time (T); however, there is no way to measure these variables with the exception of (T). The force is measured "using simple everyday thinking" (p.47). The social level in his model reflects the overall feelings of the civilization's inhabitants, and not necessarily their population size, energy use, material resources, production of goods, technological advancement, and so forth. Stephen Blaha, as a noted contributor in the elementary particle theory of physics, perceives history as a continuum composed of wave oscillations with peaks and valleys. It is interesting to notice that he found that the interval of time between the breakdown of a civilization (the point at which growth stops) and the beginning of the universal state (at the end of the time of troubles) is approximately T=400 years. This is a similar interval time as was found by Snyder (1999) as well as this author, who calls it a cycle of human curiosity. The model assumes that the interval time between consecutive peaks of waves of a civilization is approximately T=267 years, and Blaha calls it a general feature of civilizations. He assumes that it takes four generations to go from the top to the bottom of a cycle (a rout) and another four generations to reach the top again (a rally). This means that if one generation is approximately 33.375 years then eight generations would total the approximate 267 years. Another interesting feature of the model is the assumption concerning the startup phase of civilization, which takes 133.3 years before the breakdown of the civilization. He compares his theory with various major events of a civilization; in many cases he is right, but in others he is wrong, according to Mark Hall (2003).

Needless to say, every model in science simplifies reality which is particularly true for such a complex reality as the dynamics of civilization and history. Even if a model does not identify reality in a 1:1 isomorphic relationship, the model introduces us to a new way of analyzing and synthesizing civilization. The Blaha model is designed for long-lasting civilizations, which is the case of the majority of old civilizations. What about short-living civilizations such as the Soviet Civilization and Nazis Civilization, which lasted less than a century? This problem can be solved by defining what a civilization is. If civilization is an entity guided by a special set of values then those mentioned units are civilizations in the Empire Phase of Toynbee's Disintegration Phase. Thus, the Blaha model cannot be applied to them.

So, the quest for the answers regarding why civilizations rise and fall is still valid as well as questions concerning in what general or generic phases and stages they rise and fall.

WHAT IS THE PATTERN OF THE EVOLUTION OF WESTERN CIVILIZATION?

Western civilization, like every living and vibrant organism, has a pattern of dynamics and a life cycle. There is no question that it has risen and is declining, which has taken 1200 years thus far. The question is, what is between these two extreme phases? The life cycle of Western civilization is shown in Figure 3.2.; This figure shows that Western civilization is special in that it does not have a phase of stabilization (consolidation) at a certain point of maturity as is held explicitly or implicitly by the majority of civilizational scholars.

Perhaps the lack of stability and instead a phase of conflict even at the peak of its civilizational development is the driving force of Western civilization as the most dominant civilization in the world in the last 500 years. This civilization's life cycle is similar to Toynbee's four-phases (genesis, growth, breakdown, and disintegration) but extended by three: rise, growth-conflicts, and wars-peace. It is interesting that Toynbee also did not see a phase of stabilization (consolidation), but nor did he see the phase of conflicts.

Let's characterize each phase of the life cycle of Western civilization as follows:

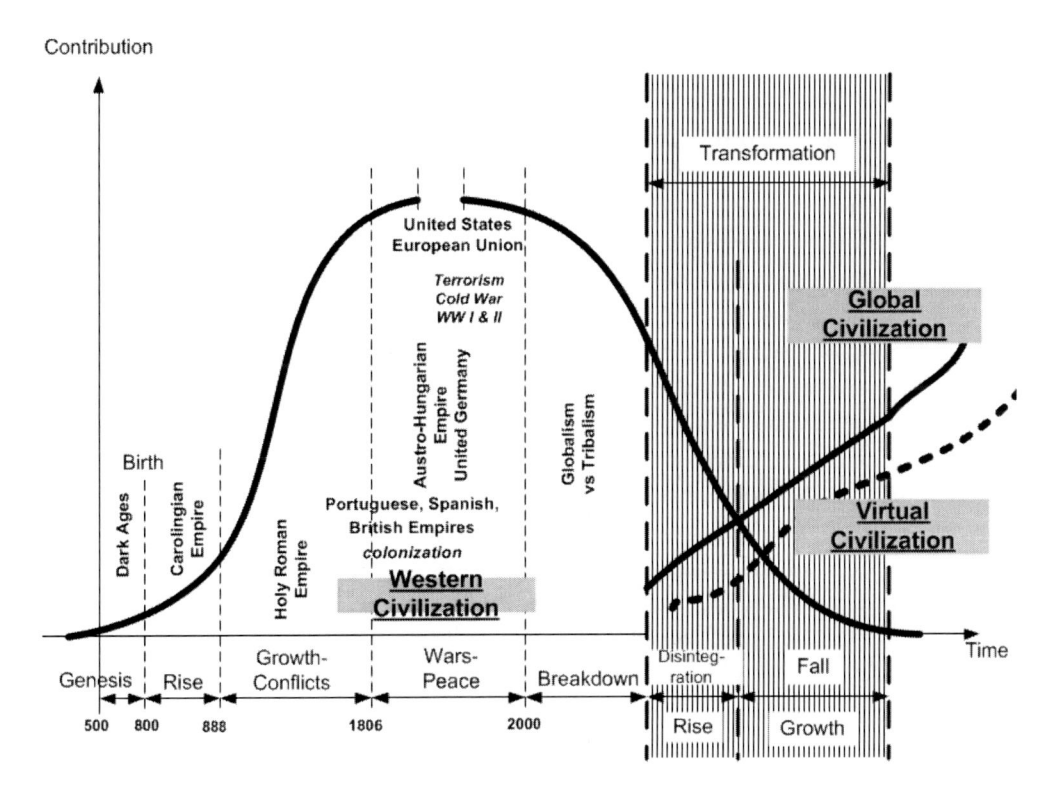

Figure 3.2. The life cycle of Western civilization in the 21st century.

1. *Genesis Phase* – the Dark Ages at the territories of the fallen Roman Empire and its vibrant periphery, within 300 years, led to the rise of the new civilization in Europe.
2. *Rise Phase* – the climbing Carolingian Empire founded in 800 in the periphery (today France and Belgium) of the previous European Empire provided military, intellectual, cultural, and economic (feudal) leadership to begin shaping the next civilization – Western civilization.
3. *Growth-Conflicts Phase* – this phase was led at the beginning by German Emperors Otto I, II, and III who knew precisely that they were "rebuilding" the Roman Empire, except from the North not from the South where it used to be. The central and largest territory of the empire was the Kingdom of Germany, though it included at times the Kingdom of Italy, the Kingdom of Bohemia (contemporary Czechoslovakia), and the Kingdom of Burgundy, as well as numerous other territories. The empire grew out of East Francia, a primary division of the Frankish (Carolingian) Empire. Its configuration was changing all the time, exemplified by the changing locations of its capital: Aachen, Munich, Prague, and Vienna. As Voltaire once stated "it was "neither holy, nor Roman, nor an empire." But due to the Germans' ambition, the Holy Roman Empire had been growing more through conflicts and revolutions than through peaceful solutions.
4. *War-Peace Phase* – this took place after Napoleon I abolished the Holy Roman Empire in 1806. The Napoleonic Wars in 1803-1815 put Europe in chaos, which was followed by the colonization of Africa and Latin America, the Franco-German War (1871), the Mexican Revolution (1910), the Bolshevik Revolution (1917) which

destabilized Eastern Europe, WWI (1914-1918) and WWII (1939-1945), the Israel-Palestinian wars and conflicts after 1948, the Cold War (1945-1991), the Korean War (1950-53), the Vietnamese War (1959-1975), the Falkland War (1982), the Clash of Civilizations (terrorism after 2001), and wars in Latin America among changing configurations of countries, drug wars, and so forth. Each war was finished with some sort of a peace and hidden, lingering conflicts. These wars and major conflicts ended with the domination of the United States as the only real superpower in the world which, however, has problems withplaying its hegemonic role successfully. This only causes wide dissatisfaction among the Americans and foreigners. The formation of the European Union in 1993 is aimed at the stabilization of Europe and containment of Germany and Russia.

5. *Breakdown Phase* – rising economic globalization flattens the world but at the same time about 5 billion people live in tribal conditions (for example every second habitant in the Sub-Saharan Africa has no access to clean water and electricity) having bad feelings towards the rapidly modernizing Western civilization. Global Business, after saturating Western civilization, is looking for new customers and found them among the bottom of the Pyramid, where 4 billion people make only 1500 dollars per year. In order to increase their purchasing power, Global Business outsources jobs to undeveloped and developing nations. As a result, Western civilization is losing its middle class and is declining. Another strong factor characterizing this phase is the declining reservoir of strategic resources (water, oil, gas, uranium) due to super-consumerism as well as the declining power of culture and political branches being unable to solve any important problem in the right time.

6. *Disintegration Phase* – if Western civilization does not correct its deindustrialized and unsustainable life policies, it will disintegrate. Perhaps it will lead towards the elimination of states and the rise of local and regional coalitions of businesses and Non-Governmental Organizations (NGOs).

7. *Fall Phase* – this will happen when Global civilization comes to fully dominate old Western civilization. However, Western civilization will be in the "DNA" of the next civilization like Classical civilization is in the "DNA" of Western civilization.

This life cycle has a helical pattern (Laszlo 1991:45) when viewed in a long-time range; there is not have a strict recurrence of the past, but certainly as a living organism Western Civilization was born, rose, grew, had conflicts, and is declining and transforming in our times. Even if some events and episodes recurs, like revolutions or wars, they do so in a new form. From a more narrow viewpoint within Western civilization's 1200 years cycle, it looks as if the life cycle has a non-linear (statistically progressive or regressive, Laszlo 1991:49) pattern, particularly since the second part of the 20th century.

The life cycle of Western civilization shows an enormous complexity whose problems cannot be solved by people at the current level of their morale and wisdom. The mechanism which generates the civilizational dynamics of Western civilization is based on permanent conflicts, triggering the development of knowledge, skills, resilience and resourcefulness of solutions. These conflicts take place among an endless number of internal and external parties and increase the need for constant development of technology and intellectual solutions. This is associated with the social advantages of democracy where each individual is free, or at least thinks that they are free, which leads to never ending discussions and situations put in limbo.

This is now leading to a declining will in society which is not able to solve any important problems.

Conclusion

1. The life cycle of Western civilization is unique, due to a greatly diversified leadership, since it was evolving under the control of 9 emperies, including several world-empires such as the Portuguese, Spanish, British Empires, U.S. superpower ("Empire"), and EU world-polity ("Empire"). The 2 last are not classic empires but play such a role.
2. Western civilization's resilience was developing due to many attacks from other civilizations like the Arab, Mongolian and Ottoman Empires which were able to control some parts of Europe for a long time. Adding to this complexity, several large and small revolutions and wars has made this civilization very resilience and resourceful through the centuries.
3. The decline of Western civilization, after reaching its peak of modernity in the second part of the 20th century, is caused by the fact that Western people are wise when, in fact, the poor and stupid are better off.

References

Blaha, St. (2002). *The life cycle of civilizations*. Auburn, NH: Pingree-Hill Publishing.
Huntington, S. (1996). *The clash of civilizations and the remaking of world order*. New York: Simon & Schuster.
Friedman, Th. (2005). *The world is flat*. New York: Farrar, Straus and Giroux.
Kobyliński, Zb. (2008). The Slavs in Paul Fouracre. *The New Cambridge Medieval History*. Cambridge: Cambridge University Press. pp. 530–537
Kreis. St. (2006). The history guide. Accessed 7-22-2014 http://www.historyguide.org/ancient/lecture10b.html.
Laszlo,E. (1991). *The age of bifurcation, understanding the changing world*. Philadelphia & Paris: Gordon and Breach.
Maddison, A. (2000). The world economy, a millennial perspective. Paris: OECD.
McNall, B. et al. (1982). *World civilizations*. New York: W.W.W. NORTHON & COMPANY.
Melko, M. (1969). *The nature of civilizations*. Boston: Porter Sargent Publisher.
Melko, M. and L. Scott. (1987). *The boundaries of civilizations in space and time*. Lanham, MD, New York, London: University Press of America.
Quigley, Carroll (1961). *The evolution of civilizations*. Indianapolis: A Liberty Press Edition.
Anderson, S. (1995). *Civilizations and world systems*. Walnut Creek, London, New Delhi: Altamira Press.
Snider, L.D. (1999). *Macro-history, a theoreticasl approach to comparative world history*. Lwiston: New York: The Edwin Mellen Press.
Spengler, O. (1932). *Decline of the west*. London: Allen and Udwin.

Stark, R. (2014). *How the West won, the neglected story of the triumph of modernity.* Wilmington, Delaware: ISI Books.

Targowski, A. (1980). *Informatyka, modele systemów i rozwoju (Informatics, models of systems and development).* Warsaw: PWE.

Targowski, A. (2004). A dynamic model of an autonomous civilization. *Dialogue and Universalism.* Vol. XIV(1-2):77-90.

Targowski, A. (2009). *Information technology and societal development.* Hershey, New York: Information Science Reference (IGI).

Targowski, A. (2014c). *The deadly effect of informatics on the Holocaust.* Mustang, OK: Tate Publishing.

Tonomura, N. (2013). *Eight Major Civilization.* Asahi Press.

Toynbee, A. (1934). *A study of history.* Oxford: Oxford University Press.

Vallance, E. (2006). The Glorious Revolution: 1688 and Britain's fight for liberty. New York: Little, Brown and Co.

Van Doren, Ch. (1991). *A history of knowledge.* New York: Ballantine.

Chapter 4

LEGACY OF WESTERN CIVILIZATION

ABSTRACT

The *purpose* of this investigation is to define the legacy of the Western civilization and its role with respect to other contemporary civilizations and the rising Global civilization in the 21st century. The *methodology* is based on an interdisciplinary big-picture view of the developments and interdependency of Western and Global civilization. Among the *findings* are: Western civilization is about 1200 years old and its major legacy is its ability to apply resilient and resourceful thinking and problem solving in developing the Whole and Universal Minds. *Practical implication:* Western civilization has a very complex history and dynamics generated by endless conflicts, wars, invasions and the impact of 9 Western empires which have been central to the development this civilization, thus supporting the argument that diversified and dynamic civilizations are more rich in solutions than monolithic and static ones. *Social implication:* Western civilization reached its developmental peak around 2010 and is now declining regardless of our positive feelings about its achievements. *Originality:* This investigation defined the legacy and trends of Western civilization which allow certain predictions of its behavior today and in the future.

INTRODUCTION

The purpose of this investigation is to characterize the legacy of the 1200+ years of Western civilization's existence, which is the dominating civilization in the world today. One of tasks will be polemical with some holding the opinion that Western civilization is a unique civilization and its success is in its modernity which began during the Renaissance. The method will be based on a review of contributions categorized by the major phases of this civilization's development from 800 through 2015. In the end, the conclusions will focus on the key factors making this civilization unique and vulnerable as far as its future is concerned.

LEGACY OF CLASSICAL (GRECO-ROMAN) CIVILIZATION AND ITS IMPACT ON WESTERN CIVILIZATION (5TH B.C.E. – 5TH C.E.)

Western Civilization has roots in two civilizations that emerged in the ancient world: the Judeo-Christian and the Greco-Roman. In the ancient world, religion was the main force in these two civilizations since it provided explanations for the acts of nature, justified moral rules applied in practice, and helped people to deal with their horror of death on Earth.

The Hebrews believed in one good god which led to a revolutionary (in those times) attentiveness to the individual. It resulted in the development of the self, or "I", among many similar or different selves. Such self-aware individuals believed that God gave them freedom in choosing between good and evil positions. In such a way the Hebrew defined the value of moral freedom and individual responsibility for our own actions. Here are the roots of human dignity which is one of the key elements in the foundation of Western Civilization.

Legacy of the Greek Civilization As the Big Bang of Western Civilization

The Greeks who settled around the Aegean sea [and were impacted by the adjacent Canaan (Semitic) Civilization (modern-day Lebanon, Israel, Palestinian, the western part of Jordan and southwestern Syria, corresponding to Bible's Levant) from the Near East], which was full of islands, liked team work in coping with the endless challenges of the sea and trade which took place all the time. They experienced many human problems and understood that their solutions must be provided not by God but by humans themselves. Eventually they emphasized the value of knowledge and wisdom in solving problems. They also understood that laws controlling their society would not come from God but must be formulated by themselves and that there are more than one solution leading to the development of their society's laws. They enjoyed free discussion on this subject which led to the concept of democracy and democratic institutions.

At the dawn of Greek Civilization, it was composed of city-states (about 100 total) ruled by nobles, where Athens (Vth century B.C.) was at the peak of prosperity and was a self-governing polity which accepted the will of free citizens not priests, kings or the commands of God. In the Assembly the Athenians discussed and voted on important issues of the city-state.

The Greek in a search for the truth about the nature and the world in general gave the birth to the queen of knowledge, philosophy (love of wisdom), which developed tools of reasoning, and eventually explained that nature is controls mankind through natural and material processes not God's will. Its first rule is that chaos is controlling nature and the human task is to minimize that chaos by knowledge and by better understanding what is going on. The Greeks developed arithmetic, measurements, and calculations of the collected data or geometric shapes in order to get the right solutions. Also their physicians saw the line between magic and medicine and tried to cure patients in a rational manner.

The Geek great philosophers laid the foundation for Western science, art and politics. Socrates took on the perfection of human character, Plato invented ideas which eventually controlled the societal processes, and Aristotle gave the foundation for a rational approach to facts and generalization of universal issues. His followers in Stoicism developed an approach for how to cope and offer answers to the problems of the loss of community and the alienation caused by declining city-states. The Stoics added *logos* (logic) to *mythos* (myth) in reasoning and assumed that everyone possesses a logical capacity, hence in effect all people are equal and significant. This assumption was accepted by Roman jurisprudence, Christian thought and modern liberalism, becoming the essence of Western Civilization.

In conclusion one can state that Geek Civilization was practicing through several centuries the following solutions which even today are applied by many states of Western Civilization:

1. A shift from aristocratic governance to democracy
2. The power of reasoning in daily life and abstract problem solving
3. The importance of ideas and perfecting one's own personality
4. The first stages of science and medicine
5. The importance to see beauty in life, which led to high art, particularly sculpture and poetry
6. A spreading out of monetary-based trade among distance parties
7. The accumulation of wealth at upper strata of the society
8. The development of colonial cities

Legacy of the Roman Civilization As the Civilizing Foundation of Western Civilization

"All roads lead to Rome." This quote holds much truth as what Rome has left to Western civilization is brought to light. The Romans made countless contributions to Western civilization, but a few are the most significant of all. Rome, the most important civilization to the Western World, left a great legacy, paving the road for the spread of Christianity, forming the basis for a republic, and allowing for a widespread diffusion of culture.

The Roman Republic left a form of government similar to the democracy of Ancient Greece but with the ability to govern large bodies of people. Rome used a representation method, where senators represented groups of people, allowing for a democracy encompassing a very large population. It contained checks and balances to ensure that power was not too highly concentrated, much as the government in the United States of America does today. Unfortunately, the Roman Republic did not last throughout all of Rome's glory due to civil unrest, but it did leave an incredible form of government for the rest of humanity to mimic. This form of government would later prove vital to the structure of the government of the United States of America and many other countries. The republic gave the general public of a large population a say in political issues, leaving a priceless gift to the Western World (Kieffer 2014).

Roman civilization successfully practiced the following solutions through several centuries which even today are applied by many states of Western Civilization:

1. A centralized state of a multi-ethnic complex of territories
2. A "check and balance" driven government of 3 branches: executive, legislative and judicial, supported by hierarchy of assemblies, magistrates and census

3   Law defining civility of habitants and government
4   Imperialist expansion as far as possible beyond its own borders
5   A large and disciplined army ready to fight and grab
6   Industrial, commercial and trade policies
7   Expansion of the road network for effective transportation
8   Elite luxury, corruption, and decadence (which led to the fall of Western Roman Empire)

After the fall of Western Roman Empire it was a period when the removal of the strong central government of Rome left Europe in chaos. The mighty empire was fragmented into small kingdoms and local lords, each of whom exercised power only in the immediate vicinity of his own castle. This was a time of poverty and hardship and declining learning.

However, on the peripheries of the Roman Empire, particularly in the Near East, learning was flourishing while the religion of Islam was a unifying force. The Chinese Civilization and in the American civilizations (Aztec, Mayan, Incas, and Indian) were flourishing as well.

LEGACY OF THE POST-ROMAN CIVILIZATION TIMES AND THEIR IMPACT UPON THE BIRTH OF WESTERN CIVILIZATION (6TH – 9TH CENTURIES)

Legacy of the "Dark Ages" (500-800) As the Stimulus of Western Civilization's Birth

While the Roman Empire was weakening, a new religion, Christianity, was reaching across the Mediterranean world. Christianity was based on the teachings of Jesus Christ, a Palestinian Jew who was crucified by the Roman authorities governing Palestine. Jesus Christ was a successor to the ethical monotheism of the Hebrew prophets. He was telling people that God was coming and that they had to ask forgiveness for their sins in order to go to Heaven. His message was short and clear, "People must love God and their neighbors." It was a new message, since thus far everyone hated their neighbors and had a vague understanding about God. Christianity was the expansion of Greco-Roman civilization which emphasized the individual's ability to be reasonable and ethically autonomous. Christian thinkers enhanced Classical civilization's goal of perfecting the individual by the far reaching goal of achieving salvation in a heavenly city.

Therefore, in the "Dark Ages", Christianity was the bridge between Greek Civilization and the future Western civilization which continued the flow of humanistic ideas making people more advanced and civilized.

The conquest of Christianity and the formation of Germanic kingdoms on once-Roman territories established the next phase in European development. In the ancient world Greco-Roman civilization functioned in southern Europe around the Mediterranean Sea; now the future Western Civilization is moving to northern Europe with a colder climate. The future history of this civilization indicates that advanced civilization took place in a cooler rather than a warmer climate, even creating a political issue North versus South.

Legacy of the Middle Ages (800-1350) As the Life Impulse of Western Civilization's Birth

A German from the Franks, Charlemagne (768-814) was crowned by Pope Leo in 800 as "Emperor of the Romans." Since the pope crowned him, the Emperor was obliged to defend the Christian faith. Later he showed respect for the Greco-Roman and Christian tradition while merging it with the German *modus operandi*. During his time in power the distinct Western Civilization took origin, but it took long time to see this civilization on its own feet running well.

The successors of charismatic Charlemagne could not keep the Empire together. Not only internal power struggles but also invasions of Muslims, Vikings from Scandinavia, and Magyars (from Western Asia) devastated villages, towns, ports, and killed many people. European trade and economy collapsed, kings disappeared, and culture and learning declined. But the Europeans again invented *Feudalism* which established a hierarchy of vassals who were obliged to provide military service for the landlord who in return protected his vassals. Feudalism was economically based on *manorialism*, which was a village community (manor), consisting of serfs (peasants) who were obliged to work for free for the landlord who in return allowed them to cultivate their small lands. A serf was obliged to work every 10 days for free for the church. This system provided good social stability with huge social inequality.

In the High Middle Ages (11-14th centuries) external invasions ended, kings repossessed their kingdoms, towns and trade flourished, and a commercial revolution surpassed the good times of the *Pax Romana*. Wars against Muslims integrated the Christian world. Christian thinkers were integrating Greek philosophy with Christian revelation within the school of *scholastics*. However, this medieval mind rejected the principles of Greek philosophy and modern thought under the form of autonomy and superiority of reason, since reason was seen as weak and was not able to provide a unified understanding of nature and humans without including in it the higher order being.

The process of transforming the medieval world into the modern world based on reason and science took the next centuries. Despite of the shortcomings of medieval scholastics, the Church was decisive in the birth of Western Civilization.

THE TRIUMPF OF MODERNITY AND ITS IMPACT ON WESTERN CIVILIZATION (15-19 CENTURIES)

Legacy of the Italian Renaissance As the Culture-oriented Modernizing Force of Western Civilization

The word renaissance means "rebirth", and it is used to denote the attempts by artists and thinkers to recuperate and relate again the ancient understanding and ideals of Greece and Rome. This movement was born in the city-states of northern Italy and spread to the rest of Europe in the years 1350-1600. In those times the rest of Europe was still in the scholastic boundaries of thinking and acting.

Metropolitan College of NY,
Library - 7th Floor
60 West Street
New York, NY 10006

Figure 4.1. Dome of Florence Cathedral designed by F. Brunelleschi.
(Photo: Wikipedia).

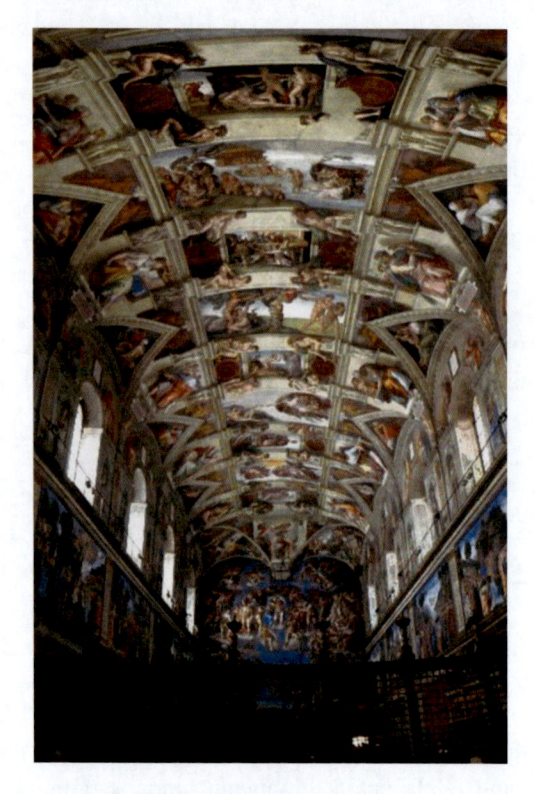

Figure 4.2. Sistine Chapel's ceiling in the Vatican painted by Michelangelo between 1508 and 1512 is today one of the most important artistic achievements in the world.
(Photo: Wikipedia).

The Italian Renaissance was successful in triggering the following ideas which are applied by many societies of Western Civilization today:

1. *Humanism* – learned from the Greek and Roman literature guiding principles for a successful secular good, active, and interesting life, without questioning the Bible. This approach was aimed at fostering the good citizen attitude, supported by good communication skills for the public good. It also triggered a method of critical inquiry to undermine traditional loyalties and institutions. The honor, fame, and even glory if achieved for meritorious effort were worth the effort. These ideas were formulated by Baldassare Castiglione (1478-1529) in his *The Book of the Courtier* and supported by Lorenzo de' Medici (1449-1492), an Italian statesman and de facto ruler of the Florentine Republic during the Italian Renaissance.
2. *Revolution in political thought* - triggered by Niccolò Machiavelli (1469-1527) for whom religion was not the foundation for society but merely a useful tool in the *Prince's* struggle for success. In the book *the Prince*, he formulated a fundamental political truth that politics (seen as the relationship between ruler and ruled) if successful must be based on will and virtue but adapted to the actual needs. Ever since this principle has been called Machavelism and widely applied today.
3. *Art* – the most graphic images of the Renaissance are exemplified through its art, architecture, sculpture, and painting. Their common characteristics were expressed in proportion, balance, and harmony. Filippo Brunelleschi (1377-1446) was one of the foremost architects and engineers of the Italian Renaissance. He is perhaps most famous for his development of linear perspective and for engineering the dome of the Florence Cathedral, which recaptures the splendor of classical dome structures, such as the Pantheon.

    New perspectives and a new approach in painting were developed by the three great artists of the Renaissance: Leonardo da Vinci (1452-1519), Michelangelo Buonarotti (1475-1564), and Raphael Santi (1483-1520). All of them lived in Medici's Florence and were contemporaries.
4. *Printing* – invented in Europe by Johann Gutenberg (1398-1468) helped in spreading *Humanism* to Germany, France, England, and Spain. This new technology of making books helped spread ideas more quickly, numerously, and cheaply. It also made literacy easier to realize

The Renaissance world view was bold and novel, but it was the exclusive prerogative of a small well-educated urban elite and did not reach to include masses (Perry et al., 1989:281). It was the best example of the power and potential of High culture.

The Renaissance set an example of what people might achieve in art and architecture, taste, and refinement, education, and urban culture (Perry et al., 1989:281). In many areas, the Renaissance established the cultural standards which are still present in Western Civilization.

Legacy of the Religion-oriented Reformation Made Some Countries of Western Civilization Wealthier than Others

Due to the Renaissance of learning, the Reformation of the Christian Church took place The leadership and administration of the Church was already being criticized, and the Church's massive wealth and far reaching political power looked as though they took predominance over its mission to search for holiness and salvation in the world. The

Reformation began in Germany in 1517 when the Augustinian monk, Marthin Luther (1483-1546), nailed a protest (95 thesis) against the sale of indulgences (pardons for sins) on the door of a church in Wittenberg.

Switzerland, Scandinavia, Scotland, some small German states, and some Eastern European states soon adopted the new religion, calling it Protestantism because its followers were protesting against abuses in the Roman-Catholic Church. The Roman Catholic Church responded with a Counter-Reformation initiated by the Council of Trent.

The Reformation has had a wide-ranging influence on personal life up to the present, such as the following:

1. The sole authority of Scripture
2. Justification by faith alone, not by anything the church does for us
3. Priesthood of the believer, since all believers are priests, hence there is no necessity for an earthly mediator
4. The rejection of the authority of the Pope
5. Hard work ethic
6. Accumulated wealth's majority should be spent on investments
7. Fashion should be more sober and dignified
8. Aesthetics in general should be less wasteful

Protestantism with its faith and ethics strongly contributed to the economic success of Western-West (Atlantic) civilization. There is a saying that Protestants eat better but Catholics sleep better.

Legacy of the Commercial Spreading-out As the Societal-oriented Modernizing Force of Western Civilization

During the times from 1450 to 1750, Western Civilization entered an era of overseas explorations and economic expansion the transformed Western society. The Europeans learned new ways to grasp the opulent centers of India by sailing around Africa, and they conquered and colonized the New World in America. These new discoveries of resourceful lands increased business activities resulting in a higher level of supplied money (as gold and silver from colonies) which stimulated the rise of *Capitalism* in Europe and the colonies.

The exploration-driven commercial expansion-out impacted Western Civilization in the following manners:

1. The time of secluded manors and walled towns was ending.
2. A world economy was emerging, depending on Eastern spice for conserving food, African slaves, and American silver.
3. Western civilization was generating commercial dynamism which dominated other civilizations in the world.
4. The quality of life was rising but the population was also rising (particularly at the level of the low class people) and the only beneficiary of it were *nouveaux riches* (the new rich).

5. Modern Europe of those times looked like an underdeveloped country today, with two classes, upper and lower.
6. The progress in agriculture was triggered by the lease of fields system, which penalized small farmers who could not effort a new lease of land; eventually a landlord could combine small fields into a large one and increase productivity and profit.
7. The rising population needed more clothes, hence woolen and linen textiles were in demand and causing a rise of prices.
8. The growing commerce needed good merchants-employers who needed banks to support their operations and development which replaced ancient *Feudalism* by *Mercantile Capitalism*, since good merchant could accumulate capital. It paved the way for the coming Industrial Revolution.
9. Besides the high culture practices at the royal courts, the feudal lords, and the educated clergy, popular culture was developing at the communal and country side by "inferior" people who to certain degree were better off in comparison to medieval times.
10. Puritanism was promoted by the upper class as to way of reforming popular culture which eventually could unite the poor against the rich. Hence, some leaders like Girolamo Savonarola (1452-1498) in Florence or Philip Stubbe (1555-1610) in England were promoting "the triumph of Lent" (church-oriented culture) over "the world of Carnival" (Figure 4.3).

Figure 4.3. The Fight between Carnival and Lent is an oil-on-panel work painted by Pieter Bruegel in 1559. It presents the contrast between two sides of contemporary life, as can be seen by the appearance of the inn on the left side (for enjoyment) and the church on the right side (for religious observance). (Photo: Wikipedia).

11. The divide between the elite and poor was well established with two high and popular cultures hostile to each other.

The rising role of commerce/business and the conflict between the elite and poor has ever since became the number one issue of Western civilization up to the present and threatens the well-being of Western Civilization today.

Legacy of the Scientific Revolutions As the Modernizing Force of Western Civilization

With the arrival of the Renaissance, a new generation of scholars began to contest medieval conventions about human beings and nature, equipped with the Greco-Roman contributions. The following key scholars of this new generation discovered mechanisms governing humans and nature:

Natural sciences:
1. Nicolaus Copernicus (1473-1543): a Polish scientist who displayed courage in thinking by reversing the theory of cosmology based on heavenly motion by formulating the theory of a heliocentric universe supported by mathematical evidence. This theory is held up to the present.
2. Johannes Kepler (1571-1630): a German scientist who searched for harmonic movements of planets which was defined in three basic laws of planetary motion. He defined these laws in mathematical formulas. In addition he mathematically proved Copernicus' theory. Although, he did not explained what keeps planets in orbits.
3. Isaac Newton (1646-1723): an English scientist who discovered universal gravitation, a phenomenon that he described mathematically. This discovery characterizes the contributions of the Scientific Revolution and has captured the interest of European intellectuals of those and even contemporary times, such as Albert Einstein (1879-1955).
4. Philip von Hohenheim Paracelsus (1493-1541): a Swiss-German physician who defined the concept of diagnostic medicine. He discredited the ancient orthodox medicine.
5. Andreas Vesalius (1514-1564): a Belgian surgeon who opposed the ancient Galenic practice by applying anatomical dissection as the key to know how the human body works.
6. William Harvey (1578-1657): an English physician who discovered the system of blood circulation due to the mechanical pump—the heart. This to certain degree had characterized the paradigm of the mechanical worldview, which had been gradually discovered in this revolution concerning nature and humans.

Social sciences
1. Giordano Bruno (1548-1600): an Italian monk and philosopher who found Hermetic philosophy of a new religion which should reflect the laws of nature (like Copernicus's heliocentric theory) not on supernaturally stimulated dogmas taught by the clergy. He also speculated that there may be life on other planets too. The Inquisition found him guilty, and in 1600 he was burned at the stake in Rome's

Campo de' Fiori. After his death he gained considerable fame, particularly among 19th- and early 20th-century commentators who regarded him as a martyr for science (Labriola 1952).
2. Francis Bacon (1561-1626): an English scholar who, in his Advancement of Learning (1602), argued that science must be open and free and all ideas must be allowed a hearing. He also argued that university education should replace ancient texts by a new method of learning about humans and nature. His view of progressive science led to the intensified scientific discoveries in years to come.
3. René Descartes (1596-1650): a French philosopher who is considered as the father of modern philosophy and science. He believed in the potential of the human intellect and its ability to achieve scientific knowledge. He defined the foundation of the scientific method in his book *Discours de la méthode*. He explained his method of reasoning through even the most difficult of problems. He illustrated the development of this method through brief autobiographical sketches interspersed with philosophical arguments. His method is still applied as the most optimal for scientific works.

Figure 4.4. Giordano Bruno (1548-1600), the martyr for science and Isaac Newton (1646-1723), the father of the Scientific Revolution.
(Photo: Wikipedia).

The Scientific Revolution of the 15th -17th centuries replaced the motionless earth by a mechanized one. The universe was ever since understood as giant machine functioning according to natural-universal laws that could be formulated with mathematical precision. This new worldview even claimed that nature could be mastered. In fact there may be some truth to this claim as space travel, including landing on the Moon and Mars, has shown in the coming 20th and 21st centuries.

Gradually Newtonian science became the science of Western Civilization as well as the whole world, and its mechanistic paradigm led to the development of mechanizing technology under the forms of water pumps, engines, automobiles, railroads, and factory systems which characterize the coming Enlightenment (in terms of social mechanisms) and Industrial Revolution (in terms of mechanical products and processes).

Legacy of the Enlightenment and Revolutions As the Idea-oriented, Modernizing Force of Western Civilization

The intellectual ferment in the 18th century is called the Age of Enlightenment or the Age of Reason. The thinkers of those times, mostly philosophers, were under the influence of the Scientific Revolution which developed a new understanding of nature as a mechanism. Hence, also mostly the English, French and American philosophers wanted to improve life through the reasoning-thinking mechanism of public institutions which controlled people. The institutions in those times functioned in darkness and for the convenience of the ruling class. Now, through the application of reason, this darkness should be lifted.

Towards the Better Society

The legacy of the Enlightenment is summarized in Table 4.1.

Table 4.1. The Key Legacies of the Age of the Enlightenment (the 18th century)

No	Area of enlighten-ment	Main leaders	Contribution	Lasting results
1	Christianity under scrutiny	Pierce Boyle (1647-1706) Voltaire (1694-1778)	Critique of dogmas, superstition, and blind obedience, because they defied logic and civil law	Freemasons' Masonic Lodges as an alternative form of religion
2	Political Thought	J. Locke (1632-1704) Montesquieu (1689-1755) J.J. Rousseau (1712-1778)	Challenged the divine power of kings and wanted checks to power	Democracy
3	Social Thought	Locke, Voltaire, Rousseau, C,. Beccaria (1738-1794) Mary Wollstonecraft (1759-1797)	Humanitarianism calling for better education, no torturing of prisoners, slavery as immoral, equality for women	Human rights
4	Economic Thought	A. Smith (1732-1790)	Science of economics	"Invisible hand of the market"
5	Universal Thought	D. Diderot (1713-1784) J. d'Alembert (1717-1783)	The Encyclopedia (1751) As the catalog of learning and universal laws. The philosophers became cultural heroes.	American and French Revolutions
6	American Revolution	George Washington (1789-1797) John Adams (1735-1826) Thomas Jefferson (1743-1826) James Madison (1751-1836) Al. Hamilton (1755-1804) Benjamin Franklin (1706-1790)	1765-1783 Uprising against the British for independence and democratic nation	Democracy Bill of Rights Electable Government with Check and Balance mechanism

No	Area of enlightenment	Main leaders	Contribution	Lasting results
7	French Revolution	Jean-Paul Marat (1743-1793) Georges Danton (1759-1794) Maximilien Robespierre (1758-1794)	1789-1799 Uprising against the monarchy and feudalism	Democratic Republic Rights of Man Individualism Citizenship

Table 4.2. The Key Inventions of Science and Engineering Enlightenment

Science	Scientist/Engineer	New invention	Lasting Result
Physics	Gabriel Fahrenheit (1686-1736)	Mercury thermometer and scale	These inventions are still used today
	Anders Celsius (1701-1744)	Temperature scale	
Chemistry	Joseph Black (1728-1799)	Discovered carbon dioxide and latent heat	This is the main pollutant today
	Joseph Priestley (1733-1804)	Discovered oxygen. He answered age-old questions of why and how things burn.	This element is the main component of organic chemistry broadly applied today
	Henry Cavendish (1731-1810)	He discovered hydrogen or what he called "inflammable air" and measured the Earth's density	This element it the main component of organic chemistry broadly applied today
Engineering	Thomas Newcomen (1663-1729)	Steam engine to pump water from mines (1710)	Electrical engines are applied for the same purpose
	James Watt (1736-1819)	Improved the steam engine (1763) and defined the concept of horsepower	In some parts of the world steam engines are still applied
	Stephen Grey (1666-1736)	Experimented with electrical conduction, rather than simple generation of static charges and investigated the static phenomena.	Electricity runs contemporary civilization
	Charles Cisternay du Fay (1698-1739)	He discovered the existence of two types of electricity later known as positive and negative charge respectively. He noted the difference between conductors and insulators.	This is basic knowledge about electricity
	Alessandro Volta (1745-1827)	He invented the battery	The energy source of electrical cars and mobile devices today.

Towards the Enlightened Science and Engineering

The Renaissance was born in Italian cities which traded between West and East and contributed to the growth of upper class which could sponsor painters and architects in creating beautiful artifacts. These achievements also enlightened engineering which eventually led to the Industrial Revolution in the 19th century. The key legacies of enlightened science and engineering which contributed to the development of science & engineering in coming centuries are characterized in Table 4.2 and those which improved civilizational infrastructure are characterized in Table 4.3.

Table 4.3. The Key Technological Inventions of Engineering Enlightenment

Areas of infrastruc-ture	1700	1750	1800	Results
Key invention and discoveries	Meissen porcelain	Kay's flying shuttle	Spinning cotton mule	Textile industry industrialized
Prime movers	Severy's fire engine	Newcomen's beam engine	Watt's improved engine	Muscle-driven civilization transformed to mobile civilization
Transport	*École des Ponts et Chaussees*	Iron rail tramways	Balloon flights Steamboats	Constant improvements of air travel
Mining & metals	Iron smelted with coce	Crucible steel	Cort's pudding process	Metallurgy
Agriculture	Seed-drill in Europe	Curved mould-boards	Self-sharpening ploughshare	High productivity farming
Domestic life	Smallpox inoculation introduced in England	Lightning conductor	Oil lamp Food preservation	Thinking about electricity

Source: Williams (1987:84) and the author.

The Enlightenment's ideas felt the impact of the Renaissance artists and humanists who criticized the medieval worldview and gave value to individual achievements and the rational life. It was a direct effect of the Scientific Revolution which provided the empirical method of the inquiry and demonstrated self-sufficiency of the human mind in rational reasoning.

Legacy of the Industrial Revolution As the Infrastructure-oriented Modernizer of Western Civilization

The term Industrial Revolution symbolizes the shift from an agrarian, handicraft, labor-intensive economy to one dominated by machine-driven manufacturing, specialization of tasks (at the shop-floor and in office where bureaucracy was born), a free flow of capital, and the concentration of people in cities as the emerging *Industrial Society*.

The following legacies of the Industrial Revolution can be perceived from about a 200 years-long perspective:

1. *Factory system and bureaucracy* - technological progress in the cotton and iron industries created a factory system based on the *engine* which provided centralized power to machines.
2. *Railroads* - transportation rapidly was growing as workers from the country side had to be taken to the factories in cities through a network of railroads which became the core of a new public transportation infrastructure.
3. *Steam boats* – transportation through seas and oceans was developing fast as the colonies needed products and services, and Europe could provide them but at the same time needed raw materials and free labor (slaves and immigrants).
4. *Post office and telegraph* – communication of information was necessary to control the rapid flow of material, products, and services. The first post office was organized in England in 1840, and the first telegraphic message was sent from Baltimore to Washington DC in 1844. Very soon, in 1851 a cable was laid down under the English Channel connecting England with continental Europe, and in 1866 the transatlantic cable allowed electrical communication between the United States and Europe.
5. *Financial system* – developed under a form of stock companies with some controlled liability, which allowed for a more effective concentration of capital for savings and investments.
6. *Urbanization* – concentration of industrial businesses in cities led to their rapid growth. By the end of the 19th century 52 percent of the British, 25 percent of the French, 36 percent of the Germans, 7 percent of the Russians and 10 percent of the Americans in the U.S. lived in cities (Perry 1989:470). Before industrialization, most workers could grow their own food; however, in cramped towns they had to rely on all sorts of services, which were developing the landscape of those towns. Cities were developing without any planning into zones of better off and poor inhabitants, where the latter lived in long rows of houses, close to factories. These harsh conditions of living triggered the awareness of class straggle.
7. *Bourgeoisie versus proletariat* – a new social structure was formed, composed of the affluent middle-class people characterized as conventional, conservative, or materialistic in outlook, which according to Marxist theory, owns the means of producing wealth and is regarded as exploiting the working class. The latter ever since is known as the workers, working-class people, wage earners, the working classes, the common people, the lower classes, the masses, the rank and file, the third estate, the plebeians, the lumpen, the lumpen-proletariat, and so forth. The latter class soon organized themselves into political parties and international workers organizations to protect their work and income.
8. *Per capita income* – since 1820 world industrializing development has been much more dynamic, and more "intensive," than in the years 1000-1819. Per capita income rose faster than the growing population; by 1998 it was 8.5 times as high as in 1820 (Maddison 2000:27). This growth created discretionary income which fueled the further development of industrialization and population growth.
9. *Population growth* – once the industries could provide large quantities of products they needed a steadily growing number of customers. In addition, people working in industries made more money and felt secure to have more children and could afford some sort of health care. All these factors led to consumerism and to population

growth. From 1820 to 1998 the population was growing 5.6 times fasters than in the years of 1000-1819 (Maddison 2000:27).

Figure 4.5. James Watt's steam engine (1763) which transformed muscular into mobile civilization and Charles Babbage's (1791-1871) Differential Engine (1832) which, like the computer in the 21st century, makes civilization better informed and communicated. Two key lasting legacies of the Industrial Revolution.
(Photo: www.uh.edu and www.gloster.com).

Figure 4.6. Michael Faraday, English scientist (1791-1867) in 1831 designed the electric dynamo (a simple power generator), which solved the problem of generating electric current in an ongoing and practical way. This opened the door to American Thomas Edison (1847-1931) and British scientist Joseph Swan (1828-1914) who each invented the incandescent filament light bulb in their respective countries in about 1878. Ever since dark civilization transformed into bright civilization.
(Photo: Wikipedia).

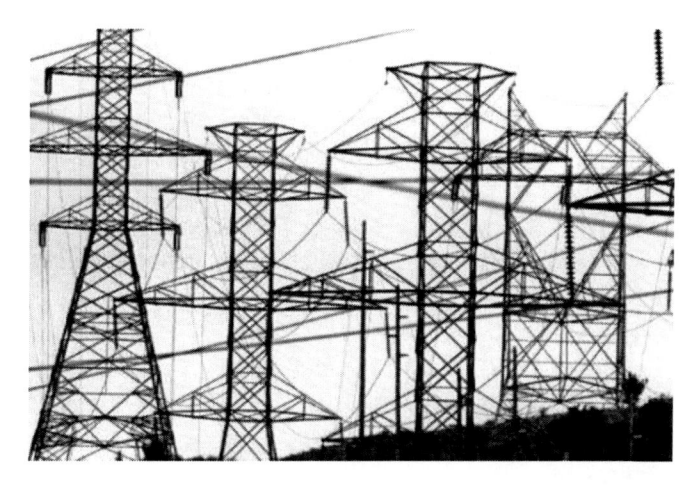

Figure 4.7. The electric lines became a lasting part of Western Civilization's landscape since the Industrial Revolution.
(Photo: Wikipedia).

The Industrial Revolution is proving how men can steadily and purposefully apply the theories of natural science to the methods of economic life. The earlier progress in engineering and economics were achieved by craftsmen and entrepreneurs who had little understanding of natural science. During the 19th century, the Industrial Revolution schools for engineers ascended where theory and practice were integrated and theoretical scientists began to pay more devotion to the practical problems of agriculture and industry.

The French and American Revolutions liberated individuals from closed-minded monarchies and the dogmatic Church and left an everlasting legacy for mankind's development in terms of human rights; the Industrial Revolution similarly left an everlasting legacy with respect to how humans can take advantage of natural and universal knowledge and wisdom to feel comfortable in advanced mobile and bright civilization.

FERMENT-ORIENTED SOCIETAL IDEAS AS THE LASTING TRANSFORMING FORCE OF WESTERN CIVILIZATION (19TH CENTURY)

The ideals of the French Revolution were not implemented in Europe, even in France, after the revolution since Napoleon Bonaparte (1769-1821), as the dictator of France, waged numerous wars against the enemies of the revolution but eventually lost at Moscow (1812) and Waterloo (1815). In fact, those wars were his quest for personal power and for the elevation of friends and family members to rule other European countries as French vassal states. His defeat led to a strengthening of some European empires like the British, Austro-Hungary, Russian, and united Germany (1871), which stopped the revolutionary ideas and achievements for about 100 years. The rulers of those European empires supported the status quo and were afraid of the next Robespierres who could send them to the guillotine.

The only country which was able to implement the revolutionary ideals in the 19th century was the new born United States of America which intercepted world leadership from Europe up to the present. But this country was also in turmoil due to the American Civil War

(1861-1865), when out of 3 million fighting soldiers, 600,000 were dead. This amount of dead soldiers was 50 percent higher than similar American loses during WWII in Europe. It was a very a high price for the abolishment of slavery.

In addition to this political unrest in Western Civilization, the Industrial Revolution with its new industrial society created a new demand for social justice in the conflict between capital and workers.

All these conflicts and wars triggered intellectual reaction by concerned societal leaders which defined the following new ferment generating ideas:

1. *Conservatism* – in the face of revolutionary forces for change there is also a preference of tradition over reason, hierarchy over equality, and the community over the individual. This position is also critical of proposals for radical social change. Some Conservatives seek to preserve the status quo or to reform society slowly, while others seek to return to the values of an earlier time. Edmund Burke (1729-1797) was an Anglo-Irish; he was a leading philosopher, statesman, and political theorist who promoted this philosophy in the Age of Enlightenment which was base for its application in the 19th century. Benjamin Disraeli (1804 - 1881) a British Prime Minister gave the conservative Tory party a political ideology, advocating a return to an idealized view of a corporate or organic society, in which everyone had duties and responsibilities towards other people or groups ("One Nation" Conservatism).

2. *Liberalism* – aimed at liberty and equality as proclaimed by the English (1688), American, and French Revolution. This ideology was a critique of the rising wave of conservatism in imperial Europe in the 19th century. Liberalism rejected the notions, common at the time, of hereditary privilege, state religion, absolute monarchy, and the Divine Right of Kings. Liberals opposed traditional conservatism and sought to replace absolutism in government with representative democracy and the rule of law. The primary intellectual influences on 19th century liberal trends were those of Adam Smith and the classical economists, and Jeremy Bentham (1748-1832) and John Stuart Mill (1806-1873). Adam Smith's *The Wealth of Nations*, published in 1776, was to provide most of the ideas of economics, at least until the publication of J. S. Mill's Principles in 1848 where he argued for laissez-faire. Jeremy Bentham thought that public policy should provide "the greatest happiness of the greatest number". It could be interpreted as a justification for state action to reduce poverty in times of Darwinian economic relations.

3. *Romanticism* – argues for the liberation of human emotions and the free expression of personality, contesting the Enlightenment's focus on rationality. Unlike Classicism, which emphasized harmonic order and established the foundation for sculpture, architecture, literature, painting and music, Romanticism allowed people to get away from the restricted, rational views of life and concentrate on an emotional and sentimental side of humanity. These attributes were acquired by the French painters who created a very strong trend in the arts—*Impressionism*. G. W. F. Hegel, a German philosopher, rejected the rational philosophy of the 18th century because he believed in *Idealism*. For him ideas were more important in life than materialism and wealth. By advocating *Idealism*, Hegel concluded that mankind could be led by his spirit, his soul, rather than the establishment or the *status quo*.

Wolfgang von Goethe in Germany (1749-1832) wrote a loosely autobiographical novel, *"The Sorrows of Young Werther"*, which epitomized what *Romanticism* stood for. His character expressed feelings from the heart and gave way to a new trend of expressing emotions through individuality as opposed to collectivism. Goethe's poetic work served as a model for an entire movement in German poetry named *Innerlichkeit* ("introversion"). Goethe's words inspired a number of music composers, including: Wolfgang A. Mozart (1756-1791), Ludwig van Beethoven (1770-1827), Franz Schubert (1797-1828), Fryderyk Chopin (1810-1849), Franz Liszt (1811-1886), Hector Berlioz (1803-1869) and others. *Romanticism*, by its emphasis on human feelings, emotions, spontaneity, instinct, passion, will, and empathy, opened human nature which so far was considered mostly in terms of anatomy applied in medicine. This trend led later to psychoanalysis pioneered by Sigmund Freud (1856-1939) and post-modernism at the end of the 20th century.

4. *Socialism (Utopian)* – asks for a new society based on the spirit of cooperation rather than on competition. Among early utopian socialists were Saint-Simon (1760-1825), Charles Fourier (1772-1837), and Robert Owen (1771-1858). One key difference between "utopian socialists" and other socialists (including social-democrats) is that utopian socialists generally do not believe any form of class struggle or political revolution is necessary for socialism to emerge. Utopians believe that people of all classes can voluntarily adopt their plan for society if it is presented convincingly (Draper 1990:1-21).

5. *Communism* - claims that human societies progress through class struggle: a conflict between an ownership class that controls production and a dispossessed laboring class that provides the labor for production. Karl Marx (1818-1883) and Frederic Engels (1820-1895) published The Communist Manifesto in 1848 which provides an analytical approach to the class struggle (historical and present) and the problems of capitalism, rather than a prediction of communism's potential future forms (Stangroom and Garvey 2005). Marx's *Capital*, published in 1867, defined the critical role of capital in the capitalist mode of production and gave the foundation for *Marxism* which very much impacted the 20th century's world order.

6. *Nationalism* – calls for the liberation of subject people and the unification of broken nations in Europe. It argues that one's loyalty and devotion should be given to the nation. It provides the individual with a sense of national community and with a cause worthy of self-sacrifice. The romantic liberals were natural leaders of nationalism and called for the unification of Italy and Germany, the revival of Poland, the liberation of Greece from Turkish captive rule, and the autonomy of Hungarians from the Austrian Empire. The nationalistic idea led to national awaking and eventually to the formation of nation-states in the 19th century like Greece and Belgium in 1831, unified Italy (1861) and Germany (1871), Hungary's autonomy (1869), the liberation of Serbia, Romania, and Montenegro from the Ottoman Empire (1887), the liberation of Norway from Sweden (1905), and the formation of Bulgaria (1908) and Albania (1912). There were also several Polish uprisings in 1830-31, 1848 and 1863 which were unsuccessful. Finally, even more captive nations were liberated in Europe after WWI in 1918, like Finland, Estonia, Latvia, Lithuania, Poland, Czechoslovakia, and Hungary. Nationalism under the form of the German superior race led Germany to WWII and about 60-85 million dead.

Figure 4.8. The impressionists showed *romantic* feelings in their art. Claude Monet's Sunset (1891). Museum of Fine Art in Boston. Pierre-August Renoir's *Dance de la Galette* (1876). *Musee d'Orsey*. Their art is worth tens of millions dollars per painting in the 21st century, mostly in investment-oriented selling.
(Photo: Wikipedia).

All these trends of societal ideas, *Conservatism, Liberalism, Romanticism, Socialism, Communism,* and *Nationalism*, are still active in the 21st century and create ferment in politics and societal-oriented thinking in the so called New World Order after the fall of *Communism* in 1989-1991.

Figure 4.9. Ludwig van Beethoven (1770-1827), Karl Marx (1818-1883)[40], Claude Monet (1840-1926) leaders from the 19th century who set the everlasting standards in their professions of music, economics & sociology, and painting.
(Photo: www.biography.com, Spartacus-educational.com, Wikipedia).

Perhaps only Communism and Nationalism have lost their early meanings, since *Communism* as practiced in the Soviet Block in the 21st century discredited its ideas as too doctrinal and barbarian since they led to 94 million dead and much more displaced and negatively affected. On the other hand *Nationalism* is still active today, particularly in European Union which straggles whether to be a unified set of states or a federated set of

---

[40] Karl Marx as a scholar contributed to the theory of capital which is widely recognized by world scholars today. On the other hand *Marxism*, under the form of *Leninism-Stalinism*, also contributed to the development of the Soviet Block in the 20th century and its crimes against humanity.

nation-states. However, nationalism now is not seen as it was in the 19th century as a positive societal force but as a force for the sake of a nation which is willing to subvert individual liberty for national grandeur. It also promotes love for the past and hatred for other nationalities and is based on extreme views questioning the open-minded concepts of reason, freedom, equality, and individualism.

COMMUNISM, NAZISM, FASCISM, AND CAPITALISM IN THE DEADLY STRUGGLE FOR LEADERSHIP IN WORLD CIVILIZATION (20TH CENTURY)

The legacy of Western Civilization in the 20th century is the fact that it was the most deadly century in the 6,000 year long history of civilization. Due to the Bolshevik Revolution (1917) and 2 world wars (1914-1918 and 1934-1945), about 200 million were killed, largely caused by the Germans (who waged 2 wars) and Russians/Chinese (who wanted to spread *Communism*).

The legacy of Western Civilization in the 20th century is as follows:

1. Western Civilization's *Democracy and Capitalism* took 73 years to beat *Totalitarianism* and *Communism* which challenged the West and world at all levels of living, such as ideology, military, economic, societal, cultural, and so forth.
2. *Communism* promoting egalitarianism and class struggle under the form of terror-driven *Leninism-Stalinism* was discredited as unhuman and ineffective doctrine which in fact was the dictatorship of a one party state, which functions similar to a mafia as the example of North Korea has shown in the 21st century. Such a political system is de facto *Red Fascism* (Targowski 1982).
3. *Fascism* practiced in Italy, Spain and Portugal in the 1930s as the politics of law and order showed that Europeans raised on Christian and liberal values cannot be ruled by an ideology-less dictatorship which abuses power by police dominance and neglects economic conditions and national culture.
4. *Nazism* - political and economic doctrines held and put into effect by Adolf Hitler in Germany from 1933 to 1945 included the totalitarian principle of government, predominance of Germanic ethnic groups, an assumption of racial superior, and supremacy of the Führer. This ideology was discredited as a criminal regime which broke with Christian values and applied barbarian values, leading to the Holocaust and massive killings of Jews, Gypsies, Poles, Ukrainians, Russians, and others.
5. *Atomic Bomb* – was used twice in August 1945 by the U.S. against Japan; ever since it has become the strongest threat and deterrence in world politics.
6. *Industrial-Military Complex* – triggered the development of scientific and technological progress resulting in the formation of the *Technological Society* where a civilization increasingly is dominated by technique: a tragedy as argued by Jacques Ellul (1964).
7. *Capitalism* – at its best when it was confronted by *Communism* and wanted to show its human face. After the fall of Communism in 1989-1991, it transformed into

Turbo-Capitalism which has been leading to the rise of inequality within society which may result in civil unrest and possibly a social revolution.

8. *Internetization* – triggered the next Wave of Globalization which transforms Western Civilization into Global Civilization.

Figure 4.10. Three key political leaders in the 20th century, who wanted to outmanouver each other. Eventualy the American President out-manipulated both during WWII (1939-1945). Russian- Josepf Stalin (1878-1953), German- Adlof Hitler (1888-1945), American-Franklin D. Roosevelt (1882-1945). (Photo: Public domain).

POSTMODERNITY AS THE PUZZLING FORCE OF WESTERN CIVILIZATION (21ST CENTURY)

Postmodernity, or the postmodern condition, is generally used to describe the economic or cultural state or condition of society which is said to exist after modernity. Some schools of thought hold that modernity ended in the late 20th century, sometime in the 1980s or early 1990s. The idea of the post-modern condition is sometimes characterized as a culture stripped of its capacity to function in any linear or autonomous state as opposed to the progressive state of mind of *Modernism* (Jameson 1991). The latter is the period from the Renaissance though the Industrial Revolution and up to the beginning of the Information Wave (1980-1990), where the majority of the society is now employed in information processing and handling, while in *Modernity* the majority was employed in material processing and handling. The postmodern period is also termed as post-industrialism (Bell 1973).

The "chaos" and "anxiety" exemplified in architecture, art and music was just the sensitive and romantic reflection of the situation taking place in the society and its socio-political life. This took place when industrial society transformed into *service society* or post-industrial society due to the rapid application of computers and networks[41] which allowed for rapid off shore outsourcing of tens of thousands of factories from the U.S. and Western

---

[41] The creeping Revolution of Personal Computers began in the 1980s when Apple and IBM PCs invaded offices and shop-floors. Within few years millions of PC(s) were connected through tele-communication networks both private and public like the Internet

Europe to Asia. The outsourcing of manufacturing from Western Civilization resulted in the decline of the middle class with good discretionary income since employment in service industries provides low pay and part-time jobs. All these factors create "chaos" in politics since it is driven by lobbyists of global big-business and "anxiety" in the 99% of inhabitants whose well-being is in question and unsecure.

Figure 4.11. Post-modern architecture broke with linearity and harmony of modernity and replaced it by some "chaos" an "anxiety" since it reflects that kind of mood in the post-industrial society. (Photo: www.belleinterior.com)

Figure 4.12. Post-industrial Detroit, once the industrial capital of the U.S, and post-industrial pop culture set the mood of the post-industrial (service) society's anxiety about its well-being. (Photo: www.scott.net and www.live2times.com) .

As the result of post-industrialization the following legacy of this period is defined as follows:

1. The Service Society with a limited middle class cannot support the developed Western Society at a high level of living, as it once was the highest in the world, since the service economy is based on low pay and imported goods which lead to the growth of all sorts of debts and a socio-political game between the rich and poor.
2. Global business supports the service economy since it expands the customer base outside of Western Civilization's boundaries by outsourcing manufacturing and research & development, where to generate consumption it must create jobs.
3. The globalization of the world economy is powered by info-communication technology under the form of e-commerce which leads to the constant invention of digital tools and systems in which return on investment comes from the steady and uncontrollable replacement of labor by computers and machines (it is a case of returning manufacturing to the U.S. under the form of "dark factories" fully automated and robotized). This is what Neil Postman (1992) has called *Technopoly*, when culture surrenders to technology. It has created a new and dangerous situation in Western Civilization where the "technopoly" is granted sovereignty over humanity's well-being, institutions and national life, and in addition, it has become self-justifying, self-perpetuating, and omnipresent.

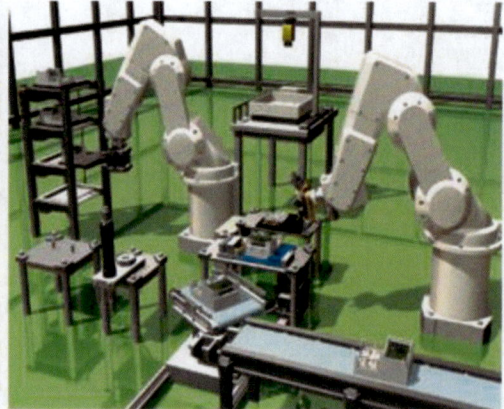

Figure 4.13. Is an automated and robotized factory without labor and taxation the future of well-to-do Western Civilization?
(Photo: Wikipedia and www.bynas.com).

4. This omnipresence of info-communication technology created the *Information Society* which at the same time became the *Virtual Society* in which reality can be controlled by virtual alliances with their own opinion and interests. Eventually it may lead to a limited role for representative government and a growing role for direct democracy which may solve some problems but in the end will create socio-political chaos.
5. Highly advanced technology as the result of highly developed scientific knowledge has created a situation where humankind declines since it cannot apply knowledge

which has created in a wise manner. Since humankind is in fact a super developed animal with its embedded "animal territory", behavior, and strategy, the poor are wise and the better-off are stupid.

6. Global and electronic economy is driven by super-consumerism which requires constant growth of business and supply of strategic resources such as: oil, gas, uranium, coal, and others. It is not a sustainable economic strategy since the volume of such resources is limited on the small planet Earth.

7. The rapid growth of super-consumerism in the world at the cost of depleting natural resources such oil in the Near East has caused the clash of civilizations (Huntington 1996) where the weaker side applies terrorism with some success.

Figure 4.14. The clash of civilizations in the 21st century about values and morality, where Western Civilization's super-consumerism, decadency (sex, drags & rock and roll) and the glory of earthy happiness is contested by Islam Civilization's conservatism and the glory of death to reach happiness. (Photo: www.albertahistoricplaces. chrismaverick.deviant.com, wordpress.com, www.classism.org, tripwow.tripadvisor.com).

CONSOLIDATED LEGACY OF WESTERN CIVILIZATION

"The Uniqueness of Western Civilization"

Ricardo Duchesne (2011) in his book with the above title argues that the singular emergence (among all other civilizations) of democratic culture, including the capacity for self-criticism, makes Western Civilization unique. Furthermore, the ability and desire to rationalize so many spheres of life from science, medicine, and law to technology created the culture of innovation and widespread competition. The political climate in Europe was for long time controlled by the aristocratic-egalitarian spirit among the elite which contributed to the unique development of Western Civilization since European kings were just one among equals, in a contrast to Japanese Emperors who were said to be of divine heritage and superior to the aristocratic elite. Even in feudalism, an overlord had obligation to vassals.

Duchesne shows quite interestingly that most of the unique features go back millennia to the Indo-European bands that gradually conquered much of Europe sometime in the 3rd millennia B.C.E. These bands then became the warrior aristocracies and slowly superimposed their languages, and also to a large extent their spirits, on the European Neolithic and copper population at large which had settled in today's Turkey and Greece about 8000-7000 B.C.E.

Although Duchesne's conclusion about the unique character of Western Civilization has value, its uniqueness comes from many other important factors too.

"How the West Won – The Neglected Story of the Triumph of Modernity"

Rodney Stark (2014) debates in his book with the above title that Modernity, 1000 years after the Italian Renaissance, developed only in Western Europe and North America. Nowhere else did science and democracy arise; nowhere else was slavery outlawed. Only Westerners invented chimneys, musical scores, electric lights, aspirin and soap. He reminds us that mostly the West demonstrates the primacy of uniquely Western ideas – among them the belief in free will, the commitment to the pursuit of knowledge, the notion that the universe functions according to rational rules that can be discovered by men, and the emphasis on human freedom and secure property rights.

Ian Morris (2010) investigates a similar topic in his book *Why the West Rules-For Now*. But the failure of one civilization only allowed another to arise somewhere else. He thinks that the Roman Empire, Renaissance Europe and the Britain of the Industrial Revolution came along, got a lift under their wings from new technologies, social innovations or a creative organizing principle and pushed the whole process of development forward another notch. However, "patterns established in the past suggest that the shift of wealth and power from West to East is inexorable" and that we may even be moving from "bankrupt America to thriving China." But what really worries him is not whether the West may be outdone by the East, but whether mankind's Promethean collective developmental capabilities might not end up as our common self-destruction abilities.

A Critique of Views of Western Civilization's Uniqueness

Duchesne's arguments that victorious democracy, self-criticism and an aristocratic spirit are unique for Western civilization do not reflect well with respect to the historic development of this civilization since democracy has only been practiced in the last 200 years in countries such as the U.S. and even perhaps much shorter if one takes into account that only since the 1960^s have civil rights been recognized universally in this country. In nations colonized by the West, some democratic features were established after the end of WWII in 1945 and at the start of decolonization. However, this process usually replaced the Western rules by dictatorial ones. Since Western Civilization is about 1215 years old, those positive features last a small percentage of this civilization's life time. Furthermore, the aristocratic spirit was drastically replaced by the plutocratic spirit after the Industrial Revolution's growth of capital and its power in shaping world attitudes. Needless to say that for long centuries the aristocracy was controlled by the Church, and whoever wanted to contest the religious dogma could perish at the stake (like G. Bruno did and thousands of women during the Inquisition). Even Nicolaus Copernicus was afraid of such an outcome, and he shared his revolution theory with a German Cardinal when he was on his death bed. Likewise, the French philosopher René Descartes to promote his revolutionary views on *La Method* had to escape from France to the Netherlands to avoid risking his life. Just to end such an "aristocratic spirit" the French Revolution sent the French King Louise XVI and his wife Marie Antoinette to the guillotine in 1793. Democracy was the antidote of the "aristocratic spirit."

Spark's argument that the modernization and technology differentiates Western Civilization from others civilizations is only the result of deeper factors which will be presented later. In addition, Morrison's argument that successful European empires applied innovation and technology, and therefore the West won is not convincing. Of course these are very important factors which make humans so powerful in comparison to other animals, but these factors are not the key ones.

The Legacy of Western Civilization and Its contribution to Mankind's Development

Homo sapiens differentiate from animals by having a more complex brain and mind which have been developing through stimuli-response processes under the form of language and memory-storage "devices," called the INFOCO System (Targowski 2009:92) like contemporary computers, which do the same. Eventually, humans in the 21st century apply four minds which can be grouped in the following clusters (Figure 4.15):

- BASIC MIND (Intuitive, Communicative, Practical), which allows humans to effectively function in civilization
- WHOLE MIND (Basic Mind, Theoretical), which allows for knowing through logical reasoning leading to the development of advanced science and technology
- GLOBAL MIND (Whole Mind, Connected, Digital), which allows humans to "act locally and think globally."

- UNIVERSAL MIND (Global Mind), which is the future mind if humans will try to save their civilization by cooperation rather than confrontation.

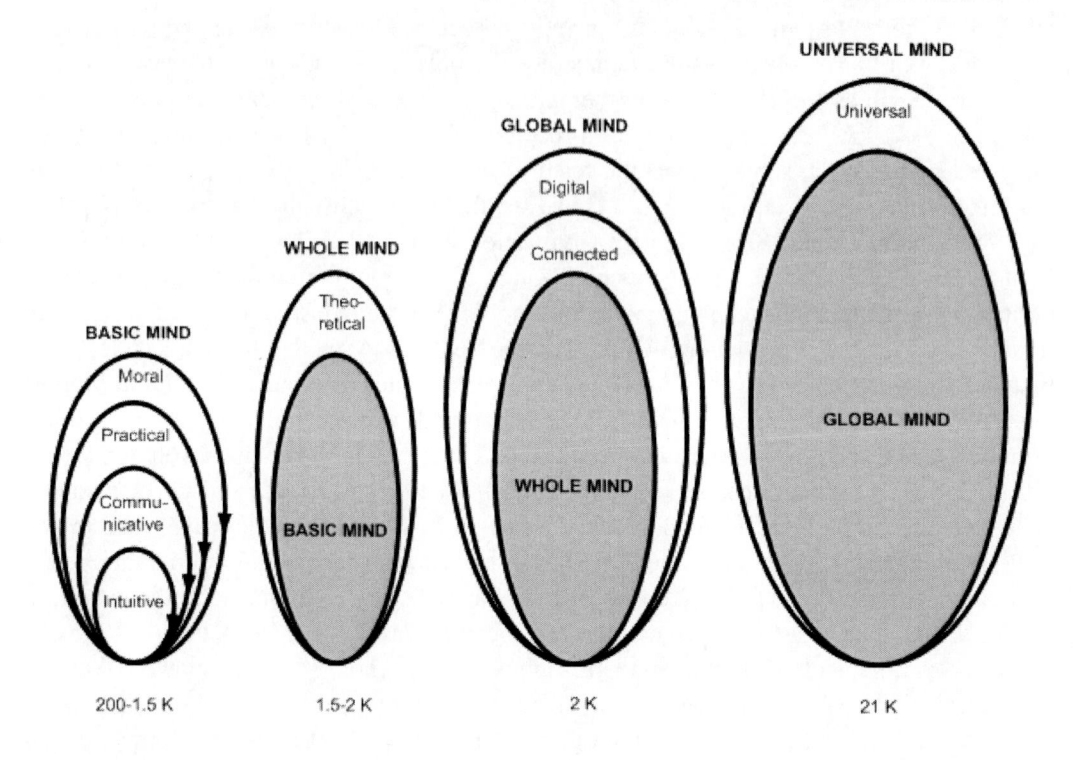

Figure 4.15. The Evolution of the mind's content (Targowski 20011:100).

According to the model in Figure 4.15, four main clusters of minds are identified which, to certain degree, shape the development of civilization. The BASIC MIND (BM) transforms humans from an uncivilized to civilized species. The WHOLE MIND (WM) allows for problem solving and decision-making based on the scientific knowledge, which both lead to the rapid development of different kinds of civilization infrastructures such as the Internet. The GLOBAL MIND (GM) is an extended mind with an access to a huge amount of digital knowledge and judgment. The UNIVERSAL MIND (UM) is a wisdom rather than technology driven mind, which can stop or slow down the decline of civilization. All minds are interrelated as the arrows indicate in a model of Basic Mind.

Western civilization is unique since during its life-time thus far it has not had a phase of stability since it is characterized by hundreds of major conflicts, wars, revolutions and disasters, and thousands of smaller ones. It developed good *resilience-resourcefulness* of individuals and their societies in problem-solving of any kind.

At the level of individual's mind

- WESTERN BASIC MIND was not unique in comparison to other civilizations until the 15th century, when it began to feel the strengthening impact of the rising GLOBAL MIND which gave it some examples of successful problem-solving because geographical discoveries provided a new understanding of the world.

CHINESE GLOBAL MIND was on the rise until 1433 when the Chinese Emperor ordered the destruction of the Chinese fleet, and China went into isolation and stagnation. Other civilizations were weak in global traveling and discovering new ways of living.

- WESTERN GLOBAL MIND was superior since the 15th century due to the experiences associated with the colonization of other civilizations such as the Aztec, Mayan, Incan, African, and later Chinese and its offspring. In the 20th and 21st centuries this mind dominates the Globalization Wave driven by global business through the Internet and global transportation networks. At this time, CHINESE GLOBAL MIND arises as the competing force with WESTERN GLOBAL MIND.

Period	Movement	Values
21	UNIVERSALISM	Goodness, Harmony, Wisdom, Dialogue, Open Society, Self-sustainability, Green Planet
21	GLOBALISM	Love, Truth, Hope, Autonomy, Responsibility, Creativity, Self-Accomplishment
20	LIBERALISM	Human Rights, Civil Rights, Nation Independence, Open Society
19	CAPITALISM	Creativity, Social Democracy, Private Ownership, Free Market
18-19	ROMANTISM	Cult of Nationality, Cult of Feeling
1789	GREAT FRENCH REVOLUTION	Liberty, Equality, Fraternity, Citizenship
1776	AMERICAN REVOLUTION	Individualism, Liberalism
1689	ENGLISH REVOLUTION	Democracy, Parliamentary Political Pluralism
18	ENLIGHTMENT	Knowledge, Rationality, Freedom of Thinking, Tolerance, Pluralism
15-16	RENAISSANCE	Complete Human Development
1 CE	CHRISTIANITY	Faith, Hope, Love
1 BCE - 4 BC	ANCIENT ROME	Law
5-3 BCE	ANCIENT GREECE	Verity, Goodness, Beauty
20-1 BCE	JUDAISM	Service to God and Man, Justice, Decalogue

DEVELOPMENT BY ACCUMULATION

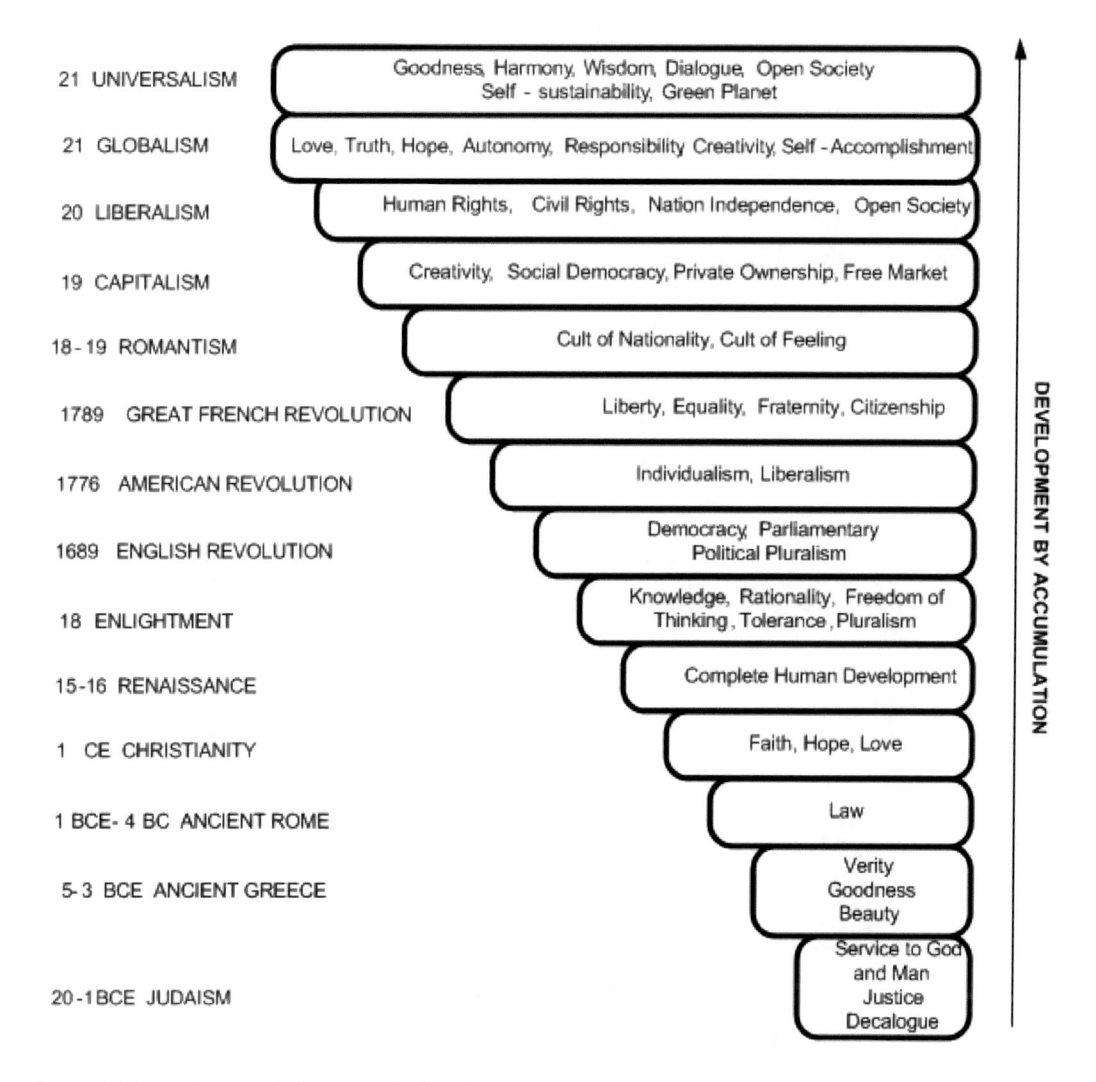

Figure 4.16. The Kawczak-Targowski Model (2000:385) of the additive process of Western values development through the centuries.

- WESTERN WHOLE MIND gained its uniqueness around the Scientific Revolution (15th -18th centuries) and was also influencing other minds through the knowledge rising and streaming from European universities which were functioning and developing since the 11th century. This mind was able to contribute to the rise of the Renaissance (15th century) and Enlightenment (18th century) which led to the Industrial Revolution (19th century) and further development of science and technology in the 20th and 21st centuries which have no comparable achievements in other civilizations. This Western mind based Western education on *critical thinking* while still in the 21st century several other civilizations' education was based on *memorization*.

- WESTERN UNIVERSAL MIND began rising as a result of the mosaic of social ideas produced by the English (1688), American (1765-1783), and French Revolutions (1789-1799) as well as the American Civil War (1861-1865), and the 19th century, full of new social trends contesting Capitalism and Monarchies & Empires, through the 20th century, with the wars involving Communism, Fascism, and Nazism. Needless to say the rising United States provided world leadership in developing the universal mind at the level of democracy, civil rights, human rights, women rights, gay rights and international law. This mind's capacity and ability is unique among other contemporary civilizations such as Chinese, Japanese, Hindu, African, Buddhist, Islam, and Eastern. The additive process of developing Western values is depicted in Figure 4.16.

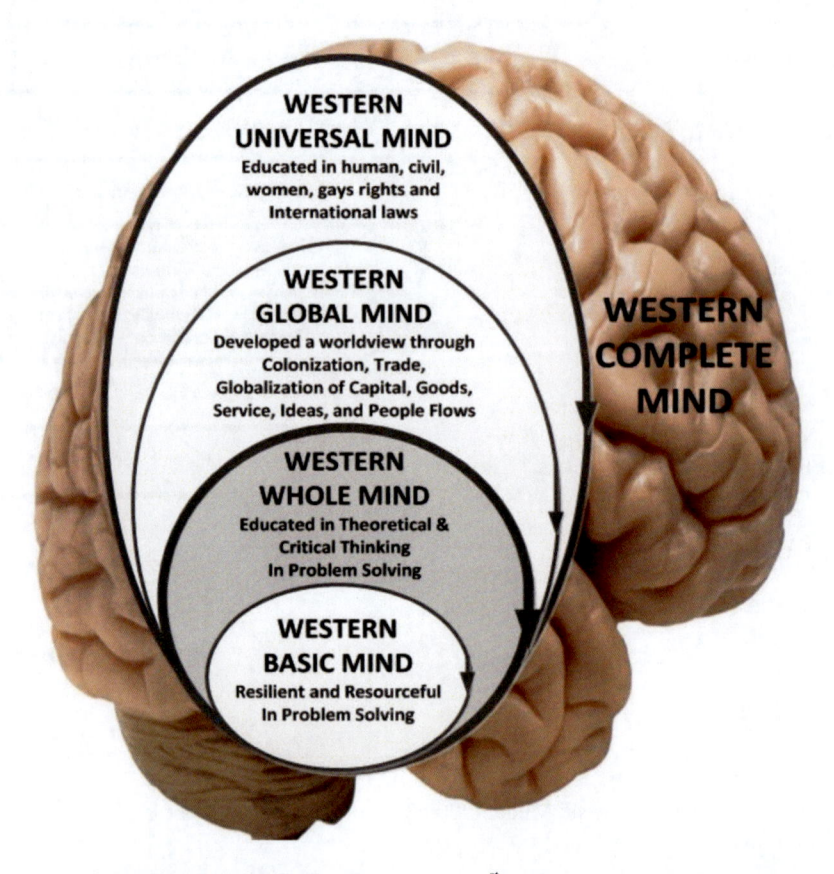

Figure 4.17. The WESTERN COMPLETE MIND in the 21st century, where WESTERN WHOLE MIND provides the solid foundation for other minds and WESTERN UNIVERSAL MIND (Targowski 2013) is a unique functioning and popular mind among other contemporary civilization.

Taking into account the synergistic sum total of these four western minds, certainly Western civilization is unique in having COMPLETE MIND (Figure 4.17) among other contemporary civilizations. How important is COMPLETE MIND? Let's compare the minds of Franklin D. Roosevelt and Adolf Hitler who were two of the main leaders in WWII. American President FDR had a COMPLITE MIND (4 minds) and Hitler had UNCOMPLETE MIND (with 1 BASIC MIND). The question is can a leader with one mind win against a leader with four minds? As the history tells Hitler lost, even having at one time a very good political and military advantage over the opponent.

CONCLUSION

1. Western civilization in the 21st century is the most developed civilization among contemporary ones due to:
   a. The richness of its trends, leaders, and events, as was characterized by about 100 major trends and the same number of key leaders identified in politics, art, medicine, science and technology, which were all characterized in this investigation.
   b. Its history which does not have the stabilization phase which results in the very well developed *resilience and resourcefulness* ability in thinking and problem solving.
   c. The development of the COMPLETE MIND composed of BASIC, WHOLE, GLOBAL, and UNIVERSAL MINDS.
   d. Among the four minds, the key mind is the WHOLE MIND which provides the foundation of thinking and problem solving based not only on conventional knowledge and wisdom but particularly on theoretical knowledge and wisdom. It gives the opportunity for educated judgment and choice in all kinds of human undertakings.
2. Western civilization due to its permanent multi-directional, non-stabilized development was able to change and adapt its society's *modus operandi* according to circumstances as follows:
   a. Level of Religion – from Christianity to Roman-Catholicism (1054)[42] and to Catholicism and Protestantism (1517) which triggered the positive work ethic and modest life of Protestants who developed the U.S. and Northern Europe to their high quality of living in the 20th century.
   b. Level of Society – shifts from the Manor Society to Feudal, Represented (English Revolution), Liberal (American Revolution), Citizenship (French Revolution), Industrial (Industrial Revolution), Technological (after WW II), Information (2000), and Virtual (2010) ones which exemplify Western civilization's progressive and sensitive attitude for change and adaptation.
   c. Level of Culture – gradual and parallel development of High and Pop-Culture, where the latter evolves from the culture of workers' protest to youth decadency (sex, drugs and rock and roll). These cultures trigger the bifurcation of society and everything associated with its bad feelings, attitudes and strategies.

---

[42] The second branch of Christianity became Orthodox Christianity.

d. Level of Infrastructure – from Roman good roads and aqueducts to the electricity and combustion engine-driven processes, megacities, automobiles, airplanes, highways, high-rises, ocean connecting channels, the global transportation and Internet – all these projects were developed by Western Civilization and later adapted by other civilizations.
3. Western civilization has two key stages of development: the first one was in the Renaissance when art and architecture reached their heights and thereafter provided standards for the development of art and architecture in the next centuries. The second key stage is about 2000, when Western society in developed nations (called sometimes the Atlantic civilization or West-Western civilization) reached a high quality of living with respect to the upper and middle class. However, due to super-consumerism and the steady depletion of strategic resources this kind of living is not sustainable world-wide.

REFERENCES

Auden, W.H. ed. (1952). *The portable Greek reader*. New York: Viking.
Bell, D. (1973). *The coming of post-industrial society: a venture in social forecasting*. New York: Basic Books.
Burckhardt, J. (2010). *The civilization of the renaissance in Italy*. Mineola, NY: Dover Publications.
Draper, H. (1990). *Karl Marx's theory of revolution, volume IV: critique of other socialisms*. New York: Monthly Review Press.
Duchesne, R. (2011). *The uniqueness of Western Civilization*. Leiden & Boston: BRILL.
Eisenstein, E. (1978). *The printing press as an agent of change*. Toronto: University of Toronto Press.
Ellul, J. (1964). *The technological society*. New York: VINTAGE BOOKS.
Farrington, B. (1961). *Greek science*. Baltimore: Penguin Books.
Gilbet, F. (1965). *Machiavelli and Guicciardini*. Princeton, NJ: University Princeton Press.
Guizot, F. (2013). *The history of civilization in Europe*. Translated by W. Hazlitt. Indianapolis: Liberty Fund.
Jameson, F. (1991). *Postmodernism or the cultural logic of late capitalism*. Durham,, NC: Duke University Press.
Labriola, A. (1952). *Giordano Bruno: martyrs of free thought no.1*. Rome: P & G.
Machiavelli, N.(1961). *The prince*, trans. By G. Bull. Harmondsworth, England: Penguin Books.
McNeill, H. (1986). *History of Western civilization, a handbook*. Chicago: The University of Chicago Press.
Maddison, A. (2000). *The world economy, a millennial perspective*. Paris: OECD
Morris, I. (2010). *Why the West rules-for now*. Goggle Books.
Perry, M. et al. (1989). *Western civilization, ideas, politics, & society from 1400*. Boston: Houghton Mifflin Co.
Postman, N. (1992). *Technopoly, the surrender of culture to technology*. New York: Alfred A. Knopf.

Stangroom, J. and J. Garvey (2005). *The Great Philosophers*. London: Arcturus Publishing.

Stark, R. (2014). *How the West won, the neglected story of the triumph of modernity*. Wilmington, Delaware: ISI Books.

Targowski, A. (1982). *Red fascism*. Lawrenceville, VI: Brunswick.

Targowski, A. and A. Ajnenkiel. (2000). *Losy Polski i świata. (The fates of Poland and the World)*. Warsaw: Bellona.

Targowski, A. (2009). *Information technology and societal development*. Hershey & New York: Premier Reference Resource (IGI).

Targowski, A. (2011). *Cognitive informatics and wisdom development*. Hershey, PA & New York: IGI Global

Targowski, A. (2013). *Harnessing the power of wisdom*. New York: NOVA Science Publishers.

Williams, T.I. (2003). *A history of inventions, from stone axes to silicon chips*. London: timewarner books.

Chapter 5

WESTERN CIVILIZATION IN TRANSFORMATION TO GLOBAL AND VIRTUAL CIVILIZATIONS IN THE 21ST CENTURY

ABSTRACT

The *purpose* of this investigation is to define the nature of the processes transforming the declining Western civilization into Western-Global-Virtual civilization. The *methodology* is based on an interdisciplinary big-picture view of the developments and interdependency of Western, Global, and Virtual civilization. Among the *findings* are: Western civilization is about 1200 years old and reached its peak at the end of the 20th century. Due to a self-defeating strategy of reducing the middle class through deindustrialization and off shore outsourcing of manufacturing jobs, Global civilization is developing which penetrates other contemporary civilizations and to certain degree is controlled by those civilizations. *Practical implication:* The Western-Global-Virtual civilization will last as long as information technology remains in existence and is unregulated. *Social implication:* Western-Global-Virtual civilization eventually will be able to solve some difficult societal problems, but at the same time it may replace the Western model of representative democracy with direct democracy leading to societal chaos. *Originality:* This investigation defined the Western-Global-Virtual civilization at the time of its birth, not at its decline, and ends by giving what should amount to some ability based on knowledge and wisdom to solve current societal problems.

INTRODUCTION

The purpose of this investigation is to analyze the symptoms of the decline of Western civilization and to synthesize the transformation process which leads to the birth of Western-Global-Virtual civilization. The scope of this investigation will be focused on religious, societal, cultural, economic, political, and technological factors. In effect this transformation will be analyzed in terms of how it impacts declining Western civilization, how the new rising Western-Global-Virtual civilization will act, and how long it will last. The method applied in this analysis-synthesis is based on the qualitative and inductive-deductive comparative approach towards different civilizations.

THE ORGANIZING PRINCIPLE SYMPTOMS OF THE DECLINE OF WESTERN CIVILIZATION IN THE 21ST CENTURY

Civilizations rise and fall. Nicholas Hagger (2008), for instance, assumes that a civilization declines when its divine Light which inspires a religion (and vice-versa) dims and fades, turns secular, and begins to fall. This rule suggests that Western Civilization's Christian religion is being replaced in the dawn of the 21st century by a secular religion identified as business which goes global with values and maxims such as: super-consumerism, winner takes all, greed, "what is good for business is good for society", constant growth, "the sky is the limit", "inequality is good for entrepreneurship" and innovations.

Furthermore, the instant dissemination of smartphones in the 21st century develops constant and instant e-communication, leading to the rise of Virtual civilization. The comparison of Western, Global (Targowski 2014a), and Virtual civilization (Targowski 2014b) is provided in Table 5.1.

Table 5.1. The General Comparison of Western, Global, and Virtual Civilizations

ATTRIBUTES OF A CIVILIZATION	WESTERN CIVILIZATION	GLOBAL CIVILIZATION	VIRTUAL CIVILIZATION
RELIGION	Christianity (Catholic & Protestant)	Business (Global and Big)	Unlimited freedom
ORGANIZING PRINCIPLE	Peace and prosperity	What is good for business is good for society	Collective intelligence to secure the common good in an alternative virtual world, since the "real" world is going in a wrong direction in the 21st century.
VALUES	Love your neighbor, honesty and ethics, win-win strategy, equality & fraternity, universal rights, including consumer rights	Super-consumerism, constant growth, winner takes all, greed, sky is the limit, inequality is good for entrepreneur-ship and innovations	Connected, expected feedback, rhythm, productivity, velocity, impatience, techno-centrism, cyber-ethics, informed, big-picture vs small-picture, global awareness, self-con-ciseness. e-behavior; net-centric, anytime, anywhere, "death" of distance, no-middle-man, curiosity, discovery, digital & virtual divide, information wealth, poverty of attention
CULTURE	Western culture (High & Pop in reality)	Global culture (Westernized)	Electronic-techno culture in virtuality
INFRASTRUCTURE	National and international linked through borders	Globally connected via the Internet and GAN over boarders and transportation networks through borders	Computer networks and storage (online invisible cyberspace as a repository for collective societal memory)

GAN – private Global Area Networks.

Western Civilization in Transformation to Global and Virtual Civilizations ...   131

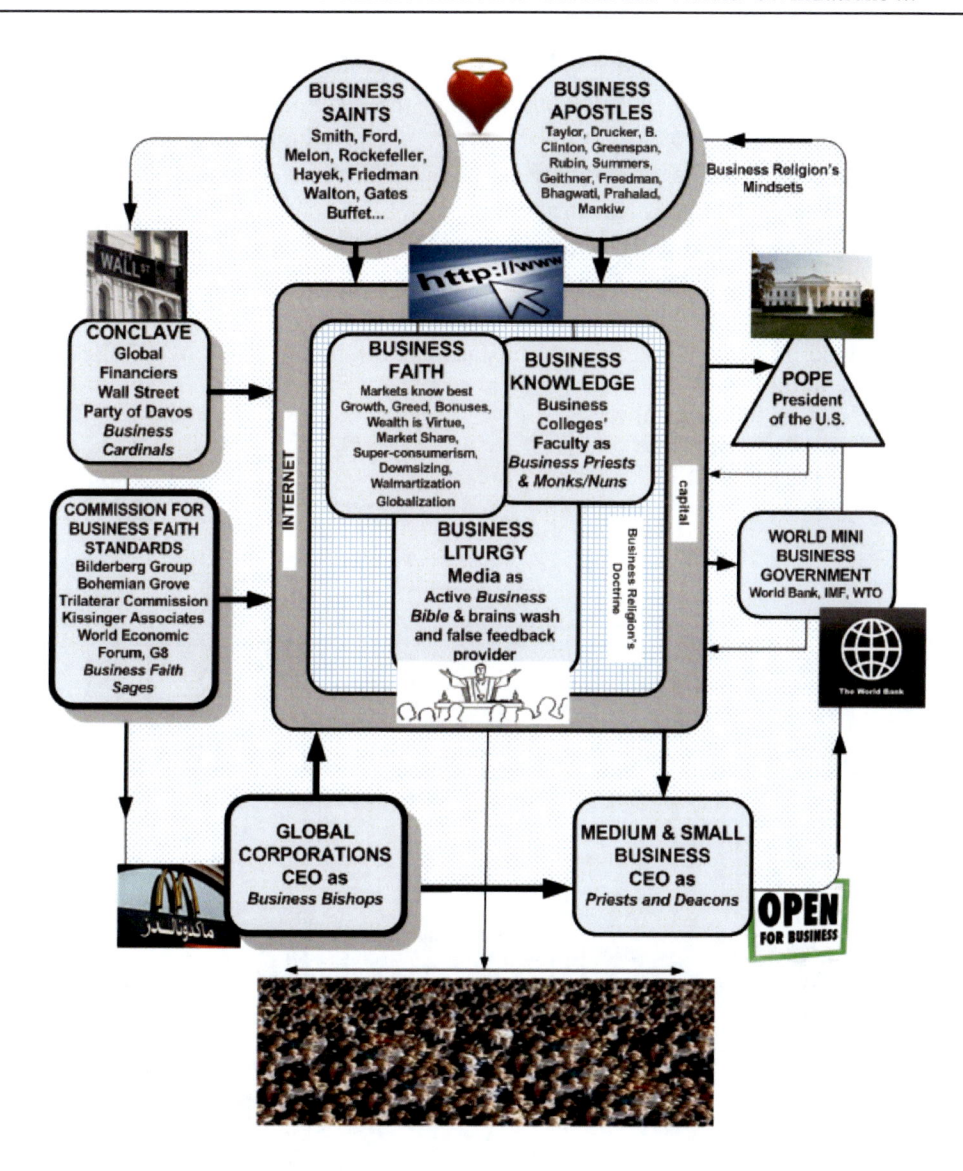

Figure 5.1. The architecture of business as a religion of Global civilization and relations among its entities.

Business Religion Doctrine is what keeps business as a religion. This doctrine is demanded by CEOs of Big Global Business who act as Business Bishops and Cardinals. As the businesses' top elite, they define the vision, goals, strategies, principles, and rules of current global capitalism, which form the Business Religion Doctrine. Later, it becomes the creed for most executives and managers of global capitalism. For example, in the 2010s this doctrine was based on the following rules:

- Rule 1: The elimination of governmental regulations is necessarily beneficial, since it encourages growth.

- Rule 2: Lowered taxation of wealthy taxpayers creates new jobs.[43]
- Rule 3: The removal of safety nets for displaced workers is justified because it minimizes business costs so as to be more competitive globally.
- Rule 4: The offshore outsourcing of manufacturing is good for consumers since prices of imported goods are cheaper.
- Rule 5: Unemployed workers do not have the right skills so it is their obligation to seek the appropriate job training to find employment elsewhere.

Figure 5.1 defines the architecture of business as a religion of Global civilization and relations among its entities.

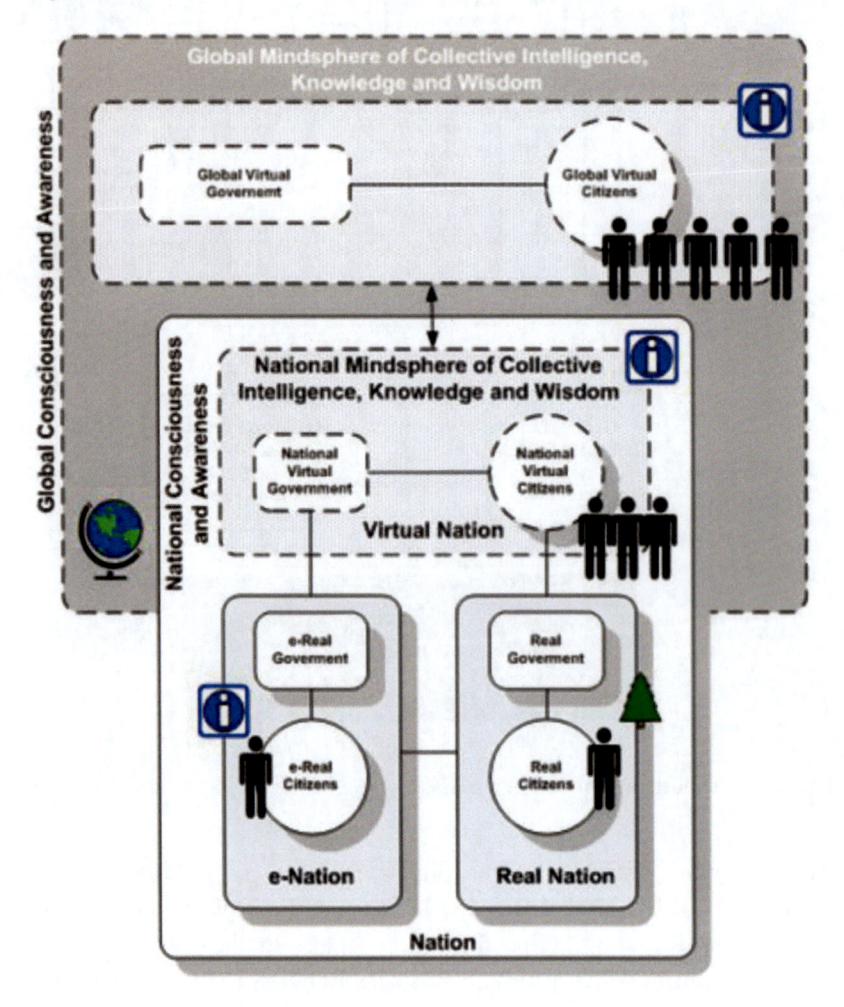

Figure 5.2. The concept of Virtual civilization.

---

[43] A March 2011 NBC News/Wall Street Journal poll found 81 percent of those surveyed would support a tax on millionaires that would be used for deficit reduction. An April, 2011 CBS/New York Times poll revealed 72 percent of people favored raising taxes on the wealthy to reduce the deficit. However, politicians refuse to listen to the people who put them into in office and continue to spout misinformation about what citizens really want.

Globalization's business religion which emphasizes a continuing pursuit of free trade and futuristic technology (Grey 2007) in order to make the rich even richer can only push Western Civilization into a severe decline which will provoke social unrest at dangerous levels. This could occur if the Great Recession 2008-11 leads to an even greater depression, which would be followed by *a necessarily conservative populist reaction* in the desperate effort to sustain law & order (Targowski 1982).

The concept of Virtual civilization is depicted in Figure 5.2.

Why is the Virtual Wave considered that which became Virtual Civilization in the 21st century? Because the latter satisfies all criteria (attributes) of a civilization, as it is defined in Table 2.1, and the latter has created its own independent virtual society, a parallel to the real one.

The architecture of Western-Global-Virtual civilization is shown in Figure 5.3.

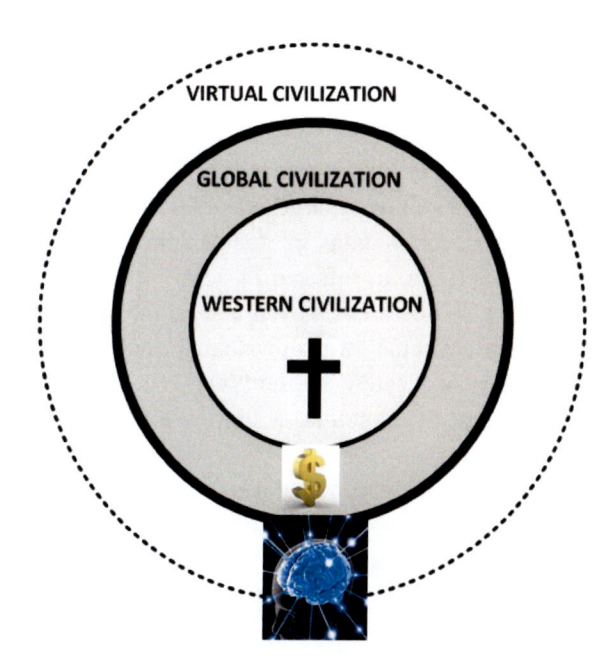

Figure 5.3. The Architecture of Western-Global-Virtual Civilization.

Today it is too soon to judge the impact of the Virtual Civilization upon the real civilizations. However, despite some positive aspects of it, such as the quest for the common good, one can notice the crisis of the young generation, exemplified by a shortened span of attention and the desire for constant (electronic in fact) fun in long-hours of playing computer games and communication tantamount to chit-chat and gossip. For example students 18-24 years old learn less, since on average they send and answer about 100 text messages every day (Smith 2011). This is about 5 times more than a faculty is reading and answering e-messages every day. Some eager students send twice as many messages per day (200).

The quest for the common good by virtual society may limit or even replace representative democracy by direct democracy which eventually could solve a few problems; however, it might also trigger permanent political chaos in real civilization.

The impressive number of e-communications among people from different parts of the world diminishes local interrelations and intensifies connectivity among international or/and distant, parochial cultures, which eventually separates, isolates and alienates individuals in their real living places.

At this time it is very improbable that virtual society can be regulated by real society. This means that on one hand Virtual Civilization can be positive, but on another hand it can also be harmful for humanity which lives in a falling civilization due to overpopulation, superconsumerism, depletion of strategic resources and environment degradation.

THE ECONOMIC SYMPTOMS OF THE DECLINE OF WESTERN CIVILIZATION IN THE 21ST CENTURY

The results of the new secular business religion penetrating Western Civilization are as follows:

Financial Perspective:
1. The structural Global Financial Crisis which started in 2007 is considered by many economists as the worst financial crisis since the Great Depression of the 1930s. It led to the risk of a total downfall of large financial institutions, the bailout of banks by national governments, and slumps in stock markets around the world. In many areas, the housing market also suffered, leading to evictions, foreclosures and prolonged unemployment. The crisis played a substantial role in the letdown of key businesses, declines in consumer wealth valued in trillions of U.S. dollars, and a decline in economic activity leading to the 2008–2012 Global Recession (Williams 2012). The same decline of economic activities took place in Western-Southern Europe.
2. There is a direct relationship between declines in wealth and declines in consumption and business investment, which along with government spending represent the economic engine. Between June 2007 and November 2008, Americans lost an estimated average of more than a quarter of their collective net worth (CNN Money 2009). Ever since only 1% of society has improved its income, while the 99% of the society has steadily lost its income.
3. The unemployment rate in the U.S. since 2007 (4.6%) was steadily rising to 2010 (9.3%) and slightly improved in the following years, reaching 7.4% in 2013.[44] However, the employment structure ever since has become typical of service economies which is based on low pay and part-time workers. Since their income is low, they do not have a discretionary income to spend and support the growth of economic/business activities.

Employment Perspective:
4. The Global Financial Crisis officially was triggered by corrupting strategies of landing and insuring loans and all sorts of investment deals. It is true that consumers could not pay off those loans, which were supposedly too easily given to them by banks. However, the main question is why they could not pay the premiums of those loans? The answer is that in the meantime, the middle class has been transformed to

---

[44] http://www.infoplease.com/ipa/A0104719.html, Retrieved 8-12-2014.

the lower class due to the loss of well paid jobs in manufacturing and research and development centers which have been outsourced offshore.

5. After outsourcing about 51,000 factories and thousands of call centers as well as some R & D centers to countries with cheap labor, Western Civilization committed suicide by self-deindustrialization (Figure 5.4) and by committing to be a service economy. However, at the same time Western global business is developing manufacturing in developing nations. Therefore, in the U.S. manufacturing employment collapsed from a high of 19.5 million workers in June 1979 to 11.5 workers in December 2009, a drop of 8 million workers over 30 years. Between August 2000 and February 2004, manufacturing jobs were lost for a stunning 43 consecutive months—the longest such stretch since the Great Depression. Manufacturing plants have also declined sharply in the last decade, shrinking by more than 51,000 plants, or 12.5 percent, between 1998 and 2008. These stable, middle-class jobs have been the driving force of the U.S. economy for decades and these losses have done considerable damage to communities across the country (Center for American Progress).[45]. In EU the same outsourcing trend is taking place. Currently, approximately one fifth of Europe's vehicles are produced in Central-Eastern Europe. According to the consultancy firm Roland Berger, 15 automakers operate 12 plants there with a total annual capacity of 3 million vehicles. This tendency is rising sharply. According to the European Auto Producers' Association (ACEA), 3 million people in Europe are directly employed by automakers, and almost 13 million in the sector as a whole, including the supply industry. Their incomes and jobs are increasingly under threat as they continue to be played off against their counterparts in Central-Eastern Europe and China.

Figure 5.4. From off shore outsourcing to the deindustrialization of Western Civilization. (Photo: www.american progress.org and www.fineartamerica.com).

6. The middle class-squeeze prevents them from maintaining a middle-class lifestyle, making downward mobility a threat to counteract aspirations of upward mobility. In the United States for example, middle-class income is declining while many staple products are increasing in price, such as energy, education, housing, and insurance

---

[45] http://www.americanprogress.org/issues/labor/news/2012/07/09/11898/5-facts-about-overseas-outsourcing/, Retrieved 8-10-2014.

(Pelosi 2006). The American middle class, long the most affluent in the world, has lost that distinction (Leonhart and Quealy 2014) and their good income (Table 5.1).

Table 5.1. Change in Median Income Since 200

Country	Change in median income since 2000
Britain	+19.7
Canada	19.7
Ireland	16.2
Netherlands	13.9
Spain	4.1
Germany	1.4
United States	0.3

Source: New York Times, April 22, 2014.

7. The lower class (Figure 5.5) in the United States has fallen behind their counterparts in at least a few other countries since the early 1980s. With slow income growth since then, the American poor now clearly trail the poor in several other rich countries. At the 20th percentile — where someone is making less than four-fifths of the population — income in both the Netherlands and Canada was 15 percent higher than income in the United States in 2010 (Leonhart and Quealy 2014).

Figure 5.5. The upper-class, middle-class, and lower-class housing.
(Photo: www.frontdoor.com, www.voiceofdetroit.com, www.wikipedia.org).

Detroit once was the industrial capital of the United States; nowadays, due to the deindustrialization strategy, about 36 percent of the city's population is below the poverty level, and, by 2010, the residential vacancy rate was 27.8 percent. With fewer people paying taxes, the city has starved financially and has struggled to maintain social services. Most of streets of the city are in total darkness because of nonfunctioning street lights. And the average police response time, including top priority calls, is 58 minutes, according to a report by the emergency manager. Poverty has been exacerbated by middle-class black families moving to the suburbs to pursue jobs or better schools and to escape crime. Meanwhile, the city's poor have stayed in Detroit (Figure 5.6). The city's unemployment rate is about 19 percent, but the lack of a transportation system has prevented residents from commuting to jobs elsewhere. A plan to cut retiree pensions, which some estimate account for $3.5 billion of the city's $18 billion in debt, could worsen the lives of some (Padinani 2013).

Figure 5.6. Detroit's once-glamorous Michigan Theater, which is now used as a parking garage and shuttered homes and businesses, lined a street in downtown Detroit in 2008.
(Photo: Sean Doerr/WNET.org and Spencer Platt/Getty Images).

THE SOCIATAL SYMPTOMS OF THE DECLINE OF WESTERN CIVILIZATION IN THE 21ST CENTURY

"Coming Apart"

Charles Murray (2013) demonstrates that a new upper class and a new lower class in the United States diverged so far in core behaviors and values that they barely recognize their underlying American kinship. The trends Murray describes do not break along lines of race or ethnicity, and the divergence between classes has nothing to do with income inequality. Murray argues that the top and bottom of white Americans increasingly live in different cultures, with the powerful upper class surrounded only by their own kind, ignorant about life in mainstream America, and the lower class suffering the erosions of family and community life that strike at the heart of the pursuit of happiness. This kind of societal divergence threatens the survival of the American project and its ideals coming from the American Revolution.

In his book, *Coming Apart* (2013), Charles Murray demonstrates that the American elite lives in SuperZips, as are characterized in Table 5.2. This elite is affluent, highly educated, highly successful, and labeled by other Americans as overeducated snobs (OES). They themselves think that they are superior to the rest of the population.

The new household of the lower class is above the poverty line, making about $14,634 in 2010 (Murray 2013:230). Most single women with children belong to this class. About 8 percent of all whites ages 30-49 belonged to this class in the 1960s but in 2010 this class embraced about 20 percent of white men in their prime age (Murray 2013:235).

Such a huge growth of the lower class in the last 50 years shows that the American project works mostly for the elite and changes the fabric of the Western (American) society. Needless to say, it appears as though the ideals of the American Revolution lasted only 225 years.

Table 5.2. Elite places to live in 1960 and what happened to them by 2000

Elite places	Median percentage of adults with college degrees		Median income (000s of 2010 dollars	
New York	1960	2000	1959	1999
The Upper East Side	23	75	$55	$183
Lower Westchester County	25	58	$87	$155
The Connecticut Corridor	27	65	$90	$191
BOSTON				
Brookline	21	77	$69	$124
The Western Suburbs	27	70	$75	$157
Philadelphia				
The Main Line	25	64	$83	$149
WASHINGTON, DC				
Northwest Washington	35	79	$88	$172
Lower Montgomery County	42	77	$94	$176
McLean/Great Falls	26	74	$74	$180
Chicago				
The North Shore	32	68	$95	$152
Los Angeles				
Beverly Hills	19	56	$115	$158
San Francisco				
Lower Marin County	26	69	$64	$158
Burlingame/Hillsborough	21	54	$89	$144
The Palo Alto Area	28	65	$72	$157
Total	26	67	$84	$163

Source: Murray (2013:77).

The Decline of Rome III

Western civilization represented by the "0.01%" with the highest income (super rich) is reminiscent of the last phase of Rome I (476 A.D.). America is falling apart, and the Western nations' super-rich are to blame for their indifference. The super-rich do not care about how much funding is needed to save this country, as long as they have their private schools, private hospitals, private airports and private places. For example, the super-rich in the U.S are squeezing working-class' income ("to be competitive"), while destroying the infrastructure of the nation that has done so much for their success. It is ridiculous that working-class Americans struggling to survive day-to-day are paying more in taxes than billionaire bankers and oil tycoons. The rich have always needed the middle class to work in their factories and buy their products. With globalization this is no longer true. Their factories can be in China, producing good for people in America, Europe and elsewhere else in the world (Buchheit 2013).

As Piketty (2014) documented, the rich nowadays are living in the inheritance society where inherited capital allows them to live without working. A 2011 study by Edward Wolff and Maury Gittleman (2011) found that the wealthiest 1 percent of families had inherited an average of $2.7 million from their parents. This was 447 times more money than the least wealthy group of people — those with wealth less than $25K — had inherited. This wealth is deliver to their owners in a passive way as unearned streams of income variously called rents, dividends, profits, capital gains, interest and so on. Those who get big inheritances can park those inheritances in investment accounts that just get bigger and bigger without them having to lift a finger. As a result, the gaping inheritance disparity actually grows even more gaping each year after the inheritances have been received (Bruenig 2014).

Unfortunately, these multi-millionaires and billionaires who have given up on America and some Western European countries (and invest in new "emerging markets") and on the working class are in control of the political process in this country. The huge inequality and inheritance of 0.01% can be compared to the Roman elite which let down Rome I. Table 5.2 compares the state of elite in Rome I with the U.S as Rome III with its rich elite's similar behavior.

Table 5.2. The Comparison of the Roman Empire and the U.S. in the 21st century

Criteria	The roman empire 5th century b.c.e	The united states the 2000s c.e.
Rulers	Insensitive	Misleading
Politicians	Irrelevant	Self-serving
Elite	Passive	Detached
Military	Dispersed	Stretched-out
Work done by	Slaves & servants	Computers and illegal immigrants working like slaves Offshore cheap labor
Ideas	Lack of ideas	Lack of ideas
Purpose of life	*Dolce vita*	The fun society
Mindset	Return to country-side and autarchy	Protectionist feelings and besieged
Viewed by others	Falling & attacked and beaten by weaker external tribes	Falling (Iraq & Afghanistan); attacked by terrorists against whom one cannot decisively win

The comparison of Rome I and Rome III (the U.S.) gives the impression that the U.S. is in bad shape from the civilizational point of view. It cannot lead Western civilization back to its previous prominent state.

The Society on Sale

In pursuing a new religion of business (what is good for business is good for the society), many schools have been privatized and have been switched to for-profit models as well as prisons. Charter schools are the fastest-growing sector of public education today, taking root in most U.S. states, thanks to a big push by the education reform lobby and the federal government's Race to the Top competition. In Michigan, the leading state with the number of charter schools (about 300), the evidence concerning charter school quality is clear: Students in charter schools perform worse on average than public school students, according to a 2007 study by Gary Miron (2014), a professor at Western Michigan University. A CREDO study on Michigan found that 80 percent of charters perform below the 50th percentile of achievement in reading, and 84 percent perform below that threshold in math. On top of that, according to the National Association of Charter School Authorizers, 26 percent of Michigan charter schools fall into the bottom 15 percent of the state's schools on 8th grade math exams and 21 percent in 8th grade reading (Resmovitz 2014).

The same issues are associated with the development of colleges for profit, particularly among law schools' which operate at the low cost due to the lack of expensive labs and projects. For example, New England Law's Dean (in fact a CEO) is paid about $873,000 per year. It is a school with a modest academic reputation, whose graduates end up as local legal practitioners. By comparison, the dean at the University of Michigan Law School, a constant top-10 institution in the country, made only $412,000 in 2013. It is evident who is profiting most from the for profit model and practice of colleges (Campos 2014:68).

As far as privatized prisons are concerned, even if the public and private sectors are cost-wise equivalent (as many studies prove it), one can argue against privatization on the grounds that—assuming it costs less—it enables greater expansion of the prison system and therefore may increase incarceration and hinder the search for alternative penal policies (Volokh 2014). Today in 2014, American society (the leader of Western Civilization in income) has a very sad image: 2.5 million people are in prison, 12-14 million are arrested every year, 30 are killed every day, and 75 million out of 316 million have a criminal record (CNN 8-17-2014). Therefore, civilians—innocent or guilty—are far more likely to be shot by police in America than in any other rich country in the world.

The process of developing common good for the society was one of main issues of several societal revolutions in the last 200 plus years. It is a measurement of the degree of the civilization development of a given society. Very often the Scandinavian countries are a prime example of people with the highest index of life happiness since the common good is at the center of their governments' legislation and execution. As has been the case in the past five years, that distinction[46] goes to countries that enjoy peace, freedom, good healthcare, quality education, a functioning political system and plenty of opportunity: Norway, Sweden, Canada and New Zealand (Helman 2013). Off course, the taxes are high in those countries, but life's happiness is not cheap, and perhaps it is worth its price. In other countries of Western Civilization profit is more important than society's happiness.

THE CULTURAL SYMPTOMS OF THE DECLINE OF WESTERN CIVILIZATION IN THE 21ST CENTURY

Culture is composed of the values and symbols that control the role models in society. Culture is expressed in behaviors in language, television, media, tourism, sports, art, fashion, music, film, and the like. Mass access to media, the Internet, cinemas and music events have transformed the 19th century elitist culture into the 21st century mass culture (pop culture).

---

[46] The saddest, least prosperous war-ravaged countries under the thumb of greedy despots and theocrats, where freedom of expression is limited, education nonexistent, violence the norm: Chad, Congo, Central African Republic, Afghanistan and Yemen (Helman 2013).

From the standpoint of the access to culture, this is a beneficial process, but on account of its mass scale, culture has lowered its quality in order to cater to and satisfy the lowest tastes.

Culture has become great business, particularly concerning film making, music (including singing), sports and fashion. In order to win a large public, the level of films and music has drastically plunged; in actuality it was adjusted to mass taste of the youths who are fascinated by crime stories, catastrophic movies and science fiction. Music is dominated by videos of half-naked soloists, singing rather poorly but presenting excellent convulsive body language.

Fashion promotes clothes or, rather, lack of clothes, particularly in male fashion, where an unbuttoned shirt without a tie is a rule. Politicians are now conforming to the fashion: the President of the United States can appear at a parade of the officers of the Navy (greatly clothed in beautiful official uniforms) looking as if he had just left the bathroom and was just about to get dressed. This style among the luminaries is geared at showing that they are cool. Alas, rather than promoting a style, they themselves yield to a vulgarized fashion and in so doing they only deepen the processes of the debasement of culture.

In terms of language, it is beneficial to use English as the international language, which facilitates global communication. Unfortunately this language is also becoming degraded, particularly among the young, who can communicate with clusters of a few words, particularly such ones as *good, exciting, cool, fun, and f...ck.*

Easy access to arms by the American society means that about 300 million weapons are now owned by individuals, the effect being at least 10,000 deaths annually or 27 people daily. The total of those killings by American civilians following 1945 is in excess of the aggregate casualties of both world wars and other wars the US fought among American soldiers. The extremely effective lobby of the *National Rifle Association* (N.R.A) blocks any legislation to limit access to arms, including machine guns, that is, military weapons. This is also why there are more and more shooting sprees in schools, cinemas, shopping malls and even in hospitals. This is undoubtedly influenced by mass "upbringing" of male youths by computer games and films, where murder is the main action. A question arises whether this culture of violence is supposed to safeguard the functioning of peaceful democracy.

Certainly, these degraded models of "cultured behavior" are controlled by the values of the Global Civilization: that is, counting everything in money and fun.

One effect of this mass culture is that society has become too debilitated to face vital challenges of civilization and the solution of the problems is being left for others. It is easier to rule such people, which is what the authorities of totalitarian systems noticed long ago and hence encouraged alcoholism.

The development of mass culture (violence) is growing and there are no signs showing that rock musicians or scandalizing actors are to cease being key role models. Intellectuals, writers, professors, prominent engineers, doctors – people of knowledge and wisdom – are ignored in this type of culture. Sure, nobody takes rock celebrities, politicians who emulate them or Hollywood stars seriously. Who then is a rank and file citizen supposed to trust?

THE POLITICAL SYMPTOMS OF THE DECLINE OF WESTERN CIVILIZATION IN THE 21ST CENTURY

The present political and economic system is characterized by solutions suitable for the 19th (when population was small) rather than the 21st century;

I. The national policy of constant economic growth to secure new jobs for the systematically growing population, which is growing owing to this policy, is leading to the problem of overpopulation and a vicious circle of self-destruction of the population.

II. The business strategy of permanently improving the methods and effectiveness of agricultural production is a fundamental paradigm of contemporary business and business schools. In consequence, it leads to a nonsensical vast concentration of businesses (as Big Business), automation, robotization, informatization and virtualization, which diminish employment in a situation where global manpower is growing.

- For example at small farms in America, after the agricultural tools are put away, the farmers leave to second and third jobs in order to keep their farms in operations. About 91 percent of all farming households depend on multiple sources of income. Receiving affordable health care, paying for their children's college, and saving for retirement are not taking place. With the majority of American farmers working at a loss — the median farm income was negative $1,453 in 2012 — farmers can barely keep the chickens fed and the lights on (Smith 2014).

III. The national policy of deindustrialization by off shore manufacturing, and eventually one of bringing back manufacturing in automated and robotized factories, diminishes the middle class and employment and by supporting the development of a service economy, based on low pay, limits the consumer power and puts the state into structural crisis.

IV. The national practiced "invisible" policy of supporting the rich by tax reliefs of all sorts (under so called tax loops) who supposedly provide jobs leads to huge political bifurcation of the society which is not in the long-term sustainable.

- A 2011 study by the CBO found that the top earning 1 percent of households increased their income by about 275% after federal taxes and income transfers over a period between 1979 and 2007, compared to a gain of just under 40% for the 60 percent in the middle of America's income distribution (CBO 2011). In 2012, the gap between the richest 1 percent[47] and the remaining 99 percent was the widest it is been since the 1920s when the Great Crisis began (Weisman 2013) (Figure 5.7).
- The gap between rich and poor lessened after World War II as labor unions discussed and achieved better pay and benefits and as the government ratified a minimum wage and other policies to support the poor and middle class in their mobility up.

---

[47] The top 1 percent of American households had pretax income above $394,000 in 2012.

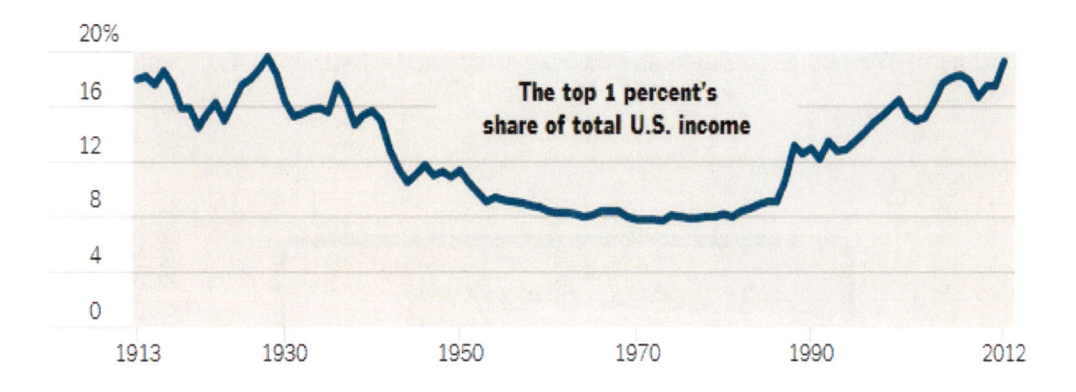

Sources: Tax Policy Center; White House Office of Management and Budget.
Figure 5.7. History repeats itself, since inequality[48] during the Great Depression in the 1930s is again at the same level in 2012.

This assessment of the plight of economic conditions is not reflected in the policies of the establishment parties, either ruling or in active opposition in both the developed and developing countries. It was until recently taken for granted that in democratic systems politics leads to rational solutions that benefit societies.

In the 21st century there are 196 countries in the world, out of which 85%, that is, 167 countries, practice the democratic system.[49] In the nations of Western Civilization, democracy has become pseudo-democracy, as the ruling classes are global financial institutions. Worse, several billionaires try to push for their doctrines as the only acceptable solutions to social and economic crises, with the parties they sponsor accepting these doctrines as their agendas. The political process is now about how fast a party can come to power (including the tycoon becoming the president), and how fast its leaders can get rich as a result of executing this power. Obviously, there are some countries, such as the Scandinavian ones, where these practices are foreign.

Following a political takeover, the triumphant parties forgot about their electoral agendas and implement policies dictated by lobbyists and sponsors of primaries within parties where the funds donated are not limited by the US Supreme Court. In Europe, the political process still has some persuasive legal accessories, but they are less and less effective. This kind of situation is getting rather worse, and there is no indication that this can be improved soon.

THE IMPACT OF RISING GLOBAL CIVILIZATION ON WESTERN CIVILIZATION IN THE 21ST CENTURY FROM WESTERN TO WESTERN-GLOBAL CIVILIZATION

Despite of the push of the global financial elite towards the globalized world, Global Civilization (Figure 5.8) makes this world more economically flat (Friedman 2005) which to

---

[48] In his best-selling "Capital in the Twenty-First Century," the French economist Thomas Piketty (2014) proposes that inequality could be tempered by returning to the tax rates of the past. Confiscatory taxes of excess incomes are, he says, "an American invention." If we could raise top tax rates to nearly 80 percent once, why couldn't we do it again?

[49] http://www.worldatlas.com/nations.htm, Retrieved 12.23.2012.

certain degree corrects the brutality of colonialism. Therefore, according to some positions, the decline of Western Civilization and the rise of Oriental Civilizations is socially justified and positive.

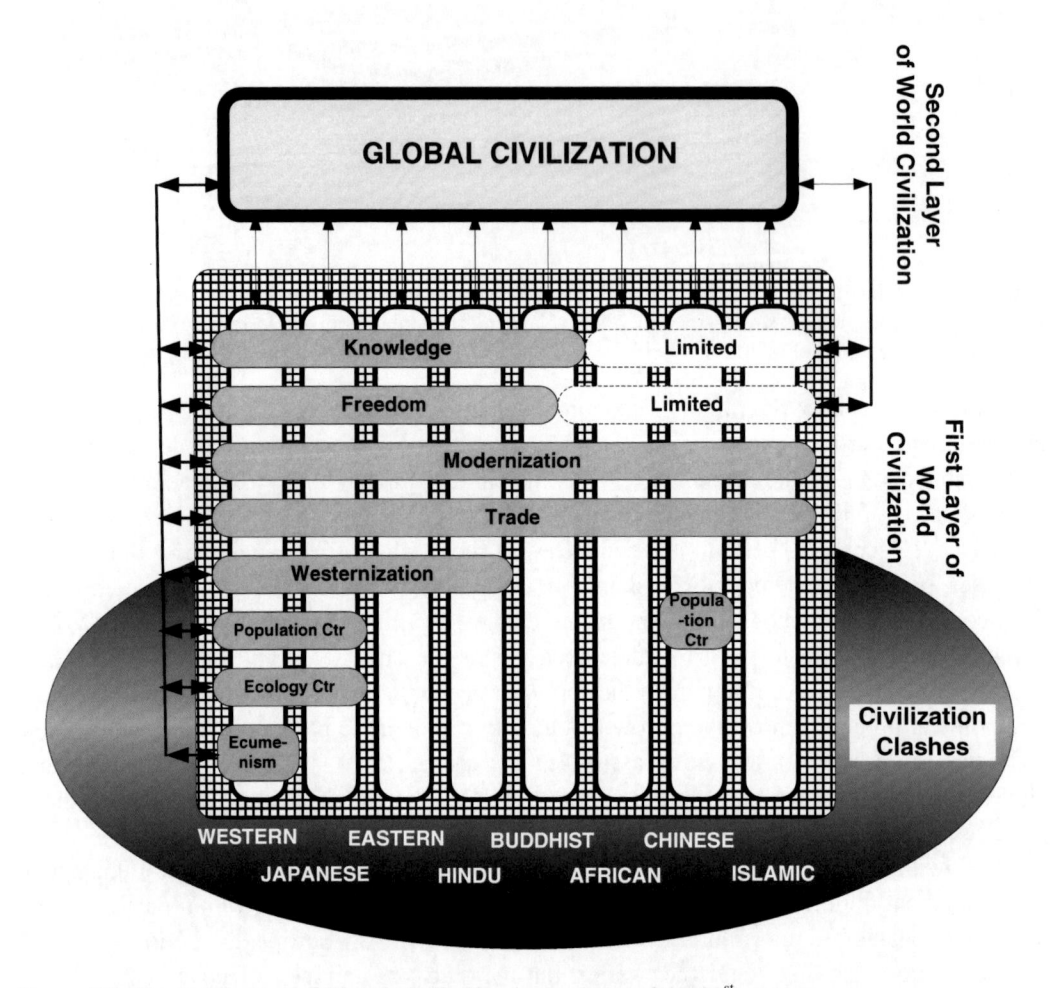

Figure 5.8. The architecture of Global civilization in the dawn of the 21st century.

In terms of economic progress globalization provides the following impact on Western Civilization:

1. Globalization has brought large economic gains to many parts of the world, above all to Asia, which has successfully exploited the ladder of development created by Western labor-intensive manufactures that outsource production to Asia.
2. Unemployment, social degeneration and difficulty of competition are the killer disadvantages on the quality of life for people in developed Western nations.
3. Some companies want to build factories in other countries because environmental laws are not as strict as they are at home. Poor countries in the Third World may have to cut down more trees so that they can sell wood to richer countries.

4. OECD's study in May 2013 said the richest 10 percent of society in OECD countries pocketed 9.5 times as much market income as the poorest 10 percent in 2010, up from 9 times in 2007. It also stated that the widest gap between rich and poor was found in Chile, Mexico, Turkey and the United States. By contrast, Iceland, Slovenia, Norway and Denmark were the most egalitarian societies (Wealth Gap 2013).
5. Inequality hardens Western society into a class system. Inequality divides people from one another in schools, in neighborhoods, at work, on airplanes, in hospitals, in what we eat, in the condition of our bodies, in what we think, in our children's futures, and in how we die. Inequality makes it harder to imagine the lives of others (Packer 2011).

The impact of globalization on Western Civilization's culture is seen as a blend of the heterogeneous and homogenous, or a "globalization" of sorts. Globalization can be understood as the development of hybrid cultures at the local level, as foreign cultures reach local soil, such as in the creation of fusion cuisine or music. In the 21st century, this impact has been felt in American movies, where foreign films like *The Departed* are remade for the U.S. market (Big Question 2013).

One of the most common arguments against globalization is that it forces American culture onto the world, Westernizing other nations. Will everyone one day wear blue jeans and eat at McDonald's? We don't know. Globalization can work both ways: Even American blue jeans were forged from different cultures. They were developed by a German immigrant; their denim comes from the name of the French town where it originated (de Nimes); and "jeans" comes from "Genes," a name used to describe a style of pants inspired by the pants worn by Geneon sailors (Legrain 2003).

THE IMPACT OF RISING VIRTUAL CIVILIZATION ON WESTERN-GLOBAL CIVILIZATION IN THE 21ST CENTURY FROM WESTERN TO WESTERN-GLOBAL-VIRTUAL CIVILIZATION

Virtual Civilization (Targowski 2014b) has transformed from the Virtual Wave into Virtual Civilization due to the advancements in info-communication technology in the 21st century, exemplified by the ability of the Internet to secure operations of virtual organizations and social networks. Therefore one can characterize the Virtual Civilization as the infrastructural character. The mission of Virtual Civilization is to control public policy of other real civilizations to secure common good in these real societies. At least such a mission has been exemplified in the practice of some virtual communities at the dawn of the 21st century.

The quest for the common good by virtual society may limit or even replace the Western model of representative democracy by direct democracy which eventually will solve positively a few good policies but may also trigger permanent political chaos in real civilizations.

The impressing many e-communications among people from different parts of the world diminishes local interrelations and intensifies connectivity among international and/or distant, parochial cultures, which eventually separates, isolates and alienates individuals in their real living places.

At this time it is very improbable that virtual society can be regulated by real society. It means that Virtual civilization on the one hand can be positive and on the another hand can be harmful for humanity which lives in falling civilization due to overpopulation, super-consumerism, depletion of strategic resources and environmental degradation.

Since each civilization is characterized by a religion, a religion of virtuality is one which "preaches" the value of unlimited freedom, cyberspace, and progress supported by collective intelligence in order to secure the common good in an alternative virtual world, since the "real" one has been going in the wrong direction during the 21st century.

The power of the virtuality religion is generated by *collective intelligence* which has infinite ability (since "the cyberspace is the limit") to develop and share among virtuality members that have a strong capacity for solving problems, based on word-wide retrievable knowledge and wisdom, kept in digital format.

As far as virtuality versus reality is concerned, one can state that a virtual life is easier than a real life, but it is really no life at all (Kite 2009). Since relationships between people who never see, touch, smell, or hear each other cannot be truly supportive, intimate, truthful and lasting. Communication and co-ordination in the virtual world is, however easy, cheap, fast, and global; therefore it is a new and lasting tool to impact social identity, governance, community and the society at large. The virtual world became in the 21st century a new landscape of social life in Virtual civilization as the parallel one to Real civilization. The use of virtual functions (applications) should take place depending on the real world's needs to improve its *modus operandi* today and in the future. To secure a positive impact of the virtuality upon reality, the former's developments and operations should be publically controlled similarly as it is done in reality. The virtual society's crime and misbehavior should be judged by the real society with the application of the latter's laws. The virtuality won't disappear as long as computers and their networks are in use.

CONCLUSION

In summary one can state as follows:

1. Western civilization reached its peak in development at the end of the 20th century, but due to the self-defeating strategy of reducing the middle class through deindustrialization and off shore outsourcing manufacturing jobs, it is developing Global civilization which penetrates other contemporary civilizations and to certain degree is controlled by those civilizations.
2. Global civilization is in fact the polity of global business which Westernizes other civilizations at the same time arguing and trying to convince Western stakeholders that what is good for global business is good for the society.
3. The rapid growth of global business is using up strategic finite resources of our small planet faster, causing the civilization to eventually "stop."

4. Global Civilization producing more goods and services for a larger customer and population base will put civilization's weather climate on the catastrophic path due to increased carbon dioxide emissions.
5. Global Civilization by transferring jobs from Western Civilization to other civilizations is triggering social unrest in the former and is triggering world instability.
6. Global Civilization reduces taxation in the developed world which is resulting in deteriorating and regressing of Western infrastructure and society. A good example of this is the failure of Detroit, which is regressing from an industrial to agricultural town.
7. Global Civilization triggers the domino effect with one failure-driven country pulling other countries with it. This is a case of the Euro crisis of the European Union in the 2010s, when failing PIGS countries (Portugal, Italy, Greece, and Spain) negatively economically impact Germany, France, and others.
8. The Virtual civilization by the rapid dissemination of e-communication and the rise of virtual society at all levels may lead within former Western-Global Civilization to the transformation into Western-Global-Virtual civilization which will be able to solve some difficult societal problems but at the same time may replace the Western model of representative democracy into direct democracy leading to societal chaos.
9. These transformation processes which are driven by greed and e-technology show that humans, when they are poor, are wise and when they are better off, are stupid. Can the latter eventually be cured by better education?

REFERENCES

Big Question: How is globalization changing culture? *CULTURE AND HISTORY*. Retrieved 10/7/2012.
Bruenig, M. (2014). You call this a meritocracy? How rich inheritance is poisoning the American economy. March 24. *SALON*. Retrieved 8-15-2014.
Buchheit, P. (2013). 5 ways super-rich are betraying America. *AlertNet*, Retrieved 8-15-2014
CNN MONEY (2009). Americans' wealth drops $1.3 trillion. *CNNMoney.com*. June 11.
Campos, P. (2014). The law school scham. The Atlantic, September.
Congressional Budget Office (2011). T*rends in the distribution of household income between 1979 and 2007*. October 2011.
Grey. J. (2007). *Black mass, apocalyptic religion and the death of utopia*. New York: Farrat, Straus, Giroux.
Friedman, Th. (2005). *The world is flat*. New York: Farrar, Straus and Giroux.
Helman, Ch. (2013). The world's happiest (and saddest) countries, 2013. *Forbes*, October 29.
Kite, M. (2009). A virtual life is easier than real life, but it is really no life at all. *The Telegraph*. Retrieved 1-23-2014.
Legrain, Ph. (2003). Cultural globalization is not Americanization. *The Chronicle of Higher Education*. May 9.
Leonhart, D. and K. Quealy. (2014). The American middle class is no longer the world's richest. *New York Times*, April 22.

Miron, G. (2014). *Multiple choice: charter school performance in 16 states*. Pal Alto, CA: Center for Research on Education Outcomes (CREDO).

Murray, Ch. (2013). *Coming apart, the state of white America, 1960-2010*. New York: Crown Forum.

Padinani, A. (2013). *Anatomy of Detroit's decline*. New York Times, December 8.

Packer, G. (2011). The broken contract. *Foreign Affairs*, November/December.

Pelosi, N. (2006). *The middle class-squeeze*. Retrieved 6-15-2010.

Pikietty, Th. (2014). *capital in the twenty-first century*. Cambridge, MA & London: The Belknap Press of Harvard University Press.

Resmovitz, J. (2014). Charter school growth in Michigan brings cautionary tale on quality. *HUFFPOST DETROIT,* August 18.

Smith, A. (2011). *Americans and text messaging*. PewResearch Center. http://pewinternet.org/Reports/2011/Cell-Phone-Texting-2011.aspx. Retrieved 10-12-2012.

Smith (2014). *Don't let your children grow up to be farmers*. New York Times, August 9.

Targowski, A. (1982). *Red fascism*. Lawrenceville, Virginia: Brunswick.

Targowski, A. (2014a). *The global civilization in the 21st century*. New York: NOVA Science Publishers.

Targowski, A. (2014b). *The virtual civilization in the 21st century*. New York: NOVA Science Publishers.

Volokh, S. (2014). Are private prisons better or worse than public prisons? *Washington Post*, February 24.

Wealth gap widens in rich countries as austerity threatens to worsen inequality: OECD. *The Huffington Post*. Retrieved 14 May 2013.

Williams, C.J. (2012). Euro crisis imperils recovering global economy, OECD warns. *Los Angeles Times*. Retrieved June 15, 2012.

Wiseman, P. (2013). "Richest 1 percent earn biggest share since '20s." apnews.excite.com/article/20130910/DA8NN7U02.html, Retrieved 8-14-2014.

Wolf, E. N. and M. Gittleman (2011). *Inheritance and the distribution of wealth or whatever happened to the great inheritance boom*? Washington, DC: U.S. Department of Labor.

Part II.
Globalizing and Virtualizing Culture and Infrastructure

Chapter 6

CULTURE FRAGMENTATION OF WESTERN-GLOBAL-VIRTUAL CIVILIZATION

ABSTRACT

The *purpose* of this investigation is to define how culture fragmentation and the state of modus operandi impact the decline of Western civilization in the 21st century. The *methodology* is based on an interdisciplinary big-picture view of several cultural ways which Western, Global, and Virtual civilization function. Among the *findings* are: 25 specific cultures can be grouped in 4 major cultures. *Practical implication:* The biggest impacts on the decline of Western civilization are seven specific cultures, such as: folk, popular, mass, pop, global, middle, and hybrid. *Social implication:* It is difficult to reverse this declining process in a democracy in which there is also deterioration. *Originality:* This investigation is conducted through a big picture versus small picture view at the level of synthesis. The focus is placed on the role of "entertainment culture" in this declining process.

INTRODUCTION

The purpose of this investigation is to analyze the impact Western culture fragmentation on Western-Global-Virtual civilization in the 21st century. Culture is a very important element of civilization which reflects society's response to its challenges along political, economic, military, social and other lines. Culture is comprised of the beliefs, values and symbol-driven patterned behaviors of people and institutions dealing with all sorts of challenges, both spiritually and materially, facing them. Since civilization is about 6000 years old culture also stretches the same time span. Western civilization is about 1200 years (thus, so is its culture), although has deep roots in Classical civilization (Greek and Roman) which began about the 8th century B.C.E. Unfortunately its impact on the future European civilization was interrupted for 300 years in the Dark Ages which took place after the fall of Western Roman Empire in 476 C.E.. In those times the state was reduced almost to a vanishing idea, and the Classical culture of citizenship and public law were turned off.

THE RISE OF WESTERN CULTURE

Formally, Western culture began function once Western civilization was born in the 8th century when the Carolingian Empire was born as the home for the newly rising Christian religion which promoted Christian values. Ever since, the complex and far reaching relations have powerfully connected Western culture with Christianity. A different process took place in China where Confucianism defined a secular social order and likewise in India, where the caste system did the same. Surprisingly that secular order created a closed, stagnant society in these countries, and today they are the largest and relatively poorest in the world. On the other hand, Christianity in Europe, with some religious obstacles (such as dogmas and Inquisition) along the way, allowed for the development of a Humanist culture. Particularly since the Renaissance (15th century) and Enlightment (18th century), Western culture began developing open-minded values, symbols and patterns of human and institutional behavior in solving all sorts of problems.

One of strong key features of Western culture is its missionary character allowing for the transmission of Western spiritual movements from one people to another and from one nation to another even penetrating other civilizations. From the very beginning of Christianity in Europe, it came from the Hellenic cities of the Levant (Palestine, Jordan, Lebanon, and Cyprus). After the fall of Western Roman Empire this transmission took place from Western provinces to the barbarian people in the North, reaching Gaul (Frankish Empire), Ireland (St. Patrick's mission), England, German and Dutch pagans, and Belgium.

Fortunately for its further development, the spread of Western cultural leadership was parallel to the extension of its political power and dominance which was one of the main factors that produced freedom and the dynamic activities of Western culture (Dawson 1950:18).

The rise of Western culture took place during the reign of Charlemagne (c.742-814) and his successors who stimulated a religious, intellectual and artistic renaissance. Dozens of monasteries, cathedrals, and palaces were built in this period, particularly north of the Loire in France, in Germany and in Italy. Schools and scriptoria were established in the monasteries. Some of 8,000 manuscripts from this period are still extant; thanks to them, numerous classical authors have been saved from oblivion.

In the 10th – 13th century Monasticism was defining a way of life, distinct from that of laymen and clerics living in the community. It characterized the main feature of Christianity which impacted the society and its *modus operendi*. The Benedictine order, the leading order since the 6th century, was contested by the Dominican order. The latter was more effective in combating rising heresy and the promotion of the spiritual value of poverty as a reaction to the growth in the wealth of the monasteries and of the church. This followed the rules established by St. Augustine (354-430) who preached "*a City of God and City of Man*" which separated religion from secular governing (an became the rule for Western culture up to the present) and St. Francis (c.1181-1226) who devoted his life to poverty. Today Pope Francis (1936-) practices a similar way of life in the 21st century.

In those times the West was rapidly expanding to the East and simultaneously was confronting the Easterners coming to Europe like Islam (in Spain), the Slavs and Magyar paganism, and the Great Schism (1054) in Christian Orthodoxy and Jewish isolationism. It triggered an attitude of social exclusion, which was also directed against the poor, lepers, prostitutes, and homosexuals. This attitude is still present in Western culture, more visible in bad times when the native habitants protect their territory and resources. The First Crusade (1096-1099) in the Near East (Anatolia, Palestine) was accompanied by numerous pogroms, which were attributed to Christian anti-Judaism; there was as not yet anti-Semitism as we know it today.

The number of towns in Western Europe in the Middle Ages grew rapidly. Many sprang up along the sides of the road on the trading routes. War between barbarian tribes had declined, but there were many bandits. Towns were more of a grouping of traders, each with a permanent shop: that is, traders who had banded together to protect themselves from outside attack. There were some inns to house travelers, and some stables to take care of the horses, and maybe a doctor or two. In spite of bad sanitary conditions, more and more people arrived in the towns, eager to escape their life as serfs on the manors (Doon - 2014). But towns provided space for worship, places for displaying arts in churches and expensive buildings, and sponsors for arts.

Approximately 1000 C.E. is beginning of Romanesque architecture and art. The name of this trend is based on the Roman accomplishments which in this time were expanded and improved. New materials like stones were used to construct large scale buildings with large arches. In church art, a harmony of color was designed to synchronize with the liturgical chant. Gold and silver and illuminations represent the most precious expression of the spirituality of the times.

The transfer of learning from monasteries to city schools also transferred the content of learning from objects to intellectual activities at rising universities. This trend was reflected in the rising Gothic style of architecture whose characteristics included the pointed arch, the beamed vault and the flying reinforcement. Gothic architecture is most familiar as the architecture of many of the great cathedrals, abbeys and churches of Europe (Figure 6.1). It is also the architecture of many castles, palaces, town halls, guild halls, universities and to a less prominent extent, private dwellings.

Figure 6.1. Gothic architecture; Cathedral of Reims (France) and Rheinstein Castle (Germany). (Photo: Wikipedia).

During the late Middle Ages, Italy was positioned in the middle of many important trading routes between the Near East and the rest of Western Europe. With increased trade between east and west, pioneered by sea traders such as Marco polo, Italy developed a prosperous commercial sector. By the end of the 14th century, the city of Florence, in Italy's central-north, had established itself as the center of the European wool industry. Prosperous textile merchants, such as the Medici family were the beneficiaries of this successful industry. Along with other well-to-do families, they began investing their money in the banking sector to increase the revenue they were gaining from trade. As the result, Florence had also grown into the center of European finance.

Table 6.1. Major cultural contribution provided by key social events in the last 500 years

Key events	Century	Contribution	State of contribution in the 21st century
Geographical Discoveries	15-16	Open world, slavery, and natural resources drainage	Same view on geography
Era of Merchants	15-16	Trade, wealth, and arts sponsorship	Similar standards
Renaissance	15-16	Beautiful art and architecture, High Culture, Folk Culture, and open mind	Similar standards
Scientific Revolution	16-17	Truth about the Universe	Similar views
Protestant Reformation	16	Modesty and work ethics	Same standards
English Revolution	1688	Parliament and legal rights of real estate owners	Similar standards
English and French Colonialism	18	Colonial imperialism and wealthy upper class's life style	Capital imperialism
Enlightment	18	Reason, freedom, tolerance	Similar standards
American Revolution	1765-1783	Freedom, democracy, individualism	Same standards
French Revolution	1789-1799	Citizenship, freedom, equality, popular cowboy culture	Same standards
Industrial Revolution	19	Engine, electricity, products, capital, High vs Low Cultures, life poetry, nationalism, racism, liberty challenge, liberalism, conservatism, idealism, socialism, Marxism, science of society, dissolving certainties.	Same standards
Technological Revolution	20	Mobility, productivity, High Culture, Popular Culture, Folk Culture, technology supporting culture, decadence, elite theory, intellectual freedom, existentialism, Man depersonalization,	Same attitudes
Information Wave	21	Networked society, unlimited digital freedom, super-consumerism, multiculturalism, post-modern culture, technology conquering culture, solving social problems by technology	Confused options

These merchants (or traders) became the new 'rich' class, steadily captivating power and status away from the nobility (the land-owning upper class). In this class of merchants, fortune was usually held within families. One such rich family was the Medici family, the most esteemed of all the merchant families of Renaissance Italy. They held a great scope of power and impact in the city of Florence for a substantial part of the 15th and 16th centuries. The Medici family was also the patrons of some of Italy's most famous artists and intellectuals. Lorenzo de Medici sponsored some of the most significant artists and inventors of the Renaissance, including Leonardo da Vinci and Michelangelo Buonarroti.

It was the Era of Merchants but also it was the Era of Artists, since society had wealthy members who sponsored the needed income of artists. This business model of art is applied nowadays.

In the Middle Ages Western culture was developing by the church and wealthy merchants and mostly took place in rising towns. This cultural triangle was changed during the Modernity Ages, which were triggered by the Italian Renaissance and the Scientific Revolution. Table 6.1 characterizes the major stages of Western culture development till the 21st century.

As the effect of these legacies of Western Cultural development in the last 500 years, one can recognize many platforms of culture as it is defined in Figure 6.2.

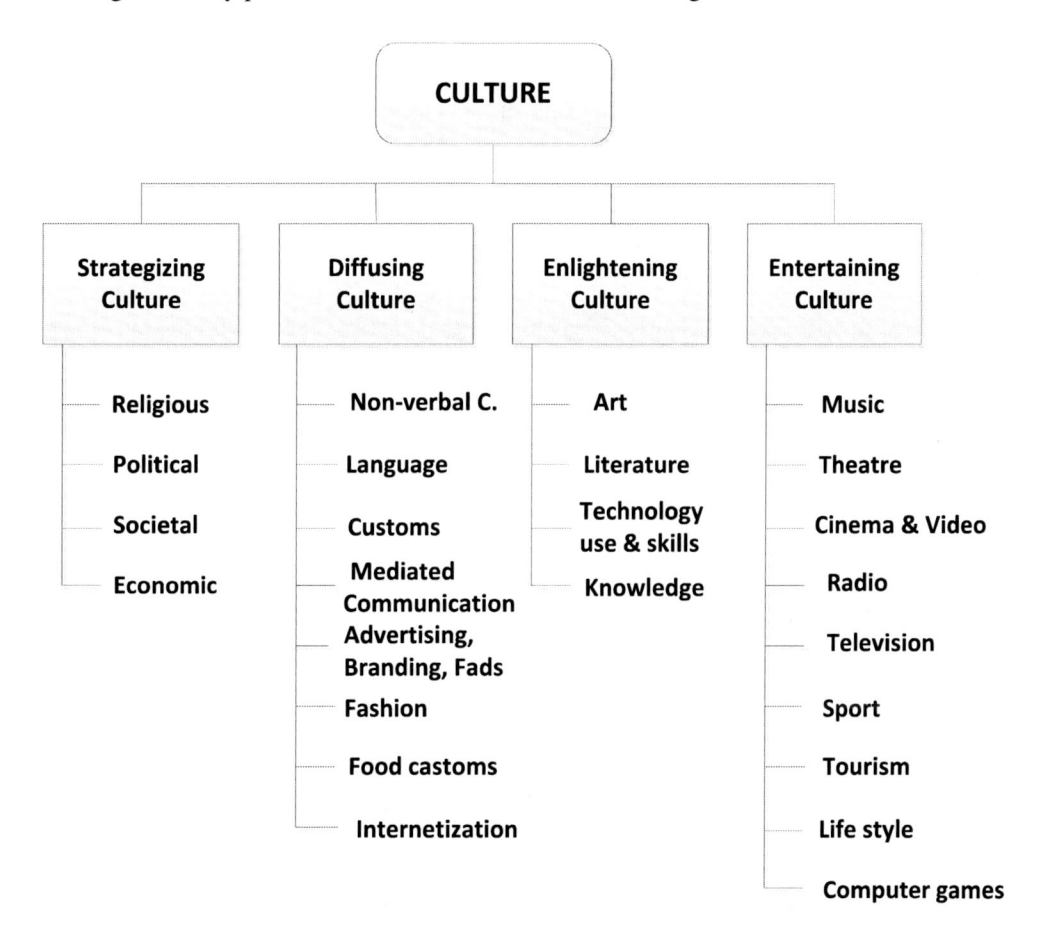

Figure 6.2. The platforms of Western culture in the 21st century.

Further in this investigation the focus will be put mostly on entertaining culture and in addition to some others such as painting, language, fashion, advertising, and Internetization that is manifested in everyday life of society. This is most visible culture which sets the tone for society's way of living.

MULTI- FORCUTION OF WESTERN ENTERTAINING CULTURE IN THE 21ST CENTURY

Entertainment and some other kinds of Western culture are developing and function in the following six key areas in Western civilization in the 21st century:

- *High culture* - the set of cultural products and services, mainly in the arts (painting, music, theatre, and opera), held in the highest esteem by a culture. It is the culture of an upper class such as an aristocracy, plutocracy, and intelligentsia.
- *Folk Culture* – local values, fashion, music, crafts, customs, food dishes, dinks of the lower class people which are the counter-parts to the concurrently developing High culture of the landlords and rich merchants.. This is rooted in regional/national identity.
- *Popular culture* - the totality of ideas, perspectives, attitudes, memes, images, and other phenomena that have been within the mainstream of Western culture since the beginning of the 20th century through the dawn of 21st century. Pop culture is profoundly impacted by mass media like television, which sets the ways of acting.
- *Mass culture* –a commercial culture, mass-produced for mass consumption driven by mass media. It is the marketing machine. This may be compared to American and West European culture. Its goal is to provide large markets for products and services that can (or should) be consumed as broadly as possible, and as the result, to bring large profits for business. Mass culture comes under heavy disapproval from religious and old-timer groups which perceive it as shallow, consumerist, melodramatic, and degraded. This culture is in some contexts a synonym of popular culture.
- *Pop-culture* – conveys non-traditional forms of popular culture where one such form is counter-culture. Pop-culture became fashionable in the second part of the 20th century and in the 21st century. Since the 1950s one can distinguish such periods of social change as *the Big Band era, the Rock era, the Beatles era, hippie era, the Woodstock era, the disco era, the punk era, the hip-hop era, the video era, the rappers era, sexuality & drug era, Twitter-Facebook era, computer games era, the casual dress era* and so forth. Some of these eras take place concurrently.
- *Global culture* – this includes recognizable symbols like "CNN," "Wall Street Journal," "Martini," and values; instant electronic communications (i-phones, e-mail), the Internet, the "dollar/euro" in international businesses and banks, and behavior; speaking English (Globish") and Western dress code. This is a new layer upon the national culture layer applied during professional (business, education, sport, art, etc.) dealings with people abroad or at home. In effect, global culture

makes the world like a "global village" which makes it appear as though the world is "shrinking" every day.
- *Middle culture* – the adapted values of assimilated immigrants, symbols, and behavior from the national culture of the country where they have settled. It is a blend of at least two cultures or even more if a family has multi-cultural roots.
- *Complementary culture* – reflects a set of complementary values from contemporary civilizations which is aimed at promoting tolerance and peace world-wide. Table 6.2 specifies this universal set of values.
- *Hybrid culture* – integrated set of such cultures as; national, middle, global, and complementary. Figure 6.3 illustrates this kind of culture which is sometimes practiced in the 21st century in Western civilization as well as others (Targowski 2014:157).

Table 6.2. The Common Universal – Complementary Values of Universal Civilization of a World Citizen

Civilization	contributed values
African	Ancestral Connection
Buddhist	Morality
Eastern	Self-sacrifice
Hindu	Moderation
Islamic	Reward and Penalty
Japanese	Cooperation and Nature Cult
Chinese	Authority Cult
Western	Freedom and Technology
Global	Free Flow of Ideas, Goods, Services and People according to *Pax Orbis*
Universal-complementary	Wisdom, Goodness, Access, Dialogue, Agreement (on main principles), Forgiveness upon Condition, Human and Civil Rights, International Law, Green and Self-sustainable Planet

Each of these kinds of culture has some impact upon the declining Western civilization in the 21st century.

CULTURE'S IMPACT ON DECLINING WESTERN CIVILIZATION IN THE 21ST CENTURY

Western High Culture in the 21st Century

High culture is the culture of the elite and its development and functioning is supported by a well off aristocracy, plutocracy and intelligentsia. Since the 19th century it has had an international character since it is the agglomerate of contributions made by geniuses of painting, music, theater/opera, and film coming from different countries. Among them are artists such as: Rembrandt, Rafael, van Gogh, Picasso, Dali, Bach, van Beethoven, Mozart,

Chopin, Liszt, Tchaikovsky, Rachmaninoff, Gershwin, Shakespeare, Goethe, Verdi, Puccini, Offenbach, Strauss, Chaplin, Bergman, De Sica, Fellini, Goddard, Lucas, Hitchcock, Cameron, Spielberg, Allen, Wajda, Polanski, and others.

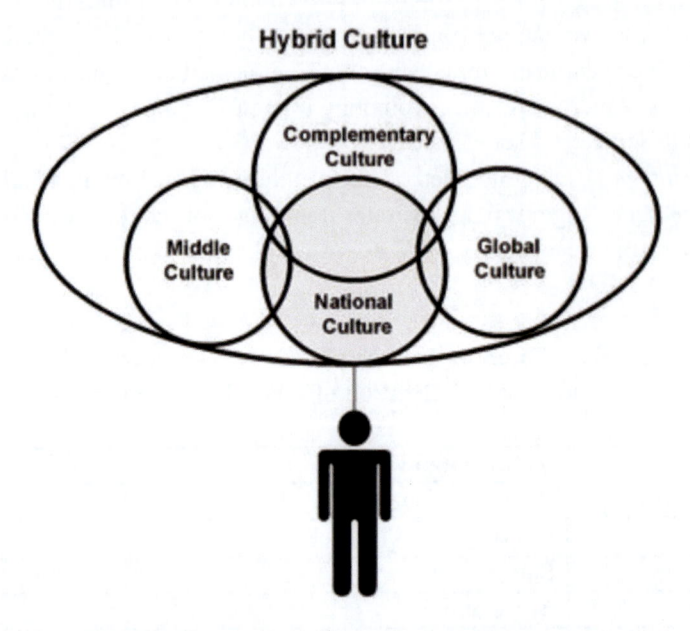

Figure 6.3. A concept of hybrid culture in the 21st century to secure cultural diversity, universality, and belonging.

Figure 6.4. High culture (symphony concert and opera house in Paris) sustains Western Civilization in the 21st century.
(Photo: Wikipedia).

The peak of High culture's contributions was about 200+ years ago while today these contributions are in use as the mark of good taste. Most of these contributions were created in Western civilization; therefore, High culture sustains the Westernization of society in the 21st century. But does it promote and sustain globalization? High culture always was internationally oriented not globally minded in the sense of its meaning today. If Western High culture is spreading around the world today, it is caused mostly by the Westernization of the tastes of the foreign elite who would like to experience the greatness of Western High Culture in their native countries. On the other hand, for long time American film has been globalizing since its entertaining professionalism is liked by people world-wide. This is in spite of the fact that the local film industry is suffering, as is the case of French and Italian movie industries which were well developed after World War II but today have been reduced mostly to TV serials productions. Sometimes American movies abroad are identified with American cultural imperialism. For example in the Soviet Union only American Westerns could be shown, since the Communists did not want to show local viewers American's abundant homes and life styles.

Certainly High culture does not contribute to the decline of Western civilization; rather, it sustains this civilization's Western character.

Western Folk Culture in the 21st Century

The folk culture of Western civilization in the 21st century is strong and active at all levels: local, regional, national (Figure 6.5), and international. The latter three are manifested in the form of all kinds of festivals, some supported by special funds. Folk culture is practiced by families, communities, towns, cities, regions and so forth. On the other hand, at the neighborhood level one can notice a slight decline of folk culture, particularly among the younger generation.

Figure 6.5. Carnival in Rio (Brazil) and grilled hamburgers are examples of Western Folk culture practiced in the 21st century.
(Photo: Wkikipedia.org).

Young people are obsessed with texting electronic friends who far away from them. They are curious about foreign settings and affairs and dream about hearing what is going on there. In the long-term this kind of folk culture will decline and a certain form of isolation will rise, causing many negative effects like problems with dating and marriages as well as suffering depression and other illnesses. Texting has a tremendous impact on young people who constantly send e-texts to their peers (about 100-150 per day), which becomes an addiction and waste of otherwise time spent on learning and more valued activities. Texting while driving is becoming more prevalent even if it results in paying a ticket or accidents and death (Figure 6.6).

Figure 6.6. "Click it or ticket".
(Photo: www.newsadvance.com).

On the other hand, Western Folk culture under the form of American culture penetrates other civilizations and Western cultures with the grill and fast food meals.

Western Popular Culture in the 21st Century

Western Popular culture of the Affluent society in the 21st century is gearing towards the "Nice society" (Lerner 1980) where the most important value is comfort, fun and taking easy life challenges. The current generation of Westerners, particularly Americans, has quietly assimilated a new human right - the right to be constantly entertained - which is loaded upon us by the mass media and the Internet, transmitting all sorts of business-motivated entertainments. This has modified the old Western level of needs, aspirations, satisfactions, and the criteria of judgment and choice which successfully work in society. The consequence of this new attitude is the misbehavior of young people (even at the criminal level) as the result of movies, comics and poor taste-oriented TV serials loaded with violence (Lerner 1980).

The Nice society also applies a politically correct attitude, agreeing with the idea that people should be careful to not use language or behave in a way that could offend a particular group of people, particularly not touching sensitive issues of politics, sex and race. Politically correct thinking has done more damage to the reality of politics, business and education than any other cultural trend in current times (Figure 6.7). A new generation of politically correct leaders who assume that they have a moral and ethical responsibility to be politically correct are carelessly leading to the moral and ethical deterioration of Western society.

To have fun first one must secure comfort in life. To achieve this way of life, for example a typical goal of the young generation in Germany is to be employed by government, have a BMW car, and go on 6 week vacations at the Mediterranean Sea. With such an attitude young people lose entrepreneurial spirit and aim low instead of high.

Greg Lukianoff, the author of *Unlearning Liberty*, was interviewed in *The Wall Street Journal* on the subject of politically correct speech in colleges and universities. Lukianoff, the president of the Foundation for Individual Rights in Education, is alarmed by the loss of free speech on university campuses. He says baby boomers who remember universities as institutions of free thinking would not recognize today's schools. Where once there was freedom of speech, now there are strict speech codes determined by extreme political correctness (Williams 2013).

The current Western Popular culture meaningfully contributes to the decay of Western Civilization in the 21st century since it makes the truth a relative judgment. In this way it eliminates truthful feedback from society and becomes the "blind society" losing its awareness and directions for being sustainable and well off in reality and world's matters.

Figure 6.7. Is the truth politically correct?
(Photo: www.styleonsite.com and www.christianstandard.com).

Western Mass Culture in the 21st Century

Western Mass Culture is controlled by big business and media is supported by streaming business commercials. To be able to constantly buy the new generation of gadgets (like iPhones) or new collections of clothing, the consumers must have easy credit provided by banks and credit cards businesses. Eventually, consumers with illusionary buying power through easy credit fall victim to the addiction of super-consumerism and debts.

The total market of consumer debt using credit cards shows our addiction to borrowed money; its level globally reached $53 trillion in 2013. If one looks at Greece as a microcosm of the bigger issue, one can realize they are treating a solvency issue as if it were a liquidity issue. Let us be sure that all of this debt will never be paid off. Since most intelligent people understand this, the banking sector is leveraging central banks to basically print money, for no person would lend money out knowing they would never be paid back. One must include in consumer debts also mortgage credit and students loans which per year are equal to credit cards debts. Therefore about 77 million Americans out of 220 million who have credit cards with a debt in collections in 2013 (Washington Post July 28, 2014).

In summary the mass culture driven by super-consumerism strategy triggers the following debts in 2014 (nerdwallet finance 2014):

- U.S. household consumer debt profile:
  - Average credit card debt: $15,480
  - Average mortgage debt: $156,474
  - Average student loan debt: $33,424

In total, American consumers owe in 2013:

- $11.74 trillion in debt (73% of the 2013 GDP), an average increase of 5% from year to year:
  - $872.2 billion in credit card debt
  - $8.24 trillion in mortgages
  - $1,131.7 billion in student loans

What does this mean? Credit card debt is holding fairly sound, but whether or not that is a good thing is up for consideration. On the one hand, higher consumer spending puts the economy on a positive growth. Higher spending leads to more jobs and higher incomes, which in turn lead to higher spending. However, if wages and employment are improving at the sluggish pace like in the 21st century, this might well be an indication that families are borrowing to make ends meet rather than a reflection of a well-founded increase in consumer sustainable confidence.

The debate on whether more credit card debt is a good thing is trivial: of course it is bad. If 10% of a consumer's monthly income goes to credit card bills, it would actually need to be increased to 25% of their monthly income to actually pay off the debt over several years, which is unsustainable due to the steady decline of income of the Middle class in the 21st century.

Western Popular culture is based on super-consumerism which in addition to putting this civilization on credit card debt has also increased the pace of depleting strategic resources which eventually may be the ruin of this civilization and perhaps others as well (Figure 6.8). Already Western civilization uses the Eco-system twice much it should be since it spends about 8 gha/capita of the bio-capacity instead 4 gha/per capita (ecological footprint-2014).

Figure 6.8. Western Popular culture through super-consumerism is deteriorating citizens' health. (Photo: www.eco-say.com).

Western Pop Culture in the 21st Century

Pop culture is nonconforming. It is a culture by people for the people from the same social class. It contrasts to old-fashioned other cultures, for it rejects both the authority of customs and conventional rules as well as the affectations of intellectual inclinations within High culture represented by such great artists as Rembrandt, Michelangelo, Bach, and Shakespeare. In pop culture one does not have to dress up to listen to the symphonic music and sit silently or visit the Metropolitan museum and not touch any artifact.

Pop culture is not popular culture or folk culture since the latter transpires from specific places like the Indian community, Black churches, Amish farms, Louisiana cuisine, Southern cooking, Creole folklore, Marlboro county, Country style, Basque folklore, Alpine folklore, German folklore, Dutch folklore, Polish folklore, Hungarian folklore and so forth. Folk culture reflects the *particular* (Outsborne 2013:2). In divergence, popular culture reflects the *attitude*; mass culture reflects the *corporate standards* (McDonald's Big Mac). While Western pop culture reflects *authenticity, spontaneity*, and *democracy* (Outsborne 2013:2), it can also be a form of counter-culture in a protest to the elite's political culture and well-being. It also reflects nostalgia for better times or the lost past. It reflects the voice of the poor against of the rich as it does in rap lyrics. To certain degree it reflects the clash between "high" and "low" culture from the times of the Industrial Revolution and its Bourgeoisie versus Workers class conflicts.

In the 21st century pop culture reached the following intensities almost at the level of life vulgarization:

- *Music* – the Hard Rock, Rap and Techno Era is limited to the 40 radio hits which are eclectic, where words are more important than music and where instead of listening, one should watch it to see Lady Gaga's costumes or Madonna's moves. The most popular vocalists such as Tupac Shakur, Eminen, Jay-Z, and the Beastie Boys sell albums in tens of millions as big business. Apple's iTunes are almost constantly heard by young people who look possessed by that "music without melody" (Figure 6.9).

Figure 6.9. Rock concerts will make you deaf playing music without melody! (Photo: www.thehealth side.com) .

- *Cinema and Video* – movies are produced mostly for audiences 15-40 and are full of action scenes, mostly computer-made, and violence. Among such films are: Ichi the Killer (2001), The Haunted World of El Superbeasto (2009), Machete (2010), Martyrs (2008) and so forth. Video streamed via the Internet mostly presents "Rock, drugs and sex." These media used to be art but now apply the money rule of cinema mostly showing what sells: that is, "girls and guns" as a famous French director, Jean-Luc Goddard, noticed.
- *Television* – "In Beverly Hills they don't throw their garbage away. They make it into television shows" once said Woody Allen, a sophisticated American movie director and jazzman. Today, sitcoms like "Everybody Loves Raymond" (2000) and "Will & Grace" (2000) continue to be popular. However, to cut production costs, TV networks produce reality shows where low paid amateurs share their daily activities or compete for some good prize. Among them are: "The Real Housewives of New Jersey," "The Swan," "The Will," "Megan Wants a Millionaire," "Bridezillas," "Temptation Island," "Married by America," "My Big Fat Obnoxious Finance," "Who is Your Daddy," and so forth, not to mentions "Keeping up with the Kardashians." All these productions are mostly trash.
- *Computer games* – by the time teenagers today reach the age of 20, they will spent an average of 10,000 hours playing video games (Wallace 2013:391). It is like spending 5 years being a full time employee just to play those games the whole working day. What a loss of real live. Such games develop good reaction skills and encourage constant pursuits among young people; however they build a new behavior of players who expect that life should be like a computer game: fast, clashing, engaging, and providing constant fun. Even many schools and colleges are promoting a curriculum which minimizes the content but emphasizes computer games like simulated experience. It reminds one of travel by a fast car whose driver does not know the destination. Needless to say that the particularly young male generation almost all the time plays computer games and is not interested in their looks and dating. Unfortunately what is going on in virtuality is not going in reality. This means that young computer games players are not well prepared to work and live in reality (Figure 6.10).

Figure 6.10. Should Computer games define real life?
(Photo: www.nerdraector.com and www.news.heartland.com).

- *Sport* – this is a very strong part of pop culture at all levels of age. In schools Friday football is the most important activity which is even more important than learning since it is about a school's prestige and players' popularity among teachers and girls (Figure 6.11). Therefore, American school graduates rank very low on the international indexes of learning achievements. Many of them are drop-outs either at school or later at the college level. Professional sports like football and baseball matches provide a holiday with full stadiums, liquor boxes, huge incomes and high pay which make the players behave like gods who become the spectators' icons. The current sport atmosphere reminds one of the Roman times with gladiators and the ruling policy "bread and circuses." The most watched "sport" show of WWE wrestling in particular reminds one of those gladiators' sad competitions, since wrestling has transformed from a script fight to a real street fight whose loser lands in a hospital and spends several months in rehabilitation. Supposedly such violence is "good for business."

Figure 6.11. School football games are more important than learning.
(Photo: www.erganicliving.com and www.weblogs.baltimoresun.com).

- *Life style*-dress code – this has social significance since it conveys the message of who one is. Today in pop culture it is the backlash against the traditional social norms under the form of rebellion. In the 21st century, Western societies have adopted more casual dress codes in the workplace, school, and leisure. At schools and during leisure times young people wear: tie-dye T-shirts, sneakers, bags bought at local markets, head caps, have long hair regardless of gender, and even have beards, piercings, and tattoos (Figure 6.12). The last attribute is even called body art. They look unattractively but certainly there must be a purpose. This dress code passes to the work place which has resulted in a lowered quality of work and manners.
- *Life style*-language – Television shows, rap music, and violent movies are many peoples' favorite pasttime. Nowadays should the media label a woman a "bitch" or use "f-word", it is not the end of the world like it was sixty years ago. Teens often choose the slang and use it in their daily vocabulary. The vulgar language is becoming more and more popular in the media and everyday talk and all have a blind eye if what has been said is bad. In general, such vulgar language is limited to buzz words and in texting to a few graphic symbols.

Figure 6.12. Pop culture's dress code in the 21st century.
(Photo: www.third-and-four.com and www.enterprenuer.com).

Contemporary pop culture has the following features: non-melodic music, violence, rock, drugs and sex, trash TV programs, life as a computer game, unattractive fashion, importance of sport rather than learning, and addiction iPhones, even while driving or sleeping. Such pop culture vulgarizes humanity and deteriorates Western Civilization and has even engaged it in the deadly clashes of civilizations which are in fact value-driven, cruel wars.

Global Culture in the 21st Century

Western-Global culture has replaced Christian values and promotes global business values which are causing the transformation of Western civilization into Western-Global civilization. It is matter of fact that Western-Global culture Westernizes and globalizes other contemporary civilizations. This is a very confusing process, since Western culture's symbols and behavior (but not values) are globalizing and the Westerners at home feel that nothing is changing.

Middle Culture in the 21st Century

Middle culture should be a culture of immigrants who, as it is the case in France, do not want to assimilate and like their ghettos; and as is the case in France, they would rather the French accept their culture which is foreign to French culture. The same problems are facing more European countries like the United Kingdom, Germany, and Italy. The United States accepted "hyphenated" citizens and to certain degree suffers the transformation from the nation to the political society. Middle culture puts Western civilization at the cross-roads of being successful or failing.

Hybrid Culture in the 21st Century

Western Hybrid culture should be a culture of all the world's inhabitants since the flow of people is at the world scale and impacts all contemporary civilizations. There is some progress in learning and applying this culture but this process is very slow and is mostly implemented by the elite, due to its good tolerant education. This culture, if applied wisely, can sustain almost every culture.

CONCULSION

The transformation of Western civilization into Western-Global-Virtual civilization in the 21st century is a process which takes place from within since it is driven by the impact of several cultures and is characterized in the scope of key contributions as it is shown in Table 6.3.

In summary one can state that the decline of Western civilization in the 21st century is a fact and is caused mostly by its internal cultural processes. This process is not new, since a usually large organism deteriorates from within, like empires. Can Western civilization re-engineer its own culture by itself? The scope of deteriorations and democratic culture won't allow for any top-down social engineering today.

One must be aware that human kind is part of nature's chaos and randomness and therefore is not the ultimate master of the world.

Table 6.3. The Impact of Western culture on the decline of Western civilization in the 21st century

Culture kind	Key contribution	Deteriration level of Western civilization
High culture	High esteem	Sustains
Folk culture	Tradition, fast food, texting	
Popular culture	The Nice society (comfort and fun) political correctness, relative truth	Very high impact
Mass culture	Super-consumerism, unhealthy food, and depletion of strategic resources	Very high impact
Pop culture	Vulgarization of humanity	Very high impact
Global culture	Christian values replaced by global business values	Very high impact
Middle culture	Very slow assimilation of immigrants living in ghettos and transformation from the nation to political society	Significant impact
Hybrid culture	Tolerance and complementary values, accepted mostly by the elite	Sustains

REFERENCES

Barzun, J. (2001). *From dawn to decadence*. New York: Perennial.

Danesi, M. (2012). *Popular culture*. Lanham & New York: Rowman & Littlefield Publishers, Inc.

Dastin, K. (2014). Pop culture freaks, identity, mass media, and society. Boulder, CO: Westview Press.

Dawson,Ch. (1950). *Religion and the rise of Western culture*. New York: Image Books, Doubledy.

Donn (2014). *Mr. Donn's social study site. http://www.mrdonn.org/index.html,* Retrieved 8-25-2014.

Ecological footprint. (2014). *List of countries by ecological footprint*. Retrieved 8-24-2014.

Lerner, D. (1980). *Comfort and fun, morality in a nice society*. The paper presented at the Faculty Seminar of the MIT Institute for religion and Social Studies. Cambridge, MA: MIT. Retrieved 8-26-2014.

Mosse, G.L. (1988). The culture of Western Europe, the nineteenth and twentieth centuries. Boulder, CO: Westview Press.

Nerdwallet finance (2014). *American household credit card debt statistics*: 2014. Retrieved 8-17-2014.

Outsborne, J. (2013). *Reading pop culture*. Boston: Bedford'/St. Martin's.

Targowski, A. (2014). *Global civilization in the 21st century*. New York: NOVA Science Publishers.

Wallece, L. (2013). Can video games teach us how to succeed in the real world? In Outsborne, J. (2013). *Reading pop culture*. Boston: Bedford'/St. Martin's.

Williams, P. (2013). Is the truth politically correct? ChristianStandard, March 6. Retrieved 8-26-2014.

Chapter 7

FROM MULTICULTURALISM TO HYBRID CULTURE IN WESTERN-GLOBAL-VIRTUAL CIVILIZATION

ABSTRACT

The *purpose* of this investigation is to define how multiculturalism impacts Western civilization in the 21st century. The *methodology* is based on an interdisciplinary big-picture view of how contemporary Western civilization interacts among its members. Among the *findings* are: Western civilization is strongly weakened by multiculturalism and virtualism. *Practical implications:* The most significant impact on the decline of Western civilization comes from within since multiculturalism breaks social cohesiveness. *Social implication:* If Western society would like to interact wisely, it is necessary to maintain diversity at the level of the individual and develop a Hybrid Culture. *Originality:* This investigation is defined through the big picture versus small picture judgment at the level of synthesis. Focus is put on multiculturalism, transculturalism, plurality, separatism and their role in this declining process, affecting contemporary Western civilization.

INTRODUCTION

The purpose of this investigation is to synthesize the impact of internal interactions among members of Western society. The focus will be on such modes of societal interactions as: *diversity, culturalism, multiculturalism, transculturalism, pluralism, virtualism,* and *separatism*. It will be indicated that almost none of these communication modes have a positive impact on globalizing Western civilization. After reviewing the practice of diversity in the long-term context of civilization, a role of diversity in Western society's internal interactions will be defined. Furthermore, a new mode of societal internal interactions it will be defined which should be practiced today by Western society if it would like to sustain its existence.

HUMAN DIVERSITY AT THE ROOTS OF HUMAN DEVELOPMENT

Diversity is the foundation of life forms for the entire Earth. Biodiversity is often used as a measure of the health of biological systems. Biodiversity found on Earth today consists of many millions of distinct biological species, the product of four billion years of evolution. Hence, socio-diversity is one of the dimensions of biodiversity. There is general understanding that biodiversity is necessary in the sense of one diverse group aiding another in developing resistance to catastrophes. In the political arena, the term diversity is used to describe political entities (neighborhoods, cities, nations, ethnicities, cultures, etc.) with members who have identifiable differences in their backgrounds, behavioral patterns, lifestyles, and positions on certain issues.

The use of the term diversity may encompass differences in racial or ethnic classifications, age, gender, religion, philosophy, physical abilities, socioeconomic background, sexual orientation, gender identity, intelligence, mental health, physical health, genetic attributes, behavior, attractiveness, place of origin, cultural values, or political views as well as other identifying features. Some political creeds which promote these diverse cultures may aid communication between people of different backgrounds and lifestyles because doing so should lead to better understanding and peaceful coexistence. In contrast to diversity, other political creeds promote cultural assimilation as the process leading to these ends.

Population movements and social formations (e.g.: cities, city-states, states, empires, nation-states, civilizations) from family to global society took millennia. The process was driven by different cultures, particularly by their concepts of diversity, under a form of key values which were at stake for a given society or civilization. In this study we limit our scope of considerations to civilization, which in a broad and large-scale sense of space and time is composed of a large society, a cultural system and an infrastructural system, creating an autonomous fuzzy reification that is not a part of a larger unit, with exception to the World Civilization.

Table 7.1 illustrates the civilizational elements (society, culture and infrastructure), emphasizing the role of key diversity elements and factors.

What lessons of diversity might be learned from history? Here are some examples:

1) Early civilizations (4000-3000 BC)
   - Diversity was limited to a ruler and the ruled, interacting according to the patrimonial rule, organizing society within a framework of patronage and clientage within a caste system.
   - Differences were arising among the ruled who began to specialize in certain crafts and administration, including the military. However, the society was ruled as one *corporation* bringing profit to the ruler.
   - Rulers were less interested in people's ethnicity as long they paid taxes and were ready to work and *accommodate* themselves to the way of life of the civilization.
2) Colonial civilizations (500 B.C.-1800s AD)
   - Diversity was welcomed mostly with respect to ethnicity, which led to masters and slaves who provided cheap labor. It led to domination of one ethnic group over another.

Table 7.1. The Evolution of Civilizational Components, Determining Social Diversity

Civilization stage	Society	Culture	Key diversity factors	Infrastructure
Pre-Civilizational, 9000-4000 B.C.	Families, Tribes	Value of Territory	Family-Tribe	Nomads, Hunters-Gatherers, Settlers,
Early Civilizations (*Mesopotamian, Egyptian*) 4000-3000 BC	City-State, Empire, Rulers, Warriors, Priests, Cultivators, Craftsmen, Traders	Interest of Castes, Patrimonial Rules	Wealth (Discovering and Protecting), Accommodation	Farms, Irrigations, Cities
Colonial Civilizations [Roman, Macedonian, Western (Portugal, Spain, Netherlands, U.K., France)] 500 BC-1800 AD	Empire Rulers, Military, Priests, Elites (aristocracy, specialists), migrants	Value of Ethnicity & Slavery Colonial Law	Domination-Ethnocracy, Hierarchal Access to Power or Wealth Profiting	Merchant Capitalism Navy
Imperial Civilizations [Western (*France, U.K.*), Eastern (*Russia*), *Japanese, Nazis, Soviet*] 1800 – 1991 AD	Empire Rulers, Military, Elites (aristocracy, apparatchiks intellectuals, specialists), Migrants	Value of Uniformity & Race Interest of Classes Imperial Law	Domination-Ethnocracy, Hierarchical, Inclusive Ethnic Cleansing, Profiting	Commercial Capitalism Industry Imperial Corporations
Post-imperial Civilizations [(*Western: U.S., France, Germany, Italy, Poland..*), *Japanese, Chinese*] 1776 AD -	Nation Politicians, Military, Elites, Classes, Specialists, Migrants	Value of Ethnicity, Interest of Classes National and International law	Nation, Religion & Nationalism, Homogeneity-Monoculturalism, Ethno-nationalism Exclusive, Competitive, Profiting, Minority	Regulated Capitalism, Competition Education National & Transnational Corporations
Globalizing Civilizations (Western, Japanese, Hindu, Chinese…) 2000th AD +	Global Elite Politicians, Military, Classes, Elites, Specialists, Migrants	Value of Multiculturalism Interest of Classes National, International, Global Laws	From Nation to Society Race, Ethnicity, Class, Gender Tolerance, Inclusive and Self-enclosing	Global Capitalism, Knowledge Stateless Corporations Transportation and Information Technology
Universal Civilization 2000th + AD	Universal Society	Value of Complementary Multiculturalism, Interest of Classes Eco-system Law	Values & Symbols Shared and Diversified at the same moment, Hybrid Nation	Ecologism Wisdom

- Differences were arising within the society, triggered by emerging capitalism (of the merchant kind), which was, and still is, based on competition. It led to rising hierarchies within society based on either access to power or wealth.

3) Imperial civilizations (1800s-1900s)

- Diversity was limited, since the elite protected its homogeneity. For example, an aristocracy or a party leader's cliques (e.g.: Nazists & Communists) were closed systems, and they expected that the ruled from different nations would *accommodate* or *assimilate* (a case of the Soviet Union) rather than fight the rulers.
- Difference was limited to labor specialization, which had to be productive and submissive.
- Uniformity was the rule since it was supporting law and order, including even ethnic cleansing. This factor usually led to the fall of empires since, as a closed system, it in fact was producing social chaos and disobedience.

4) Post-imperial civilizations (1776 AD – till the present day)
- Diversity in ethnicity in a given region was the driving force in creating nation-states; oriented by *monoculturalism*, it led to the triumph of ethno-nationalism (Euro-centrism) in modern Europe in the following ways:

i) In Eastern Europe, ethnic groups with largely peasant backgrounds, such as the Czechs, the Poles, the Slovaks, and the Ukrainians found that key positions in the government and the economy were already occupied – often by the ethnic Armenians, Germans, Greeks, or Jews. Therefore, they come to demand a nation-state of their own, in which they would be their own masters, dominating politics, staffing the civil service and controlling commerce (Muller 2008).

ii) During the Balkan Wars of 1912-13, Muslims left regions under the control of the Bulgarians, Greeks, and Serbians; the Bulgarians deserted Greek-controlled areas of Macedonia; the Greeks fled from regions of Macedonia, passing to Bulgaria and Serbia.

iii) After World War I (1914-18) strong ethno-nationalism was unleashed; mass deportations and ethnic cleansing of Armenians took place in the declining Ottoman Empire, and the Greek government invaded Turkish territory in 1919 to expand a "greater Greece" to Constantinople, which was stopped by the Turks. Atrocities were committed due to policies on both sides of ethnic cleansing, ending in the transfer of 1.5 million Greeks and 400,000 Turks to their core territories as the result of the 1923 Treaty of Lausanne.

iv) The National Socialists (the Nazis), who came to power in Germany in 1933, based their policy on a "Germanness" in contrast to "Jewishness;" the latter was eliminated by the genocide of the Jews. The Germans also used their own ethnic minorities to control Central and Eastern European states.

v) After World War II, in 1945-47 (Muller 2008):
(1) Five million ethnic Germans fled from Eastern Europe westward to escape the conquering Red Army and seven million Germans were expelled from Czechoslovakia, Hungary, Poland, and Yugoslavia in response to their collaboration with the Nazis. It was the largest forced population movement in European history, with hundreds of thousands of people dying along way.

(2) 200,000 Jews left Central and Eastern Europe due to still existing anti-Semitism, despite the fact that this region was the center of Jewish life since the 16 century.
(3) 1.5 million Poles were transferred from eastern Polish territories, taken by the Soviet Union, and 500,000 Ukrainians were transferred from Poland to the Ukrainian Soviet Socialistic Republic. Also Slovaks were transferred out Hungary, and Magyars were sent away from Czechoslovakia and Yugoslavia, and Serbs and Croats were moving in the opposite direction.

vi) After the fall of communism in 1989-91:
(1) East and West Germany were unified,
(2) Czechoslovakia was split peacefully into Czech and Slovak republics,
(3) The Soviet Union broke apart into several nation-oriented states,
(4) Germans in Russia have moved to Germany,
(5) Magyars in Romania have moved to Hungary,
(6) Jews in the Soviet Union (about one million) moved to Israel
(7) Yugoslavia has broken into mono-ethnic states.

- Difference was limited to economic *competition* if capitalism was applied. At the level of society, difference was replaced by *homogeneity* leading to the *assimilation* of like-minded people and the creation of a common culture and identity with an integrated nation-state. Difference in some countries was demonstrated if a definition of the nation was based on blood, kinship, and language. Based on this criterion, the Czechs were rejected from the unifying Germany in the 19th century. In the 20th and 21st centuries this criterion is strictly applied in most Muslim countries.
- The ethno-nationalist principle was largely accomplished, and for the most part, each nation in Europe has its own state.

5) Globalizing civilizations (2000th + CE)
- Diversity is strongly welcomed due to the active global *migration* of people, which brings in needed knowledge and skills to be more effective; migrants should rather quickly adapt to the targeted country's society rather than become an isolated minority.
- Difference is supported by a policy of multiculturalism of a multiethnic country which supports inclusiveness but cannot stop the emergence of ethnic ghettos and gated communities. Hence, the noble aim of inclusiveness is deconstructing the nation and transforming it into society with fragmented ethnic groups.
- Difference in life styles is developing freely along the lines of subcategories such as gender.

6) Universal Civilization (2000th AD+) this civilization does not yet exists and ideally should avoid the challenges of the previous civilizations. Its attributes will be presented by the end of this book.

Table 7.2 summarizes lessons learned from diversity evolution in civilization.

Table 7.2. The Evaluation of Diversity's Impact on the Humanity Development

Civilizations	Diversity	Differences	Positive impact on humanity development	Negative impact on humanity development
Early Civilizations (4000-3000 BC)	Ruler vs. the ruled	Increased through crafts & administration specialization	Beginning of social complexity	Privileged casts
Colonial Civilizations (500 BC-1800 AD)	In ethnicity, Masters vs. Slaves	Increased through competition in wealth creation	Competition leading to higher complexity	Slavery
Imperial Civilizations (1800s – 1900s AD)	Homogeneity of elites	Minimized through accommodation and assimilation or increased by racism	Accommodation & assimilation within empire	Closed state system, racism, Nazism, fascism, communism, totalitarism..
Post-Imperial Civilizations (1776+ AD)	Regional diversity of ethnicity	Minimized through accommodation and assimilation	Development of monoculture within a nation-state	Too much homogeneity leading to rejection of others, ethnic disaggregation from population transfer to genocide
Globalizing Civilizations (2000th + AD)	Immigrants, minorities & multi-ethnicity	Increased through multiculturalism	Inclusiveness & tolerance, civil & human rights	Segmentation and transformation from nation to political society
Universal Civilization (2000th + AD)	Immigrants, minorities & multi-ethnicity	Balanced through some shared, complementary values of ethnic groups	Inclusiveness, tolerance & dialog, multiculturalism controlled, hybrid human family,	Less eager? Nation or Global Society?

In conclusion, with respect to the evolution of historic diversity one can state the following:

A. Diversity, as a way of making society more complex and sophisticated, was applied through the whole development of civilization, beginning with the caste formation and jobs specialization and ending with multiculturalism in the present day.
B. Opposite to diversity is a polity of homogeneity of elites and nations which led to closed systems which were very often hostile internally and/or externally through acts such as slavery, racism, nationalism, and, ethnic cleansing. These acts, which should be rejected forever by humanity, were endorsed by Nazism, Fascism, Communism, and other forms of Totalitarianism.
C. Forced migrations of peoples generally panelize the expelling countries and reward the receiving ones (Muller 2008).
D. So far none of the mentioned diversity tendencies are secure for the optimal development of humanity. Even promising multiculturalism leads to serious failures; hence, the quest for better social solutions is the task for all of us.

THE COMPLEXITIES OF RACIAL IDENTIFICATION

The theory of identifying a person's racial roots is a product of post-World War II psychological research. According to this approach, identification leads to a better understanding of one's self and better developmental opportunities. The approach became popular after Eriksson developed his theory of the eight stages of human development. This human development theory is closely related to culture which is driven by a given ethnicity. Hence, understanding one's ethnicity leads to understanding one's culture and one's self. In effect it supposedly eliminates identity confusion. Perhaps this is true, but is it welcomed by all the people as the ultimate way of controlling one's own development? Certainly not!

Needless to say that ethnicity played a very important role in World War II (1939-1945) which was waged by the German Nazis and was based on the idea of German racial superiority and privilege for having a larger space for living. It implemented under the form of the Lebensraüm and the Holocaust in which knowing somebody's ethnicity, coded as "8" (for a Jew) in the column 4 on an IBM card, led to the killing of 4 million people (Targowski 2014).

In the 19th and 20th century, economic problems in Europe led to economic competition, which eventually led to racial/ethnic hostility in Germany, Poland, Russia, and in another countries, where the Jews were singled out as the main cause of this problems, which was not true. Hence, increased economic global competition is leading to the next wave of ethnic tensions in the 21st century, regardless what the psychological theory of development and social theory of multiculturalism may teach us.

The ill-treatment of ethnic minorities is a recurrent theme in Western civilization. The "ethnic cleansing" practiced by Serbians in Bosnia is a recent example which happened in the center of Europe just 40 years after the tragic and systemic massacre of Jews by Nazi Germany had taken place. In fact, many European countries have demonstrated very high levels of intolerance especially toward immigrants of color who have entered their workforces in recent decades, particularly in France, Germany, and Italy. Throughout much of the 20th century, Australia experienced an exclusionary immigration policy which beset all non-Caucasians. Racism was customary by apartheid in South Africa until the 1990's. In contrast, the experience of the United States (which includes a high-fatality civil war arraigned by whites trying to abolish slavery) appears enlightened but imperfect, since about 100 years after the Civil War, the Civil Rights movement led to the gradual improvement of social status of Black Americans in society. Surprisingly, perhaps even for President Abraham Lincoln, a black politician was elected twice President of the U.S. – Barak Obama (2008 and 2012). Furthermore this President, whose middle name is Hussein, had a grandfather who was a Muslim, defeated a woman candidate (Hilary Clinton), and later defeated a Mormon (Mitt Romney) in his reelection.

With the U.S. in a continuing economic downturn since 2007, the issue of ethnicity is rising which is exemplified by the anti-immigration attitude of many Americans. The American residents in southern states are upset since they do not want their tax money to be spent on the 2014-2015 wave of undocumented children who have been flooding across the Mexican border. In 2014 more than 60,000 unaccompanied children have entered the U.S. illegally, and they are burdening an already burdened system. Most of these children are coming from Guatemala, Honduras and El Salvador, and some of the children making the dangerous journey have been toddlers. Border patrol stations are backed up, so thousands of kids are being sent to detention centers on military bases.

Figure 7.1. A U.S. Border Patrol officer oversees a group of women and children who crossed the border from Mexico.
(Photo: John Moore, AFP).

TYPOLOGY OF IDENTITY: CULTURALISM, TRANSCULTURALISM, MULTICULTURALISM, PLURALISM AND VIRTUALISM

Western civilization historically has been and still is the most dynamic civilization among the contemporary civilizations. One example of this dynamism is social activism which has been constantly launching and transforming Western society in its 1200 years of existence. It has been passing through such stages as: family, tribe, ethnos, chiefdom, society, people, proto-nation, nation, state, empire, power, superpower, hegemonic power, political society, transnational community, spherical community, global society, global polity, and so forth (Targowski 2009:15). Furthermore, it took six revolutions (English-1688, American-1776, French-1789, Industrial-19th century, Mexican-1910, and Polish-1989) and several wars (American Civil War, World War I and II) to conclude that liberal democracy is the most optimal social solution. However, liberal democracy may have several shades of ethnic tolerance, also called diversity, which are practiced in the 21st century. Among them one can mention: *Culturalism, multiculturalism, transculturalism, pluralism,* and *virtualism.* Let's take a look at what they offer nowadays.

Culturalism - this term is used in anthropology to denote a theory that all societies are trying to create different cultural identities. Since humans acquire culture through the learning processes of enculturation and socialization, people living in different places or different circumstances develop different cultures. Anthropologists have also pointed out that through culture people can adjust to their environment in non-genetic ways, so people living in different environments will often have different cultures. Much of this anthropological theory has originated in an appreciation of and interest in the tension between local cultures (Figure 7.2) and cultures in other places or cultures coming from different circumstances (Rosaldo 1993).

Figure 7.2. In defense of *Culturalism*.
(Photo: catholic-caveman.blogspot.com).

Multiculturalism it is the view that the various cultures in a society merit equal respect and scholarly interest. Multiculturalism became a significant force in American society in the 1970s and 1980s as African-Americans, Latinos, Chinese (Figure 7.3) and other ethnic groups explored their own history.[50] Multiculturalism is often contrasted with the concept of *assimilation* and has been described as a "salad bowl" or "cultural mosaic" rather than a "melting pot" (Burgess, A. C. and T. Burgess 2005).

Figure 7.3. Chinatown in New York City exemplifies *multiculturalism* in American practice in the 21st century.
(Photo: Wikipedia).

---

[50] The American Heritage® New Dictionary of Cultural Literacy, Third Edition Copyright © 2005 by Houghton Mifflin Company.

Transculturalism goes beyond race, religion, sexuality, class, and every sort of classification known to sociologists and marketers. Transculturalists lead lives some may consider unusual. They often think, consume, date, or marry outside of their race, religion, or nationality. They travel on a whim to a faraway lands, dress unconventionally and codify their own styles. They live in areas their parents were once barred from and take jobs previously considered outside of their leagues. They are comfortable listening to, creating and criticizing music outside of their original cultures and often display high levels of creativity in various progressive disciplines. Some call transculturalists heretics; many call them the future (Grunitzky 2004).

The centrality of *Transculturalism* in the experience of contemporary urban citizens is at the heart of one of the first urban media projects with a transcontinental focus. Trace TV is a Franco-American urban media network that was founded in 2003 by Claude Grunitzky, Olivier Laouchez, and Richard Wayner with the specific aim to target young urban populations and their lives of in-betweenness across cultures and milieus. With a target audience of 18-35 year-old urban youths, Trace TV was originally intended as the broadcast extension of the homonymous American-British magazine created by Grunitzky in London in 1996.

Urban media projects like Trace TV focus on a growing pressure between the cultural fullness of the city and the former ethnic homogeneity of the nation. The city can be a site of wrongdoings, disjointedness, and new openings which often disorders the smoothing dynamics of the narrative of the nation-state. Trapped between the polarizing forces of the global and the local, these inventors use old and new media technologies to re-design spaces whose original public function has been undermined by the commercialization of the urban understanding. In doing so, they provide a platform for more elastic and, perhaps, an uncontrolled communicative role of the city (Ardizzoni 2009) for the common good of diversified inhabitants.

Figure 7.4. *Transculturalism* in action at the college campus where students from different cultures pray together.
(Photo: www.sethskim.com).

Figure 7.5. A pluralistic collaboration in making. An international day of action on climate change brought hundreds of thousands of people onto the streets of New York City on Sunday, September 21, 2014, easily exceeding organizers' hopes for the largest protest on the issue in history. (Photo: News.yahoo.com).

Pluralism – "e pluribus unum" ('one from many')" - the traditionally understood meaning of the phrase was that out of many states (or colonies) emerge a single American nation. However, in recent years its meaning has come to suggest that out of many peoples, races, religions, languages, and ancestries has emerged a single people and nation—illustrating the concept of the melting pot (Figure 7.5). As Thomas Friedman (2014) reminds us "pluralism is not diversity alone, but the energetic engagement with diversity, since mere diversity without real encounter and relationship will yield increasing tension in our society." Pluralism means that one's own culture does not have to be left behind in a new society (after immigrating into one) but should be engaged in this society as a positive synergetic contribution in promoting positive change and innovations in collaborating on needed solutions. For example, the American atomic and hydrogen bombs were in fact developed in the 1940s by Hungarian and Polish physicists and mathematicians who brought knowledge and skills gained in their countries of birth. The call for pluralism in Western civilization is needed since this civilization, through overused multiculturalism, has lost the sense of being one nation (for example, the U.S., Canada, United Kingdom or Spain) and has become a political society with diverse ethnic interests prevailing over the common good. When the U.S. was a more unified nation in the 1960s, President John Kennedy asked "My fellow Americans, ask not what your country can do for you, ask what you can do for your country." Unfortunately, in the 21st century elections, when, for instance, presidential candidates visited Miami, they were asked "what he/she can do for the local ethnic society?" This is an example how the American nation has transformed into a political society today.

Virtualism – this is triggered by the intensive Internetization of the young generation which escapes from reality and electronically practices *transculturalism* as an antidote for local separatism and loneness. Despite its mere technological application, it is generating a tremendous impact upon Western society whose future leaders may be addicted to constant texting and be afraid of face-to-face communication as too personal. Needless to say that today the young Western generation is so addicted to e-communication that it needs hospitalization and serious medical treatments. Internet addiction is described as an impulse control disorder which does not involve use of an intoxicating drug and is very similar to pathological gambling. Some Internet users may develop an emotional attachment to on-line friends and activities they create on their computer screens. Internet users may enjoy aspects of the Internet that allow them to meet, socialize, and exchange ideas through the use of chat rooms, social networking websites, or "virtual communities." Other Internet users spend endless hours researching topics of interest online or "blogging". Blogging is a contraction of the term "web log", in which an individual will post commentaries and keep a regular chronicle of events. It can be viewed as journaling and the entries are primarily textual. Similar to other addictions, those suffering from Internet addiction use the virtual fantasy world to connect with real people through the Internet, as a substitution for real-life human connection, which they are unable to achieve normally. Internet addiction results in personal, family, academic, financial, and occupational problems that are characteristic of other addictions. Impairments of real life relationships are disrupted as a result of excessive use of the Internet (Figure 7.6). Individuals suffering from Internet addiction spend more time in solitary seclusion, spend less time with real people in their lives, and are often viewed as socially awkward. Arguments may result due to the volume of time spent on-line. Those suffering from Internet addiction may attempt to conceal the amount of time spent on-line, which results in distrust and the disturbance of quality in once stable relationships.[51]

Figure 7.6. Internet addiction means that face-to-face communication is too personal. (Photo: www.interventionsupport.com).

The relationships among contemporary social interactions are shown in Figure 7.7. After World War II (1939-1945) *culturalism* took place as victorious nations celebrated their triumph and were rebuilding their countries. Once the economy was blossoming the need for more workers opened the doors for immigrants as it was the case of the U.S., Germany, France, and the United Kingdom. The inflow so many new people with new cultures triggered liberal policies for *multiculturalism* and diversity in general. The rapid application of the Internet triggered a new Wave of Globalization in the 21st century which transformed

---

[51] http://www.addictionrecov.org/Addictions/index.aspx?AID=43, Retrieved 9-24-2014.

multiculturalism into *transculturalism* and the later into *Virtualization*. Globalization also triggered outsourcing of manufacturing from Western to Asian and Eastern civilizations, minimizing the Western middle class. It is resulting in the rise of unprecedented inequality when 1% of society takes all the benefits of 99% of the work. This has triggered antiglobalization movements and sentiments for *Separatism* and a return to *culturalism*. This cycle indicates the strong role of economy and education in social inter-actions driven by diversity. Good economy and education support diversity-driven inter-actions and vice-versa. Poor economy and education (often the result of poor economy) evolves into *separatism* and *culturalism* also known as *nationalism*.

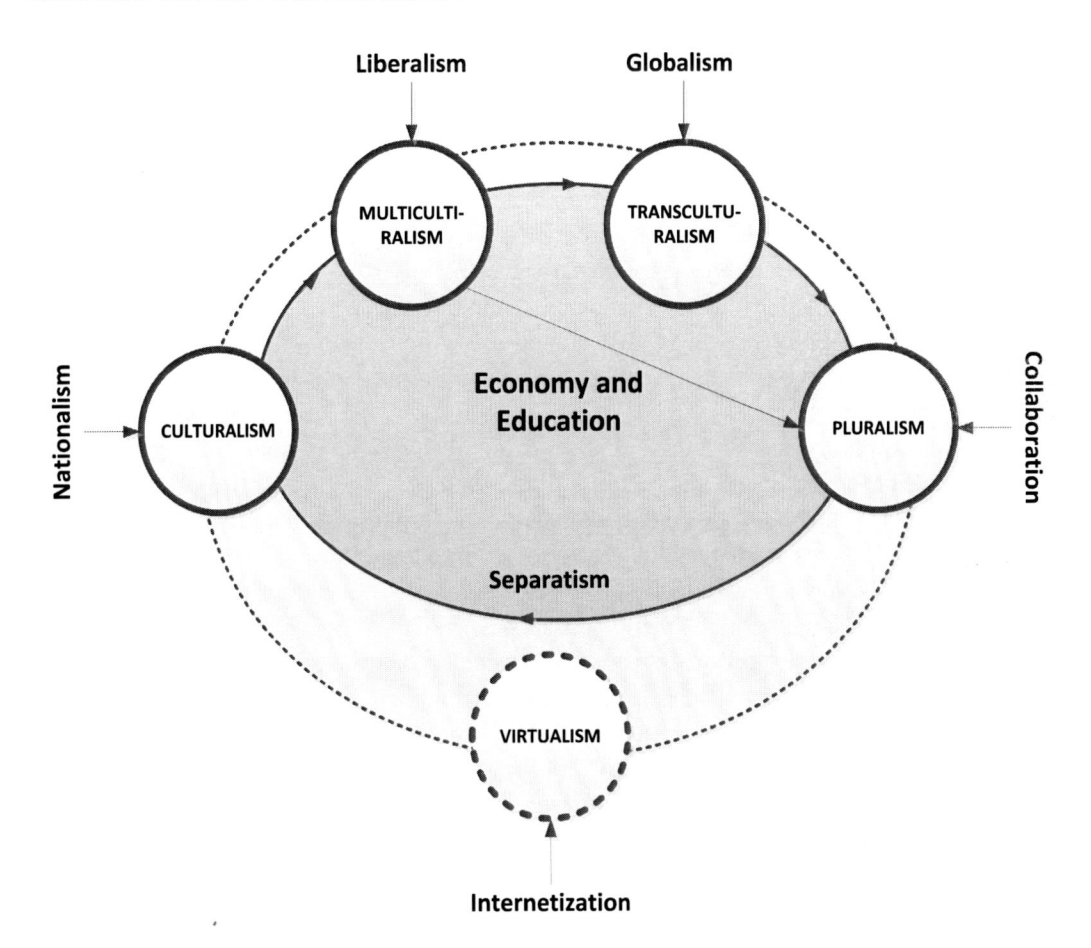

Figure 7.7. The cycle of social inter-actions driven by diversity in Western civilization in the 21st century.

THE RISE OF MULTICULTURALISM

In the United States, multiculturalism became associated with political correctness and with the rise of ethnic identity politics (so-called Hyphenated Americans). A prominent criticism in the US, later echoed in Europe, Canada and Australia, is that multiculturalism has undermined national unity, hindered social integration and cultural assimilation, and led to the fragmentation of society into several ethnic factions, also referred as "Balkanization" (Miller 1988).

Schlesinger, Jr. (1992) states that a new attitude — one that celebrates difference and abandons assimilation — may replace the classic image of the melting pot in which differences are submerged in democracy. He argues that ethnic awareness has had many positive consequences in uniting a nation with a "history of prejudice;" however, the "cult of ethnicity," if pushed too far, may endanger the unity of society. According to Schlesinger, multiculturalists are "very often ethnocentric separatists who see little in the Western heritage other than Western crimes." Their "mood is one of divesting Americans of their sinful European inheritance and seeking redemptive infusions from non-Western cultures."

Huntington (1998) has described multiculturalism as "basically an anti-Western ideology." According to Huntington, multiculturalism has "attacked the identification of the United States with Western civilization, denied the existence of a common American culture, and promoted racial, ethnic, and other subnational cultural identities and groupings."

In the United States, the belief in cultural relativism, implicit in multiculturalism, has attracted criticism. Often this has been combined with an explicit preference for Western Enlightenment values, understood as universal values. In his 1991 work, *Illiberal Education*, Dinesh D'Souza argues that the entrenchment of multiculturalism in American universities undermined the *universalist* values that liberal education once attempted to foster. In particular, he was disturbed by the growth of ethnic studies programs (e.g., African-American Studies).

Criticism of multiculturalism in the U.S. was not always synonymous with opposition to immigration. Some politicians did address both themes. Notably Pat Buchanan (2002) described multiculturalism as "an across-the-board assault on our Anglo-American heritage." Buchanan and others argue that multiculturalism is the ideology of the modern managerial state, an ongoing regime that remains in power regardless of what political party holds a majority. It acts in the name of abstract goals, such as equality or positive rights, and uses its claim of moral superiority, power of taxation and wealth redistribution to keep itself in power and citizens reduced to the labor force as a commodity.

Perhaps some of the high regard for the post-modern societal concept stems from confusing the word "multicultural" with "multiracial". If you want to run a successful business in the 21st century, it could mean hiring an Indian IT manager, a Chinese engineer, an American accountant, an Italian designer, and a South African salesman. Refusing to hire people because of their skin color may be unethical, but it first makes one a bad capitalist. The U.S. can either remain a powerful, multiracial country of dynamic individuals, or it can disintegrate into a multicultural chaos of clashing tribes (Bruno 2005). This opinion supports Miller (1998) in his book with a very straightforward title – *The Unmaking of Americans, How Multiculturalism has Undermined America's Assimilation Ethic*.

THE SOCIAL COEHESION AT RISK – FROM MELTING TO BOILING POT

In the 21st century, globalization is leading to a massive worldwide movement of people, with at least 3 percent of the world's population now living outside their country of birth.

This mass migration is driven by the inequality between nations; people from poor countries who are seeking out an income for their families are drawn towards richer countries for cheap labor. Industrialization is also causing a movement from rural to urban environments, often resulting in areas of mass poverty surrounding the new megacities of the developing world (Burman 2007).

This migration trend to Western Civilization, also called the IVth Globalization Wave (Targowski 2014), has triggered opposite views on multiculturalism:

- Europe is very unhappy with multiculturalism as it is practiced, particularly in France (as evidenced by protests in which cars are burned), Holland (as evidenced by killed people who criticized societal segmentation), the United Kingdom (as evidenced by the presence of terrorist cells), and Germany (as evidenced by presence of ethnic ghettos).
- The German chancellor, Angela Merkel, has courted a growing anti-immigrant opinion in Germany by claiming the country's attempts to create a multicultural society have "utterly failed". Speaking to a meeting of young members of her Christian Democratic Union party, Merkel said the idea of people from different cultural backgrounds living happily "side by side" did not work. She said the onus was on immigrants to do more to integrate into German society. "This [multicultural] approach has failed, utterly failed," Merkel told the meeting in Potsdam, west of Berlin, on October 16, 2010. Her remarks will stir a debate about immigration in a country which is home to around 4 million Muslims. Merkel said too little had been required of immigrants in the past and repeated her argument that they should learn German in order to cope in school and take advantage of opportunities in the labor market. The row over foreigners in Germany has shifted since former central banker Thilo Sarrazin published a highly-controversial book[52] in which he accused Muslim immigrants of lowering the intelligence of German society.[53]
- British Prime Minister David Cameron launched a devastating attack on 24 September, 2014 on 30 years of multiculturalism in Britain, warning it is fostering extremist ideology and directly contributing to home-grown Islamic terrorism. Signaling a radical departure from the strategies of previous governments, Mr. Cameron said that Britain must adopt a policy of "muscular liberalism" to enforce the values of equality, law and freedom of speech across all parts of society. He warned Muslim groups that if they fail to endorse women's rights or promote integration, they will lose all government funding. All immigrants to Britain must speak English and schools will be expected to teach the country's common culture. Mr. Cameron blamed a doctrine of "state multiculturalism" which encourages different cultures to live separate lives. This, he says, has led to the "failure of some to confront the horrors of forced marriage". But he added it is also the root cause of radicalization which can lead to terrorism. Instead of ignoring this extremist ideology, we – as

---

[52] In his 2010 book *Deutschland schafft sich ab* ("*Germany Is Doing Away With Itself*" or "*Germany Is Abolishing Itself*"), the most popular book on politics by a German-language author in a decade, Thilo denounces the failure of Germany's post-war immigration policy, sparking a nation-wide controversy about the costs and benefits of the idea of multiculturalism.

[53] http://www.theguardian.com/world/2010/oct/17/angela-merkel-german-multiculturalism-failed.

governments and societies – have got to confront it. Instead of encouraging people to live apart, we need a clear sense of shared national identity, open to everyone.[54]

- French President Nicolas Sarkozy declared on February 10, 2011 in a nationally televised debate that multiculturalism was a "failure" in France warning that such a concept fostered extremism. "We have been too concerned about the identity of the person who was arriving and not enough about the identity of the country that was receiving him," Sarkozy said. The French leader said that while it is important to respect cultural differences, France should be a place with a national community - not a place where different cultural communities just coexist. "'If you come to France, you accept to melt into a single community, which is the national community," he continued. "And if you do not want to accept that, you cannot be welcome in France."[55]
- The U.S. is accepting multiculturalism as politically correct social solution, but their elites are against it since it disintegrates the nation, which is transforming into a political society.
- Stanley Renshon (2011) argues that "Multiculturalism [in the U.S.], by reposing political problems in terms of culture or faith, transforms political conflicts into a form that makes them neither useful nor resolvable. Rather than ask, for instance, 'What are the social roots of racism and what structural changes are required to combat it?' it demands recognition for one's particular identity, public affirmation of one's cultural difference and respect and tolerance for one's cultural and faith beliefs. It was within this contextual legacy that the multicultural demand for 'recognition' gathered traction. Multiculturalism in the United States has always reflected two strands of thought. The first, more prosaic and culturally benign strand, simply stated the obvious: America is a country in which many diverse cultures exist, co-exist and find common ground as Americans. The second more divisive strand has argued that people do, and ought to, gain their primary identities from attachment to their racial or ethnic groups. In this view the role of the government is not only to accept that 'fact,' but to facilitate it. Advocates of such views insist not only on their right to recognition, but also on their exclusivity along with government policies that ensure it. It is hard to have a primary identity as an American if all you really care about is yourself. And it is also hard to have a primary national identity if all you really care about is your own group."

If globalization and immigration cannot be stopped in the near future, then one must find a new solution which can address the issues of assimilation, isolation, and national homogeneity in general.

---

[54] http://www.independent.co.uk/news/uk/politics/cameron-my-war-on-multiculturalism-2205074.html, Retrieved 9-24-2014.

[55] http://www.cbn.com/cbnnews/world/2011/February/Frances-Sarkozy-Multiculturalism-Has-Failed/ Retrieved 9-24-2014.

DIVERSITY WITH HYBRID CULTURE

Diversity has been embedded in human development since its early stages. Furthermore, nature is so rich since is so diverse. Therefore diversity should be promoted in social development if that development is to be natural and not artificially engineered. Each individual is called an "individual" since he/she is different. This kind of diversity should be practiced.

On the other hand *multiculturalism*, as cultural equality in a country which has accepted immigrants with their cultures, is in question, particularly if a new "arrived" culture is pushing aside the local culture and pretends that is better than latter. Many presented examples of *multiculturalism* in Europe and the U.S. show that it is an idea which makes local society weaker and prone to be invaded, despite its hospitality for new comers. But if new comers think that a local culture is bad, and they do not want to accept its standards, why did they come here? Why did they not stay at a home where they could practice a "better" culture?

The following *hybrid culture* as a complex of the following cultures can serve as a solution to mentioned problems:

- Sustaining the *mother culture* at home in a new country,
- Development of *middle culture* - the full assimilation of immigrants, particularly in the first generation is difficult. Therefore, in order to minimize their isolationist tendencies, one must require that these individuals accept the given state's culture, which is referred to as the *middle culture*. This kind of culture includes awareness and skills of the following:
  - National values (expressed in the Constitution),
  - National symbols (expressed, for example, in the pride of a national flag and military service),
  - Official language as a means of communication out of the original culture,
  - Inter-cultural communication – skills to communicate with another culture,
  - Cross-cultural communication – skills to communicate with many cultures,
  - Other
- Development of *global culture* – to avoid isolation and ghetto tendencies, minorities as well as local people should acquire awareness and skills to be a Global Citizen:
  - English (called also "Globish"),
  - Applying e-mail, e-commerce, e-news and so forth by having an access to the Internet,
  - Traveling abroad,
  - Cross-cultural communication,
  - Other
- Development of *complementary culture*, which would allow for peaceful coexistence among civilizations, regardless of geographic location. In the 21st century these may be religion-oriented and have strong sets of their own values, very often competing among themselves. Therefore, this new culture should be based on selected values from each civilization and shared by them. Table 7.3 provides an example of possible set of complementary-shared values (Targowski 2008), applied by a World Citizen.

The model of Hybrid Culture is shown in Figure 7.8.

Table 7.3. The Common Universal – Complementary Values of Universal Civilization of a World Citizen

Civilization	Contributed Values
African	Ancestral Connection
Buddhist	Morality
Eastern	Self-sacrifice
Hindu	Moderation
Islamic	Reward and Penalty
Japanese	Cooperation and Nature Cult
Chinese	Authority Cult
Western	Freedom and Technology
Global	Free Flow of Ideas, Goods, Services and People according to *Pax Orbis*
Universal-complementary	Wisdom, Goodness, Access, Dialogue, Agreement (on main principles), Forgiveness upon Condition, Human and Civil Rights, International Law, Green and Self-sustainable Planet

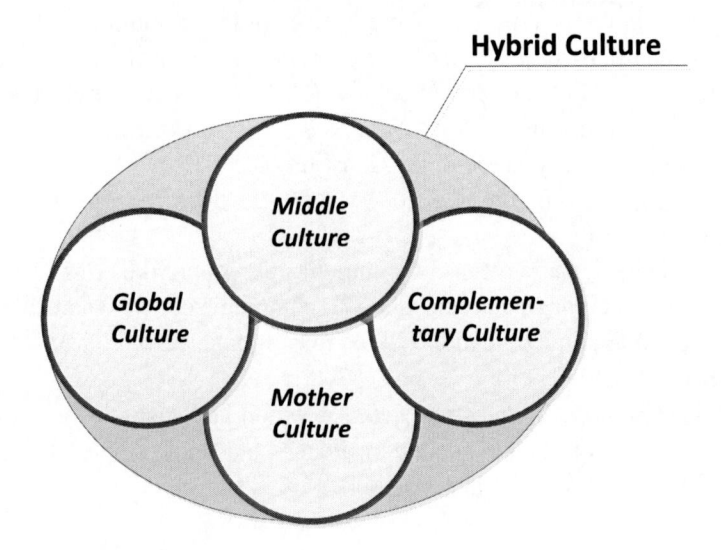

Figure 7.8. The model of Hybrid Culture.

CONCLUSION

1. Western civilization's liberal democracy in the 21st century is so liberal that it has allowed for the development of *multiculturalism* and *virtualism* which can destroy this civilization by breaking its societal cohesion and ability to be sustainable.
2. Other modes of societal inter-actions such as *culturalism* and *transculturalism* as well as *pluralism* are very sensitive to economic and educational conditions in the

sense that when the economy is good, education is good and *transculturalism* and *pluralism* are satisfactory; however, when the economy is bad, education declines and societal inter-action looks to *separatism* and *culturalism* in a world which has just opened for global interactions of all kinds.

3   Western civilization in the 21st century is mastering the development of technology but at the same time is experiencing problems with the cohesiveness of its society which results in a loss of the ability for positive changes and survival. Perhaps, humans have reached such a complex level of development that they cannot cope successfully with the latest issues and challenges.

4   To seek an optimal mode of societal inter-action in contemporary Western civilization, which is proud of its liberal democracy and open to the dynamic globalizing world, perhaps Western society should apply diversity at the level of individuals and the complementary *hybrid culture*, composed of *mother*, *middle*, *global*, and *complementary* cultures in a given nation.

5   Teachers must teach pupils and students about how to develop and behave in *national cultures* within the scope of *mother (hosting)*, *middle*, *global*, *and complementary cultures,* which all together create *hybrid culture*.

REFERENCES

Ardizzoni, M. (2009). *Mediating urban cultural borders*. http://flowtv.org/2009/05/mediating-urban-cultural-borders-by-michela-ardizzoni-university-of-colorado-boulder/ Retrieved 9-23-2014.

Becker, J. (2007). *Dragon rising: an inside look at China today*. Des Moines, IA: National Geographic.

Brown, J. M. (1994), *Modern India: the origins of an Asian democracy*, Oxford and New York: Oxford University Press.

Butler, J. and G. Ch. Spivak. (2007). *Who signs the nation-state? Language, Politics, Belonging.* Salt Lake City, UT: Segull Books.

Bruno, W. (2005). *Multiculturalism – Tribalism Recycled.* http://wolfgangbruno.blogspot.com/2005/10/multiculturalism-tribalism-recycled.html, retrieved 2-6-2008.

Buchannan, P. Jr. (2002). *The death of the west: how dying populations and immigrants invasions imperil our country and civilization*. New York: St. Martin's Press.

Burgess, A. C. and T. Burgess. (2005). *Guide to Western Canada* (7th ed.). Globe Pequot Press. p. 31.

Burman, St. (2007). *The state of the American Empire*. Berkley, Los Angeles: University of California Press.

Cooper, D. (2004). *Challenging diversity*. Cambridge, UK: Cambridge University Press.

Cromwell, O. C. (1970). *Caste, class, and race*. New York: Monthly Review Press.

Dogakinai, A. http://www.lclark.edu/~krauss/advwrf99/causeeffect/akikocause.html, retrieved 2-9-2008.

D'Souza, D. (1991). *Il liberated education*: *the politics of race and sex on campus*. Glencoe, Ill: Free Press.

Friedman, Th. (2014). Three cheers for pluralism over separatism. *New York Times*, September 21, Sunday Review, p.1.
Gellner, Ernest. 1983. *Nations of nationalism*. Ithaca: Cornell University Press.
Goldberg, D. (1994). *Multiculturalism, a critical reader*. Oxford & Cambridge, UK: BLACKWELL.
Gordon, A. A. and Gordon, D. L. (1996). *Understanding contemporary Africa*. Boulder, CO: Lynne Rienner Publishers.
Gress, D. (1999). Multiculturalism in the World History. *The Newsletter of FPRI's Marvin Wachman Fund for International Education*, Vol. 5, No. 8.
Grillo, R.D. (1998). *Pluralism and the Politics of Difference*. Oxford, UK: Oxford University Press.
Grunitzky, Cl (2004). *Transculturalism: how the world is coming together*. London: True Agency.
Harvey, P. (1990). *An introduction to Buddhism: teachings, history and practices*. Cambridge and New York: Cambridge University Press.
Huntington, S.P. (1998). *Clash of civilizations and the remaking of world order. The*. New York: Simon & Schuster.
Hechter, M. (2001). *Containing nationalism*. New York: Oxford University Press.
Hobsbawm, E. and Ranger, T. (1983). *The invention of tradition*. Cambridge, UK: Cambridge University Press.
Jack, A. (2006). *Inside Putin's Russia*. Oxford, New York: Oxford University Press.
Malik, K. (2013). *Multiculturalism and its discontents*. London, New York, Calcutta: Seagull Books.
Macionis, J. J. (2006). *Society: the basics*. Upper Saddle River, NJ: Prentice Hall.
Moynihan, D. P. (1994). *Pandemonium: ethnicity in international politics*. New York: Oxford University Press.
Muller, J. (2008). Us and them. *Foreign Affairs*, 87(2):18-34.
Neary, I. (1997). Japan's minorities: the illusion of homogeneity. London: Routledge.
Parekh, B. (2000). *Rethinking multiculturalism: cultural diversity and political theory*. Basingstoke: Palgarve.
Pieterse, J. N. (2007). *Ethnicities and global multiculture*. Plymouth, UK: Rowman & Littlefield Publishers, Inc.
Renshon. St. (2011). *Multiculturalism in the U.S.: cultural narcissism and the politics of recognition*. Center for Immigration Studies. http://cis.org/renshon/politics-of-recognition.
Philips, A. (2007). *Multiculturalism without culture*. Princeton, NJ: Princeton University Press.
Rosaldo, R. (1993). *Culture and truth*. Beach Press.
Schlesinger, Jr. A. M. (1992). *The disuniting of America: reflections on a multicultural society*. New York: W.W. Norton & Co. Inc.
Smedley, A. (1999). *Race in North America: origin and evolution of a worldview*, 2nd ed. Boulder, CO: Westview Press.
Simon, D. R. (2007). *Elite deviance*. Boston: Allyn & Bycon.
Schmidt, A.J. (1997). *The menace of multiculturalism, Trojan horse in America*. Westport, CT & London: PRAEGER.
Smith, A., D. (1987). *The ethnic origins of nations*. Malden, MA: Blackwell.

Targowski, A. (1982). *Red Fascism*. Lawrenceville, VA: Brunswick Publishing Co.

_____. (2006). The emergence of global civilization. *Comparative Civilizations Review*. 55, Fall, 91-107.

_____. (2008). *Information technology and social development*. Hershey, PA: IGI Global.

_____. (2014). Global civilization in the 21st century. New York: NOVA Science Publishers.

UN International Convention on the Elimination of All of Racial Discrimination, New York 7 March 1966.

Ward, C. (1997). On difference and equality. *Legal Theory* 3, 470-5.

Chapter 8

THE EXPANDING INFRASTRUCTURE OF WESTERN-GLOBAL-VIRTUAL CIVILIZATION

ABSTRACT

The *purpose* of this investigation is to define Western-Global-Virtual civilization's infrastructures which are becoming global in the 21st century. The *methodology* is based on an interdisciplinary, big-picture view of Western-Global-Virtual civilization's developments and interdependency. Among the *findings* are: Western-Global-Virtual civilization, out of 11 civilizational infrastructures, is developing the following 7: financial, information, cyberwar, knowledge, production, service, and transportation infrastructure. Other civilizational national infrastructures are: authority, military, urban-rural, and education. *Practical implication:* The Western-Global-Virtual civilization's global infrastructures impress one as technologically progressive; however and they are worrisome as being socially irresponsible. *Social implication:* The global information infrastructure is aiming at a labor-less economy, and the global transportation infrastructure is unsustainable due to its huge consumption of energy. *Originality:* This investigation defined the Western-Global-Virtual civilization's infrastructure through graphic modeling which allows one to be better aware of its nature through its components and relationships. The focus is put on the social responsibility and sustainability of global infrastructures.

INTRODUCTION

The purpose of this investigation is to analyze the civilization infrastructures of rising Western-Global-Virtual civilization in the 21st century. As the father of civilization studies, Arnold Toynbee stated (1935) that civilizations respond to challenges of nature and society. He did not mention "infrastructure" since he did not investigate current civilizations in the 21st century, and in those times there were only a few infrastructures, such as: authority, military, and rural.

In the 21st century, Western civilization became "Technological civilization" dispossessed of culture with a governing soul. Today Western-Global-Virtual civilization functions within 11 key civilization infrastructures which required responses by its society. These civilization infrastructures are challenging the *modus operandi* not only this one civilization but all remaining ones, such as: Eastern, Chinese, Japanese, Hindu, Buddhist, African, Islam, and Global.

The scope of this investigation will be focused on the infrastructures of global civilization such as: financial, information, cyberwar, knowledge, production, service, and transportation. The method applied in this analysis-synthesis is based on the graphic modeling of their sets, components, and relations. Focus will be put on their social responsibility and sustainability.

THE GLOBAL FINANCIAL INFRASTRUCTURE (GFI)

The global financial system is the worldwide framework of legal agreements, institutions, and both formal and informal economic actors that together facilitate international flows of financial capital for purposes of investment and trade financing. The system has evolved substantially since its emergence in the late 19th century during the first modern wave of economic globalization (James and Patomäki 2007).

During the Industrial Revolution (1800s to early 1900s), accelerated world migration and enhanced communication technologies like telegraph assisted in exceptional growth in international trade and investment, triggering early financial globalization. At the beginning of World War I (1914-1918), trade and investment shrunk as foreign exchange markets stopped due to a lack of liquidity in money markets. Countries like the United States and European sought to guard against external shockwaves with protective trade policies and world trade virtually froze by 1933, even deteriorating the effects of the worldwide Great Depression until a set of mutual trade agreements in the 1930s and late 1940s slowly reversed trade protectionism and reduced tariffs worldwide. Between 1934 and 1947, the U.S. signed 29 bilateral trade agreements and the average tariff rate was reduced by approximately one-third during this same period.

After the WWII in 1945, the Bretton Woods Agreement was signed by 44 nations which favored pegged exchange rates for their flexibility. Under this system, nations would peg their exchange rates to the U.S. dollar, and the U.S. dollar would be convertible to gold at $35 USD per ounce (Carbaugh 2005). The Bretton Woods agreement provided the financial order after WWII in the Free World, which did not include nations belonging the Soviet Block, where the flow of currencies was regulated by the standard of the Russian rubble and planned "paper money."

An important component of the Bretton Woods agreements was the creation of two new international financial institutions: the International Monetary Fund (IMF) and the International Bank for Reconstruction and Development (IBRD). The creation of these two organizations was a crucial milestone in the evolution of international financial architecture, and some economists consider it the most significant achievement of multilateral cooperation following World War II (Elson 2011).

As the other result of the Bretton Woods Agreement, the World Bank was created at the 1944 Bretton Woods Conference. The World Bank and the IMF are both based in Washington D.C. and work closely with each other. The mission of the World Bank is to provide loans to developing countries for capital programs. The World Bank requires sovereign immunity from the countries it deals with (World Bank 2007). Sovereign immunity waives a holder from all legal liability for their actions. It is proposed that this immunity from responsibility is a "shield which (The World Bank) wants to resort to, for escaping accountability and security by the people"(IFI Watch 2004). As the United States has veto power, it can prevent the World Bank from taking action against its interests.

In 1947, 23 countries concluded the General Agreement on Tariffs and Trade (GATT) at a UN conference in Geneva. GATT became the de facto framework for later multilateral trade negotiations that followed. Participating countries emphasized trade reciprocity as an approach to lowering barriers in pursuit of mutual gains (Bagwell and Staiger 2004).

During the Marrakech Agreement (a round of GATT negotiations) which was signed in April 1994, the World Trade Organization (WTO) was established. The WTO is a chartered multilateral trade organization, charged with continuing the GATT mandate to promote trade, govern trade relations, and limit or prevent damaging trade practices and policies. The WTO became operational in January 1995.

In 1998 the European Central Bank (ECB) and European System of Central Banks were established. Very soon a common currency for circulation known as the Euro was adopted by eleven members of the fifteen-member European Union in January 1999. In doing so, they disaggregated their sovereignty in matters of monetary policy. In 2002 the ECB began issuing official Euro coins and notes. As of 2011, the European Monetary Union comprises 17 nations which have issued the Euro and 11 non-Euro states. The United Kingdom has opted in favor of monetary autonomy, Denmark, Latvia, and Lithuania are members of the ERM II, and Sweden, Poland, the Czech Republic, Hungary, Romania, Bulgaria and Croatia are either not complying with all convergence criteria or do not want to apply for ERM II (Dunn and Mutti 2004).

Figure 8.1. Wall Street (the financial capital of the world), the UAE-based Global Financial Center, Rothschild's London Headquarters (Old Money) and Global Financial Center in Shanghai (New Money). The last ones implement new projects which reflect the power of their capital.
(Photo: www.cityreality.com, www.gfmag.com, www.openbuildings.com, www.evolo.us).

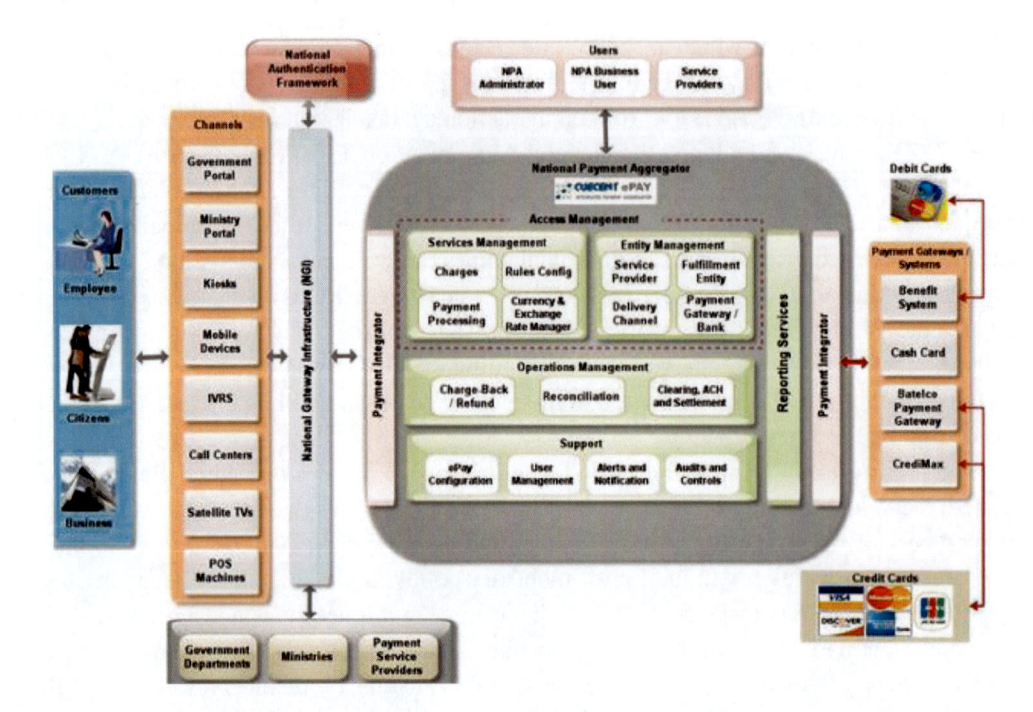

Figure 8.2. The Financial Systems Architecture of the Ministry of Finance – Kingdom of Bahrain showing the National Gateway Infrastructure (NGI) which connects with other countries' NGIs. (Photo: www.mof.gov.bh).

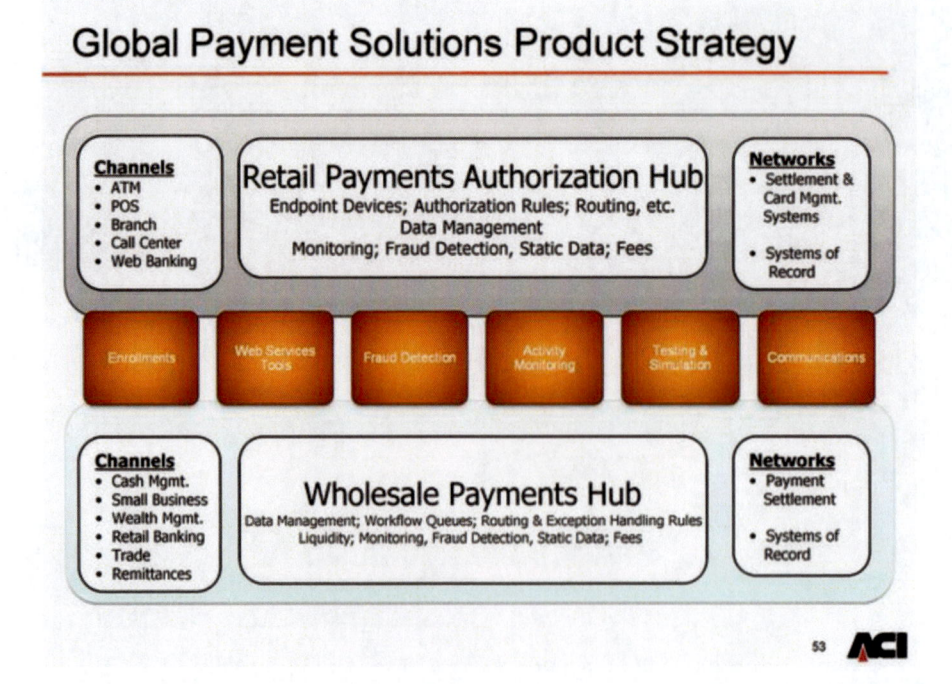

Figure 8.3. The Global Financial Information Systems Architecture for retail and wholesale business offered by the ACI software company.

The world economy became increasingly financially integrated in the 1980s and 1990s through capital account liberalization and financial deregulation due to growing globalization, triggered by the instant electronic flow of digital money through the private Global Area Networks and public Internet. The National Finance System Architecture of the Kingdom of Bahrain is illustrated in Figure 8.2, showing how the National Payment Aggregator has to function in order to process all tools of the global financial system and to be compatible with this system in processing global flows of money.

This National Finance System must interact with all kinds of commerce and consumers. The financial services software architecture (ACI firm's) for retail and wholesale business is shown in Figure 8.3.

The architecture of the Global Financial Infrastructure is shown in Figure 8.4.

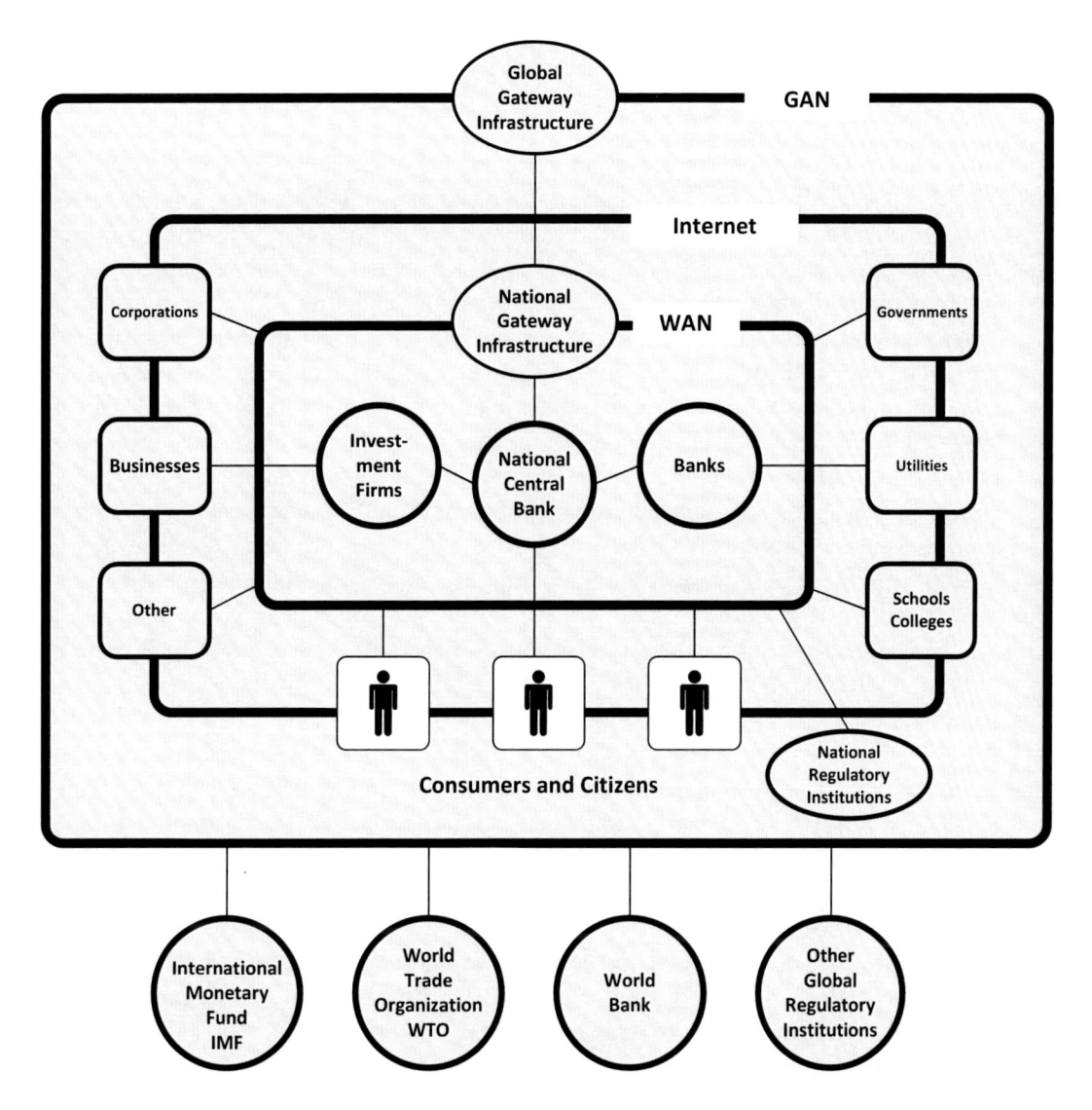

Figure 8.4. The architecture of the global financial infrastructure.
(WAN-private Wide Area Network, GAN-private Global Area Network).

THE GLOBAL PRODUCTION INFRASTRUCTURE (GPI)

The global production infrastructure is shrinking since it has been outsourced offshore largely beginning with the emergence of the smooth functioning of the Internet (based on the World Wide Web and user-friendly browsers). Outsourcing can be analyzed from systems and/or business perspectives as follows in the coming sections.

Outsourcing system perspective – Outsourcing subsystems are engineered to accomplish a goal, and significant resources are employed to get them to work together smoothly with business core functions. Business corporations have evolved into holding economic dominance through coordination of nearly-decomposable hierarchical divisions and organizational identification (Simon 1990). Nearly-decomposable systems maximize component independence and minimize the cost and effort of coordination and communication. Companies have separate and nearly independent departments, optimizing sales, production, and logistics. Near-decomposability allows a corporate department to independently change many of its processes and procedures without concern for effects on other departments. As systems become more complex, nearly-decomposable architecture with its hierarchical subdivisions has been shown to be much more effective than architecture with less departmentalized interconnections. Simulations with genetic algorithms have confirmed the dominance of near-decomposability in complex biological ecosystems (Simon, 1990). Near-decomposability can apply to any business system of activities. Once coordination and communication demands are minimized, the responsibility for the system can be assigned to any group that can accomplish the activities effectively. As effective as nearly-decomposable systems are in business, they minimize rather than eliminate the need for coordination, communication, and control of different departments, divisions, or activities in a business. As the quality focus of the 1970s and 1980s demonstrated, there is wealth to be created, and competitive advantage to be gained, from coordination and communication of business component systems. Successful businesses ensure that the products obtained by the purchasing department perform well in production and that accounting and sales personnel know when raw materials are in transit, when production is scheduled, when shipments are made, when deliveries can be expected, and when invoices are issued. As business systems expand from individual to multiple companies, the demands of coordination, communication, and control intensify. If sufficiently robust methods of coordination, communication, and control exist, then nearly-decomposable activities can occur wherever they can be carried out most efficiently — inside or outside of the company. Outsourcing occurs when activities are executed outside of the company. An increasingly sophisticated information technology infrastructure is enabling coordination, communication, and control of activities in a business value chain even when the chain includes multiple companies in multiple parts of the world.

Outsourcing business perspective – This perspective looks for cost reduction by subcontracting a part of production or service to another party, very often off-shore. It is based on the economic rule of so called comparative advantage achieved by countries with low wages. In the our modern information technology environment, the global information infrastructure assures the fast exchange of information between cooperating parties, so fast that there are some who have declared that "distance is dead." Instant communication is accomplished in the private sector by corporate Global Area Networks and by the Internet in the public sector. The global industrial infrastructure (Figure 8.3) has been established, and there is a hierarchy of countries, where the upper level of this hierarchy subcontracts orders to lower levels. In addition to GII, two other infrastructures, the global finance infrastructure (GFI) and the global transportation infrastructure (GTI), make off-shore outsourcing economically successful. Furthermore, lottery-like rewards that executives get under the form of bonuses for lowering cost and increasing profit and stock values are a strong motivation for off-shore outsourcing.

The question is which perspective of outsourcing will prevail?

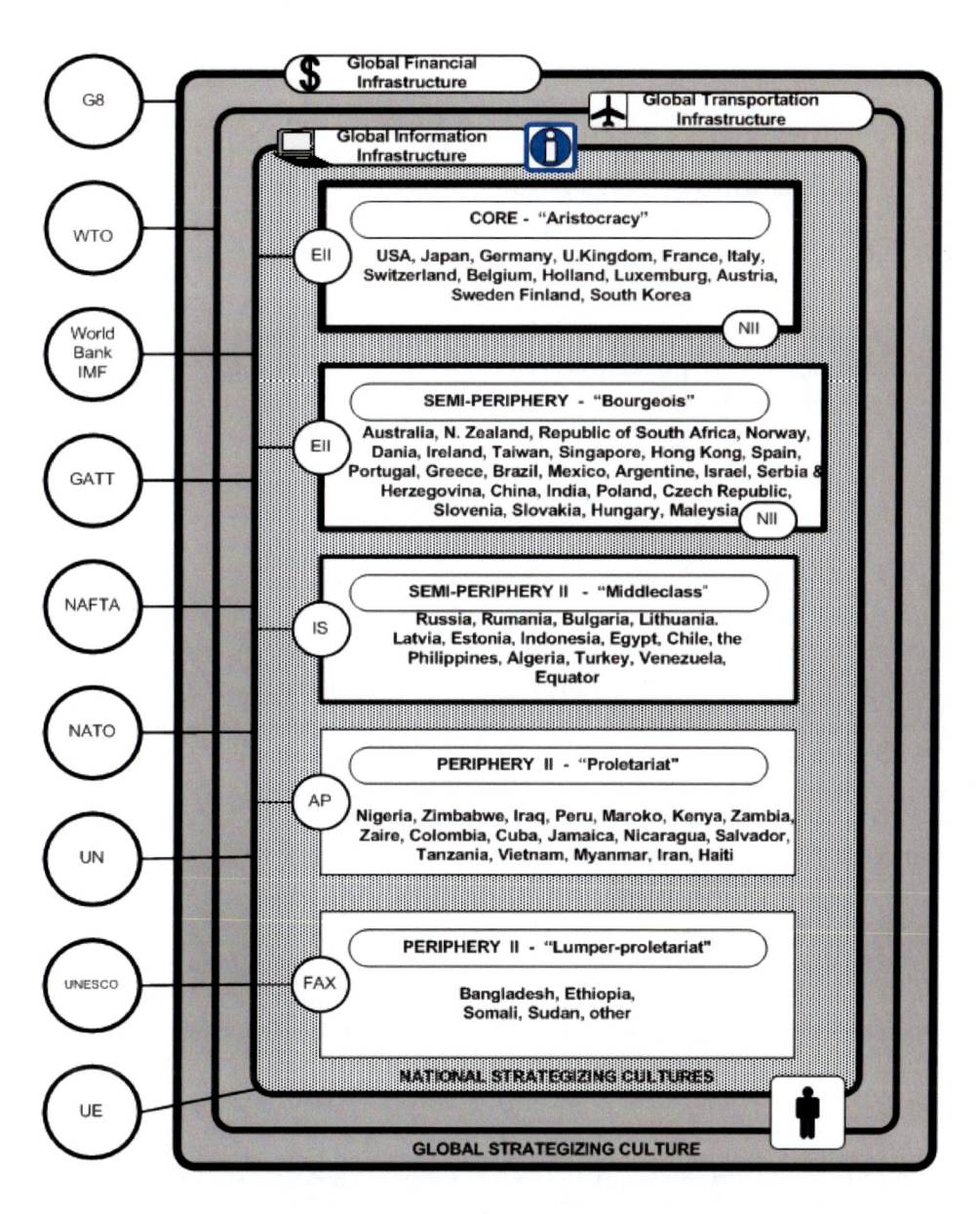

Figure 8.5. The global industrial infrastructure (21st Century)
(EII-Enterprise Information Infrastructure, NII-National Information Infrastructure, IS-Information Systems, AP- Computer Applications).

Long-Term Economic View of Outsourcing and Off-shoring

The long-term effects of outsourcing for developed countries like the United States ultimately rest with the balance reached between jobs and business costs. An estimated 50,000 American factories have been relocated to foreign countries. About 4 million direct manufacturing jobs have been lost in the United States since 1979 (Meyers 2013)[56] with about 8 million support jobs disappearing with them. This means that altogether offshore manufacturing took away about 12 million middle class jobs from the U.S. A tailspin of good jobs reduces not only opportunities for people currently in the workforce but also for future employment seekers. If job losses continue to escalate with no offsetting new opportunities, evaporating manufacturing jobs will result in:

- millions unemployed
- millions of workers in fear of unemployment
- a lower demand for complex IT systems (no CAD/CAM and integration toward CIM flexibility)
- a lower demand for engineers and IT professionals
- a lower demand for MBA graduates
- a shrinking middle class
- increasing trade deficits
- social unrest
- others

An equally foreboding scenario can be applied to information technology outsourcing. Many U.S. based airlines are linked via computers and telephone lines with reservation clerks in Ireland where labor costs are low and education is high. Many American computer firms have technology support in India. Between 2003 and 2015 an average of 37,000 IT jobs per year have been offshored from the United States, while American universities graduate about 50,000 students per year who study information technology. If entry jobs for these graduates disappear it will mean the death of IT curricula in U.S. higher education and a knowledge gap for future IT development. This symptom can already be seen today, as Bill Gates argued for more job visas for experienced foreign IT professionals to the Congress.[57] If American businesses minimize the volume of entry job positions, in what way will the American IT graduates be able to became advanced IT professionals without any practice?

Figure 8.6 describes the long-term effects of continued job losses from offshoring. Short term profits for U.S. companies improve, but long term effects include a less complex economy (like service economy) resulting from the loss of the country's manufacturing base,

---

[56] The year 1979 may very well have been the year when the middle-class in America first began its long decent into oblivion. According to a U.S. Bureau of Labor Statistics report, manufacturing in the U.S. peaked in 1979 when we had over 19.6 million manufacturing jobs in a labor force of 104.6 million. In 1979 manufacturing was 21.6% of all jobs. Now manufacturing is only 9,9% of jobs in America. Today we have 155.8 million in the labor force with 11.8 million workers unemployed. This is largely due to the outsourcing of manufacturing jobs, and it has been on a downward trend ever since, with no end in sight (Meyers (2013). A very modest calculation (without taking into account the growth of jobs due to the growth of production volume) yeilds 19.6 million (1979) – 15.4 (2013) = 4.2 million.

[57] T. Lee (2008). Gates to Congress: Microsoft needs more H-1B visas. *ArsTechica*, March 13. Retrieved 8-19-2014.

the proliferation of low paying service jobs, a shrinking middle class, and large trade deficits, producing a new world economic order in which the United States will play a much less prominent role. In this scenario, the country experiences lower national security, becomes a follower rather than a leader in technology and education, experiences a decline in the standard of living for its citizenry, and has to contend with a much more radicalized political structure.

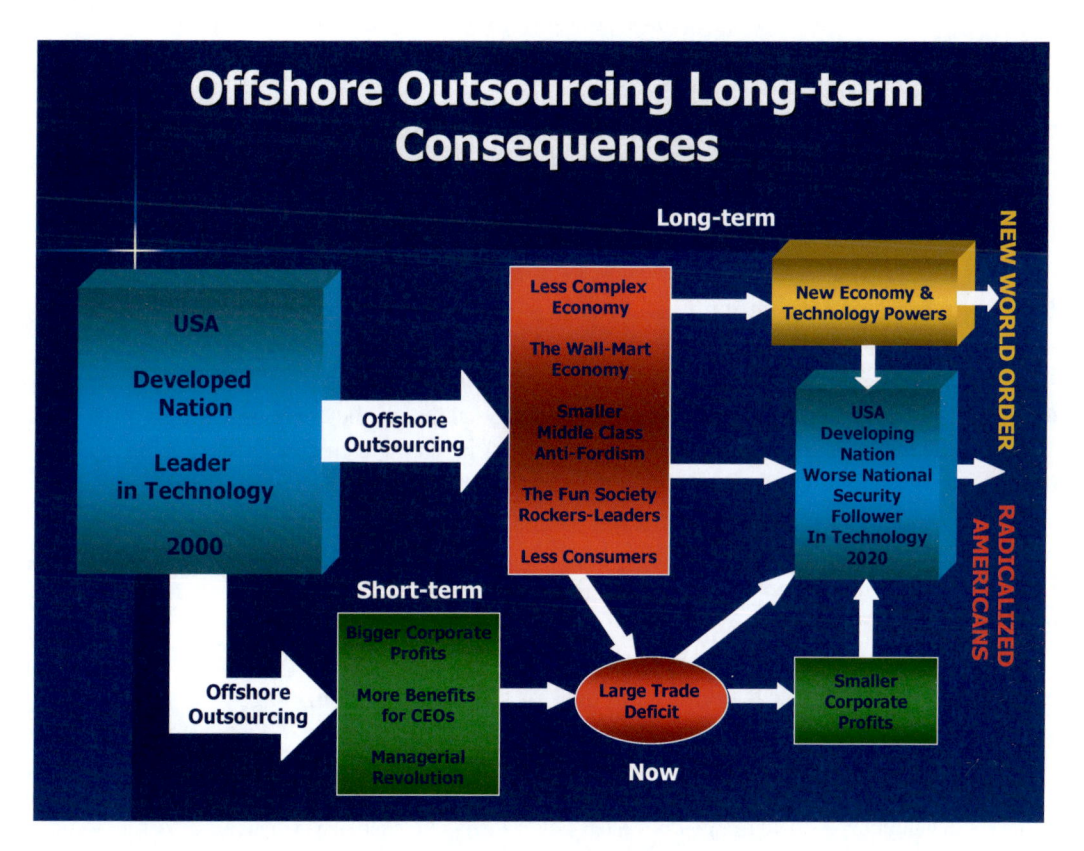

Figure 8.6. Long-term consequences of off shore outsourcing manufacturing by the U.S.

U.S.' Outsourcing Myths

1. Outsourcing and off-shoring that we are experiencing today is akin to what happened at the turn of the 20th century when we ceased being an agricultural economy and became an industrial one.
    - We did not remove agriculture. We increased productivity.
    - We are removing manufacturing which means we are potentially removing intelligence/complexity in engineering and information technology.
    - We maintain our life style by selling our "reputation", i.e., treasury bonds to foreign creditors. As "industrialists" we paid in goods. Now we pay by debts. How long can that continue?
2. The Global Economy is about free trade, and outsourcing/offshoring is the 21st century face of free trade.

- Free trade is about exporting/importing goods at low tariffs, but is it also about exporting millions of jobs?
- Americans should just learn new jobs.
  - What jobs are available? The Chinese influence on prices affects both low tech and high tech industries. Perhaps nanotechnology and biotechnology are an answer, but how many jobs will these emerging industries produce and how long will it take to develop them. They are still about 20 to 100 years away from being more fully developed.
- Americans should move to more complex jobs.
  - Which jobs are more complex? Before one can run, one must learn how to walk. We cannot teach classical music if the symphony orchestra is in another country.

Consequences of Off-shore Outsourcing

The business-related consequences of outsourcing are described in Table 8.1. Ultimately its effect depends upon the balance that industry achieves between optimized processes anywhere in the business value chain and continued investment in core competencies needed to remain competitive in the future. Balanced outsourcing can lead to cost effective processes while simultaneously maintaining in-house capabilities that will insure the ability to compete in the future. Indiscriminant offshoring leads to a race to the bottom with less competitive businesses, less reliable operations, and a gradual loss of skills needed to compete in a technological economy.

Table 8.1. Consequences of Off-shore outsourcing

Criterion	Balanced outsourcing	Radical off-shoring
Process Efficiency	Cost effective	Less competitive business in long-term
Process Reliability	IT in-house specialists' shortage compensated	Less reliable operations
IT infrastructure	Better in-house productivity of IT specialists	Less IT knowledge & skills in-house leads to less business tools, and less competitiveness in long-term

"Dark Factories"

The rising critique of off-shore outsourcing has triggered a sentiment for a strategy which argues manufacturing and other industrial jobs are more socially and economically desirable than jobs in the service sector or finance which dominate the service economy of Western Civilization. Also military or national security concerns stimulate reindustrialization policies, reflecting a need for self-sufficiency and fear for trade routes and supply lines in times of conflict. Reindustrialization policies may reflect national worries over the negative balance of trade.

Figure 8.7. Bethlehem Steel and the National Welding and Manufacturing Company, Newington, Connecticut; after their industrial might, they have been off-shore outsourced in the 2000s.
(Photo: Wikipedia).

Hence, more and more factories are returning to the U.S.; however, they are returning as "dark factories." So-called "dark factories"—otherwise known as "lights out" or "automatic" factories—are manufacturing facilities that do not depend on human labor to get work done. While they may have some benefits for the environment and save on energy usage, the machines and robots do not pay taxes, and they replace the human labor force. In Japan, FANUC Robotics operates a lights-out factory employing robots to make other robots. It looks like something out of science fiction, but it is doubtful whether it is socially justified. Figure 8.8 exemplifies such a "dark factory."

Figure 8.8. This passenger car is made by no humans; maybe it will be driven without a human steering it in a trip to get a welfare check since a "passenger" might not have a bank account for where the check could be transferred. Is this the future of a wise civilization with a happy, labor-less economy?
(Photo: www.peoplesolidarityeconomy.net).

Automation Laws

According to known facts, factory automation caused a worldwide decline in manufacturing jobs during the 2000s-2010s not only in developed countries but in developing countries as well. Hence, laws regulating automation systems should be implemented since these systems are very important with respect to the well-being of society.

The automation systems are one of the most complex systems in civilization which triggered tremendous developmental trends in science and technology in the 20th century. They looked very promising at their early stages but later gave rise to many doubts about their positive role in society. The automation systems designed for better effectiveness, reliability, and quality are positive as long as they do not harm and endanger human beings and society.

With respect to these issues, Andrew Targowski & Vladimir Modrák (2011) offered the following laws of automation in manufacturing:

> Law I. Do not implement high automation technology if you are unsure whether the same goal can be achieved by other means.
> Law II. Do not implement automation technology with the aim of totally eliminating human presence in the manufacturing process.
> Law III. Do not develop automation which harms society or endangers the human race.

In order to integrate all these laws into one coherent discipline, a new strategy should be pursued. Perhaps it should be named *Technosophie*, which would investigate *wise engineering* for a *wise civilization*. This kind of engineering should be developed now and aimed at the sustainability of our civilization in these times of shrinking strategic resources. It is widely known that the population has become too big to sustain our Western styles of life, even in the short-term future. Hence, the future is now and *Technosophie* is needed today as never before.

THE GLOBAL SERVICE INFRASTRUCTURE

The Global-National Service Architecture (NSI)

In the 21st century the advanced economies of Western Civilization are of a service nature, where about 90 percent of employed work is in service-providing businesses and organizations, as it is shown in Figure 8.9.

The national service infrastructure today is operating through the grid of networks such as private networks: LAN (Local Area Network in-house), WAN (Wide Area Network), GAN (Global Area Network) and the public Internet. This grid of networks makes the group similarly developed to the global service infrastructure. The list of services classified in six categories is characterized in Figure 8.10.

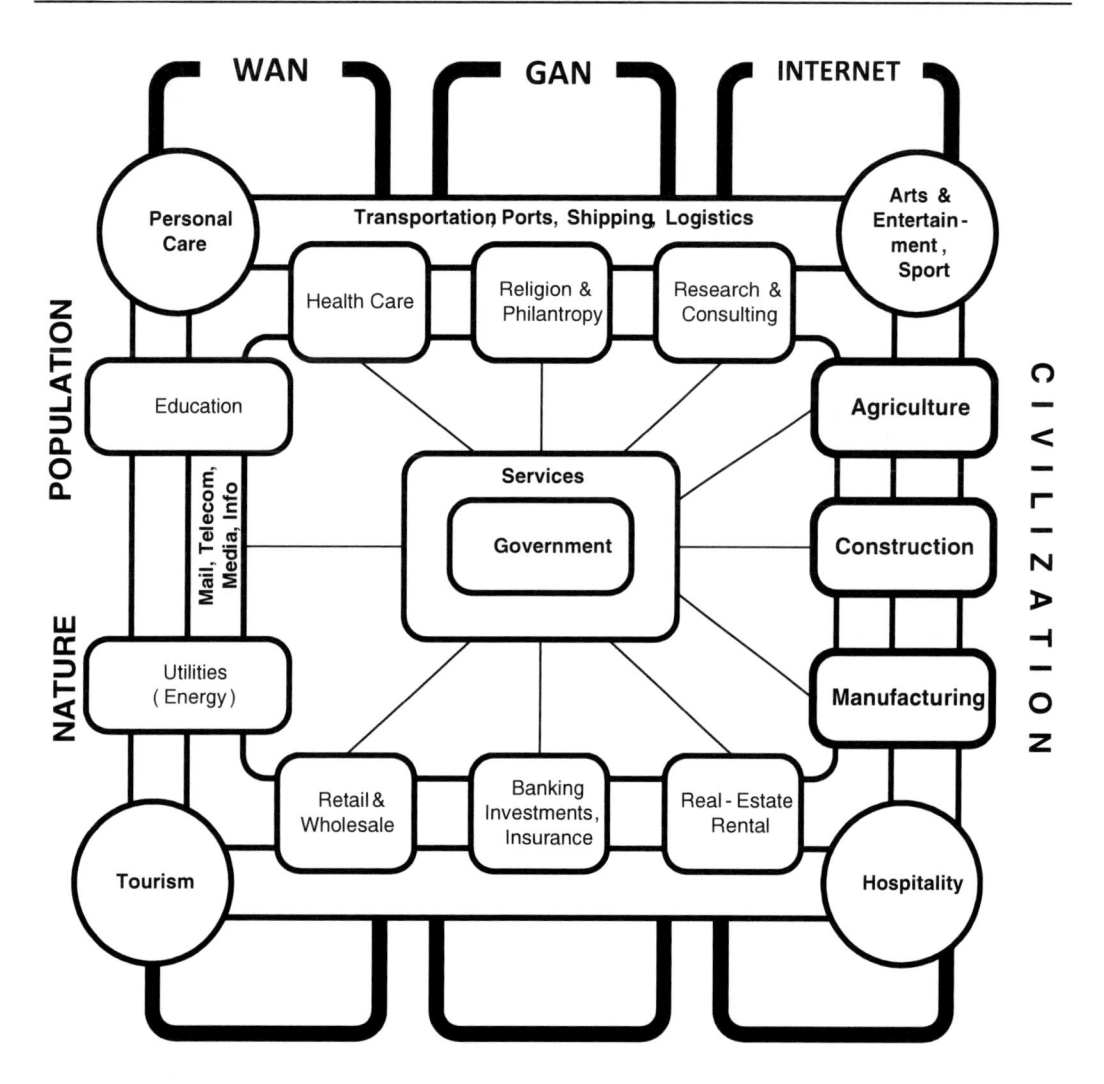

Figure 8.9. The architecture of the global-national service infrastructure functioning within the grid of WAN (Wide Area Network), GAN (Global Area Network), and the internet, instantly connecting, info-communicating, and processing with similar world-wide services.

The service systems evolve along with technological progress and cost-sensitive business strategies of development. Their evolutionary process is depicted in Figure 8.11.

The *Collaborate Model* (1970s) is staffed with experts who can troubleshoot and easily explain to the service users all the problems they may encounter since they created that particular service. Even today this is the case for start-up companies whose developers provide first-hand help to service recipients in areas such as software.

The *Augment Model* (1980s) applies service communication tools answering to the service users most "frequently asked questions" (FAQ). The first FAQ system was initiated by phone and later was applied to websites. A service user must still find out how to use the service.

Society Served	People Served	Possession Served
Services Directed at Citizens & Communities	**Services Directed at Person**	**Services Directed at Property**
Military Service Land Security Service Intelligence Service FEMA Service Immigration Service Diplomatic Service Consular Service Rangers Service Federal Postal Service IRS Service Other	Health Care Physical Therapy Social Assistance Restaurants/Bars Lodging Passenger Transportation Car Rental & Lease Tourism, Location Directions Sport Beauty Salons Barbers Fitness Centers Amusement Parks Gambling Funeral Services Charity Other	Utilities (Water & Energy) Refueling Infrastructure Maintenance Environment Protection Parks Maintenance Equipment Rental & Lease Housing Rental & Lease Real-Estate Disposal/Recycling Laundry/Dry Cleaning Cleaning Service Repair & Maintenance Landscaping/Gardening Security Service Retail Warehousing Freight Transportation Logistics Other
Services Directed at The Nation	**Services Directed at People's Awareness**	**Services Directed at Info-Communication Handling**
Political Parties Justice Legislature Governing Non-Government Organizations Scientific Societies Professional Societies Civic Societies Philanthropy Other	Religion Education Arts Museums Entertainment Media Public Relations Advertisement Other	Banking Insurance Investment Service Professional, Management, Scientific, and Technical Services Telecommunication & Mail Data Processing & Transmission Internet .Libraries Information Service Publishing Systems Repair & Maintenance Other

Tangible Service / Intangible Service

Agriculture, Forestry, Fishing, Mining, Construction, Manufacturing

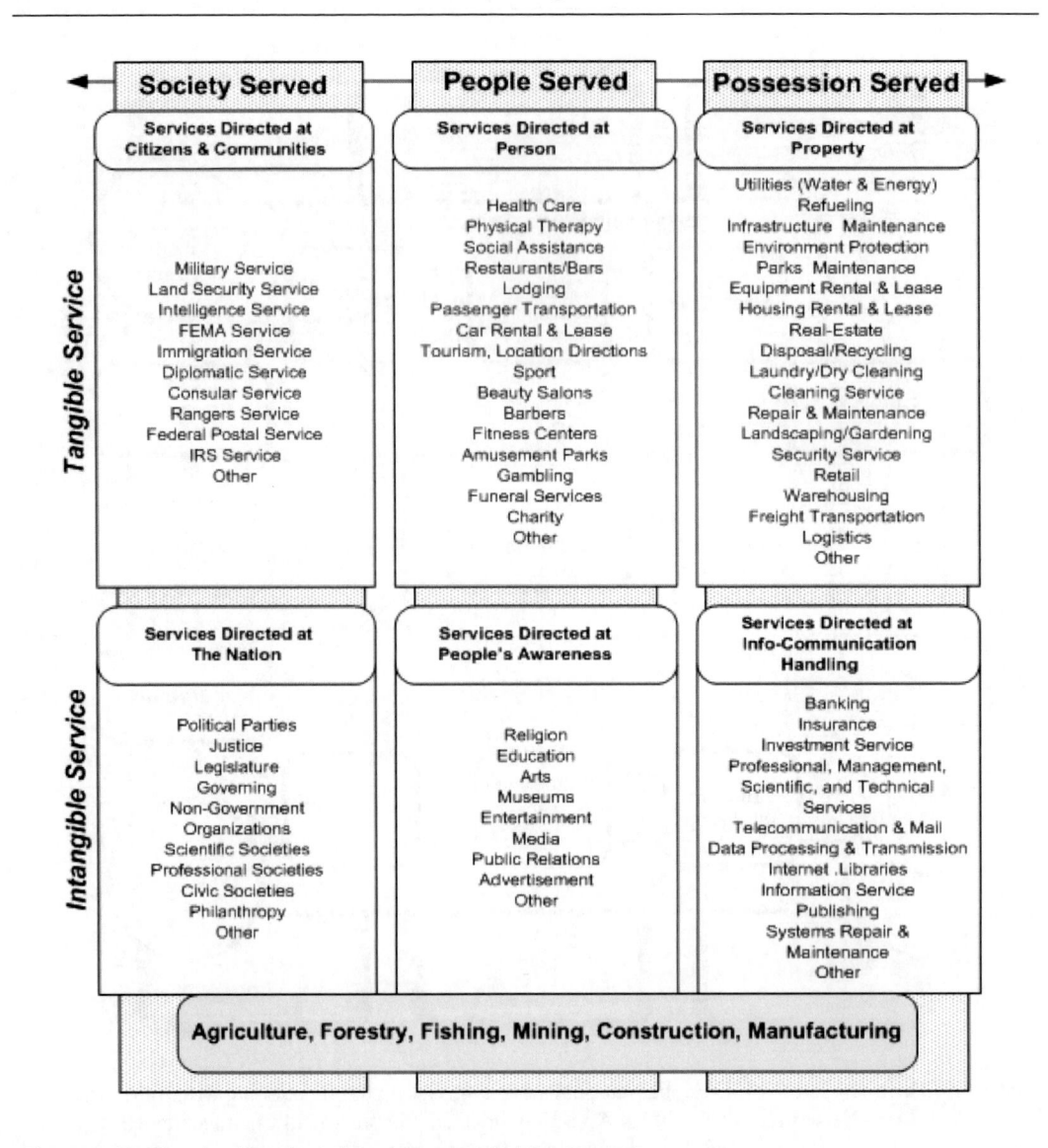

Figure 8.10. The classification of services provided for the society.

The *Outsource Model* (2000s) delegates servicing to a third party located on-shore or frequently off-shore (e.g., India). This model was triggered by the strategy of restructuring and cost-cutting by allocating manufacturing to China and IT projects and customer service to India as both countries provide low-cost labor. This model leads to the decline of middle class in developed nations, and as far as customer service is concerned, is not embraced by the American customers because the level of help and expertise provided is rather low, perhaps due to the physical distance from the places of action.

The *Automate Model* (2010s) is supported by high-tech companies which need to utilize their available (idle?) resources in the next wave of technological development. This model eliminates humans from service processes and generates a market demand for advanced technology. This is a very controversial strategy, first in terms of a right technical solution and second in terms of the right social solution. As far as the former is concerned automation of *complex* service systems cannot be a reliable solution since many factors are not known for designers. For example, the FAA does not allow pilots to use auto-pilot systems in bad weather. If we look at the control rooms of many process installations, we see a lot of instrumentation but operators who do nothing since the process control has been automated. In the case of an emergency these operators very often do not know what to do because they are without practice of how to handle crisis situations. As far as the latter is concerned, service automation should not lead to the drastic decline of employment as it has occurred in agriculture and manufacturing. People should have something to do and have the necessary income to support their lives and society (including the demand to create high-tech companies), even with the cost inefficiencies and particularly if the population is constantly growing! Technology, particularly computers, may merely further automate blue and white-collar jobs, achieving unprecedented speed and consistency, robbing workers of whatever skill and gratification they may retain and increasing the impersonality and remoteness of management.

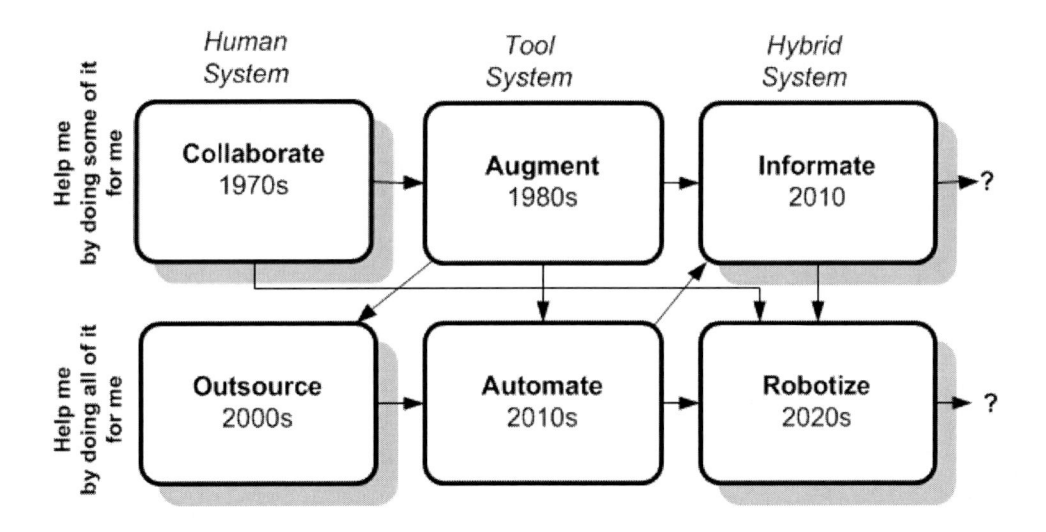

Figure 8.11. The paradigms of service evolution. (The first four stages come from a model of J. Spohrer and P. Maglio from the IBM Almaden Research Center).

The *Informate* Model (2010) empowers ordinary working people with the overall knowledge of service processes, making them capable of critical and collaborative judgment about service. This model assumes some sort of automated info-communication infrastructure. However, it is operated and supervised by humans supported by e-information which leaves room for the human operator to conceptualize status (change) and the required decisions filtered by human knowledge (very often under the form of given business knowledge, coming from data mining) leading to wise decisions made ultimately by humans. This model is particularly appropriate for semi-ill and ill-structured decisions under uncertainty. This model to a certain extent coexists with the Automate Model. A pilot who lands a plane by hand in a bad weather or a policeman who directs traffic when traffic lights fail (but is still in wireless communication with the command center) are good examples of this model.

The *Robotize Model* (2020) is a combination of the Collaborate, Automate, and Informate Models, particularly in the case of Japan. In some countries there is a shortage in the supply of labor for industrial work, which drives up investment in robotics. With the present demographic trends this shortage will be even more pronounced in years to come, which will further stimulate robotics investment in repetitive lifts involved in handling materials such as parts, beverage crates, and so forth. The number of robots is constantly increasing in the manufacturing industry: Japan has 280 per 10,000 people; Singapore 148; Rep. of Korea 116; Germany 102; Sweden 69; Italy 67; Finland 51; Benelux 49; United States 48; France 48; Switzerland 46; Austria 44; Spain 41 Australia 25; Denmark 24; United Kingdom 23; Norway 16 (UN/ECE NEWS, 2000). It is interesting that in Japan a robot does not replace a worker; rather, the worker serves as its "master," taking care of it.

"Organizations that take steps toward exclusively automating strategy can set a course that is not easily reversed. They are likely to find themselves crippled by antagonism from the work force and the depletion of knowledge that would be needed in value-adding activities. The absence of a self-conscious strategy to exploit the informating capacity of the new technology has tended to mean that managerial action flows along the path of least resistance – a path that, at least superficially, appears to serve only the interest of managerial hegemony" (Zuboff 1988: 391).

The automation strategy of service creates the environment of jobbers, who are also required to act "automatically," leading in its conclusion to the deadliest, most sterile passivity in history since the fall of the Roman Empire (476 AD). This strategy will push humans into the bifurcation stage when complex systems designers will be very sophisticated people and the users of this systems will be very simple people. This has occurred previously in the history of the human race, when the language-speaking *Cro Magnions* replaced the *Neanderthals*, who could only bark, about 40,000 years ago in Europe.

The current role of universities is to launch service-oriented programs, whose systemic components to certain degrees are available and technologically are in the reach of the faculty and students. However, the most important role of the university is to research and teach the social, corporate, and personal responsibility in developing and managing ethical complex service systems!

In order to fulfill this noble task, the Three Laws of Service Systems defined by Andrew Targowski cannot be violated by their developers and operators. These laws are similar to Isaac Asimov's approach to robotization but directed towards service automation and should be a subject of broader discussions among specialists in ethics, law, and other appropriate disciplines:

Law I - Do not develop service systems without a human presence.
Law II - Do not develop service systems which harm society.
Law III - Do not develop service systems which endanger the human race.

The Law I protects people against passivity. Law II protects society against structured unemployment. Law III protects the human race against the bifurcation into two kinds of species. It would be necessary for governments, scientific, professional, trade and industrial associations to sign the Service Systems Agreement based on these laws to be sure that service systems are developed and managed in a responsible manner.

Figure 8.12 depicts a model of six service categories and their developmental paradigms. The role of the science of service is to constantly update these paradigms and implement into research, reaching, and consulting.

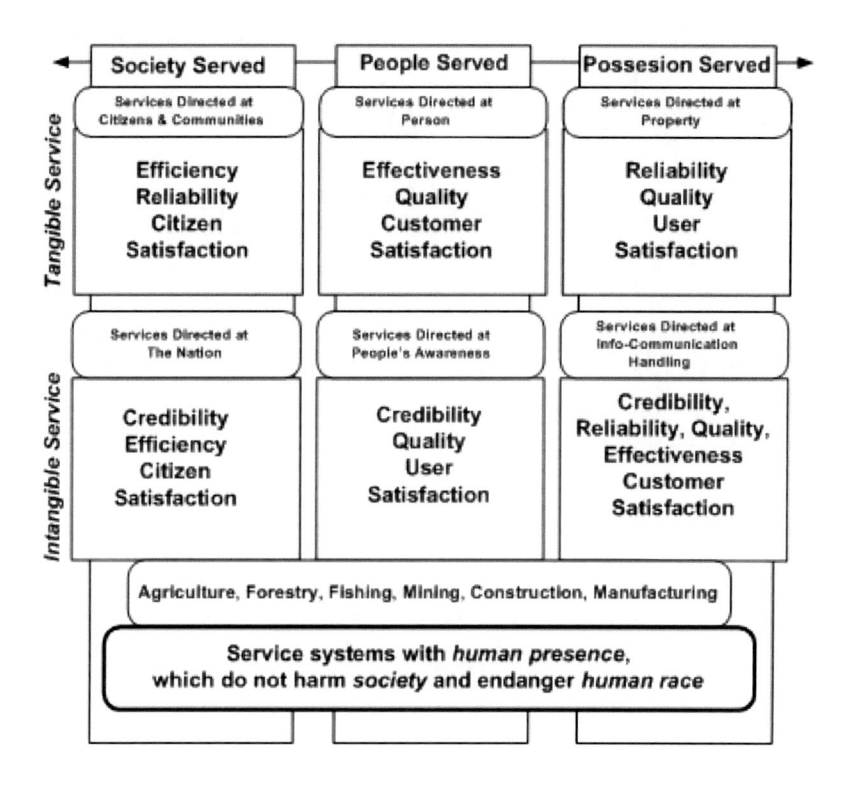

Figure 8.12. The Developmental Paradigms of Six Categories of Services.

THE GLOBAL-VIRTUAL INFORMATION INFRASTRUCTURE

Electronic Global Village (EGV)

Global Village is a term invented by Marshall McLuhan and spread in his books *The Gutenberg Galaxy: The Making of Typographic Man (1962)* and *Understanding Media (1964)*. McLuhan described how the globe has been contracted into a village by television and the instantaneous movement of information and images coming from/to every corner of the world at the same time. In bringing all social and political functions together in a sudden implosion, electric speed heightened human awareness of responsibility to an intense degree (McLuhan 1964).

McLuhan was impressed with the rising overwhelming presence of television in homes in the 1960s and its involvement in political issues, investigative journalism and popular entertainment under the form of serial shows and the transmission of sport events. Therefore, he noticed this new societal tool and its new ability of promoting "image as the message." Figure 8.13 illustrates that the Global Village has the powerful ability to disseminate "image as message", which was apparent during the clash of civilizations in summer 2014.

Figure 8.13. The Global Village is powerful in its ability to disseminate "image as a message" which can be seen during the clash of civilizations, reflecting globalism versus tribalism on August 19, 2014.

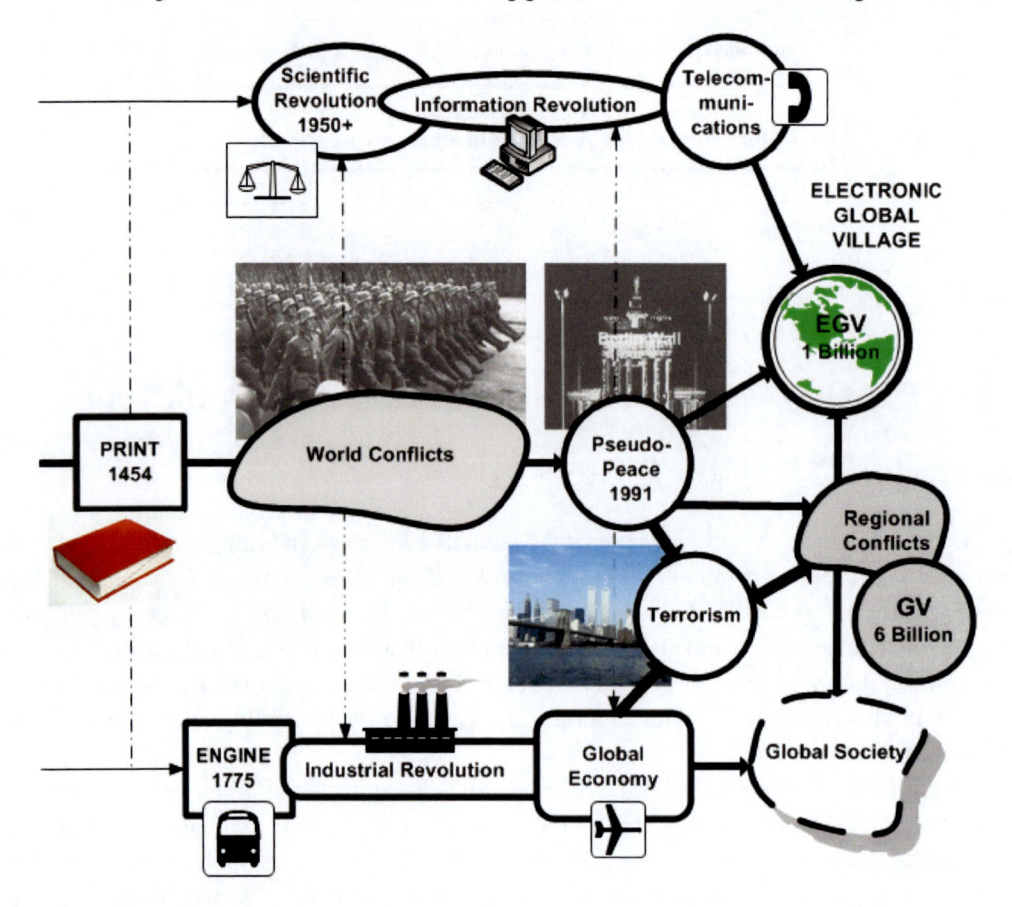

Figure 8.14. The world-wide bifurcation process of contemporary society in the 21st century.

Marshal McLuhan, however, passed away in 1980 just before the telecommunication boom and creeping revolution of micro-computers ("PS"), so he was not able to see all that would become of the Global Village. Targowski (1991) extended McLuhan's term into Electronic Global Village. The new EGV is different than GV since in the latter information is disseminated top-down, while in EGV information is dispersed in both directions with a very strong tendency that the volume of information sent bottom up surpasses the volume of information sent top-down. One can even state that the power of the EGV leads towards the bifurcation of the world population into voice active habitants of EGV and voiceless passive habitants of GV. Today there are about 1 billion inhabitants with a voice and about 6 billion habitants without a voice. The former have become electronic global citizens and the latter are still tribesmen involved in regional conflicts. This bifurcation process of today's society is illustrated in Figure 8.14.

The architecture of the Electronic Global Village is depicted in Figure 8.15. It shows the following new civilization conceptual realities:

- Cyberspace as a new electronic real estate where digital information is stored, processed, accessed, and communicated globally through tele-computer networks.
- Virtual schools, colleges, and universities which teach and graduate students but do not have buildings, although they have strong information infrastructure.
- Virtual businesses which make profit but do not have buildings; they nonetheless have strong information infrastructure.
- Online governments which communicate electronically with their stakeholders through strong information infrastructure.
- Electronic global citizens (EGC) who study, do business, and collaborate with others in a variety of issues in cyberspace.
- Digital libraries which have world-wide accessible and spread-out collections of e-books.
- Cyber money which is a new emerging currency to make all sorts of deals in cyberspace. One of its forms is Bitcoin which is in question now and has a global circulation worth of more than $1.4 billion on paper. Yet almost no one, it seems, knows the true identity of its creator. In the United States, this mysterious money has become the darling of antigovernment libertarians and computer wizards prospecting in the virtual mines of cyberspace. In Europe, meanwhile, it has found its niche as the coinage of anarchic youth (Faiola and Farnam 2013).
- e-Commerce – online buying and selling.
- Telemedicine – healthcare services provided online.
- Telicity – a city which communicates online and handles the duties, requests, issues, etc., of citizens and the city online.
- e-Republic – a nation which communicates online and handles the duties, requests, issues, etc., of citizens and the nation online.
- Information Superhighway (INFOSTRADA) – the paradigm of a new economy applying computer networks.
- Global digital consciousness which is constantly developing and transforming into collective intelligence which can be applied by electronic global citizens and their organizations.
- Altogether, these new conceptual realities contribute to the development of the mediasphere as the new layer of the human mind, perhaps digital mind.

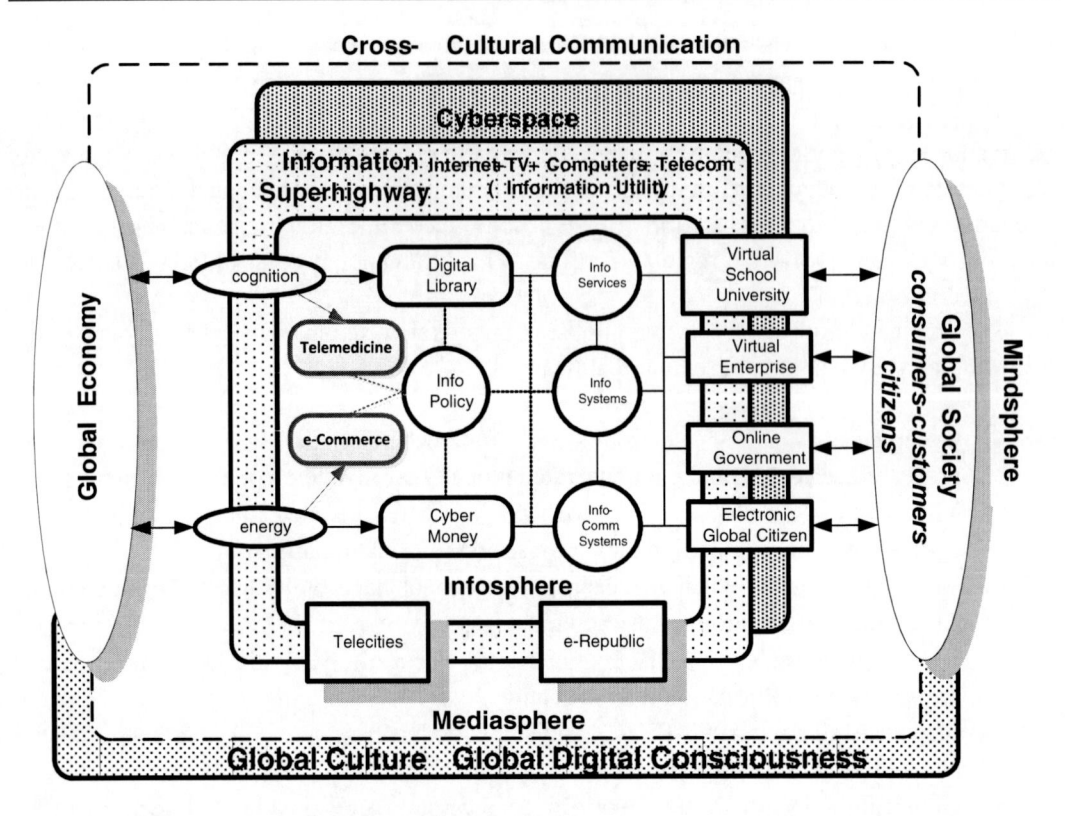

Figure 8.15. The architecture of Electronic Global Village.

The Internetization of Civilization

The universal Internetization in the 21st century is spectacular and in fact enjoys a great appreciation by most of its users as a remedy for all socio-economic diseases. And indeed, the model of the Internetization, depicted in Figure 8.16 shows a number of benefits, but it also contains many disadvantages.

The advantages include the following:

- Empowers users,
- Empowers organizations,
- Empowers global business,
- Empowers the society in reacting to negative issues.

Some disadvantages, in developed nations include:

- Increased unemployment, caused by the outsourcing of manufacturing,
- Decreased income of the middle class,
- Triggers economic crisis due to the above-mentioned causes,
- Prompts political crisis due to the above-mentioned causes,
- Activates civic unrest, due to the above-mentioned causes.

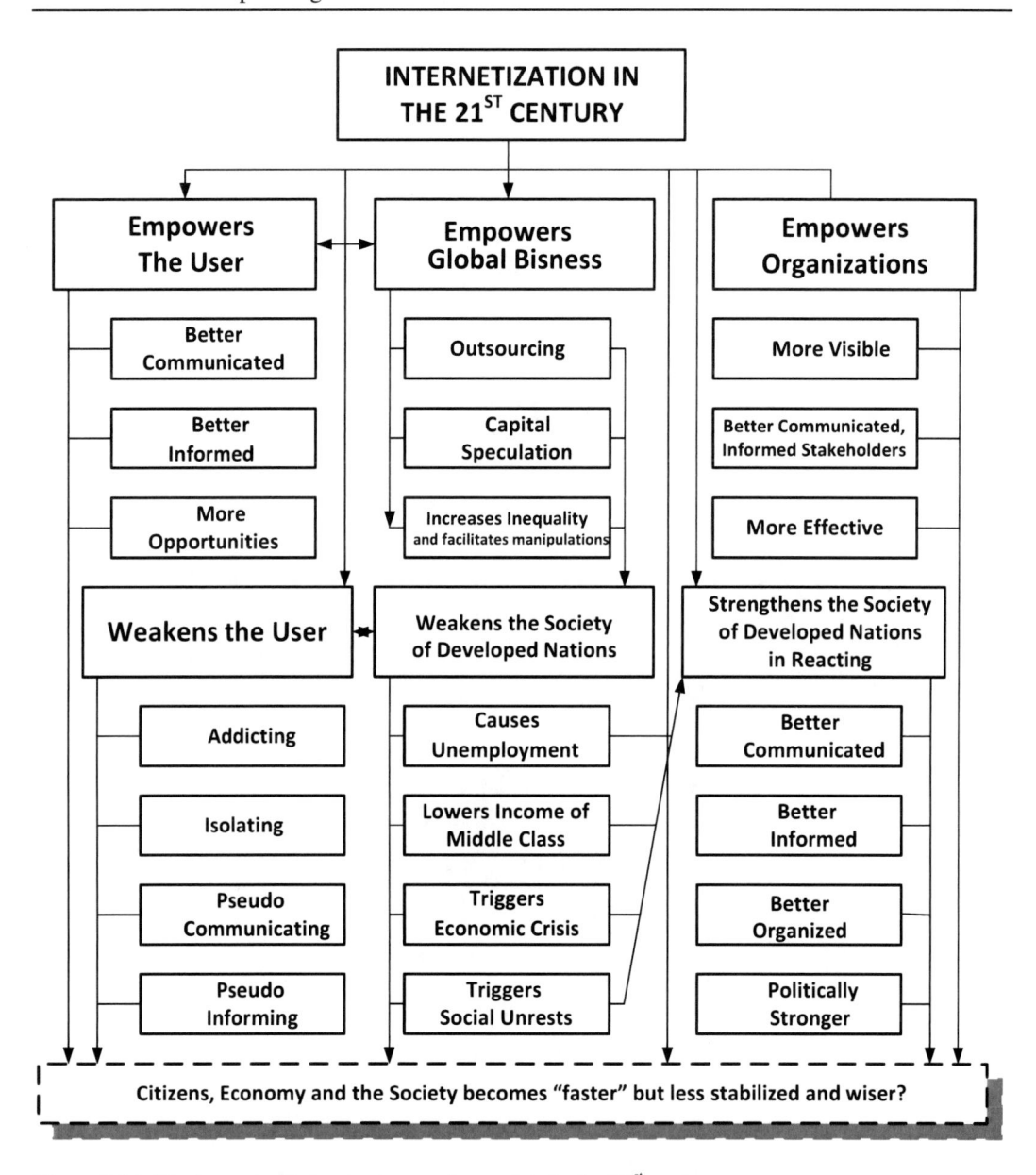

Figure 8.16. The impact of Internization on the society in the 21st century.

It can be concluded with a high degree of rational certainty that the Internetization has led Western Civilization to its fall and has transformed it into a global civilization, which is mostly beneficial for developing countries and disadvantageous for developed ones. However, the "99%" of the population of the developed countries do not agree with this state of affairs. This leads to riots, and possibly to social revolution (e.g., "Occupy Wall Street"), by way of which the kind of democracy and capitalism that we now know and practice today might be corrected.

Perhaps we shall soon see whether this correction is positive, and therefore whether the Internet as the main perpetrator has created a positive macro-scale technopoly (Postman 1992) for mankind.

The Internet of Things

The Internet of Things (IoT) is the next platform of universal connectivity, after the first platform which connects the people (IoP). It refers to the interconnection of devices, systems, and services with the digital interfaces to conduct machine-to-machine communications (M2M) through a variety of platforms, protocols, domains, and applications. Almost every modern object with the digital interface can be connected with another objects and supervising people.

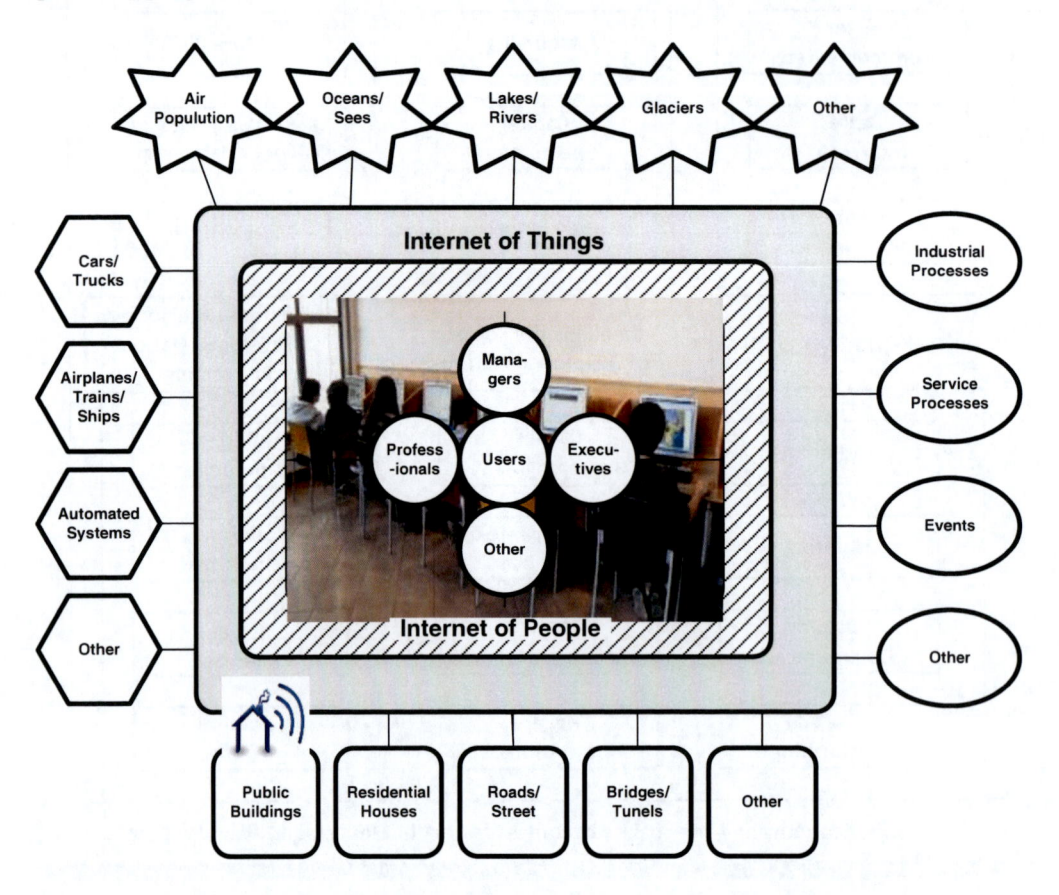

Figure 8.17. The architecture of the Internet of Things which world-wide connects trillions of sensors monitoring and supervising things like machines, vehicles, trains, facilities, and so forth.

Today it is at the early conceptual stage of development like the Internet of People was in the 1960s. Among the potential applications one can recognize the following;

- Environment monitoring for sustainable planet life.
- Infrastructure supervision for breakdowns and preventive maintenance.
- Industrial applications to monitor manufacturing operations particularly in the area of complex chemical processes.
- Energy control for optimizing its consumption.
- Medical and health systems for their reliability.
- Cars, trucks, buses, and transport systems for their reliability.

- Roads and bridges for their breakdowns and maintenance.
- Other

The architecture of the Internet of Things is provided in Figure 8.17. It is mostly composed of event-driven and machine-focused protocols.

The Internet of Things will connect millions of new devices to monitor and supervise them. As these "things" add capabilities like context awareness, increased processing power, and energy independence, and as more people and new types of information are connected, civilization will quickly enter the Internet of Everything (IoE), where things that were silent will have a voice. As billions and even trillions of sensors are placed around the globe and in our planet's atmosphere, humans will gain the ability to literally hear the world's "heartbeat." Without a doubt, we will know when our planet's climate and environment are healthy or sick. With this intimate understanding, perhaps humans can begin to eradicate some of our most pressing challenges, including hunger and ensuring the availability of drinkable water.

The Enterprise Information Infrastructure (EII)

The goals of EII are to support the development and operations of an enterprise as follows:

1. To empower an enterprise in better positioning itself in the marketplace through the optimization of using resources from other infrastructures (urban, agricultural, industrial, etc.),
2. To empower an enterprise's workers and executives in broadening their cognition about operated/managed processes and resources.
3. To connect with other e-enterprises and institutions locally, regionally, nationally, and globally through appropriate information infrastructures, such as LII, RII, NII, and GII, including also HII (Home Information Infrastructure).

The strategy of EII should lead towards the gradual development of a comprehensive, compatible, reliable, secure, and safe complex of digital resources, processes and services according to the master plan. These new computer-driven systems and services require a new approach towards IT applications in the enterprise. The set of these systems and services is called the Enterprise Information Infrastructure (EII). This is a new civilization infrastructure, which is composed of the following electronic invisible layers (Figure 8.18):

1. Telecommunications Layer – physical information transmission over public telecommunications lines and facilities,
2. Computer Networks Layer – managed on-line information transmission among clusters of computers,
3. Internet Layer – public cyberspace for information exchange in the global publicsphere.
4. Computing Layer – physical electronic processing of information,
5. Communication Layer – facilities and systems of providing on-line information,

6. Application Layer – application systems of info-communication handling and processing applied by the end-users in the enterprise.
7. Intelligence Layer – a management dashboard containing key performance indicators in the areas of global, business, and sustainability intelligences.

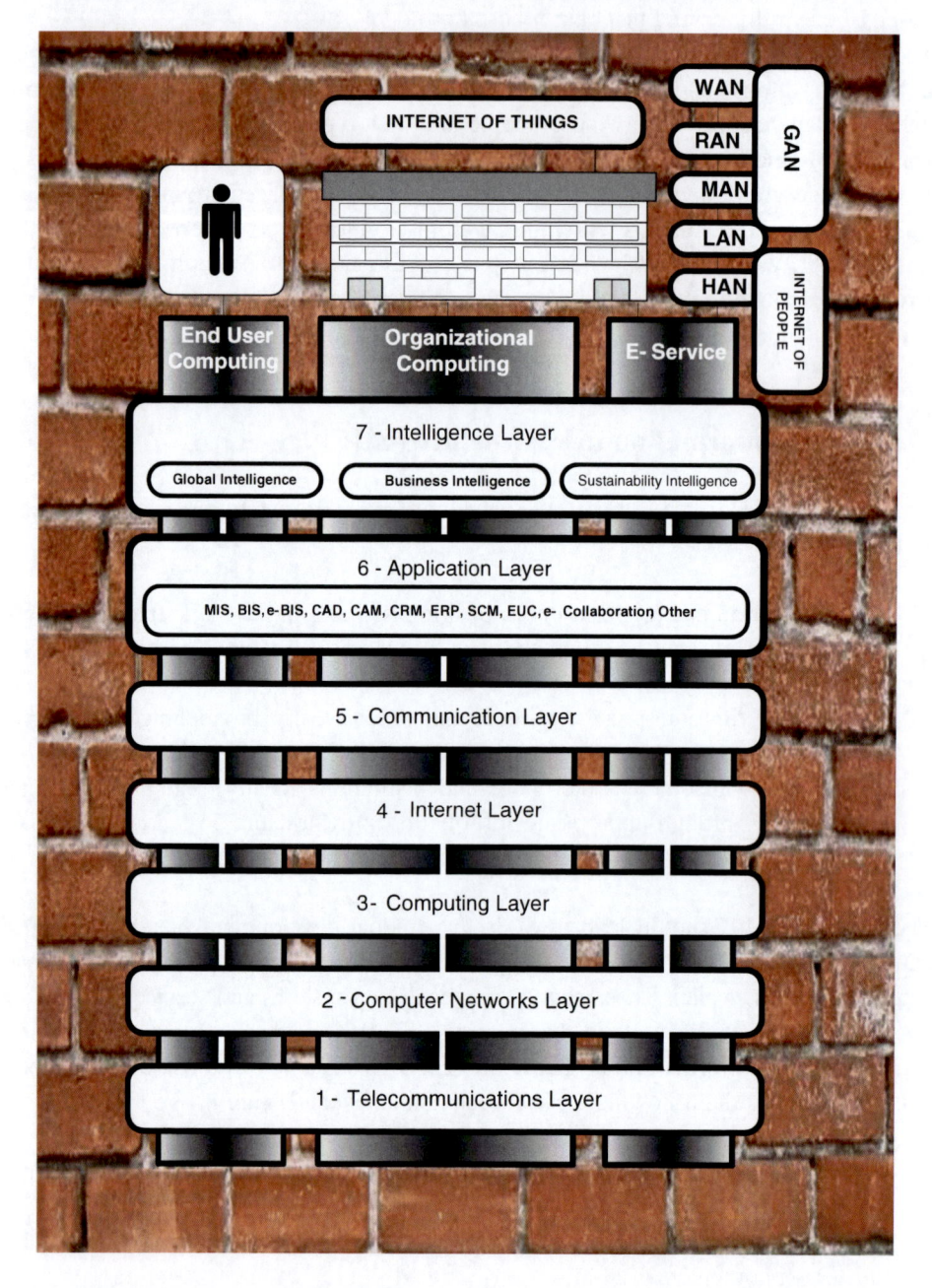

Figure 8.18. The architecture of the Enterprise Information Infrastructure in the dawn of the 21st century with electronic and mortar bricks joined.
(HAN-Home Area Network, LAN-Local Area Network, MAN-Metropolitan Area Network, RAN-Rural Area Network, WAN-Wide Area Network, GAN-Global Area Network).

These layers are new electronic "bricks" which work within the brick and mortar or click and click or mixed environments. These electronic "bricks" are invisible to the human eye, but they are there and monitor and control the physical and information infrastructures.

Western Civilization is the world leader in developing and operating the Enterprise Information Infrastructure. It brings in cost effectiveness in business/organization development and operations in the world-wide competiveness race.

The Global Information Infrastructure (GII)

The Global Information Infrastructure (Targowski 1996) (Figure 8.19) is mostly developing today in Western Civilization where the technological mantra that technology is the remedy for all societal problems dominates the minds of politicians and businessmen. This kind of an information infrastructure allows for instant communication and paperless bureaucracy between citizens & customers and institutions & businesses locally, regionally, nationally and globally. It looks as though strong progress in social engineering has been achieved. On the other hand it makes these dealings and infrastructures vulnerable for espionage, break downs, and cyber warfare which are taking place among world powers today.

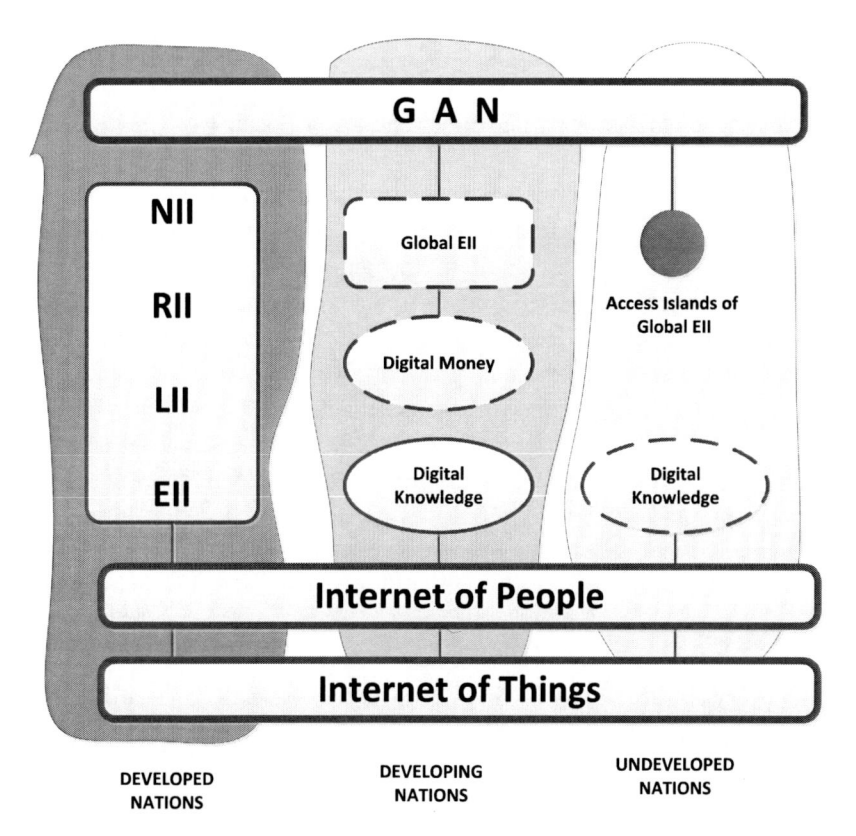

Figure 8.19. The architecture of the global information infrastructure in the dawn of the 21st century (EII-Enterprise Information Infrastructure, LII-Local Information Infrastructure, RII-Rural Information Infrastructure, and NII-National Information Infrastructure).

Today, from the sustainability point of view, it is difficult to decide which civilization is more sustainable: traditional (less developed) or electronic/virtual (more developed)?

Robots versus Humans

The number of robots in the world today is approaching 1,000,000, with almost half in Japan and just 15% in the USA. couple of decades ago, 90% of robots were used in car manufacturing, typically on assembly lines doing a variety of repetitive tasks. Today only 50% are in automobile plants, with the other half spread out among other factories, laboratories, warehouses, energy plants, hospitals, and many other industries. Robots are used for assembling products, handling dangerous materials, spray-painting, cutting and polishing, and inspection of products. The number of robots used in tasks as diverse as cleaning sewers, detecting bombs and performing intricate surgery is increasing steadily and will continue to grow in coming years (Automation.com).

The useful potential of robots include domestic tasks like mowing the lawn and vacuuming the carpet, which are rather easy job for many unskilled people. Many robots are also applied in underwater projects, demolition projects, and in medical surgical treatments. A big increase is predicted for domestic robots used for vacuum cleaning and lawn mowing. A robot for cleaning a floor can be bought for about $200. In the wake of anthrax alerts at post offices, robots are increasingly used in postal sorting applications. There is huge potential to robotize the US postal service. Some 100,000 robots eventually can sort the mail of the U.S. Post Office. This means that at least the same amount of postal workers or even more may lose their jobs.

Since thousands of IT professionals work every day in advancing microprocessor speed, image processing, and human jobs simulation, this will result not only in minimizing the cost of business operations, but it will result in the automation of most uninteresting, low-intelligence, low-paying jobs.

Marshall Brain, founder of HowStuffWorks.com, has written a couple of interesting essays about robotics in the future which are impressive and scary. He thinks that it is quite believable that over the next 35 years robots will displace most human jobs. According to Brain's projections in his essay *Robotic Nation* (2014) humanoid robots will be widely available by 2030. They will replace jobs currently filled by people for work such as fast-food service, housecleaning and retail sales. Unless ways are found to compensate for these lost jobs, Brain estimates that more than 50% of Americans could be unemployed by 2050, replaced by robots. Marshal Brains predicts the following huge job losses by 2040 or 2050 as robots move into the workplace will be as follows

- Nearly every construction job will go to a robot. That's about 6 million jobs lost.
- Nearly every manufacturing job will go to a robot. That's 16 million jobs lost.
- Nearly every transportation job will go to a robot. That's 3 million jobs lost.
- Nearly every hotel and restaurant job will go to a robot. That's 10 million jobs lost.

M. Brain reminds us that during the Great Depression at its very worst, 25% of the population was unemployed. In the robotic future, where 50 million jobs are lost, there is the potential for 50% unemployment. The conventional wisdom says that the economy will create 50 million new jobs to absorb all the unemployed people. However, nobody seems to know what kind of jobs these supposedly new jobs will be.

Perhaps the scariest prediction is that the Singularity Era is coming and human intelligence will become increasingly non-biological and trillions of times more powerful than it is today—in other words, the dawning of a new civilization that will enable us to transcend our biological limitations and amplify our creativity. In his book *Singularity is Near*, Ray Kurzweil (2006) predicts that by about 2045 computers will think faster than humans and a new race of cyborgs will replace *homo sapiens*. Even if Kurzweil's prediction about the artificial speed of thinking turns out to be correct, does it mean that humans will be wiser? Those who think fast do not necessarily think wiser than slow thinkers.

We must also ask whether it is wise for us (and for Ray Kurzweil also) to promote such technological progress which eventually will endanger the human race. Should we not apply Isaac Asimov's (1950) Three Laws of Robotics? The Three Laws are as follows:

I. A robot may not injure a human being or, through inaction, allow a human being to come to harm.
II. A robot must obey the orders given to it by human beings, except where such orders would conflict with the First Law.
III. A robot must protect its own existence as long as such protection does not conflict with the First or Second Law (Isaac Asimov. I, Robot (Asimov, Isaac - I, Robot.pdf). p. 85. Retrieved 11 November 2010.

Figure 8.20. Robots versus humans in thinking and moving.
(Photo: www.contently.com).

Western Civilization today is blind and for the sake of technological progress is ready to replace humans by robots, neglecting all voices who advocate that technological progress should be regulated by society not by business which in pursuing low labor cost solutions is ready to eliminate its customers.

THE GLOBAL KNOWLEDGE INFRASTRUCTURE (GKI)

From Data to Knowledge and Wisdom

Information is the key factor in modernizing civilization since the invention of printed book in the 15th century. Today the Internet has the same role as the first book, since it handles and disseminates information around the world. It can be called *book.2*. Ever since the invention of the Internet, the concept of the Information Wave is overtaking the way of thinking today and is promising that digital knowledge will be available world-wide for the benefit of mankind. However, what is information and knowledge? In many situations they are seen as a synonymous. But this, of course, is not true. Figure 8.21 depicts the Semantic Ladder (Targowski 2003) which explains the set and hierarchy of cognition units.]

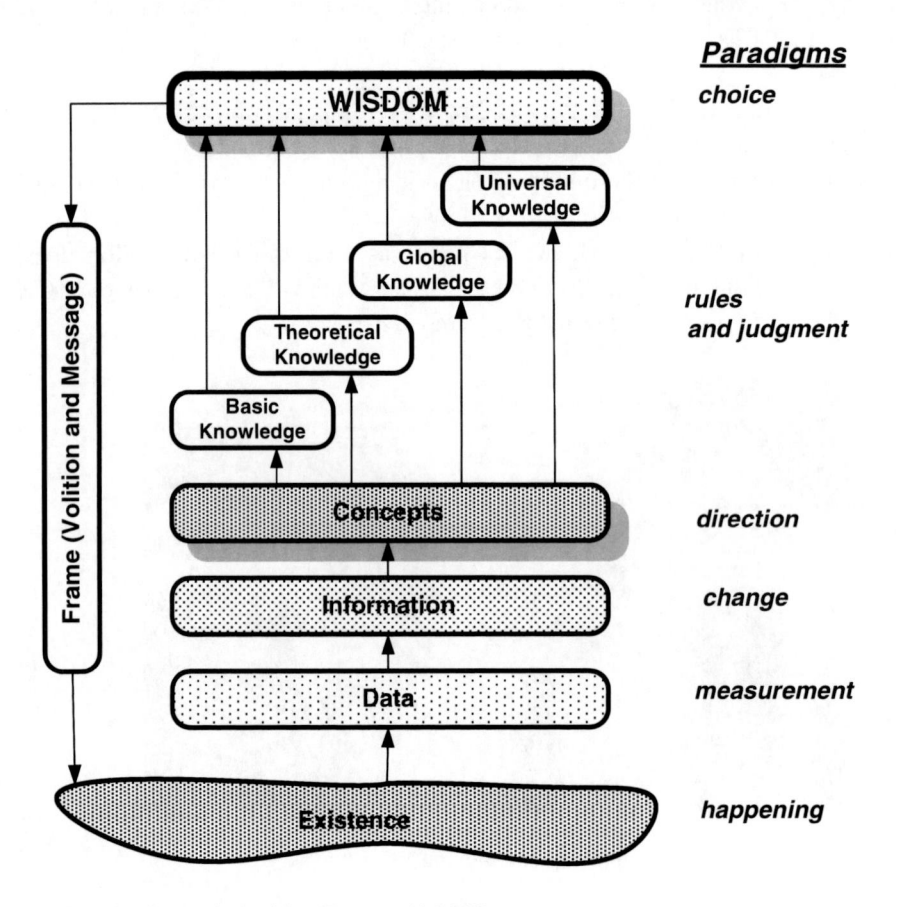

Figure 8.21. The Semantic Ladder (Targowski 2003).

The Semantic Model explains that wisdom is not knowledge, neither is it information nor data. Wisdom is judgment and the choice of concepts of thinking and action. Moreover, in order that the concept is properly formulated, one needs to be well-informed; that is, one has to have verifiable data. In order to make a wise assessment, one needs to have good knowledge: basic, theoretical, global and universal. Not all have such kinds of knowledge, and therefore their judgments are not wise within the range of knowledge that a decision-making subject has. This is not to say that if one has a wide the range of knowledge at their disposal, one is guarantee of a wise judgment. There are other factors, such as emotions, intuition, luck or the will to implement a wise action. All these attributes reflect an art of living. The word 'art' used here refers to an intuitive and innovative approach to the known and right principles of judgment and an ability to create new principles and breaking rules when outdated for the case in question.

The theory of the Semantic Ladder is a contemporary approach to units of cognition in the 21st century. It clearly distinguishes knowledge and wisdom from the remaining units of cognition. In approaches from centuries ago, wisdom was a concept of the totality of the wisdom of mankind, which an individual man was incapable of attaining, and therefore was not wise. In a contemporary psychological approach, wisdom is an expert attitude, inaccessible to the rank and file. In this cognitive IT approach, wisdom can be possessed by any sane individual (Targowski 2013).

The Semantic Ladder clearly indicates that it is not easy to convert information into knowledge and wisdom. However, data mining "Big Data" may provide some rules about a given business or institution's development and/or operations. For example Walmart found that on Mondays the best selling goods are baby pampers and beer. Hence, a store manager is more knowledgeable and can select amongst possible strategies: 1) to satisfy a customer - baby pampers and beer should be kept in the same alley, 2) to satisfy business - these two items should be spread apart to different alleys to stimulate a customer to buy other items on impulse.

From Minds to Global Knowledge Infrastructure

Information is a cognitive entity which supplies the human brain with the external mental state of reality based upon the input which the human mind processes under the forms of thinking, memorizing, judgments, and choices which can be kept or share with external parties. To do so, humans (from Western Civilization) use the following four specialized minds (Targowski 2013):

- Western Basic Mind – developed in practice and school age, responsible for common sense thinking in terms of morality & ethics, the art of communication, and basic life functions and problem solving.
- Western Whole Mind – educated in theoretical & critical thinking and problem solving at a higher level of sophistication than the Western Basic Mind.
- Western Global Mind – developed a world-wide view through colonization, trade, and the globalization of capital, goods, services, ideas, and people.
- Western Universal Mind – educated in human, civil, women, and gay rights and international law.

If somebody has these four minds, they also have the Western Complete Mind. In the Industrial Age all of these minds were developing mostly through traditional schooling, higher education, and international experience. In the dawn of the 21st century, in the

Information Age, these minds have a chance to be developed faster and perhaps deeper through the digitalization of information and its distribution.

A set of digital information services is provided in Figure 8.22 under the form of the global knowledge infrastructure which is composed of virtual schools and colleges, online courses, digital libraries, databases, digital references, digital press, digital TV, digital films (video), and so forth. Certainly, the online users, regardless of their education status, have almost unlimited instant world-wide access to data and information provided by the mentioned digital services. Eventually, this should lead to better conceptualization and common sense knowledge and wisdom. However, only some will be able to apply theoretical knowledge and make more sophisticated judgments and choices based upon that knowledge.

Intensive application of information-communication technology (ICT) together with the Internet at the dawn of the 21st century is leading to a strong divergence among users of digital media. Among them one can distinguish (Targowski 2014):

- • Digital Illiterates apply traditional (old) ICT. They are uninformed and reason poorly; however, if they improve their knowledge/skills they may advance to Digital Migrants who work on adapting to new conditions of handling information. They may improve their skills in using the Internet and its resources as Digital Tourists. The global information infrastructure should improve their Basic Mind.
- • Digital Migrants have good knowledge/skills in handling information but mostly apply old ICT. They only occasionally apply new ICT, usually with the help of other people. They may improve digital skills to advance to Digital Tourists or to Digital Natives They are able to reason well at the level of common sense. The global information infrastructure should improve mostly their Basic Mind but other minds can be improved as well.
- • Digital Tourists are good Netizens (mostly members of the younger generation) who spend hours using the Internet, but their knowledge/skills of handling and understanding cognition units is shallow, as is their level of reading. They collect a lot of data and become "Datamaniacs," but their reasoning is pseudo-reasoning, sometimes good, but mostly questionable. If they improve their knowledge and skills of handling information, they may become Digital Natives. The global information infrastructure should improve their Basic Mind.
- • Digital Natives (Prensky 2001) belong to the information elite and apply new ICT. They reason very well. If those specialists do not practice their knowledge/skills, they may lose them. The global information infrastructure should improve all of their Minds.

It is wrong to say that since Digital Natives reason best, we should educate only this kind of graduate. One cannot forget that they are not only good in digitalization but also belong to the information elite. This kind of elite has a very comprehensive education in humanities and given professions, and ICT knowledge/skills is the second layer of their education. Furthermore, in order to belong to the information elite, they cannot be separated from nature in a simulated virtual/digital environment since they may lose their biologically-driven humanity.

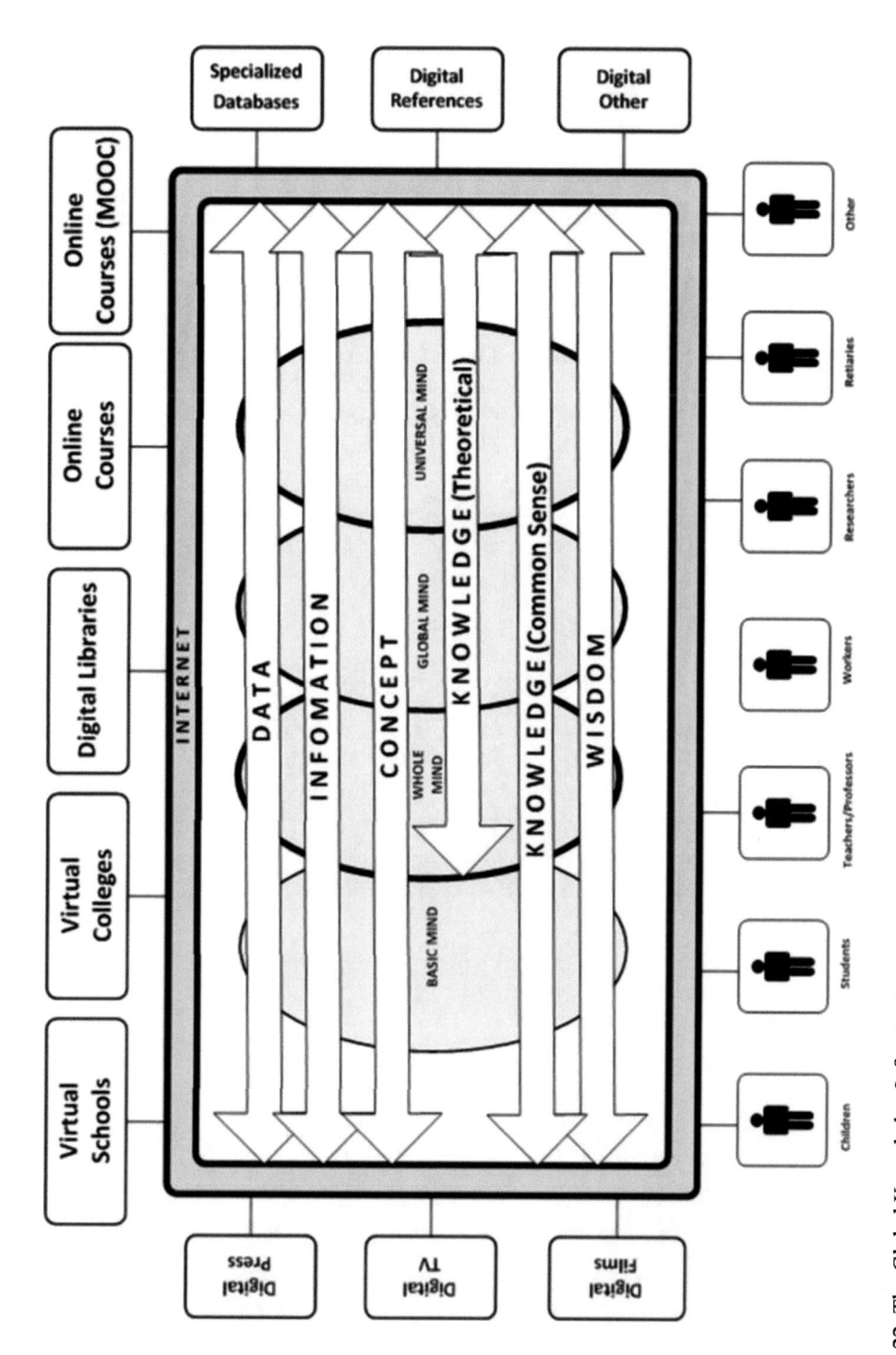

Figure 8.22. The Global Knowledge Infrastructure. (MOON-Massive Open Online Courses).

Hence, it is not a "done deal" (according to some commentators) with the traditional way of handling information, since F2F (face to face), P2F (paper to face), or F2P (face to paper) communication is still richer in information than electronic communication.

Therefore, it is important to keep equilibrium in society between old and new ways of handling/processing information in order to minimize the disparity between people's digital knowledge/skills. This should be done by the intensive development of *Technopsychology*, *Technophilosphy* and regulations for how intensively and broadly ICT should be applied. The required regulations may dramatically challenge many already well-established values in certain civilizations. Certainly they will challenge the values of Western civilization.

THE GLOBAL TRANSPORTATION INFRASTRUCTURE (GTI)

When Western Civilization's business began rapidly off-shore outsourcing their manufacturing factories at the end of the 20th century, mostly to Asian nations, the global transportation infrastructure began to develop rapidly within the so called global supply chain systems, which apply air and sea cargo shipping at the world-wide platforms illustrated in Figure 8.23.

Figure 8.23. The elements of the global transportation infrastructure for a global supply chain. (Photo: www. francoelecuteru.com, www.ouroffset.com, www.fungglobalinstitute.org).

These Global Supply Chains are impressive in their scope and volumes transported with good timing, efficiency (containers) and professionalism (highly computerized). Needless to say that the most successful business major at business colleges world-wide is the major of supply integration systems, since it is a business which constantly employs business graduates today. Besides global transportation, within major nations there takes place intensive transportation of goods produced in centralized facilities or transported form ocean ports, where goods are coming from abroad. Also, food is made in centralized food factories and large farms which result in food being sold at large food stores which on average have traveled 1500 miles before it arrives at a consumer's table! This means that the local farmers are neglected in this kind of business.

This new transportation phenomenon is not sustainable in the long-run since it consumes too much energy which is limited thus far, despite some optimism that supposedly humans are always able to solve such threats.

As far as global passenger and freight land travel is concerned, there is a prediction that it will double until 2050, and non-OECD regions will account for nearly 90%. As a consequence of this surge, global mobility will grow 80%. Also associated emissions of gases will increase 40% by 2050. About 45,000 to 77,000 square kilometers (km^2) of new parking spaces must be added to accommodate passenger vehicle stock growth (Dulac 2013).

If the transportation of goods and people by air through the Atlantic and Pacific Oceans are concerning, then the cost is shocking. Over the Atlantic Ocean there are about 2000 flights per day (Brunton 201) while through the Pacific Ocean there are about 3000 flights per day (passenger and cargo). Each such flight consumes about 20,000 gallons of fuel which means that per day this over-oceans air transport uses about 100 million gallons of fuel/day[58]; in order to make this much fuel in refineries, one must use about 5.3 million barrels of crude oil/day. Until 2050 this consumption may double, and it will require about 10 million barrels/day which will be more oil per day than the U.S. consumes for all its applications today (about 8.77 million barrels/day).

This estimate is very modest since does not include all the resources consumed by the global transportation infrastructure which includes sea transportation, roads, bridges, parking lots, storage and so forth. This escalating usage of limited resources challenges the benefits which are coming from the global supply chain because in all of these kinds of calculations only business cost is included while the costs of environment deterioration and labor minimization are excluded from business cost controls. In other words, if the shallow economy were to be replaced by a deep economy then it would be much more evident that the global transportation infrastructure, in how it is currently used, is unsustainable.

THE GLOBAL CYBERWAR INFRASTRUCTURE (GCI)

As the national information infrastructure grows and evolves into everyman's information superhighway, electronic doors are opened for cyber warfare. Cyber warfare is a politically and economically motivated hacking to conduct sabotage, espionage, terrorism, and cyberattacks. It is becoming a very efficient and dangerous warfare which is able to provide comparable effects to conventional warfare.

---

[58] 5,000 flights/day x 20,000 gallons/flight = 100 million gallons of fuel/day.

Today cyberwar takes place at almost of all levels of the society, particularly at such levels as: personal, corporate, government, and global (Schwartau 1996).

- At the personal level cyberwar neglects an individual's electronic privacy and is aimed at the repossession of an individual's records, files, communication messages and interests, passwords, credit card numbers, and so forth. In result this information can be sold to marketing businesses, and other information can be used to gain some financial benefits.
- At the corporate level cyberwar is a new way of carrying out traditional industrial espionage in order to get a competitive advantage. Western Civilization's corporations are still more advanced than other civilizations' corporations; therefore, they are subject of thousands of cyberattacks per day.
- At the government level, particularly the military, it is a very interesting area where all civilizations aim their cyberattacks in thousands per day. Therefore, each major military power has established command centers which are in charge of defending against such invisible attacks. The following cyberattacks have taken place:
  - In April 2007, Estonia came under cyberattack in the wake of the relocation of the Bronze Soldier of Tallinn. The largest part of the attacks came from Russia and from official servers of the authorities of Russia. In the attack, ministries, banks, and media were targeted (Csmonitor 2007).
  - On 4 December 2010, a group calling itself the Pakistan Cyber Army hacked the website of India's top investigating agency, the Central Bureau of Investigation (CBI). (NDTV 2010).
  - In October 2010, Iain Lobban, the director of the Government Communications Headquarters (GCHQ), said Britain faces a "real and credible" threat from cyberattacks by hostile states and criminals, and government systems are targeted 1,000 times each month; such attacks threatened Britain's economic future, and some countries were already using cyber assaults to put pressure on other nations (Glob and Mail 2010).
  - In September 2010, Iran was attacked by the Stuxnet worm, thought to specifically target its Natanz nuclear enrichment facility. The worm is said to be the most advanced piece of malware ever discovered and significantly increases the profile of cyberwarfare (AFP 2011).
- At the global level cyberwar can be waged by any invisible interest group from anywhere as it is convenient.

To protect people, organizations, and governments against such warfare, each group must develop global cyberwar infrastructure which includes special software, computer servers, and highly specialized centers and professionals. This infrastructure is invisible for the public but very active at all levels of cyber warfare, small and big. The most efficient such infrastructures are those which use supercomputers for ultrafast simulations of password and access codes. Needless to say, the U.S. and China are leaders in developing such computers today.

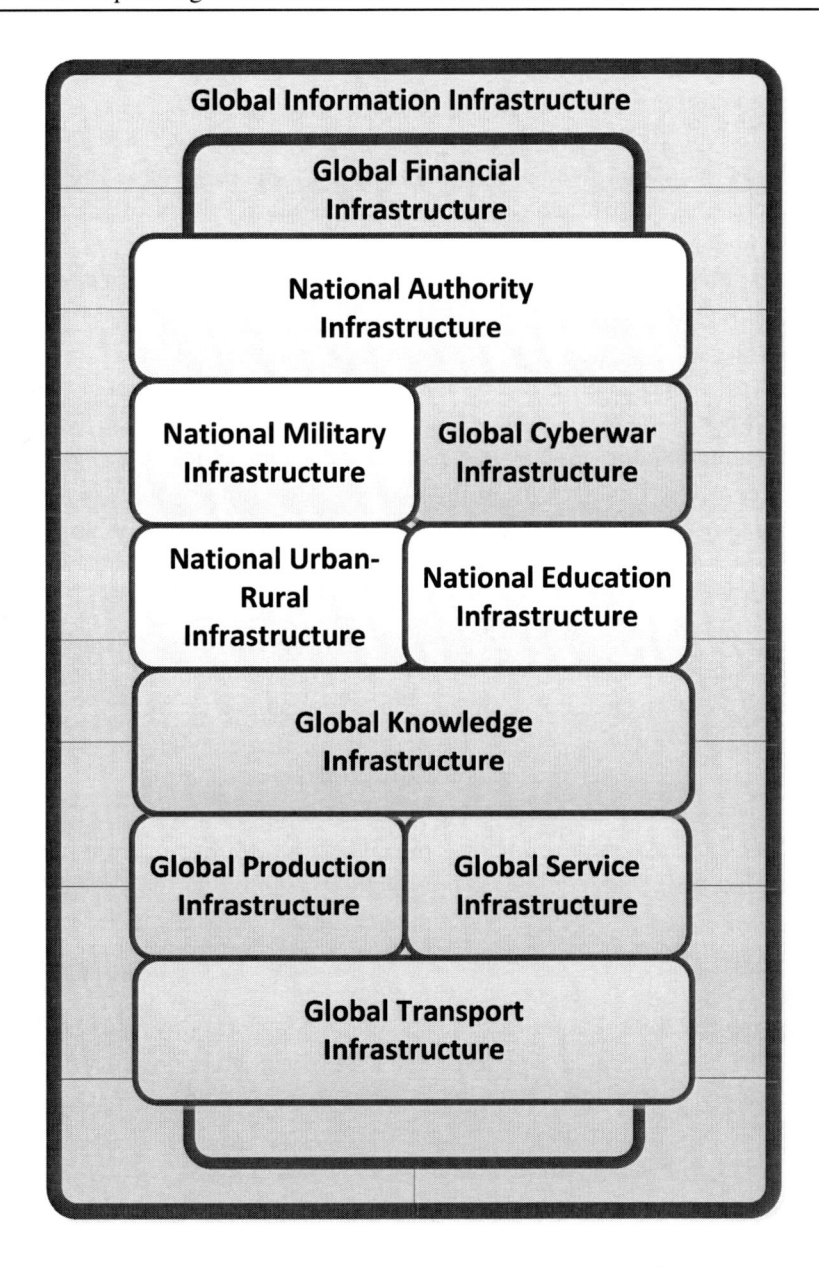

Figure 8.24. The Western Civilization's Infrastructure in the dawn of the 21st century.

CONCLUSION

Western Civilization is a civilization which responds to challenges triggered by its infrastructure in the 21st century. It functions by applying 11 key civilization infrastructures, with 5 traditional, nation-oriented infrastructures: authority, military, education, and urban-rural infrastructures. Another 7 infrastructures are developing mostly in the 21st century and have global-orientation. Among them one can distinguish the following: global cyberwar, global knowledge, global production, global service, global transport, global finance, and global information infrastructures. Figure 8.23 depicts their main relations, where the global financial and global information infrastructures play the key integrational role towards the remaining infrastructures.

These new 7 civilization global infrastructures create serious a challenge for society and the other 4 nation-oriented civilization infrastructures. This challenge is in understanding their functioning, potentiality, and limitations and understanding the level of skills which would allow society to use them rightly and effectively.

The impact of these new globalizing civilization infrastructures upon Western Civilization is as follows:

1. The global financial infrastructure has a powerful an influence in its dealings with a nation since the best profit is today gained globally, not nationally. This infrastructure is transforming Western civilization into Global civilization where the market economy has been used improperly to develop a market society and where everything is for sale. For example, a prison cell upgrade costs $82 per night; access to the car pool lane while driving solo costs $8 during rush hours; the cell number of your doctor costs $1,500 and up per year; staying in a line overnight on Capitol Hill to hold a place for a lobbyist who wants to attend a congressional hearing costs $15-$20 per hour (Sandel 2012:3-4). There is no sign that this infrastructure could lose its grip upon Western and Global civilization today and in near future.
2. The global information infrastructure provides a technological platform for the functioning of other civilization infrastructures electronically in instant e-communication over the Internet and private computer networks [LAN, MAN, RAN, WAN, GAN, and VAN (service)]. This civilization infrastructure provides effective support for most of the computer information systems and their users. On the other hand, its information technology conquers human culture, claims superiority over everything else, and is leading to a labor-less economy. Within the same technological platform robots are being developed to replace almost every kind of human job by 2050. The voices of workers and societal professionals for limits on this technology is treated as a voice against technological progress by business and politicians who care about the low cost of products and services. They only forget who will be able to buy them.
3. The global knowledge infrastructure may better inform society through digital libraries and references but not through virtual schools and colleges which, at lower costs, deliver content but limit students' socialization and are triggering fire out of their minds. Virtual education graduates 2D specialists, who were born at home, study at home, marry via the Internet, work at home and pass away at home not knowing the 3D world outside of their homes.
4. The global production infrastructure of today minimized the middle class and consumer base by outsourcing manufacturing jobs from Western civilization and created a destabilizing economy.
5. The global service infrastructure of today is trying to computerize most of their services, eliminating the convenience of face-to-face contacts. To a certain degree, customer service is almost dead in the U.S. due to online expert systems trying to fix customers' problems.

6. The global transport infrastructure is efficient in supporting the global supply chains and flow of people world-wide. Unfortunately, due to the huge consumption of energy, in the long run this is not sustainable.
7. The global cyberwar infrastructure is planned and functions to protect other civilization infrastructures against cyberattacks, espionage, and cyberwars, but in practice such protection is not 100% reliable due to many unknown factors and the complexity of electronic systems.

The response of nation-oriented civilization infrastructures to the challenges of global civilization infrastructures is as follows:

1. The national authority infrastructure is steadily the deciding voice in global corporations which established the opinion that what is good for business is good for society. This eventually led to the market society.
2. The national military infrastructure in the U.S. still has a high priority in politics; it needs technological progress and a huge budget and needs to keep a close eye on buying too many materials from abroad since production has decreased in their own country.
3. The national urban-rural infrastructure in the area of cities is suffering from low income due to stakeholders and unbalanced budgets which cannot support efficient services and the maintenance of roads, bridges, and facilities. In the rural areas, unemployment is high and soil is becoming depleted in the central states due to climate change and abandoned small farms which cannot support themselves. In Europe the state of this infrastructure is in better shape since the European Union supports agriculture, and urban areas have been traditionally in good shape in the several centuries of their existence.
4. The national education infrastructure is confused about which kind of education it should provide for the declining Western civilization and the rising Global civilization. Low state budgets trim education resources and promote charter schools which look more for profit than for curriculum. For-profit schools leave students with heavy debts and worthless credentials. New "innovative" business models of schools, including online ones, are bad substitutes for teachers in person.

In summary one can argue that the state of Western Civilization's infrastructures may impress as far as technological progress is concerned; however, they are worrisome with respect to the lack of societal responsibility which determines this civilization's transformation into Global civilization and is a bad solution for Western society.

REFERENCES

AFP (2011). Stuxnet worm brings cyber warfare out of virtual world. *Google.com*. Retrieved 8-15-2014.

Assimov, I. (1950). *I robot*. New York: Genome Press.

Automation,com (2014). http://www.automation.com/library/articles-white-papers/articles-by-jim-pinto/robotics-technology-trends, Retrieved 8-21-2014.

Bagwell, K. and R. Staiger (2004). *The economics of the world trading system*. Cambridge, MA: The MIT Press.

Brown, M. (2014). Robotic nation. http://marshallbrain.com/robotic-nation.htm, Retrieved 8-21.

Brunton, J. (2014). North Atlantic skies – the gateway to Europe. *NATS Blog*. Retrieved 8-22-2014, http://nats.aero/blog/2014/06/north-atlantic-skies-gateway-europe

Carbaough, R. (2005). *International economics*, 10th edition. Mason, OH: Thomson South-Western.

Csmonitor (2007). Estonia accuses Russia of 'cyberattack'. *Csmonitor.com* 17 May. Retrieved 8-10-2014.

Dulac, J. (2013). *Global land transport infrastructure requirements*. Vienna: IEA.

Dunn, R.M. and J.h. Mutti. (2004). *International economics*, 6th edition. New York: Routledge.

Elson, A. (2011). *Governing global finance: the evolution and reform of the international financial architecture*. New York: Palgrave Macmillan.

Faiola, A. and T.W. Farnam (2013). The rise of the bitcoin: virtual gold or cyber-bubble? *Washington Post*.

Globe and Mail (2010). Britain faces serious cyber threat, spy agency head warns. October 13, Retrieved 8-14-2014.

IFI Watch (2004). "The World Bank and the question of immunity". IFI Watch - Bangladesh 1 (1): 1–10. Retrieved 7-14- 2004.

James, P. W. and H. Patomäki. (2007). *Globalization and economy, Vol. 2: Globalizing finance and the new economy*. London, UK: Sage Publications.

Kurzweil, R. (2006). *Singularity is near*. New York: Penguin Books.

McLuhan, M. (1964). *Understanding Media*. Berkley, CA: Gingko Press.

Meyers, B. (2013). 2013 Offshoring from sea to shining sea. *The Economic Populist*, July 29.

NDTV (2010). Hacked by 'Pakistan cyber army', CBI website still not restored. Retrieved 8-22-2014 http://www.ndtv.com/article/india/hacked-by-pakistan-cyber-army-cbi-website-still-not-restored-70568?cp

Prensky, M. (2001). Digital natives, digital immigrants. *Horizon*, vol. 9(3).

Postman, N. (1992). *Technopoly, the surrender of culture to technology*. New York: Alfred Knopf.

Sandel, M.J. (2012). *What money can't buy the moral limits of markets*. New York: Farrar, Straus, and Giroux.

Simon, H. A. (2001). Complex systems: the interplay of organizations and markets in contemporary society. *Computational & Mathematical Organization Theory*, (7):79-85.

Schwartau, W. (1994). Chaos on the electronic superhighway, information warfare. New York: Thunder's Mouth Press.

Targowski, A.(1991). Strategies and architecture of the Electronic Global Village, The *Information Society*, 7(3):187 – 202.

Targowski, A. (1996). *Global information infrastructure*. Harrisburg, PA: Idea Group Publishing.

Targowski, A. and I.V. Modrak. (2011). Is advance automation consistent with sustainable economic growth in developed world? *Communications in Computer and Information Science Series*, Springer, 2011, vol. 221.

Targowski, A. (2013). *Harnessing the power of wisdom.* New York: NOVA Science Publishers.

Targowski, A. (2014). *Global civilization in the 21st century.* New York: NOVA Science Publishers.

Toynbee, A. (1935). *A study of history*, 2d ed. Oxford: Oxford University Press. I: 44-45.

World Bank (2007). *Sovereign immunity.* Washington, DC: World Bank Group Report.

Zuboff, Sh. (1988). *In the age of the smart machine: the future of work and power.* New York: Basic Books.

Chapter 9

WESTERN-GLOBAL-VIRTUAL CIVILIZATION AND THE CLASH OF CIVILIZATIONS IN THE 21ST CENTURY

ABSTRACT

The *purpose* of this investigation is to define how the clash of civilizations impacts Western civilization in the 21st century. The *methodology* is based on an interdisciplinary big-picture view of how contemporary civilizations interact among themselves. Among the *findings* are: Western civilization is strongly weakened by clashes with other contemporary civilizations and could even be considered as being at war with Islamic civilization. *Practical implication:* the largest sources of the decline of Western civilization are its vulgarizing popular culture, the unfixed conflict between Israel and Palestine, and global business' push for the privatization of democracy and society. *Social implication:* it is difficult to reverse this declining process when the truth is considered relative and there is no political will to do so. *Originality:* This investigation is defined through the big picture versus small picture judgment at the level of synthesis. Focus is put on the role of the culture of entertainment in this declining process.

INTRODUCTION

The purpose of this investigation is to analyze and synthesize the impact of the clash of civilizations on Western civilization in the 21st century. In this century, the world is just 25 years past the 46 year long Cold War (1945-1991) which was an ideological war between Capitalism and Communism. In fact it was a war between two civilizations, Western and Eastern, in which military confrontation was replaced by propaganda and wars by proxy wars and economic competition.

The first who noticed the New World Order after the fall of Communism was Samuel P. Huntington, who in the summer of 1993 in *Foreign Affairs* published an article entitled "The Clash of Civilizations?" No article, according to the editors of that distinguish journal, has generated more discussion since George Kennan's "X" article on containment (of Communism) in the 1940s. In 1996 S.P. Huntington published a best-selling book titled *The Clash of Civilizations and the Remaking of World Order.* Huntington's hypothesis was right, and today world politics is controlled by the clashes of civilizations, not at the level of countries, but at the level of cultures of civilizations (including religions) which want either non-discrimination or domination.

Today, in the post-Cold War world, the critical distinctions between people and nations are not economic or political but cultural in the scope of values and morality. They are almost of a religious character. As Arnold Toynbee argued, civilizations are defined by religions since a religion, either sacred or secular, determines the purpose of life and behavior for a group of people which, in turn, shape both society's culture and infrastructure.

Due to the strong economic development of Western civilization in the last 100 years, it must use a large amount of energy based on oil which is mostly supplied by other civilizations like Islam civilization since the Middle East is the most secure source of that type of energy and likes the large payments it receives from the West. This trade has created huge wealth in some countries in the Middle East, accumulated mainly at the "palace". Hence, one can see the rising disagreement between the "palace" and "street." To protect this wealth, the "palace" provides education for the youth in the Madras schools which teach only religion dogmas and mostly hatred against the Americans. After graduation, young people do not have any professional knowledge and skills to sustain their lives; they become desperate and turn their anger against the Americans (Westerners) who are guilty of paying too much to the palace and exploiting their natural resources for a decadent life style. Eventually this anger is intercepted by the Islamic clergy who dreams about diffusing their religion around the world.

This process - oil for wealth, the Islamic population explosion, and the spread of the "good life" of Western society through the Internet - radicalizes Islamic society, wounds Western civilization and changes global politics today.

Table 9.1. Percentage of world population that was killed in events lasting less than 30 years

EVENT	TIME	PERCENTAGE OF KILLED
Genghis Khan	1206-27	11.1
An Lushan Rebelion	755-63	5.9
Xin Dynasty	9-24	5.9
Timur	1370-1405	4.7
Fall of the Ming Dynasty	1635-52	4.6
Second World War	1939-45	2.6
Fall of the Yuan Dynasty	1340-70	2.1
Taiping Rebelion	1850-64	1.7
Thirty Years' War	1618-48	1.4
Mao Zedong	1949-76	1.3

Source: M. White, The Great Big Book of Horrible Things (1997).

FROM ALL KINDS OF HUMAN SUFFERING AND WARS TO CIVILIZATION CLASHES

The 6,000 year long history of civilization is mostly a record of human suffering caused by institutional oppression, dynastic wars, failed states, despots, colonial wars, religious wars, civil wars, international wars, ethnic cleansing, genocides, the Holocaust, and so forth. The bloodiest events which lasted a maximum of 30 years are listed in Table 9.1.

Out of these bloodiest events, the Thirty Years' War (1618-48) falls into the category of cultural war, since it was a religious war between the Protestant and Roman Catholic princes of Germany regarding who should become the next Holy Roman Emperor. A less bloody religious war took place in France in 1562-98 and lasted 36 years, even longer than the Thirty Years' War. This was a war between Huguenots (French Protestants) and Roman Catholics. During this war between 2,000,000 and 4,000,000 people were killed (Users.erols.com-2012).

Another example of culture war is ethnic cleansing which is the effort to remove (through discrimination, deportation, displacement or even mass killing) members of an undesirable ethnic or religious group in order to establish an ethnically homogenous geographic region. Nevertheless "cleansing" crusades for ethnic or religious motives have occurred throughout history. The growth of extreme nationalist movements during the 20th century led to an exceptional level of ethnically inspired cruelty, including the Turkish massacre of Armenians during World War I, the Nazi Holocaust's extermination of some six million European Jews, and the forced displacement and mass killings carried out in former Yugoslavia and the African country of Rwanda during the 1990s.

In his 1993 article "A Brief History of Ethnic Cleansing," published in the magazine "Foreign Affairs," Andrew Bell-Fialkoff marks that the purpose of the Serbian crusade was "the expulsion of an 'undesirable' population from a given territory due to religious or ethnic discrimination, political, strategic or ideological considerations, or a combination of those." Expanding this definition, Bell-Fialkoff and many observers of history consider the forceful dislocation of Native Americans by European settlers in North America in the 18th and 19th centuries as fitting the category of ethnic cleansing. By comparison, the relocation of thousands of Africans from their inborn lands for the purpose of slavery cannot be categorized as ethnic cleansing, as the aim of this trade was not to oust a particular group but to make money on human trafficking, which is a big crime as well.

Most of these examples of atrocities took place within the same civilizations, mostly in Chinese and Western civilizations respectively, though there are some examples of atrocities that took place between civilizations, such as:

- Genghis Khan (1206-1227) led the Mongol invasions that resulted in the conquest of most of Eurasia, creating vassal states out of all of modern-day China, Korea, the Caucasus, Central Asia, and substantial portions of modern Eastern Europe, Russia, and the Middle East. Certainly these wars took place between Mongol civilization and Chinese, Islamic, and Eastern civilizations, although these wars were aimed at territorial and natural resource acquisitions. Culture-wise Mongol civilization was encouraging religious tolerance.
- The Turkish massacre of Armenians during World War I (1914-1918) in the years 1915-18 resulted in 1,500,000 deaths (Figure 9.1) since the Christian (Orthodox)

Armenians were considered non-believers in Islam. This massacre was a strong example of the clash of Islamic and Eastern civilizations.
- The Communist conquest of Eurasia in 1918-1991 was a cultural war, also commonly considered an ideological war, in which the sacred religion of Communism took in total the lives of almost 95 million people in many different countries over the span of 74 years (Courtois 1997). This is the largest atrocity to have taken place in the history of world civilization. (The Mongol wars lasted less than 30 years and longer political events were not ranked in the cited above table). The communist regime was based on a sacred religion with all sorts of liturgy and ideology as well.
- The Nazi-German genocide of Slavs and the Holocaust of Jews and Gypsies in World War II (1939-45) took the lives of 10 million civilians. The Nazi-German regime was in fact a civilization founded on a different set of values and morality than Western civilization. The Nazi-German civilization was based on a secular religion whose most important value was the superiority of the German race and culture which, according to them, deserved more land (Lebensraum). Therefore it was a clash/war between Nazi-German civilization and Western (Slavs and Jews) and Eastern (Russian, Ukrainians, Byelorussians, Bulgarians) civilizations. This was a war rather than a clash of civilizations since the Poles, Russians, Ukrainians, and Byelorussians were militarily fighting the Nazi-Germans. In fact, Hitler consciously applied the practice of the Turkish massacre of Armenians in this war.
- The Muslim-Bosniak genocide at Srebrenica in 1995 was committed by Bosnian-Serb forces (Figure 9.2). About 8,000 Bosnian Muslim men and boys were killed in Srebrenica in addition to the mass expulsion of another 25,000-30,000 Bosniak civilians. The ethnic cleansing in Bosnia and Herzegovina included unlawful confinement, murder, rape, sexual assault, torture, beating, robbery and inhumane treatment of civilians, the targeting of political leaders, intellectuals and professionals, the unlawful deportation and transfer of civilians, the unlawful shelling of civilians, the unlawful appropriation and plunder of real and personal property, the destruction of homes and businesses, and the destruction of places of worship (International Tribunal 1995). It was a clash between Eastern (Serbs) and Islamic (Bosniaks) civilizations.

Figure 9.2. The Muslim-Bosniak massacre in 1995.
(Photo: news.co.au and news.bbc.co.uk).

As the list of the civilization clashes/wars indicates that from a strict religious criterion (excluding secular religions) two major clashes of civilizations have taken place in the last 100 years. Among them there are the Turkish massacre of Armenians during World War I and the Muslim-Bosniak genocide in former Yugoslavia in 1995. These were clashes between Islamic and Eastern civilizations. The wars between the Ottoman Empire and Western nations in the 16th and 17th centuries were international wars aimed at the expansion of territory and the acquisition of resources (treasures, slaves, and women among others). Those wars were not driven by religious passion. The same aims was present during the Muslim conquest of Spain in 711-18 which led to the 754 year reign of the independent Caliphate in what is today Andalusia (Figure 9.3) which used to belong to Roman civilization which along with Greek civilization is the root of Western civilization, born in 800. Eventually, this Caliphate fell to the Catholic Monarchs in 1472.

Figure 9.3. Islamic arts and architecture in Andalusia (Spain).
(Photo: www.islamic-arts.org and www.all-that-is-interesting.com).

This short review of historic wars and clashes in Europe shows that Islamic civilization had and still has tremendous energy and will try to promote its way of living in the world.

THE CLASH OF WESTERN AND ISLAM CIVILIZATIONS

New York 2011

On September 11, 2001, 19 militants associated with the Islamic extremist group al-Qaeda hijacked four airliners and carried out suicide attacks against targets in the United States. Two of the planes were flown into the towers of the World Trade Center in New York City, a third plane hit the Pentagon just outside Washington, D.C., and the fourth plane crashed in a field in Pennsylvania. Often referred to as 9/11, the attacks resulted in extensive death and destruction, triggering major U.S. initiatives to combat terrorism and defining the presidency of George W. Bush. Over 3,000 people were killed during the attacks in New York City and Washington, D.C., including more than 400 police officers and firefighters.

The attackers were Islamic terrorists from Saudi Arabia and several other Arab nations. Reportedly financed by Osama bin Laden's al-Qaeda terrorist organization, they were allegedly acting in retaliation for America's support of Israel, its involvement in the Persian

Gulf War and its continued military presence in the Middle East. Soon after takeoff, the terrorists commandeered the four planes and took control, transforming ordinary commuter jets into guided missiles.

Operation Enduring Freedom, the American-led international effort to oust the Taliban regime in Afghanistan and destroy Osama bin Laden's terrorist network based there, began on October 7. Within two months, U.S. forces had effectively removed the Taliban from operational power, but the war continued as the U.S. and coalition forces attempted to defeat a Taliban insurgency campaign based in neighboring Pakistan. Osama bin Laden, the mastermind behind the September 11th attacks, remained at large until May 2, 2011, when he was finally tracked down and killed by U.S. forces at a hideout in Abbottabad, Pakistan. In June 2011, President Barack Obama announced the beginning of large-scale troop withdrawals from Afghanistan, with a final withdrawal of U.S. forces tentatively scheduled for 2014 (History of 9/11 Attack).

Figure 9.4. The terrorist attack on the World Trade Towrs, September 9, 2001 which triggered the clash of Western and Islamic civilizations in the 21st century.
(Photo: Wikipedia).

As a result of the 9/11 attacks, many governments across the world passed legislation to combat terrorism. However, terrorism is only a weapon of the weaker side. For example during the Cold War, it was not referred to as "the war with the atomic bomb" since it was a war between Capitalism and Communism and between the political West and East. This 9/11 attack was an example of the clash between Western and Islam civilizations which passed into long wars between the civilizations in Afghanistan and Iraq.

Unfortunately Western civilization did not notice that perhaps some of its values and policies should be updated for the sake of the peace in the world.

The Arab Spring-2011

The Arab Spring was a series of anti-government protests, uprisings and armed rebellions that spread across the Middle East in early 2011. Their purpose, relative success and outcome remain passionately disputed in Arab countries and world-wide, among foreign observers, and between world powers looking to the possible benefits of a shift in the political map of the Middle East.

Figure 9.5. The Arab Spring in 2011.
(Photo: www.vopiceeducation.org, www.npr.orh, and www.vox.com).

The Arab Spring or Revolution was an allusion to the Polish Revolution and its spread in Eastern Europe in 1989, when the supposedly impenetrable Communist regimes began falling apart under pressure from mass popular demonstrations leading to a domino effect. In the next few years all countries in the former Soviet Bloc accepted democratic political systems with a market economy. Hence, such outcomes were expected from the Arab Spring as well.

But the events in the Middle East departed in a less forthright direction: Egypt, Tunisia and Yemen entered an uncertain transition period; Syria and Libya were drawn into a civil conflict; and the wealthy kingdoms in the Persian Gulf remained largely unshaken by the events. The use of the term the "Arab Spring" has since been criticized for being mistaken and naïve, although the authoritarian and corrupted regimes took notice of their "awakened" citizens.

Western civilization's foreign policy is driven by short-term gains from crisis to crisis and in fact is reactionary; therefore, it was not prepared to reasonably deal with the Arab Spring challenge. Its main message is to promote democratic change while those countries are not mentally ready to do so. Eventually, the Arab Spring also triggered extremism across the Middle East and its political destabilization.

The Arab Spring of 2011 was not a clash of civilizations, but it involved the U.S. and European Union in providing military assistance and involvement (in Libya) including some expertise which has had some repercussions in the invisible semi clash of the two civilizations.

From Al-Qaeda to Taliban and ISIS – From Clashes to War of Civilizations or Against Civilization?

After the terrorist attacks of September 11, 2001, al-Qaeda (or al-Qa'ida, pronounced al-KYE-da) surpassed the IRA (Irleand), Hamas, and Hezbollah (Palestine) as the world's most infamous terrorist organization. Al-Qaeda—"the base" in Arabic—is a network of extremists organized by Osama bin Laden from Saudi Arabia. The principal aims of al-Qaeda are to drive Americans and American influence out of all Muslim nations, especially Saudi Arabia, to destroy Israel, and to topple pro-Western dictatorships around the Middle East. Bin Laden also said that he wishes to unite all Muslims and establish, by force if necessary, an Islamic nation adhering to the rule of the first Caliphs. The death of bin Laden, who was killed in a joint operation by U.S. troops and CIA operatives in May 2011, complicated the future of al-Qaeda. Some speculated that the group will be encouraged and seek revenge, while others speculated whether it might function without its supreme leader. In June, U.S. officials said that after searching through the documents and computer files taken from bin Laden's compound, they are sure of their assumption that al-Qaedain Afghanistan and Pakistan has been truly damaged as a result of U.S. counterterrorism actions carry out in Pakistan.

More than a month after bin Laden's death, al-Qaeda named Dr. Ayman al-Zawahiri, al-Qaeda's theological leader, as its leader. Ever since 1988, Al-Qaeda has served as "the base" for worldwide jihad and is known all for its various crimes. However, when they are not making headlines for blowing up buildings, Al-Qaeda terrorists are dreaming up business schemes, devising some pretty weird plots, and generally acting, well, strange. For example, in 2009, the group said they were sorry for murdering Muslims, and in 2007, bin Laden apologized for killing Muslims in Iraq. Of course, these videos probably have more to do with appearances than guilt. It's a move to gloss over the fact that Al-Qaeda kills more Muslims than non-Muslims. Between 2004 and 2008, Muslims made up 85 percent of the group's casualties. For an organization that is supposedly protecting the faithful, that is a pretty bad track record.

The Taliban is a Sunni Islamist organization operating primarily in Afghanistan and Pakistan. Solitary leader Mullah Mohammed Omar has been leading the Taliban since the early 1990s. "Taliban," in Pashto is the plural of Talib, which means student. Most Taliban's members are Pashtun, the largest ethnic group in Afghanistan. The exact number of Taliban forces is unknown. The group's aim is to impose its interpretation of Islamic law on Afghanistan and remove foreign influence from the country. After the Soviet Union's invasion in 1979-89 and occupation of Afghanistan, Afghan resistance fighters, known collectively as mujahedeen, faught back. In 1997 the Taliban issued an edict renaming Afghanistan the Islamic Emirate of Afghanistan. The country was only officially recognized by three countries: Pakistan, Saudi Arabia and the United Arab Emirates. In 1996-2001 the group imposed strict Islamic laws on the Afghan people. Women had to wear head-to-toe coverings, were not allowed to attend school or work outside the home, and were forbidden to travel alone. Television, music, and non-Islamic holidays were banned also. In 1997 Mullah Omar established a relationship with Osama bin Laden, who then moved his base of operations to Kandahar. In March 2001 the Taliban destroyed two 1,500 year old Buddha figures in the town of Bamiyan, saying they were idols that violated Islam. In October-November 2001, after a massive U.S. bombardment as a part of Operation Enduring Freedom, the Taliban lost Afghanistan to the U.S. and Northern Alliance forces. Ever since, a war with Taliban guerrilla forces has been taking place in Afghanistan. Western civilization is represented by military forces from the U.S., Canada, the United Kingdom, France, Germany, Spain, Italy, Denmark, Netherlands, Poland, Hungary, Bulgaria, the Czech Republic and many other countries which have provided service support under the form of hospitals, airports, and so forth. In June 18, 2013 an official political office of the Taliban opened in Doha, Qatar's capital city. The Taliban announce that they hope to improve relations with other countries, head toward a peaceful solution to the Afghanistan occupation, and establish an independent Islamic system in the country (CNN Facts). In 2014 Western civilization's military forces were gradually withdrawing from Afghanistan and passing governing rules to the national liberal government which is under permanent treat from the active Taliban.

ISIS is the Islamic State of Iraq and the Levant (ISIS) which became, in the 2014, the most powerful and effective extreme jihadi group in the world. ISIS now controls or can operate with impunity in a great stretch of territory in western Iraq and eastern Syria, making its army the most successful jihadi movement ever. ISIS is more violent and sectarian than the "core" of al-Qaida, led by Ayman al-Zawahiri, who is based in Pakistan. ISIS is highly fanatical, killing Shia Muslims and Christians whenever possible, as well as militarily efficient and under tight direction by top leaders. ISIS's aim is to create a Caliphate in northern Syria and Iraq, surrounding countries such as Jordan, Saudi Arabia and Turkey which would become targets of the aggressive Sunni troops. ISIS's war tactics is to launch surprise attacks, inflict maximum fatalities and spread fear before retreating without heavy losses. This tactic reminds one of the Mongol's tactics which successfully conquered many Eurasian territories 800 years ago. ISIS concentrates on using militarily unexperienced foreign volunteers (some from United Kingdom and the U.S.) as suicide bombers either moving on foot wearing suicide vests, or driving vehicles packed with explosives. ISIS's military operations are supported by Iraq's Sunnis since Iraq's Shia-dominated government became convinced that the protesters want not socio-economic reforms but a revolution returning their ethnic group to power. Hence, about six million of Iraq's Sunni became more isolated and kind towards ISIS.

ISIS is a mixture of the past and contemporary since it is applying recent practices in successfully recruiting young fighters from Western Europe and intimidating enemies by their extraordinary command of American weaponry and state-of-the art videos.

ISIS today is gruesomely violent yet skillful, as they have made propaganda videos showing how families with sons in the Iraqi army have to dig their own graves before they are killed. The message is that their rivals cannot expect mercy. The leader of ISIS is an intellectual Abu Bakr al-Baghdadi, also known as Abu Dua, who has rapidly and surprisingly emerged as the political figure who is shaping the future of Iraq, Syria and the wider Middle East. He was born in 1971 in Samarra, a largely Sunni city north of Baghdad, and is well educated. He has a degree in Islamic Studies, containing poetry, history and genealogy, from the Islamic University of Baghdad. He remains in control of a great stretch of territory in northern Syria and Iraq. His competition is split and dysfunctional; hence, he is almost unopposed as he moves recklessly towards establishing himself as Emir of a new Islamic state in the Middle East which is in war with Western civilization.

Figure 9.6. On November 4, 2013 an upscale mall popular with the Kenyan elite and the foreign diplomats and businesspeople who call Nairobi home turned into a war zone on Saturday, as Al Qaeda's gunmen opened fire on shoppers in an apparent terrorist attack, killing at least 20 people and wounding dozens more.
(Photo: www.warscerotic.wordpress.com).

Figure 9.7. The Taliban fighters in Afghanistan.
(Photo: www.khaama.com).

x x x

Al Qaeda is a small terrorist organization with membership from all over the Arab world. It opposes the state of Israel and its allies. Its main purpose is to get non-Muslims out of the Middle East. It places little value on human life, including the lives of its members.

Figure 9.8. ISIS in Iraq is gruesomely violent.
(Photo: www.thetimes.co.uk).

The Taliban is a religious group which gained political control over Afghanistan after the Russian withdrawal. They are Islamists who set up a strict Islamic political system in Afghanistan. While they have often inflicted terrifying Islamic penalties, they were not by their nature terrorists. They did, however, allow the Arab terrorist group al Qaeda to train and maintain a permanent base within the borders of Afghanistan. Afghanistan is not an Arab nation and does not speak Arabic. After the al Qaeda attacks on 9/11, both the Taliban and al Qaeda were driven out of Afghanistan. The Taliban have been fighting their way back ever since.

ISIS is worse than All-Qaeda and any other terrorist group that came before it. For absolute, vicious efficiency, ISIS is several stages above Hamas, Hezbollah, Boko Haram or even the Taliban. The closest analog is the Khmer Rouge, the Cambodian movement that killed more than two million people (about 30 percent of the population since they were educated and came from cities where money was used) in the mid-1970s. In its enthusiasm for genocide, ISIS appears to copy Adolf Hitler's genocide and Holocaust strategy in WWII. ISIS, like the German Nazis, has identified entire groups of people for annihilation. Its fighters thoroughly encircle groups of "unbelievers", which can mean anybody including their related Sunnis, and they act in a manner Heinrich Himmler (a German Nazist) would have recommended. Online videos of these mass killings clearly show the fanatical pleasure with which the killers go about their effort.

From the clashes and wars of civilizations one can draw the following conclusions:

- Al Qaeda is a political group which applies terrorism as a weapon to make the world aware of the plight of the Palestinians in Israel. Its principal aims are to drive Americans and American influence out of all Muslim nations, especially Saudi Arabia; destroy Israel; and topple pro-Western dictatorships around the Middle East. This group is similar to many Western groups of freedom fighters like: the Polish Home Army AK during the German occupation in 1939-45, the IRA in Ireland, and Basque freedom fighters or West Bengal fighters. They all were called bandits (by Germans) or terrorists by actual political rulers in the contrast to being called national heroes by their nations' compatriots. This group has no territory of its own

and is limited to making terrorizing clashes between Western and Islamic civilizations.
- The Taliban is a religious group fighting to set up an Islamic conservative state in Afghanistan. Their purpose is legitimate although is not liked by Western civilization which would like to Westernized this country which is not an Arabic nation and typically practices a very strict Islamic religion. This group has its own territory which was invaded by Western civilization with the purpose of building a nation which would practice Islam with a human face. The question is what do Afghan citizens think about practicing a very restricted version of Islam? Are they free to make such a choice? Certainly they are reluctant to practice Western liberal democracy. However, should they support the terrorist hub settling on their territory? If they are ready to do so, are they ready to face foreign pre-emptive strikes against the terrorists operating world-wide from Afghanistan?
- ISIS is a religious-political rising state led by an intellectual who applies genocide to accomplish the group's historic mission. In the past, the genocide strategies practice by Stalin, Mao Zedong and Pol Pot did not work and today are called crimes against humanity. While ISIS has a legitimate political goal, its strategy is unacceptable by the civilized world which in general is or should be tolerant for every humanistic religion practiced world-wide. The religious-ethnic conflict triggered by ISIS in 2014 is unavoidably transforming into a war of civilizations.
- If Western civilization would like to care for sustainable world peace and stability, it should fix the Israeli-Palestinian conflict first and secure a free choice of self-government in the Middle East. This strategy should minimize the civilizational clashes, perhaps at the cost of one civilization war in this region, aimed at the establishment of a universal humanity-driven world civilization.

THE POSSIBLE CLASH OF WESTERN AND CHINESE CIVILIZATIONS

According to popular opinion, China surpassed the U.S. as the world's largest trading nation in 2013, and by 2028, it will become the largest economy in the world. This poses a question: Will China surpassing the U.S. as the world's largest trading nation and with the largest economy be in conflict with the United States and European Union? As the history of civilization indicates, such conflict is very probable. It probably will take place as a civilization clash on the following platforms:

- Political platform – China will expand its influence in the Sinosphere challenging Japan for solving territorial (island) claims as a way of saving face and expanding its fishing rights on the whole South China Sea. It will be a prelude to move the Americans out of Taiwan and integrating it with the middle land as was done with Hong Kong in 1999.
- Economical platform – China will ask for repayment of the U.S. and EU's huge commercial debts acquired as a result of outsourcing manufacturing to China and making it the World Factory. In 2014 the United State's biggest foreign creditor is China which is holding an estimated $1.3 trillion in American government debt (US

Census Bureau). Already today China is a vocal critic of what it considers Washington's politicized recklessness. In 2028 China will hold about $6 trillion which is not possible to pay off in the 21st century. China may push the U.S into a default country and trigger all sorts of civilization clashes. Another clash perhaps will be if China will push to replace the dollar by the yuan in trading and international payments which is already taking place among the BRIC countries (Brazil, Russia, India, and China).

- Military platform - no country is increasing its military might faster than China. But it is still far behind the United States in usable military capability, since Chinese military strength is limited almost entirely to lands and seas bordering its own territory. The United States is still the only global military power. It is difficult to see what Beijing might calculate as worth a war or even the risk of war. It has boundary disputes with Vietnam, the Philippines and others in the South China Sea, and with Japan up north. Troubles should be expected there, and China will certainly be testing Washington's will in both places (Gelb 2013).
- Cultural platform – Chinese economic superiority and top-down governing style may trigger some anti-Chinese attitudes among "invaded" consumers of the World Factory. It may lead to some local and international clashes of civilizations.

THE CLASH OF WESTERN AND EASTERN CIVILIZATIONS

Since Peter the Great (1672-1725) Eastern civilization has been in a civilizational unbalance. Peter led a cultural revolution that replaced some of the traditionalist and medieval social and political systems with one that was modern, scientific, Europe-oriented, and based on the Enlightenment. Among many things which he learned working in the Dutch shipyards and visiting Dutch craftsmen and artists as well as families, he was impressed by European customs which in some areas were superior to Russian traditions. He commanded all of his courtiers and officials to cut off their long beards—causing his Boyars, who were very fond of their beards, great upset (D'Or 2008) — and wear European clothing. Boyars who sought to retain their beards were required to pay an annual beard tax of one hundred rubles. He also sought to end arranged marriages, which were the norm among the Russian nobility, because he thought such a practice was barbaric and led to domestic violence, since the partners usually resented each other (Dmytryshyn 1974:21).

The following centuries, Russia was confronting Poland from Western civilization, and since the Russian civil war in 1918, it was confronted by the Western Allied (including the Americans and British and others) intervention in Northern Russia and Siberia. Later in 1920 the Polish army stopped the Red Russians' march toward Germany at the Vistula River which is considered as one of the 20 most important battles in the history of world civilization, since it stopped the diffusion of Communism into Central and Western Europe.[59] In fact this war was a war between Western and Soviet (Eastern) civilizations. Later this war continued semi-openly and transformed into the Cold War 1945-91.

---

[59] The war between Germany and the Austro-Hungarian Empire and Russia during WWI was a war for territory and resources, not a war of civilizations.

Figure 9.9. A railroad station in Shanghai and fast trains in 2014 reflecting Chinese civilization's great potential.
(Photo: China News).

After the fall of the Berlin Wall and Communism (1991), Russia and Bulgaria began to Westernize again and accepted a market economy. Bulgaria soon joined the European Union and embraced democracy while Russia entered a stage of hesitation, slowly confronting the Westernization process and promoting nationalistic and imperial politics. Eventually, in 2014, President Vladimir Putin began slowly but decisively expanding Russia's territory once again into that of the former members of the Soviet Union. First, in 2008, Georgia was destabilized, and its two provinces, South Ossetia and Abkhazia, were taken into a close relationship with Russia.[60] In 2014 Crimea was annexed from Ukraine and later began the process of destabilizing Ukraine and Moldavia.

Figure 9.10. The two mostly Russian speaking eastern regions and the corridor between them are Russia's aim for the annexation in 2014.
(Photo: www.mirror.co.uk).

The main cause of the destabilization of Ukraine was its decision (2013-14) to associate itself with the European Union and to soon join the Western polity. In 2014 Ukraine expressed its desire to join NATO also. This means that Ukraine wanted to remove itself from the embracement of Eastern civilization and wanted to Westernize. Russia saw having a democratic and economically successful neighboring country which belonged to Western civilization as a danger. It would be a bad example for the "top-down" rule of Russia where the pride of having a strong country is more important than the well-being of citizens ("pride is more important than food").

The Russian-Ukrainian-Western Civilization (EU and the U.S.) conflict in 2014 is representative of the clash of civilizations.

---

[60] August 26, 2008, Russian President Dmitry Medvedev signed an order recognizing the independence of South Ossetia and Abkhazia, the two breakaway regions in Georgia. In response, U.S. President George W. Bush released a statement saying, "The United States condemns the decision by the Russian president to recognize as independent states the Georgian regions of South Ossetia and Abkhazia. The territorial integrity and borders of Georgia must be respected, just as those of Russia or any other country. Russia's action only exacerbates tensions and complicates diplomatic negotiations."

THE CLASH OF WESTERN CIVILIZATION WITH OTHER CIVILIZATIONS

Modernization

Since the Scientific Revolution in the 16th-17th centuries, modernization has been a continuous process which has been led by Western civilization and has been happening in almost every corner of the world. Modernization means: education and research improvements, industrialization, urbanization, trade expansion, wealth growth, cultural standards development, social mobilization, and so forth.

After the rapid spread of the use of the Internet in the world, people have been becoming more aware about society's development in other countries and want to follow their approaches. There is a widely accepted rule of leveling up to the best, perhaps among all civilized people. Hence, all current civilizations (excluding their extremists) accept modernization and in particularly modern technology. This technology mostly comes from Western civilization which is associated with Westernization, particularly among the younger generations.

Modernization means social mobility; however, it emphasizes "goodness" and "badness" while the former comes from other countries with modernizing technologies or other solutions, while "badness" comes from local places. Very often so called "good" modernization may in fact be "bad" and local solutions can be "good." This is the case with imported food produced by GMOs (Genetically Modified Organism) and locally produced, organic food.

Here a clash of civilizations is taking place when, for example, the Islamic people of Malaysia accept Western technology but reject Westernization. There are several strong cases supporting this kind of civilization clash. In Saudi Arabia there are no cinemas in order to not promote movies displaying questionable styles of living. In China the Internet is censored from foreign political influence on the state's politics with a "Chinese only" character.

Those who promote and sell Western technology world-wide to be successful should promote technology but be careful about promoting Westernization as well.

Figure 9.11. BlackBerry is popular in Indonesia, the largest Islamic country. (Photo: www.online.wsj.com).

Westernization

Westernization seems to be everywhere in China. Many young Chinese adopted English names and prided themselves on being Westernized. Coca-Cola drinks have found their way into remote villages. Kentucky Fried Chicken (KFC) has become the favorite meal for Chinese youth and children. The Starbucks at Metro City in west Shanghai was probably the busiest Starbucks in China. Most of the customers work in the nearby office buildings that lodge multinationals like Microsoft and Softbank. Every young man and woman in this cafe write something on their lap-top computers invented in the West and listen to American rock music. From clothes to coffee, to food and movies, Western culture is big and is getting bigger in China and other Asian countries. KFC is the country's most popular restaurant chain in Asia and a Buick is the top-selling car in China, as it reflects the owner's status.

Figure 9.12. Chinese rock band The Wheels is an example of a newly Westernized youth in China (www.telegraph.co.uk).

Fear of Western cultural impact, particularly on young people in China, has been a leading leitmotif in Communist Party propaganda for the past several years and resonantes the campaign against Western "spiritual pollution" of the early 1980s. This fear was voiced by former president Hu Jintao in late 2011 as follows:

> "We must clearly see that international hostile forces are intensifying the strategic plot of Westernizing and dividing China, and ideological and cultural fields are the focal areas of their long-term infiltration,"

Hu Jinato wrote in an essay published in Communist Party policy magazine Qiushi:

> "We should deeply understand the seriousness and complexity of the ideological struggle, always sound the alarms and remain vigilant, and take forceful measures to be on guard and respond."

This campaign against Western cultural "infiltration" has been sustained under China's current president Xi Jinping. In a May 2013 newspaper editorial, PLA general Zhu Heping cautioned against the influence of Western "cultural colonialism," particularly on Chinese youth:

"Western cultural infiltration techniques are very clever in their deception and hidden nature,"

Zhu wrote in the state-run Guangming Daily:

"Western hostile forces seize every opportunity to sneak attacks against us, and they are pressing harder and harder" (Eades 2014).

The Chinese government undoubtedly needs Western capital, knowledge, skills, and technology, but is alarmed at the Western cultural and political influence that emanates with these. If there really is an encounter happening in the "hearts and minds" of the Chinese people, the Communist Party seems to be in fear of losing that encounter (Eades 2014). These examples depict the intra-country cultural clashes of Western and Chinese civilizations.

GLOBALIZATION

Globalization both enlightens and pacifies, both widens horizons and contracts vision, although it does look that the tale of globalization told by the media is defenseless to increasing cognitive dissonance as its idealistic image of broadening prosperity is undermined by images of scarcity and sidelining and by an increasing surge of uncertainty and concern in Western and other civilizations (Lerche III-2014).

As Austrian economist, Joseph Schumpeter (1942), argued, capitalism inevitably involves a process of "creative destruction." Competition stimulates firms to innovate, both in products and in production, in order to outdo their rivals. However, entire industries and regions in Western civilization in the 21st century are "destroyed," or marginalized, as more manufacturing is outsourced to the countries with cheap labor forces. The liberal argument is that despite the somewhat Darwinian way, outsourcing produces inexpensive goods and services for Western consumers. In this sense economic globalization is regarded as the reasonable extension of the "flattening world" (Friedman 2005) that also very much improves the level of living for people in developing nations.

Economic globalization is controlled by global corporations and its mostly unethical value that "what is good for business is good for society". Their goal is to get a bigger market share in the global market which is causing super-consumerism and unsustainability for world civilization. The biggest promoters of economic globalization are Western corporations which prompt the intra-country civilization clashes. This takes place particularly among the intelligentsia of different civilizations which is well educated and aware of the shortcomings of the business strategies of global corporations.

Tribalization

Tribalization is characteristic for less developed societies where a few families are kept together to facilitate their existence. A tribe is a rather closed community which is far away from the main stream of social development in the world. In Western civilization the Amish serve as an example, which is a group (tribe) of traditionalist Christian church fellowships, closely related to but distinct from Mennonite churches, with whom they share Swiss Anabaptist origins. The Amish are known for simple living, plain dress, and reluctance to adopt many conveniences of modern technology. Today tribal society is active in less developed civilizations and Islam civilization recommends following its rules in an extreme way. In this case, *Tribalism* is a matter of religious beliefs and top-down order since such *Tribalism* should emphasize the rejection of decadent life styles practiced in Western civilization.

Democratization

Democracy is a form of government in which all eligible citizens are intended to participate equally either directly or indirectly through elected representatives in the proposal, development and establishment of the laws by which their society is managed. This means freedom of speech, free elections, electable government, and free markets. This political system is considered as the best system ever developed in history of world civilization. It has been continuously practiced in the United States for more than 200 years, and this nation recommends this system to every nation in the world. However, to apply this system, good social maturity is required, and therefore it cannot be applied immediately in every nation today. Furthermore, *democracy* in Western civilization is weakening visibly since in the strong lobbyist culture corporations have become citizens and politically set limits on corporate spending are seen as a form of censorship. Since democracy means free markets, socially imposed constrains on money are unconstitutional, and it is also considered wrong to expect political and economic equality within the society. The last (21st century) opinions of the U.S. Supreme Court have defined these conditions in the name of the Constitution, which is nothing else than the privatization of democracy (Kuhner 2014). Today (2014) in the U.S. the cost to be elected as President is about $1 billion, a Senator $10 million, and a Congress member $1.5 million. The donation by an individual for the budget of a candidate for a political office is unlimited which means that one can buy for the right amount of money whatever policy one wants. In 2008 the limit was $2,600. Is what is good for business good for society? Of course such privatized democracy is questionable and can prompt the clash of civilizations.

Terrorism

Terrorism is systematic use of violence and intimidation to create fear in order to achieve some political goal. Terrorism is a weapon of the weaker side in a conflict/clash/war. The first decade of the 21st century was dominated by terror and terrorists. No one man was responsible, although the pre-eminent face was that of Osama bin Laden. The global jihad of terror struck from New York to New Delhi. The center of the storm was and still is South Asia, and the epicenter of the storm is Pakistan, Afghanistan, Iraq, Yemen, Syria, and India. The whole world changed dramatically on September 11, 2001, when al Qaeda pilots (trained in Germany and in the U.S. for two years) hijacked four airplanes and attacked the World Trade Center in New York City (killing 3,000 people), the Pentagon, and tried to strike the U.S. Capitol. The attack was masterminded by a Pakistani, Khaled Shaikh Muhammad, and Bin Laden from Saudi Arabia. The 9/11 attack eventually lead to two wars (in Afghanistan and Iraq), followed by the downfall of the Taliban's Islamic Emirate of Afghanistan, and a global war on terror, mostly between Western and Islam civilizations. Ever since *Terrorism* has taken place almost everywhere in the least expected places and times. *Terrorism* is in fact unconventional war between a message sending group and a resisted society.

The relationships between Western Civilization and other civilizations are depicted in Figure 9.13.

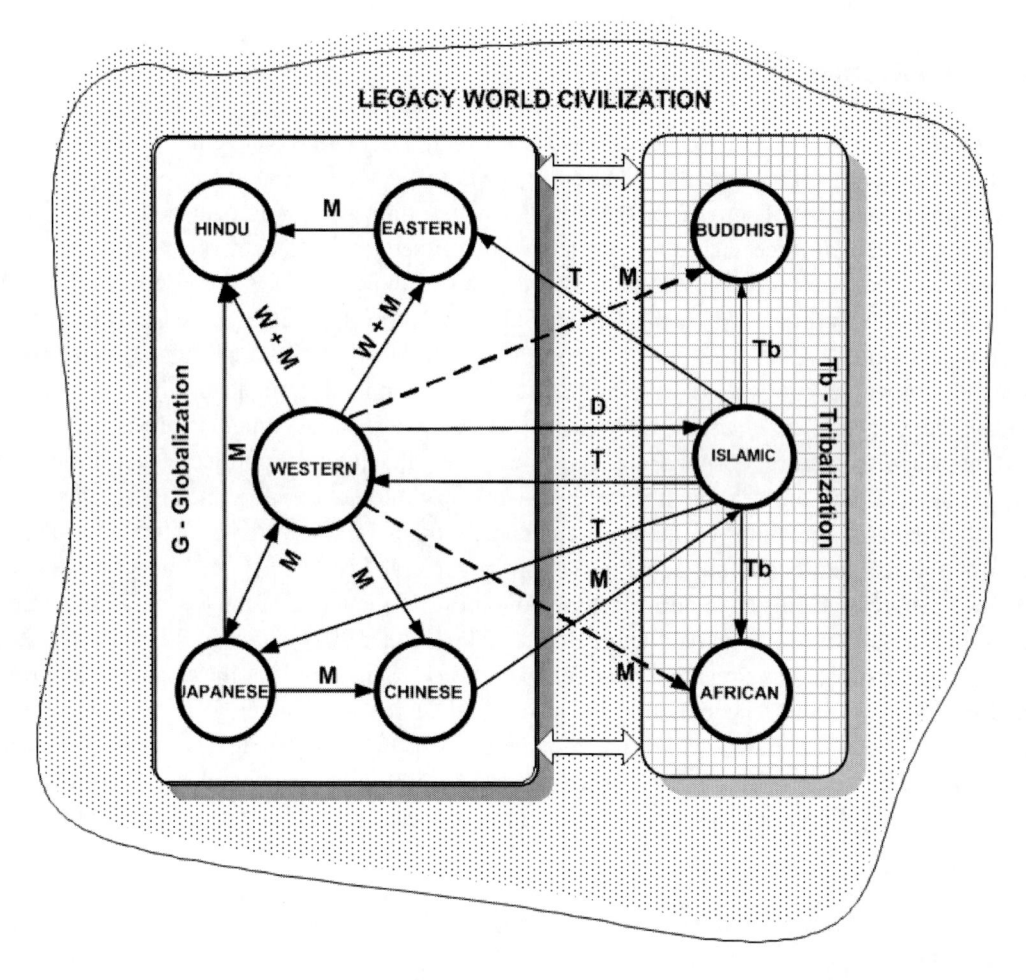

Figure 9.13. The relationships among particular civilizations in the 21st century. G-Globalization, Tb-Tribalization, D-Democratization, M-Modernization, T-Terrorism, W-Westernization.

CONCLUSION

The clashes of civilizations weaken Western civilization as it is defined in Table 9.2.

In the 21st century Western civilization has visible and invisible clashes with all contemporary civilizations (Islam, Buddhist, Eastern, Chinese, and African) except for Hindu civilization which accepts modernization, globalization, and Westernization. The most dangerous clashes, which could even result in war, are with Islam civilization. These make Western civilization unsecure and weakened by permanent threats and loses, despite its technological and military superiority.

These clashes and wars reflect the conflict between *Globalization* and *Tribalization* in the 21st century.

Table 9.2. The impact of the clashes of civilizations on Western civilization

CLASHES' BETWEEN	CLASHES' SYMPTOMS	CLASHES' IMPACT ON WESTERN CIVILIZATION
Western and Islam Civilizations	From clashes to war	Weakened and unsecured civilization
Western and Chinese Civilizations	Coming economic, cultural, and military confrontation	Weakened and world leadership, losing civilization
Western and Eastern Civilizations	Territorial, military, and political crises	Confronted world-wide and limited in international rational dealings due to sabotaging Easter civilization
Western and other Civilizations	Rejected westernization and some forms of globalization	Weakened by its global corporation that support saturated service economy and minimizing the middle class thru exporting jobs

REFERENCES

Courtois, S. (1997). *The black book of communism.* Cambridge, MA: Harvard University Press.
Dmytryshyn, B. (1974). *Modernization of Russia under Peter I and Catherine II.* Hoboken, NJ: Wiley, p.21.
D'Or.O.L. (2008). Russia as an empire. *The Moscow News weekly.* Retrieved 21 8-24-2014.
Eades, M. (2014). China targets western cultural threats. *Foreign Policy Association*, January 15. Retrieved 8-29-2014.
Gable, L.H. (2013). Is a military conflict between China and the United States possible in the future? *Council on Foreign Relations Blog.* Retrieved 8-29-2014.
Huntington, S.P. (1996). *The clash of civilizations and the remaking of world order.* New York: Simon & Schuster.
History of 9/11 Attack (2014). *Follow history.* Retrieved 8-20-2014.

International Tribunal (1995). ICTY; Karadzic indictment. Paragraph 19. *ICTY.org.* Retrieved 8-20-2014.

Kuhner, T.K. (2014). *Capitalism v. democracy, money in politics and the free market constitution.* Stanford, CA: Stanford University Press.

Lerche, Ch.O. (2014). *The conflict of globalization.* The International Journal of Pease Studies. Retrieved 8-29-2014.

Robertson, R. (1992). *Globalization: social theory and global culture.* London: Sage.

Rosenau, J. (1990). *Turbulence in world politics: a theory of change and continuity.* Princeton N.J.: Princeton University Press.

Scholte, J. A. (1997). *"Constructions of collective identity in a time of globalization."* http://nexxus.com.cwru.edu/amjdc/papers/76.

Schumpeter, J. (1942). *Capitalism, socialism and democracy.* New York: Harper.

Sorokin, P. (1937). Social and cultural dynamics, vol iii, fluctuations of social relationships, war and revolution. New York: America Books Co.

Spybey, T. (1996). *Globalization and world society.* Cambridge U.K.: Polity Press.

Steingard, David S. and Dale E. Fitzgibbons. 1997. *Challenging the juggernaut of globalization: a manifesto for academic practice.* http://nexxus.com.cwru.edu/amjdc/papers/85, April 6, 2014.

Toynbee, A. (1956). *A study of history.* Abridgement of Volumes 1-6 by D.C. Somervell. New York: Oxford University Press.

Waters, M. (1995). *Globalization.* London: Routledge.

Users.erols.com (2012). *Huguenot religious wars, Catholic vs. Huguenot (1562–1598).* Retrieved 2-15-2012.

White, M. (2011). *The great big book of horrible things.* New York: W.W. Norton & Company.

AFTERWORD

Western civilization occupies the central territories of the world, such as Europe and America, as well as peripheral lands like Australia and New Zealand. All the people in these places are integrated by shared values, culture, and infrastructure despite specific local differences. This means that Western civilization is widely accepted by those people and has been developed with close inter-relations in the last 1200 years, leading other civilizations in terms of modernization and Westernization. On the other hand, while the latter is accepted only by Hindu and Japanese civilizations other ones like Eastern, Chinese, Islamic, Buddhist, and African civilizations are impacted by Western modernization; however, they reject its dominance and "superiority" with respect to its values and culture.

The fall of the Berlin Wall and the Soviet Empire as well as *Communism* in 1991 led to the New World Order and the expectation that it was the *End of History*, as stated by Francis Fukuyama (1992), with everlasting liberal *Capitalism* with *Democracy* everywhere. Eventually, in the 21st century Russia, led by Vladimir Putin, waged a second Cold War, invading territories of the USSR's former satellites, such as Georgia (2009) and Ukraine (2014), destabilizing Moldavia and Latvia, and confronting NATO and all of Western civilization, including the U.S.

The future of the globalizing world is increasingly dependent on shrinking natural resources, especially energy sources, which implies that the geopolitical center in the 21st century is shifting from Young Europe (Central-Eastern Europe) to the oil-rich Middle East. This translocation is driven by the mounting civilization clashes between Western Civilization and Islamic Civilization in which traditional Western weaponry is attacked by terrorism, bringing incalculable harm to the entire world, particularly at the level of humanity.

The 21st-century world is going over from being partitioned to global, but it is non-united; hence, tolerance for cultural difference is a necessity. In effect, peaceful coexistence should be founded on tolerance-oriented cross-culture communication skills which are currently lacking. The increasingly globalized world has thus become a kaleidoscope of various "frontier zones" constituting a new challenge for the dynamically-growing world and its peoples. In this world centers evolve into a network of frontiers, which calls for mutual understanding and coexistence. Perhaps the center, which supposedly was and wants to be Western civilization, is itself turning into a frontier driven by a "bottom-up" strategy instead of the "top-down" strategy to which the center is accustomed. An example is the dwindling political position of the United States, heretofore a global center resembling Rome, which despite their military might evidently cannot handle many of the world's frontiers. A case in point is the difficult relations between the U.S. and EU, and the U.S. and Russia, Iran, Syria, Iraq and North Korea.

Taking into account all these conflicts, clashes, and wars, one can state that the long expected defeat of *Communism* at the end of the 20th century did not bring in the New World Order but rather a New World Disorder and such international and intra-national complexities that are far beyond societies' ability to control them. Furthermore, despite better education and ruling experiences in the 6000 years of civilization, humans are perhaps too limited as creatures of nature and are losing the game of survival within their place in the Universe.

Globalization works for global corporations but not for citizens of developed nations whose jobs are being exported to countries with low costs of labor. Also, the model of turbo-Capitalism of the 21st century promotes super-consumerism which leads to the depletion of strategic resources and to an unsustainable civilization. In effect Western civilization, as a declining civilization, is at the same time transforming into Global and Virtual civilizations whose *modus operendi* is solely in *status nascendi*. The decline of Western civilization, after reaching its peak of modernity in the second part of the 20th century, is caused by the fact that Western people are wise when they are poor and stupid when they are better off.

Western civilization in the 21st century is the most developed civilization among contemporary ones due to:

- The richness of trends, leaders, and events characterized in this investigation, including about 100 major trends and the same number of key leaders identified in politics, art, medicine, science and technology.
- Its history which does not have the stabilization phase that results in the well-developed abilities of *resilience and resourcefulness* in thinking and problem solving.
- The development of the COMPLETE MIND composed of the BASIC, WHOLE, GLOBAL, and UNIVERSAL MINDS.
- Among the four minds, the key mind is the WHOLE MIND which provides the foundation of thinking and problem solving based not only on conventional knowledge and wisdom but particularly on theoretical knowledge and wisdom. It gives the opportunity for educated judgment and choice in all kinds of human undertakings.

Western civilization, due to its permanent multi-directional, non-stabilized development, was able to change and adapt its society's *modus operandi* according to circumstances as follows:

- Level of Religion – from Christianity to Roman-Catholicism (1054)[61] and from Catholicism to Protestantism (1517) which triggered a positive motivation for work ethic and a modest life which developed a high quality of living in the 20th century in the U.S. and Northern Europe.
- Level of Society – shifts from the Manor Society to Feudal, Represented (English Revolution), Liberal (American Revolution), Citizenship (French Revolution), Industrial (Industrial Revolution), Technological (after WWII), Information (2000),

---

[61] The second branch of Christianity became Orthodox Christianity.

and Virtual (2010) ones exemplify Western civilization's progressive and sensitive attitude for change and adaptation.
- Level of Culture – gradual and parallel development of High and Pop-Culture, in which the latter evolves from the culture of workers' protests to youth decadency (sex, drugs and rock and roll). These cultures triggers the bifurcation of the society and all associated with its bad feelings, attitudes and strategies.
- Level of Infrastructure – from the good roads and aqueducts of the Romans to the electricity and combustion engine-driven processes, megacities, automobiles, airplanes, highways, high-rises, ocean connecting channels, global transportation and the Internet, all of these projects were developed by Western Civilization and later adapted by other civilizations.

Western civilization has two key stages of development; the first one was in the Renaissance when art and architecture reached their heights and ever since have provided standards for the development of art and architectural. The second key stage is about 2000, when Western society in developed nations (called sometimes the Atlantic civilization or West-Western civilization) reached a high quality of living for its upper and middle classes. However, due to super-consumerism and the steady depletion of strategic resources this kind of living is not sustainable world-wide.

Global Civilization in the 21st century, by transferring jobs from Western Civilization to other civilizations, is triggering social unrest in the former and is triggering world instability. Global Civilization reduces taxation in the developed world which is resulting in a deterioration and regression of Western infrastructure and society. A good example of this is the failure of Detroit, which is regressing form an industrial to an agricultural town. Global Civilization triggers a domino effect where one failure-driven country pulls other countries with it. This is the case in the Euro crisis of the European Union in the 2010s, when failing PIGS countries (Portugal, Italy, Greece, and Spain) negatively impact Germany, France, and other economically.

Virtual civilization, by the rapid dissemination of e-communication and the rise of virtual society at all levels, may lead the former Western-Global Civilization to transform into Western-Global-Virtual civilization which will be able to solve some difficult societal problems but at the same time may replace the Western model of representative democracy with direct democracy leading to societal chaos. These transformative processes, which are driven by greed and e-technology, show that humans are wise when poor and are stupid when are better off. Can the latter eventually be cured by better education?

The transformation of Western civilization into Western-Global-Virtual civilization in the 21st century is a process which takes place from within since it is driven by the strong impact of several cultures, characterized by the scope of key contributions as it is shown in Table A.1

One can state that the decline of Western civilization in the 21st century is a fact and is caused mostly by its internal cultural processes. This process is not new, since usually large organisms deteriorate from within, like empires. Can Western civilization re-engineer its own culture all by itself? The scope of deterioration and the democratic culture will not allow for any top-down social engineering today.

Table A.1. The Impact of Western culture on the decline of Western civilization in the 21st century

culture kind	key contribution	deterioration level of western civilization
High culture	High esteem	Sustains
Folk culture	Tradition, fast food, texting	Some impact
Popular culture	The Nice society (comfort and fun) political correctness, relative truth	Very high impact
Mass culture	Super-consumerism, unhealthy food, and depletion of strategic resources	Very high impact
Pop culture	Vulgarization of humanity	Very high impact
Global culture	Christian values replaced by global business values	Very high impact
Middle culture	Very slow assimilation of immigrants living in ghettos and transformation from the nation to political society	Significant impact
Hybrid culture	Tolerance and complementary values, accepted by the elite mostly	Sustains

One must be aware that human kind is a part of nature's chaos and randomness and therefore is not the ultimate master of the world. This is particularly the case if it is true that one is wise when poor and stupid when better off, like the Westerners of today.

Western civilization's liberal democracy in the 21st century is so liberal that it allows for the development of *multiculturalism* and *virtualism* which can destroy this civilization by breaking its societal cohesion and ability to be sustainable. Other modes of societal interactions such as *culturalism* and *transculturalism* as well as *pluralism* are very sensitive to the economic and educational conditions in the sense that when the economy is good, education is good and *transculturalism* and *pluralism* are satisfactory. However, when the economy is bad, education declines and societal inter-action looks towards *separatism* and *culturalism* in a world which has just opened for global interactions of all kinds.

Western civilization in the 21st century is mastering the development of technology but at the same time is experiencing problems with the cohesiveness of its society which results in it losing its ability to make positive changes for survival. Perhaps, humans have reached such a complex level of development that they cannot cope successfully with its issues and challenges?

To seek an optimal mode societal inter-action in contemporary Western civilization, which is proud of its liberal democracy and open to the dynamic globalizing world, perhaps Western society should apply diversity at the level of individuals and the complementary *hybrid culture*, composed of *mother, middle, global*, and *complementary* cultures in a given nation.

Western Civilization is a civilization which responds to challenges triggered by its infrastructure in the 21st century. It functions by applying 11 key civilization infrastructures, with 5 traditional, nation-oriented infrastructures: authority, military, education, and urban-rural infrastructures. Another 7 infrastructures are developing mostly in the 21st century and have a global-orientation. Among them one can distinguish the following: global cyberwar, global knowledge, global production, global service, global transport, global finance, and global information infrastructures. The global financial and global information infrastructures play a key integrational role towards the remaining infrastructures.

These new 7 civilization global infrastructures create serious challenges for society. These challenges include understanding the scope of their functioning, their potential and limitations, and the level of skills which would allow society to use them rightly and effectively.

In the 21st century Western civilization has visible and invisible clashes with all contemporary civilizations (Islam, Buddhist, Eastern, Chinese, and African) except Hindu which accepts modernization, globalization, and Westernization. The most dangerous clashes, which could even result in war, are with the Islam civilization. These could make Western civilization unsecure and weakened by permanent threats and loses, despite its technological and military superiority.

These clashes and wars reflect the conflict between *Globalization* and *Tribalization* in the 21st century and define the *modus operandi* of contemporary societies.

INDEX

#

20th century, ix, 11, 12, 14, 18, 19, 20, 36, 40, 41, 44, 46, 47, 65, 67, 68, 74, 78, 83, 92, 93, 113, 114, 115, 116, 124, 125, 129, 146, 156, 175, 199, 202, 222, 233, 254
9/11, x, 235, 236, 241, 250, 251

A

Abkhazia, 245
Abraham, 28, 175
access, 13, 63, 66, 92, 122, 140, 141, 171, 185, 220, 224, 226
accounting, 40, 196
adaptation, 125, 255
advancement(s), 12, 65, 89, 145
Afghanistan, x, 30, 42, 139, 140, 236, 238, 240, 241, 242, 250
Africa, 5, 7, 14, 34, 39, 44, 53, 54, 64, 66, 91, 92, 102, 175, 188
African-American, 65, 177, 182
age, 29, 51, 52, 62, 84, 86, 88, 93, 107, 137, 164, 165, 170, 219, 228, 229
agriculture, 50, 51, 86, 103, 111, 199, 205, 227
Air Force, 79
airports, 138, 239
Al Gore, vii, xi, 79
Al Qaeda, 240, 241
Alaska, 32
Albania, 113
American culture, 41, 145, 160, 182
anatomy, 67, 79, 88, 113
ancient world, 96, 98
Angola, 65
annihilation, 77, 241
antagonism, 206
anthrax, 216

anthropology, 176
anxiety, 116, 117
architect(s), 77, 101, 108
Argentina, 34, 35
Aristotle, 56, 96
arithmetic, 96
armed conflict, 20
armed forces, 18, 33
Armenia, 9
Armenians, 172, 233, 234, 235
Asia, x, 7, 8, 14, 17, 26, 34, 37, 50, 51, 52, 53, 55, 56, 63, 99, 117, 144, 233, 247, 250
Asian countries, 247
assault, 182, 234
assessment, 143, 218
assimilation, 167, 170, 173, 174, 177, 181, 182, 184, 185, 256
atmosphere, 165, 213
attachment, 180, 184
attitudes, 12, 121, 125, 154, 156, 243, 255
Austria, 11, 14, 52, 59, 61, 66, 73, 76, 206
authenticity, 163
authority(s), 17, 32, 33, 98, 102, 141, 163, 191, 224, 225, 227, 256
automation, 73, 142, 202, 204, 206, 216, 228, 229
automobile(s), 70, 105, 126, 255
autonomy, 54, 99, 113, 193
awareness, 43, 109, 130, 161, 182, 185, 207, 213
Azerbaijan, 9

B

Bahrain, 194, 195
Balkan Wars, 172
Balkans, 9, 54
Bangladesh, 228
banking sector, 154, 161
banks, 54, 74, 103, 134, 156, 161, 224

behaviors, 137, 140, 151
Beijing, 243
Belarus, 24, 39, 42
Belgium, 20, 22, 91, 113, 152
beneficiaries, 154
benefits, 142, 181, 183, 201, 210, 223, 224, 237
Bhutan, 42
Bible, 96, 101
biological systems, 170
biotechnology, 200
Bolshevik Revolution, 74, 91, 115
Border Patrol, 176
Bosnia, 175, 234
bottom-up, 47, 253
brain, 79, 121, 219
Brazil, 32, 33, 35, 65, 159, 243
breakdown, 88, 89, 90
Britain, 9, 16, 20, 23, 26, 33, 37, 53, 54, 61, 68, 69, 70, 73, 77, 84, 94, 120, 136, 183, 224, 228
Buddhism, 188
Bulgaria, 15, 22, 39, 42, 74, 113, 172, 193, 239, 245
Bureau of Labor Statistics, 198
bureaucracy, 11, 108, 109, 215
business costs, 132, 198
business model, 155, 227
business strategy, 142
businesses, 72, 92, 109, 131, 134, 137, 142, 156, 161, 196, 198, 200, 202, 209, 215, 224, 234

C

CAD, 198
CAM, 198
Cambodia, 42, 46, 74
capital account, 195
capital gains, 139
capital programs, 192
Capitalism, vii, ix, x, xi, 12, 19, 25, 26, 27, 30, 46, 65, 72, 74, 75, 78, 83, 102, 103, 113, 115, 124, 126, 131, 171, 173, 211, 231, 236, 248, 252, 253, 254
Capitol Hill, 226
carbon, 107, 147
carbon dioxide, 107, 147
Caribbean, 34, 65
Caspian Sea, 8
catalyst, 18
catastrophes, 170
Catholic Church, 32, 102
Catholics, 68, 102, 233
Caucasians, 175
Caucasus, 8, 55, 233
CBS, 132

Central African Republic, 140
Central Asia, 14, 15, 34, 55, 233
central bank, 161, 183
Central Europe, 20, 24, 74
CERN, 79
Chad, 140
challenges, 5, 7, 43, 61, 85, 96, 141, 151, 160, 173, 187, 191, 213, 223, 225, 227, 256, 257
chaos, 9, 12, 14, 46, 55, 74, 91, 96, 98, 116, 117, 118, 129, 133, 145, 147, 167, 172, 182, 255, 256
checks and balances, 56, 97
chemical, 68, 212
Chicago, 126, 138
children, 34, 109, 137, 142, 145, 148, 175, 176, 247
China, x, 44, 46, 47, 53, 64, 65, 74, 78, 80, 120, 123, 135, 138, 152, 187, 204, 224, 233, 242, 243, 244, 246, 247, 251
Chinese government, 248
Christian morality, vii, ix
Christianity, 13, 20, 39, 42, 53, 56, 61, 64, 74, 81, 86, 87, 97, 98, 106, 125, 130, 152, 254
Christians, 55, 61, 239
circulation, 104, 193, 209
city(s), 5, 17, 47, 51, 53, 63, 86, 97, 108, 109, 152, 159, 170, 171, 177, 179, 187, 227, 235, 241, 247, 250
citizens, 31, 56, 75, 83, 96, 132, 166, 178, 182, 209, 215, 242, 245, 249, 254
citizenship, 11, 151
civil law, 106
civil liberties, 36
civil rights, 121, 124
civil service, 172
civil war, ix, 26, 31, 111, 124, 175, 176, 233, 243
class struggle, 113, 115
classes, 103, 109, 113, 137, 143, 255
classification, 47, 48, 178, 204
climate, 3, 16, 35, 83, 98, 120, 147, 179, 213, 227
climate change, 179, 227
clusters, 11, 121, 122, 141, 213
CNN, 134, 140, 147, 156, 239
coal, 22, 70, 73, 119
cognition, 213, 218, 219, 220
cognitive dissonance, 248
Cold War, ix, x, xi, 12, 17, 19, 22, 27, 31, 46, 75, 78, 79, 83, 92, 231, 232, 236, 243, 253
collaboration, 172, 179
collectivism, 74, 113
colleges, 140, 160, 164, 209, 220, 223, 226
Colombia, 35
colonization, 13, 28, 65, 66, 91, 123, 219
combustion, 70, 126, 255
commerce, 13, 23, 79, 103, 104, 118, 172, 185, 195

Index

commercial, 40, 65, 98, 99, 102, 154, 156, 242
commercials, 161
commodity, 182
Common Market, 23
common sense, 219, 220
communication, 4, 5, 19, 44, 46, 72, 79, 80, 101, 109, 116, 118, 130, 133, 141, 145, 147, 169, 170, 179, 180, 185, 192, 196, 203, 205, 214, 215, 219, 220, 222, 224, 226, 253, 255
communication skills, 46, 101, 253
communication systems, 79
communication technologies, 192
Communism, ix, xi, 12, 15, 16, 24, 27, 30, 31, 32, 46, 47, 75, 78, 83, 113, 114, 115, 124, 173, 174, 231, 234, 236, 243, 245, 251, 253, 254
Communist Party, 247, 248
community(s), 11, 97, 99, 112, 113, 135, 137, 145, 146, 152, 159, 163, 173, 176, 180, 184, 249
community relations, 11
comparative advantage, 196
competition, ix, x, 12, 113, 120, 139, 144, 171, 173, 174, 175, 231, 240
competitive advantage, 196, 224
competitiveness, 200
complexity, 11, 92, 93, 174, 199, 227, 247
composers, 41, 113
computer, 12, 18, 41, 72, 79, 80, 110, 133, 141, 156, 164, 166, 180, 198, 209, 213, 224, 226, 238
conceptualization, 220
conductor(s), 41, 107, 108
conference, 7, 193
configuration, 91
confinement, 234
conflict, 13, 14, 16, 17, 18, 20, 37, 46, 74, 88, 90, 104, 112, 113, 200, 217, 231, 237, 242, 245, 249, 251, 252, 257
confrontation, 43, 122, 231, 251
Confucianism, 152
Congress, 25, 198, 249
Congressional Budget Office, 147
connectivity, 133, 145, 212
consciousness, 72, 209
Constitution, 25, 31, 66, 69, 185, 249
constitutional law, 69
constitutional principles, 68
construction, 4, 5, 33, 216
consumers, 22, 23, 132, 134, 161, 162, 195, 243, 248
consumption, 118, 134, 156, 191, 212, 223, 227
containers, 71, 223
Continental, 25, 26
controversial, 183, 204
convergence criteria, 193
cooperation, 20, 22, 113, 122, 192

coordination, 196
corruption, x, 98
cost, 16, 75, 119, 140, 196, 200, 203, 204, 205, 215, 216, 217, 223, 226, 242, 249
cost effectiveness, 215
cotton, 108, 109
counterterrorism, 238
Craftsmen, 171
creativity, 178, 217
creep, 116, 208
crimes, 74, 114, 182, 238, 242
criminals, 33, 47, 224
crises, 143, 251
critical thinking, 124, 219
criticism, 120, 121, 181, 182
Croatia, 193
crown, 36, 58, 68
crude oil, 223
crystallization, 89
Cuba, 17, 27, 33, 65, 78, 79
cultural clash, 248
cultural differences, 184
cultural identities, 176, 182
cultural imperialism, 159
cultural values, 170
currency, 12, 23, 193, 209
curriculum, 164, 227
customer service, 204, 226
customers, 92, 109, 204, 215, 217, 226, 247
cyberattack, 224, 228
cyberspace, 80, 130, 146, 209, 213
cycles, 4, 83, 85, 89
Cyprus, 9, 52, 152
Czech Republic, 9, 11, 14, 193, 239

D

data mining, 205, 219
deaths, 74, 141, 233
debts, 118, 161, 199, 227, 242
decay, 9, 88, 161
decolonization, 28, 121
defensiveness, 13
degradation, 134, 146
delegates, 204
democracy, vii, ix, x, 11, 12, 17, 26, 30, 31, 37, 46, 56, 65, 68, 69, 78, 83, 92, 96, 97, 106, 112, 115, 118, 120, 121, 124, 129, 133, 141, 143, 145, 147, 151, 154, 163, 176, 182, 186, 187, 211, 231, 242, 245, 249, 252, 253, 255, 256
democrats, 113
demonstrations, 237
Denmark, 11, 18, 23, 145, 193, 206, 239

Department of Labor, 148
depersonalization, 154
depression, 133, 159
deregulation, 195
designers, 62, 63, 205, 206
destruction, 77, 120, 123, 142, 234, 235, 248
developed countries, 34, 36, 198, 202, 211
developed nations, 36, 83, 126, 204, 210, 254, 255
developing countries, 143, 192, 202, 211
developing nations, xi, 92, 135, 248
developmental process, 45
dictatorship, ix, 69, 115
discrimination, 232, 233
diseases, 32, 37, 65, 210
disorder, 9, 53, 180
distribution, 12, 34, 74, 80, 142, 147, 148, 220
divergence, 137, 163, 220
diversity, x, 35, 158, 169, 170, 171, 173, 174, 176, 179, 180, 181, 185, 187, 188, 256
DNA, 50, 92
dogmas, ix, 104, 106, 152, 232
domestic violence, 243
dominance, 33, 46, 74, 115, 152, 196, 253
Dominican Republic, 65
downward mobility, 135
drugs, 125, 164, 166, 255
dynamism, 102, 176

E

Eastern Europe, x, 20, 23, 34, 50, 51, 78, 92, 102, 135, 172, 173, 233, 237, 253
e-commerce, 79, 118, 185
economic activity, 134
economic boom, 52
economic crisis, 76, 210
economic development, 232
economic downturn, 175
economic growth, 73, 142, 229
economic power, x
economic problem, 175
economic progress, 144
economic reform(s), 239
economic relations, 112
economics, 106, 111, 112, 114, 228
education, xi, 13, 14, 36, 47, 59, 86, 101, 105, 106, 124, 135, 139, 140, 147, 156, 160, 167, 181, 182, 187, 191, 198, 199, 219, 220, 225, 226, 227, 232, 246, 254, 255, 256
egalitarianism, 115
Egypt, 52, 53, 237
electric current, 110
electricity, 11, 29, 66, 92, 107, 108, 126, 154, 255

electronic communications, 156
emergency, 136, 205
emerging markets, 139
employment, 38, 117, 132, 134, 135, 142, 162, 198, 205
enemies, 64, 111, 239
energy, 20, 36, 46, 89, 107, 135, 191, 201, 213, 216, 223, 227, 232, 235, 253
enforcement, 5
engineering, 57, 101, 108, 111, 167, 199, 202, 215, 255
England, 27, 48, 66, 70, 86, 101, 103, 108, 109, 126, 140, 152
enlargement, 14
entrepreneurs, 111
entrepreneurship, 12, 130
environment(s), 134, 176, 183, 196, 201, 206, 213, 215, 220, 223
environmental degradation, 146
equality, 11, 31, 56, 57, 106, 112, 115, 130, 154, 182, 183, 185, 189, 249
equilibrium, 222
espionage, 215, 223, 224, 227
Estonia, 113, 224, 228
ethics, 102, 130, 154, 206, 219
ethnic diversity, 35
ethnic groups, 115, 172, 173, 174, 177, 184
ethnicity, 42, 137, 170, 172, 174, 175, 182, 188
Eurasia, 233, 234
European Central Bank, 193
European Commission, 23
European Community, 23
European Monetary Union, 193
European Parliament, 23, 24
European System of Central Banks, 193
European Union (EU), x, 9, 10, 12, 20, 22, 23, 24, 47, 61, 86, 92, 93, 114, 135, 147, 193, 227, 238, 242, 245, 254, 255
everyday life, 156
evidence, 104, 139
evolution, 5, 20, 21, 87, 89, 93, 99, 170, 173, 174, 188, 192, 205, 228
exchange rate, 192
expert systems, 226
expertise, 204, 238
exploitation, 28, 51, 65, 78
expulsion, 233, 234
extremists, 238, 246

F

FAA, 205

factories, 70, 72, 80, 109, 116, 118, 135, 138, 142, 144, 198, 201, 216, 222, 223
failed states, 233
faith, x, 64, 99, 102, 184
families, 18, 34, 52, 136, 138, 154, 155, 159, 162, 183, 239, 243, 249
farmers, 72, 103, 142, 148, 223
farms, 142, 163, 223, 227
fast food, 160, 167, 256
FDR, 125
fear(s), 16, 18, 198, 200, 239, 247, 248, 249
federal government, 36, 139
Federal Reserve, 27
Federal Reserve Board, 27
films, 141, 145, 164, 220
financial, 3, 38, 47, 68, 134, 143, 180, 191, 192, 193, 195, 224, 226, 228, 257
financial capital, 192, 193
financial crisis, 134
financial globalization, 192
financial institutions, 134, 143, 192
financial support, 68
financial system, 192, 195
Finland, 15, 74, 113, 206
first generation, 185
flexibility, 192, 198
flight(s), 108, 223
fluctuations, 252
food, 5, 34, 71, 72, 81, 86, 102, 109, 156, 160, 167, 216, 223, 245, 246, 247, 256
force, x, xi, 14, 33, 56, 63, 64, 74, 89, 90, 96, 98, 115, 123, 135, 172, 177, 182, 198, 201, 206, 238
Ford, 29, 72, 73
Fordism, 27
forecasting, 126
foreign exchange, 192
foreign exchange market, 192
foreign policy, 237
formation, 5, 13, 22, 28, 89, 92, 98, 113, 115, 174
foundations, 7, 21, 40
France, 11, 16, 20, 22, 27, 32, 33, 46, 52, 53, 54, 66, 68, 70, 71, 73, 86, 91, 101, 111, 121, 147, 152, 153, 166, 171, 175, 180, 183, 184, 206, 233, 239, 255
free trade, 133, 199
free will, 120
freedom, ix, 12, 36, 68, 69, 86, 96, 115, 120, 130, 140, 146, 152, 154, 161, 183, 241, 249
funding, 138, 183
funds, 143, 159

G

Galileo, 64, 67
garment industry, 72
GATT, 82, 193
GDP, 76, 162
gender identity, 170
General Agreement on Tariffs and Trade, 193
genocide, 172, 174, 234, 235, 241, 242
geography, 13, 15, 154
Georgia, 9, 46, 245, 253
Germany, 9, 11, 14, 15, 16, 18, 20, 22, 27, 33, 34, 44, 59, 70, 73, 74, 75, 76, 77, 86, 91, 92, 101, 102, 111, 113, 115, 136, 147, 152, 153, 160, 166, 171, 172, 173, 175, 180, 183, 206, 233, 239, 243, 250, 255
Global civilizations, vii, 49, 85
global competition, 175
global economy, 148
global mobility, 223
global trade, 76
global village, 19, 157
global warming, 50
globalization, xi, 3, 29, 64, 79, 81, 83, 92, 118, 138, 144, 145, 147, 158, 182, 184, 192, 195, 219, 248, 251, 252, 257
God, 19, 68, 96, 98, 152
goods and services, 147, 248
governance, ix, x, 97, 146
government spending, 134
governments, 134, 140, 183, 206, 209, 224, 236
Great Britain, 16, 23, 33, 53, 61, 70, 77
Great Depression, 134, 135, 143, 192, 216
Great Recession, 133
Greece, 23, 50, 51, 52, 53, 56, 57, 97, 99, 113, 120, 147, 161, 172, 255
greed, 74, 87, 130, 147, 255
Greeks, x, 39, 52, 56, 57, 96, 172
growth, 30, 36, 44, 56, 69, 71, 73, 76, 80, 88, 89, 90, 108, 109, 118, 119, 121, 130, 131, 134, 136, 137, 142, 146, 148, 152, 162, 182, 192, 198, 223, 233, 246
Guatemala, 175
guilty, 104, 140, 232

H

Hamas, 238, 241
happiness, 57, 112, 119, 137, 140
harmony, 63, 101, 117, 153
Hawaii, 27, 31
health, 5, 109, 142, 162, 170, 212

health care, 5, 109, 142
hegemony, 75, 206
Henry Ford, 29, 72
heritage, x, 120, 182
Hezbollah, 238, 241
higher education, 198, 219
highways, 76, 126, 255
homogeneity, 172, 173, 174, 178, 184, 188
Honduras, 35, 175
Hong Kong, 78, 242
horses, 54, 70, 153
hospitality, 185
hospitalization, 180
household income, 147
housing, 134, 135, 136
hub, 50, 242
Huguenots, 233
human, ix, x, 5, 13, 47, 50, 65, 67, 74, 75, 78, 79, 81, 83, 90, 96, 104, 105, 108, 111, 112, 113, 115, 120, 124, 125, 152, 160, 167, 174, 175, 180, 185, 201, 202, 205, 206, 207, 209, 215, 216, 217, 219, 226, 233, 240, 242, 254, 256
human body, 104
human brain, 79, 219
human development, 175, 185
Human Development Index, 36
Human Development Report, 47
human right(s), 13, 111, 124, 160, 174
Hungary, 14, 15, 18, 53, 61, 73, 74, 78, 111, 113, 172, 173, 193, 239
hybrid, 145, 151, 158, 174, 185, 187, 256
hydrogen, 40, 72, 107, 179
hydrogen bomb, 40, 72, 179
hypothesis, 68, 231

I

Iceland, 7, 145
ideal(s), ix, 62, 63, 66, 69, 99, 111, 137
identification, 175, 182, 196
identity, 146, 156, 168, 170, 173, 175, 181, 184, 209, 252
identity politics, 181
ideology, x, 112, 115, 182, 183, 234
IEA, 228
illusion, 188
image(s), 71, 79, 101, 140, 156, 182, 207, 208, 216, 248
IMF, 82, 192
imitation, 11
immigrants, 33, 42, 109, 139, 157, 166, 167, 175, 180, 183, 185, 187, 228, 256
immigration, 34, 37, 38, 175, 182, 183, 184

immunity, 192, 228, 229
imperialism, 154, 159
improvements, 33, 108, 246
income, 27, 34, 36, 109, 117, 134, 135, 136, 137, 138, 139, 140, 142, 145, 147, 155, 162, 183, 205, 210, 227
income distribution, 34, 142
income inequality, 34, 137
income transfers, 142
independence, 7, 12, 25, 28, 31, 33, 48, 66, 69, 106, 196, 213, 245
India, 16, 64, 102, 152, 187, 198, 204, 224, 243, 250
Indians, 25, 26, 65
individualism, 74, 115, 154
individuality, 113
individuals, x, 40, 72, 96, 111, 122, 134, 141, 146, 182, 185, 187, 256
Indonesia, 246
industrialization, 31, 80, 109, 118, 246
industry(s), 13, 29, 33, 36, 37, 72, 83, 108, 109, 111, 117, 135, 154, 159, 200, 206, 216, 248
inequality, x, 12, 34, 35, 48, 53, 99, 116, 130, 137, 139, 143, 148, 181, 183
information exchange, 213
information processing, 116
information technology, 21, 84, 129, 196, 198, 199, 226
infrastructure, x, 3, 4, 7, 33, 37, 45, 49, 50, 71, 75, 76, 108, 109, 138, 147, 170, 191, 195, 196, 197, 200, 202, 203, 205, 209, 213, 215, 220, 222, 223, 224, 225, 226, 227, 228, 232, 253, 255, 256
inheritance, 10, 138, 139, 147, 148, 182
innovator, 62, 71
inoculation, 108
institutions, 11, 86, 96, 101, 106, 118, 134, 143, 151, 160, 192, 213, 215
181, 183, 198, 223
intelligence, 130, 146, 170, 183, 199, 209, 216, 217
interface, 212
interference, 33
International Bank for Reconstruction and Development, 192
international financial institutions, 192
international law, 124, 219
International Monetary Fund, 192
international relations, 31
International Space Station, 36
international trade, 192
interrelations, 133, 145
intervention, 31, 243
invasions, 10, 49, 61, 85, 95, 99, 187, 233
inventions, vii, xi, 53, 68, 71, 107, 127
inventors, 68, 71, 72, 155, 178

investment(s), 102, 109, 114, 118, 134, 139, 192, 200, 206
Iran, 47, 224, 254
Iraq, 21, 30, 47, 139, 236, 238, 239, 241, 250, 254
Iraqi War, x
Ireland, 23, 136, 152, 198, 241
iron, 52, 53, 109
Iron Curtain, 79
Islam, x, xi, 12, 29, 46, 55, 56, 61, 74, 78, 98, 119, 124, 152, 192, 232, 234, 235, 236, 239, 242, 249, 250, 251, 257
Islamic law, 238
Islamic society, 232
Islamic state, 31, 240
Islamist Freedom fighters, x
islands, 9, 38, 50, 96
isolation, 14, 31, 123, 159, 184, 185
isolationism, 152
Israel, 92, 96, 173, 231, 235, 238, 240, 241
issues, vii, xi, 7, 31, 89, 96, 97, 135, 140, 160, 170, 184, 187, 202, 207, 209, 210, 256
Italian Renaissance, ix, 11, 99, 100, 101, 120, 155
Italy, 9, 11, 20, 22, 33, 52, 53, 54, 55, 59, 61, 63, 66, 73, 79, 91, 99, 113, 115, 126, 147, 152, 154, 155, 166, 171, 175, 206, 239, 255

J

Jamaica, 65
Jamestown, 25
Japan, 16, 27, 37, 46, 78, 115, 188, 201, 205, 216, 242, 243
Jews, 39, 40, 41, 61, 76, 77, 115, 172, 173, 175, 233, 234
jihad, 238, 249
Jordan, 96, 152, 239
justification, 46, 112

K

Kazakhstan, 9
KGB, ix
kinship, 137, 173
Korea, 46, 47, 74, 75, 78, 115, 206, 233, 254

L

labor force, x, xi, 182, 198, 201, 248
labor market, 183
landscape, 109, 111, 146
languages, 38, 50, 120, 179
Laos, 42, 74

Latin America, x, 32, 33, 34, 35, 42, 47, 91
Latinos, 177
Latvia, 46, 113, 193, 253
laws, 12, 86, 96, 104, 105, 106, 144, 146, 202, 206, 239, 249
leadership, 5, 9, 24, 31, 33, 49, 66, 91, 93, 101, 111, 124, 152, 251
learning, 56, 59, 98, 99, 101, 105, 106, 153, 159, 165, 166, 167, 176
learning process, 176
Lebanon, 96, 152
legislation, 20, 140, 141, 236
leisure, 56, 83, 165
leisure time, 165
liberalism, 69, 97, 154, 183
liberalization, 195
liberation, 112, 113
liberty, 84, 94, 112, 115, 154
life cycle, 5, 85, 87, 88, 90, 91, 92, 93
liquidity, 161, 192
literacy, 101
Lithuania, 14, 113, 193
loans, 134, 161, 162, 192
logical reasoning, 121
Louisiana, 26, 65, 163
Luxemburg, 16, 22

M

Macedonia, 52, 172
majority, 31, 38, 42, 55, 77, 79, 90, 102, 116, 142, 182
Malaysia, 246
management, ix, 205, 214
manipulation, 5
manpower, 74, 142
manufactured goods, 36, 70
manufacturing, xi, 11, 28, 36, 38, 72, 108, 117, 118, 129, 132, 135, 142, 146, 181, 198, 199, 200, 201, 202, 204, 205, 206, 210, 212, 216, 222, 226, 242, 248
market economy, x, 31, 226, 237, 245
marketing, 156, 224
Marx, 16, 74, 113, 114, 126
Maryland, 25
mass, 29, 63, 68, 72, 73, 89, 140, 141, 147, 151, 156, 160, 161, 163, 168, 172, 183, 233, 234, 237, 241
mass media, 156, 160, 168
material resources, 89
materialism, 112
materials, 22, 109, 153, 196, 206, 216, 227
matter, ix, 65, 166, 249
measurement(s), 34, 36, 96, 140

media, 4, 140, 156, 160, 161, 164, 165, 168, 178, 220, 224, 248
median, 136, 142
medical, 180, 216
medicine, vii, 41, 67, 83, 96, 97, 104, 113, 120, 125, 254
Mediterranean, 3, 7, 50, 51, 53, 59, 63, 70, 98, 160
melting, 177, 179, 182
membership, 9, 41, 240
memorizing, 219
memory, 121, 130
mercantilism, 63
Mercury, 107
meritocracy, 11, 147
metals, 33, 51, 108
methodology, 3, 49, 85, 95, 129, 151, 169, 191, 231
Mexico, 26, 27, 31, 33, 35, 65, 145, 176
middle class, xi, 80, 85, 92, 117, 118, 126, 129, 134, 135, 138, 142, 146, 147, 148, 181, 198, 199, 204, 210, 226, 251, 255
Middle East, 3, 5, 34, 42, 46, 232, 233, 236, 237, 238, 239, 240, 241, 242, 253
migrants, 38, 171, 173
migration, 13, 55, 173, 183, 192
military, 7, 11, 14, 22, 28, 31, 47, 52, 54, 61, 64, 73, 77, 78, 79, 86, 88, 91, 99, 115, 125, 141, 151, 170, 176, 185, 191, 200, 224, 225, 227, 231, 236, 238, 239, 243, 251, 253, 256, 257
minimum wage, 142
minorities, 172, 174, 175, 185, 188
mission(s), 14, 101, 145, 147, 152, 192, 242
models, 62, 84, 94, 139, 140, 141, 227
modernity, 29, 49, 63, 73, 83, 84, 93, 94, 95, 116, 117, 127, 254
modernization, 45, 121, 246, 251, 253, 257
modus operandi, 42, 53, 88, 99, 125, 146, 151, 191, 254, 257
Moldavia, 39, 42, 46, 245, 253
Moldova, 24
monetary policy, 193
money markets, 192
monopoly, 64, 69
morality, vii, ix, 53, 75, 76, 77, 119, 168, 219, 232, 234
mosaic, 4, 124, 177
Moscow, 18, 111, 251
motivation, 197, 254
Mozambique, 65
multiculturalism, 154, 169, 173, 174, 175, 176, 177, 179, 180, 181, 182, 183, 184, 185, 186, 187, 188, 256
multi-ethnic, 97, 174
murder, 141, 234

music, 40, 41, 59, 70, 81, 112, 114, 116, 140, 141, 145, 156, 157, 163, 165, 166, 178, 200, 239, 247
Muslims, 55, 99, 172, 183, 238, 239, 240

N

nanotechnology, 200
national community, 113, 184
national culture, 115, 156, 157, 187
national identity, 156, 184
national policy, 142
national security, 199, 200
nationalism, 13, 74, 113, 115, 154, 171, 172, 174, 181, 188
Native Americans, 233
native population, 32
NATO, 9, 18, 22, 46, 82, 86, 245, 253
natural resources, 13, 46, 74, 119, 154, 232, 253
Nazi Germany, 175
Nepal, 42
Netherlands, 25, 66, 121, 136, 171, 239
networking, 80, 180
New Deal, 27
New England, 140
new media, 178
New World Disorder, 47, 254
New World Order, ix, 30, 46, 47, 78, 114, 231, 253, 254
New Zealand, ix, 3, 38, 39, 45, 78, 140, 253
NGOs, 92
Nicaragua, 27, 31
Niels Bohr, 40
NKWD, ix
Nobel Prize, 40
nobility, 155, 243
non-OECD, 223
North Africa, 15, 34, 53
North America, ix, 25, 28, 33, 36, 65, 69, 70, 120, 188, 233
North Atlantic Treaty Organization, 22
North Korea, 47, 74, 115, 254
Norway, 26, 113, 140, 145, 206
nostalgia, 163
NOW, ix, xi, 78
nucleus, 9
NWD, ix

O

Obama, 175, 236
oceans, 14, 109, 223
OECD, 36, 84, 93, 126, 145, 148, 223

Office of Management and Budget, 143
offshoring, 198, 199, 200
oil, 36, 44, 46, 73, 92, 103, 119, 138, 223, 232, 253
Operation Enduring Freedom, 236, 239
operations, 43, 71, 103, 142, 145, 146, 200, 212, 213, 215, 216, 219, 239
opportunities, ix, 34, 175, 183, 198
oppression, 13, 233
optimism, 78, 223
organism, 85, 88, 90, 92, 167
outsourcing, x, xi, 116, 118, 129, 132, 135, 146, 181, 197, 198, 199, 200, 210, 222, 226, 242, 248

P

Pacific, 36, 38, 223
Pacific Islanders, 38
Pakistan, 50, 224, 228, 236, 238, 239, 250
parallel, 89, 125, 133, 146, 152, 255
parents, 138, 178
Parliament, 23, 24, 37, 39, 68, 154
participants, 45
Pashtun, 238
peace, 7, 12, 46, 53, 90, 92, 140, 157, 236, 242
penalties, 241
Pentagon, 235, 250
per capita income, 36
percentile, 136, 140
performance indicator, 214
Persian Gulf, 30, 31, 236, 237
Persian Gulf War, 30, 31, 236
Peter the Great, 243
Philadelphia, 65, 93, 138
Philippines, 27, 243
physical health, 170
physics, 40, 89
Picasso, 157
planets, 67, 104
plants, 135, 216
platform, 59, 78, 178, 212, 226, 242, 243
Plato, 12, 56, 96
playing, 19, 133, 163, 164
pluralism, 169, 176, 179, 186, 188, 256
poetry, 97, 113, 154, 239
Poland, 14, 15, 16, 17, 18, 19, 21, 24, 33, 46, 54, 55, 60, 61, 66, 74, 78, 79, 83, 84, 86, 113, 127, 171, 172, 173, 175, 193, 239, 243
police, ix, 53, 115, 136, 140, 235
policy, 18, 33, 73, 76, 112, 142, 145, 165, 172, 173, 175, 183, 193, 237, 247, 249
political leaders, ix, 116, 234
political party(s), 109, 182
political power, 32, 77, 101, 152

political problems, 184
political system, ix, x, 12, 75, 115, 140, 237, 241, 243, 249
politics, 31, 74, 78, 96, 101, 114, 115, 117, 125, 126, 143, 160, 172, 181, 183, 184, 187, 188, 227, 232, 245, 246, 252, 254
pollution, 247
population, 7, 8, 32, 33, 34, 38, 40, 50, 53, 63, 64, 65, 73, 83, 89, 97, 102, 103, 109, 120, 136, 137, 142, 147, 172, 174, 182, 202, 205, 209, 211, 216, 232, 233, 241
population growth, 109, 110
population size, 89
Portugal, 7, 23, 32, 61, 64, 66, 83, 115, 147, 171, 255
postal service, 216
post-industrial society, 116, 117, 126
poverty, 13, 34, 35, 56, 98, 112, 130, 136, 137, 152, 183
power generation, 40
premature death, 83
preservation, 108
presidency, 235
president, ix, 15, 16, 17, 18, 24, 26, 30, 32, 33, 79, 116, 125, 141, 143, 160, 175, 179, 184, 236, 245, 247, 249
principles, 33, 63, 68, 88, 99, 101, 131, 157, 186, 219
prisons, 139, 140, 148
private dwellings, 153
private schools, 138
private sector, 140, 196
privatization, 140, 231, 249
problem solving, 95, 97, 122, 125, 219, 254
problem-solving, 122
production costs, 164
professionalism, 159, 223
professionals, 198, 216, 224, 226, 234
profit, x, 81, 103, 139, 140, 170, 197, 209, 226, 227
project, 22, 71, 79, 137
proliferation, 199
propaganda, 231, 239, 247
property rights, 120
prophylactic, 43
prosperity, ix, 18, 23, 37, 53, 75, 96, 130, 248
protection, 217, 227
protectionism, 192
Protestants, 102, 125, 233
psychoanalysis, 113
public education, 139
public policy, 112, 145
Puerto Rico, 33, 65
purchasing power, 23, 92

Q

quality of life, 36, 53, 73, 86, 102, 144
questioning, 101, 115

R

race, 17, 76, 78, 86, 113, 137, 160, 178, 187, 200, 202, 206, 215, 217, 234
racism, 77, 154, 174, 184
radicalism, 84
radicalization, 183
radio, 72, 163
rate of change, 89
raw materials, 109, 196
reading, 133, 140, 220
real estate, 154, 209
reality, x, 12, 74, 80, 90, 118, 130, 146, 160, 161, 164, 179, 219
reasoning, 96, 97, 105, 106, 108, 121, 220
recognition, 184, 188
Red Army, 16, 172
reform(s), 89, 112, 139, 228, 239
regression, 9, 255
regulations, ix, 131, 222
rejection, 102, 174, 249
reliability, 202, 212
religion, ix, x, 3, 4, 7, 11, 13, 32, 39, 42, 49, 52, 56, 75, 76, 81, 83, 87, 96, 98, 101, 102, 104, 106, 112, 130, 131, 132, 133, 134, 139, 146, 147, 152, 168, 170, 178, 185, 232, 234, 242
religious beliefs, 249
Rembrandt, 157, 163
renaissance, 83, 99, 126, 152
René Descartes, 66, 67, 105, 121
reputation, 140, 199
requirements, 228
researchers, 88, 89
resilience, 47, 83, 92, 93, 122, 125, 254
resistance, 170, 206, 238
resources, 12, 13, 14, 28, 30, 33, 44, 46, 51, 53, 73, 74, 75, 83, 89, 92, 119, 126, 134, 146, 153, 154, 162, 167, 196, 202, 204, 213, 220, 223, 227, 232, 235, 243, 253, 254, 255, 256
response, 5, 9, 22, 43, 88, 121, 136, 151, 172, 227, 245
response time, 136
restructuring, 204
retail, 194, 195, 216
retaliation, 235
retirement, 142
revenue, 154

right ventricle, 68
rights, 13, 18, 76, 106, 111, 120, 121, 124, 130, 154, 174, 182, 183, 219, 242
risk, 86, 134, 243
robotics, 36, 206, 216, 228
Roman Catholics, 233
Romania, 15, 18, 22, 113, 173, 193
Romanticism, 70, 112, 114
root(s), 49, 59, 96, 139, 151, 157, 175, 183, 184, 235
routes, 29, 63, 64, 153, 154, 200
rules, 15, 16, 23, 24, 42, 96, 120, 121, 126, 131, 152, 163, 219, 239, 249
Russia, 14, 15, 16, 24, 39, 42, 46, 47, 66, 73, 74, 92, 171, 173, 175, 188, 224, 228, 233, 243, 245, 251, 253, 254
Rwanda, 233

S

sabotage, 223
saturation, 45
Saudi Arabia, 235, 238, 239, 241, 246, 250
Scandinavia, 26, 86, 99, 102
scholarship, 56, 59
school, 31, 53, 59, 99, 111, 116, 136, 138, 139, 140, 141, 142, 145, 147, 148, 153, 160, 164, 165, 183, 209, 219, 220, 226, 227, 232, 239
school performance, 148
science, 13, 28, 41, 62, 63, 66, 68, 81, 90, 96, 97, 99, 105, 108, 111, 120, 121, 124, 125, 126, 141, 154, 201, 202, 206, 254
scientific knowledge, 105, 118, 122
scientific method, 68, 105
scope, 42, 43, 46, 129, 155, 167, 170, 187, 192, 223, 232, 255, 257
security, 193, 199, 200
self-destruction, 120, 142
self-sufficiency, 108, 200
separatism, 169, 179, 181, 187, 188, 256
September 11, 235, 236, 238, 250
Serbia, 55, 113, 172
Serbs, 173, 234
service industries, 117
services, 5, 12, 38, 73, 78, 86, 109, 136, 147, 156, 195, 202, 203, 204, 209, 212, 213, 219, 220, 226, 227, 248
settlements, 52, 65
sex, 119, 125, 160, 164, 166, 187, 255
sexual orientation, 170
sexuality, 156, 178
shade, 25, 26, 27, 30
shortage, 200, 205
showing, 68, 80, 141, 164, 194, 195, 239

Siberia, 243
silver, 10, 53, 71, 102, 153
simulation(s), 216, 224
Singapore, 78, 206
slavery, 69, 80, 106, 112, 120, 154, 174, 175, 233
slaves, 14, 28, 53, 64, 77, 102, 109, 139, 170, 235
Slovakia, 14
social change, 112, 156
social development, 48, 185, 189, 249
social events, 154
social exclusion, 152
social group, 34, 88
social hierarchy, 69
social identity, 146
social integration, 181
social interactions, 180
social justice, x, 112
social life, 146
social network, 145, 180
social norms, 165
social order, 152
social problems, 154
social relations, 252
social relationships, 252
social responsibility, 80, 191, 192
social services, 136
social status, 175
social structure, 109
social theory, 175, 252
socialism, x, 12, 113, 114, 154, 252
socialization, 176, 226
societal hierarchies, ix
socioeconomic background, 170
Socrates, 56, 96
solution, x, 44, 78, 89, 96, 141, 176, 184, 185, 204, 227, 239
South Africa, 66, 175, 182
South America, 5, 17, 32, 33, 34, 47
South Asia, 250
South Korea, 78
South Ossetia, 245
Southeast Asia, 15
sovereignty, 118, 193
Soviet Block, ix, 78, 114, 192
Soviet Union, 14, 15, 16, 17, 40, 79, 159, 172, 173, 238, 245
Spain, 9, 23, 27, 31, 32, 33, 52, 53, 61, 65, 66, 70, 101, 115, 136, 147, 152, 171, 179, 206, 235, 239, 255
specialists, 171, 200, 206, 220, 226
specialization, 108, 172, 174
species, 122, 170, 206
speech, 160, 183, 249

spending, 134, 162, 164, 249
Sri Lanka, 42
stability, 90, 99, 122, 242
stabilization, 90, 92, 125, 254
stakeholders, 146, 209, 227
standard of living, ix, 199
steel, 22, 29, 108
steel industry, 29
stock, 109, 134, 197, 223
stock markets, 134
stock value, 197
stockholders, 72
storage, 121, 130, 223
stretching, 31, 53
structural changes, 184
structure, 5, 43, 63, 68, 86, 97, 109, 134, 199
style, 52, 53, 59, 62, 141, 145, 153, 154, 163, 165, 199, 232, 243
sub-Saharan Africa, 34
suicide, 16, 135, 235, 239
suicide attacks, 235
suicide bombers, 239
Sunnis, 239, 241
superpower, x, 31, 32, 86, 92, 93, 176
supervision, 212
supply chain, 222, 223, 227
Supreme Court, 143, 249
survival, 47, 74, 137, 187, 254, 256
sustainability, 191, 192, 202, 214, 216
sustainable economic growth, 229
Sweden, 25, 61, 113, 140, 193, 206
Switzerland, 52, 59, 61, 79, 102, 206
symptoms, x, 129
synthesis, 11, 129, 151, 169, 192, 231
Syria, 47, 52, 96, 237, 239, 250, 254

T

tactics, 239
Taiwan, 242
Taliban, 236, 238, 240, 241, 242, 250
target, 7, 46, 79, 178, 224
tax rates, 143
taxation, x, 68, 118, 132, 147, 182, 255
taxes, x, 27, 132, 136, 138, 140, 142, 143, 170, 201
teachers, 165, 227
techniques, 53, 248
technological advancement, 89
technological progress, 109, 115, 203, 217, 226, 227
telecommunications, 29, 213
telephone(s), 29, 72, 82, 198
tension(s), 175, 176, 179, 245
territorial, 16, 233, 242, 245

territory, 9, 16, 19, 37, 70, 76, 86, 91, 119, 153, 172, 233, 235, 239, 240, 241, 242, 243, 245
terrorism, xi, 43, 46, 78, 92, 119, 183, 223, 235, 236, 241, 253
terrorist attack, 236, 238, 240
terrorist organization, 235, 238, 240
terrorists, 139, 235, 238, 241, 242, 249
tertiary education, 36
text messaging, 148
Thailand, 42
Third World, 144
threats, 15, 17, 44, 223, 251, 257
Tibet, 42
top-down, 47, 167, 209, 243, 245, 249, 253, 255
tourism, 39, 140
trade, 13, 18, 33, 50, 51, 53, 63, 64, 65, 66, 69, 73, 76, 86, 96, 97, 98, 99, 133, 154, 192, 193, 198, 199, 200, 206, 219, 232, 233, 246
trade agreement, 192
trade deficit, 198, 199
traditions, 32, 243
transformation(s), x, 3, 47, 80, 86, 87, 129, 147, 166, 167, 174, 227, 255, 256
transformation processes, 147
translocation, 46, 253
transmission, 152, 207, 213
transport, 212, 223, 225, 227, 228, 257
transportation, 5, 70, 81, 98, 109, 123, 126, 130, 136, 191, 192, 197, 216, 222, 223, 255
transportation infrastructure, 109, 191, 197, 222, 223
treatment, 175, 234
Tribalism, 187, 249
triggers, 43, 147, 161, 255
Turkey, 8, 17, 50, 79, 120, 145, 239
Turks, 172

U

U.S. Bureau of Labor Statistics, 198
U.S. Department of Labor, 148
U.S. economy, 135
Ukraine, 24, 39, 42, 46, 245, 253
UNDP, 47
unemployment rate, 134, 136
UNESCO, 82
unification, 28, 46, 61, 113
United Kingdom (UK), 36, 84, 166, 179, 180, 183, 187, 188, 193, 206, 228, 239
United States, ix, x, xi, 12, 23, 28, 33, 36, 37, 47, 66, 69, 71, 74, 78, 79, 86, 92, 97, 109, 111, 124, 135, 136, 137, 141, 145, 166, 175, 181, 182, 184, 192, 193, 198, 199, 206, 209, 216, 235, 242, 243, 245, 249, 251, 253

universality, 158
universe, 11, 47, 67, 104, 105, 120
universities, 123, 153, 160, 182, 198, 206, 209
university education, 105
upward mobility, 135
uranium, 73, 92, 119
urban, 4, 35, 63, 66, 101, 178, 183, 187, 191, 213, 225, 227, 256
urban areas, 227
urban population, 178
urban youth, 178
urbanization, 72, 246
Uruguay, 34, 35
USSR, 253

V

Vatican, 58, 100
vehicles, 135, 212, 239
Venezuela, 33
veto, 14, 193
video games, 164, 168
videos, 79, 141, 238, 239, 241
Vietnam, x, 27, 46, 74, 78, 243
Viking, 25, 126
violence, 140, 141, 160, 164, 165, 166, 243, 249
virtual communities, 145, 180
virtual organization, 145
virtualization, 142
vision, 9, 63, 131, 248

W

wages, 72, 162, 196
war, xi, 7, 12, 16, 18, 24, 28, 31, 33, 34, 37, 44, 46, 47, 65, 68, 69, 73, 74, 76, 77, 78, 86, 92, 140, 175, 183, 184, 231, 233, 234, 236, 239, 240, 242, 243, 249, 251, 252, 257
Warsaw Pact, 17, 22
Washington, 26, 28, 106, 109, 138, 148, 161, 192, 228, 229, 235, 243
water, 40, 66, 68, 70, 73, 92, 105, 107, 213
wealth, ix, xi, 4, 5, 11, 12, 30, 46, 53, 56, 63, 74, 97, 101, 102, 109, 112, 120, 130, 134, 139, 147, 148, 152, 154, 171, 174, 182, 196, 232, 246
weapons, 52, 141
web, 79, 180
websites, 180, 203
welfare, 19, 201
well-being, 10, 44, 85, 104, 117, 118, 163, 202, 245

Western Europe, ix, x, 9, 11, 15, 17, 20, 22, 23, 32, 33, 55, 78, 89, 117, 120, 139, 153, 154, 168, 239, 243
White House, 143
wholesale, 194, 195
wisdom, vii, xi, xii, 4, 12, 50, 80, 85, 92, 96, 111, 122, 125, 127, 129, 141, 146, 217, 218, 219, 220, 229, 254
withdrawal, 236, 241
wool, 37, 39, 53, 154
work ethic, 102, 125, 154, 254
workers, 72, 74, 109, 112, 125, 132, 134, 135, 180, 198, 205, 213, 216, 226, 255
workforce, 36, 198
working class, 74, 109, 139
workplace, 165, 216
World Bank, 34, 192, 228, 229
world order, xi, 12, 47, 83, 93, 113, 188, 251
World Trade Center, 235, 250
World Trade Organization (WTO), 82, 193
world trading system, 228
World War I, ix, 14, 16, 20, 21, 22, 27, 28, 33, 34, 37, 61, 73, 74, 76, 78, 142, 159, 172, 175, 176, 180, 192, 233, 234, 235
World Wide Web (WWW), 79, 196
worldview, 104, 105, 108, 188

Y

Yale University, 16
Yemen, 140, 237, 250
young people, 159, 160, 163, 164, 165, 232, 247
yuan, 243
Yugoslavia, 15, 61, 172, 173, 233, 235